ARTS AND MINDS

Arts and Minds

HOW THE ROYAL SOCIETY OF ARTS
CHANGED A NATION

ANTON HOWES

PRINCETON UNIVERSITY PRESS

PRINCETON & OXFORD

Published by Princeton University Press
41 William Street, Princeton, New Jersey 08540
6 Oxford Street, Woodstock, Oxfordshire OX20 1TR

press.princeton.edu

Library of Congress Cataloging-in-Publication Data

Names: Howes, Anton, author.
Title: Arts and minds : how the Royal Society of Arts changed a nation / Anton Howes.
Description: Princeton : Princeton University Press, [2020] | Includes bibliographical references and index. |
Identifiers: LCCN 2019026884 | ISBN 9780691182643 (hardcover ; acid-free paper) | ISBN 9780691201900 (epub)
Subjects: LCSH: Royal Society of Arts (Great Britain)—Influence. | Research institutes—Great Britain—Influence.
Classification: LCC T1.R855 H69 2020 | DDC 062—dc23
LC record available at https://lccn.loc.gov/2019026884

British Library Cataloging-in-Publication Data is available

Editorial: Sarah Caro and Charlie Blake
Production Editorial: Debbie Tegarden
Jacket Design: Lorraine Doneker
Production: Erin Suydam
Publicity: Tayler Lord and Kate Farquhar-Thomson
Copyeditor: Tash Siddiqui

Jacket Credit: Robert Percy Gossop, 1934. Courtesy of the Royal Society of Arts

This book has been composed in Arno

Printed on acid-free paper. ∞

Printed and bound by CPI Group (UK) Ltd, Croydon, CR0 4YY

10 9 8 7 6 5 4 3 2 1

To the public-spirited.

CONTENTS

ILLUSTRATIONS

Unless otherwise stated in the captions, all illustrations are provided courtesy of the Royal Society of Arts. Colour plates follow page 178.

Plates

Figures

INTRODUCTION

FEW PEOPLE HAVE HEARD of the Royal Society for the Encouragement of Arts, Manufactures and Commerce. Even fewer know what it does. Many assume, as its name is usually abbreviated to the Royal Society of Arts, that it is all about art. It has certainly done a lot to promote art, but it has also done much, much more than that. In fact, the Society is by its very nature difficult to define. There is no other organisation quite like it, and nor has there ever been. It is in a category of its own.

For almost three hundred years, the Society has essentially been Britain's voluntary, subscription-funded, national improvement agency. It has tried to change an entire nation, in every way imaginable. From art, music, employment and education, to food, the environment, the economy, and even Britain's morals and culture. If anything can be improved, the Society has almost certainly tried. After all, anything can always be better.

In its first hundred years the Society funded inventions that would not otherwise have been profitable, encouraged the opening of new trades with the colonies, and held the country's first dedicated exhibition of contemporary art, all while encouraging the landed aristocracy to plant over sixty million trees. It tried to abolish the use of children in cleaning chimneys, and to find a solution to the problem of banknote forgery. The list continues.

In the mid-nineteenth century it became a platform for utilitarian reformers trying to create rational systems in everything, from education and the postal service, to musical pitch and toilets. At some points, the Society even resembled a learned society—a place for expert discussion on everything from early telephones to West African goldmines. At other points, it became the focal point for social movements, from the preservation of old cottages, to workers' self-education, to the conservation of the environment.

The Society's history includes everything from the blue plaques that dot Britain's buildings, to the temporary sculptures on Trafalgar Square's fourth plinth. It was the initial mover behind the Great Exhibition of 1851, and gave birth to hundreds of other institutions, some of which survive to this day. It has tried to bridge specialisms, and to reconcile ideological divides. Its members have included Adam Smith, Edmund Burke, and Karl Marx, founding fathers of liberalism, conservatism, and communism.

There is only one thing that ties all of the Society's members and their disparate projects together: a desire to benefit the public. But to do so, it does the things that are not already being done. It has had to constantly reinvent itself. Once a project is successful it usually gives it independence and moves on: 'having blazed a needed trail it hands the axe to others to carry on while it looks for another trail and another axe'.[1] Sometimes it has succeeded, sometimes it has failed. Operating at the edges and pushing new ideas is difficult. Sometimes its members were too stuck in their ways, or misguided in their attempts, or too ahead of their time. All the same, their failures are as instructive as their successes, especially for those who wish to serve the public good in any way they can.

The older published histories of the Society were written by insiders, the equivalents of the Society's chief executives. They sometimes read like advertisements. The last published history appeared in 1954. Much has happened since then, and more about the Society's first two centuries has also since come to light. The Society's influential and often surprising history—almost three hundred years of public-spirited people who tried, in any way they could think of, to make Britain a better place—was therefore not fully told.

It began in the eighteenth century, with an idea.

ARTS AND MINDS

1

Patrons of the Nation

THE EIGHTEENTH CENTURY was an age of improvement.[1] Things did not all necessarily get better; in many ways, and for many people, it was an age of horrors. But for scholars in particular, it was an age in which knowledge seemed every day to advance. Their letters criss-crossed Europe and North America, many of them reaching as far as India or China, all sent in an active pursuit and sharing of knowledge. This 'Republic of Letters', at least as an ideal, transcended all political and social barriers: so long as they had something to contribute, anyone, of any class or nation or religion, could participate.[2] Many of the contributions, however, conformed to a specific agenda, most famously set out by an English politician and philosopher of the early seventeenth century, Francis Bacon.[3]

The 'Baconian programme', as the economic historian Joel Mokyr has termed it, was to accumulate and rigorously test knowledge, especially as it might someday be useful.[4] Scholars devoted themselves to describing what they did not yet understand: anything and everything was counted, catalogued, classified, and compared, from rocks that might contain ores for new materials or pigments, to plants that might yield better foods or fibres or medicines, to the movements of bright objects in the night sky, which might provide new ways for sailors to find their bearings at sea. Bacon's promise was that when useful knowledge was amassed, material improvements would surely follow. And with the amassing of potentially useful knowledge, even more might then be generated. From the accumulated data would emerge patterns and

1

predictable regularities—laws of nature—which might in turn be harnessed towards useful ends.[5] Knowledge, when recorded and shared, could then be interpreted and theorised, and conjectures made about the remaining gaps, all contributing to a philosophy of nature—what we now call science.

By the mid-seventeenth century, natural philosophers had begun to formalise their relationships with one another. They began to meet regularly to discuss their work and share their findings, forming organisations for the collection and diffusion of knowledge. The preeminent institution to emerge in England was the 'Royal Society of London for the Improvement of Natural Knowledge', founded in 1660, and most commonly known today as simply the Royal Society. In France an *Académie des Sciences* was soon established too, as were many other learned societies across Europe. These societies did more than just collect information; they were places for truth to be tested, for experiments to be performed and replicated before a wide audience rather than reported by letter from the privacy of the home (after all, even the most prestigious or trustworthy correspondents might deceive themselves). It was at the societies that information could become accepted as fact.[6]

The Baconian obsession with collection and cataloguing was also applied beyond natural philosophy, to history, archaeology, and ancient languages, so that the learning of distant ancestors might also be preserved and built upon.[7] In London from 1707 some scholars met to share information on British heraldry, genealogy, monuments, and ancient buildings—a group that later became known as the Society of Antiquaries.[8] Societies emerged outside of the capital cities too, often called 'literary and philosophical', catering to both the antiquarian and scientific interests of local scholars—that at Northampton, for example, was referred to as a 'Royal Society in miniature'.[9] More informally, too, scholars exchanged their theories and observations over drinks in taverns and coffee houses—after overseeing the dissection of a dolphin, for example, fellows of the Royal Society like Isaac Newton or Edmond Halley would continue their discussions at the Grecian Coffee House down the road, where they might also share a table with politicians, poets, or merchants.[10] As the historian Peter Clark has argued, with the growth of British cities in the eighteenth century, their clubs, societies, and other associations also multiplied. The groups that met to promote natural philosophy or improvement were only a few among a growing 'associational world' of mostly urban societies devoted to art, music, literature, commerce, charity, religion, and politics, as well as just socialising and having fun.[11] Alongside the scholarly pursuits, the coffee houses and taverns were places where stock prices were reported, news was exchanged, and plans were hatched.

By the early eighteenth century, however, the Baconian promises of material improvement were not being fully met. It was not enough for natural philosophers to collect knowledge that might be useful; the knowledge actually had to be put to use. In its early years many fellows of the Royal Society had recognised this. They investigated not only the works of nature, but also human artifice: 'all useful arts, manufactures, mechanical practices, engines, and inventions', as well as agriculture.[12] In addition to science, the Royal Society was supposed to devote itself to recording and advancing technology. Some of its fellows, following Bacon's programme to the letter, began work compiling a dictionary of crafts, industries, and inventions.[13] They also hoped to eventually purchase manufacturers' secrets, to reveal the best techniques and inventions to the public so that they could be more widely used. The practice of buying and revealing secrets would itself be 'a most heroic invention',[14] and in 1664 the Royal Society took out a patent covering various improvements to carriages, chairs, coaches, chariots, pistols, powder horns, textile machinery, and a newly invented pendulum to be used for navigation at sea.[15]

But the broad ambitions of the Royal Society's early fellows were soon curtailed by economic and social reality. With only limited time and funds, it made sense to specialise; and in choosing what to make a priority, the natural philosophical investigations of amateur gentlemen were more prestigious than the practical, hands-on work of the middle-class artisans. The artisans themselves often also opposed attempts to reveal their secrets, believing that it would threaten their livelihoods.[16] And besides, the reasoning went, 'pure' natural philosophy promised the discovery of universal laws, which would find general uses, whereas spending time developing particular machines and techniques would only ever benefit their specific time and place. An invention would soon be superseded and forgotten, but a scientific law was forever. So long as pure science continued to progress, the fellows of the Royal Society contented themselves with the belief that the potential applications would also multiply.[17] The practical applications could be investigated later on, and by others.

Over the course of the late seventeenth century the functions of the Royal Society shifted decidedly towards natural philosophy, with only the occasional investigation of practical applications. Although it counted artisans and merchants among its fellows, the majority were wealthy gentlemen with an interest in science, and in the 1730s it rejected proposals to once more encourage inventions.[18] Its counterparts in the rest of Europe showed a similar, but even more pronounced shift. Natural philosophers on the continent were heavily influenced by the works of René Descartes, whose approach was to logically deduce nature's laws.[19] Whereas British natural philosophy was mostly led by observation and experimentation, in France it was led by abstract mathematical reasoning.[20] France's *Académie des Sciences* excluded artisans entirely, restricting its membership to only aristocrats and scientists. Albeit less pronounced in Britain, there was a clear social divide between those who knew (the *savants*) and those who made (the *fabricants*); a separation between heads and hands.

The problem was that the ever-expanding knowledge of the savants was not so easily applied. As natural philosophy advanced, it developed its own jargon, making it more difficult to communicate to those who might put it to use. The process of application was also itself difficult and time-consuming, requiring careful experimentation. Plenty of advancements could even be made in technology without requiring any new natural philosophy. Bacon's programme had involved collecting and revealing the best practices from around the world, many of which were already in use: perhaps the secret glass-making techniques of Venice would improve the same industry in Britain; perhaps the leather-making processes of London could benefit Dublin or Edinburgh. A common 'treasure' of knowledge would then more easily be expanded upon, showing people what had already been done and hinting at what might be improved next. It would, at the very least, save the wasted effort of reinventing something that had already been invented elsewhere. Even more urgently, however, collecting and revealing the world's various arts and inventions would ensure that they were not lost—secrets were often taken to the grave, and many experiments were started but never completed for want of money or time.[21]

For Bacon's programme to be properly realised—and for his promises of material improvement to come true—a new institution was required. In 1721–22, a series of proposals circulated in London, very probably written by an inventive English watchmaker named Henry Sully, who had recently been rejected by the French *Académie* for being a mere artisan.[22] Whereas the Royal Society and its French counterpart promoted 'learning, sciences, and philosophy', Sully's proposed society would devote itself to 'preserving and improving inventions, arts, and manufactures'.[23] This society of arts—that is, dealing with human artifice—would pick up where the Royal Society had left off.[24] It would compile a register of the best practices and inventions, ensure that promising new ideas were put through proper trials, and buy from inventors those improvements that would otherwise be kept secret. It would reveal the 'mysteries' of trades and manufactures, and build upon them further. In time, Sully promised, Britain would become the 'retreat and succour of every peculiar genius for arts and inventions'. Beyond the advantage to the nation and the world, however, Sully offered private benefits too. He suggested that subscribers to the society would profit from patenting some of the more promising inventions.

But Sully's reputation was sullied. He was associated with a Scottish banker named John Law, who in the late 1710s had overseen an ambitious scheme to reorder the French government's finances. Law ran the Mississippi Company, which gradually acquired all the various other companies that had monopolies on France's intercontinental trade. In exchange for the monopolies, the company bought up the French government's accumulated war debts, allowing repayment on more generous terms—the scheme allowed the government to more easily fund itself. As the Mississippi Company absorbed its competitors, its shares became increasingly valuable. By 1719 it had agglomerated into a Company of the Indies and ran the collection of all French taxes, taking its own cut. Meanwhile, so that people could buy the company's shares, Law printed paper money. To back the paper currency, however, Law needed to amass gold and silver. For one of his strategies he enlisted Sully's aid, paying him to entice skilled British watchmakers to France, to work in factories under Sully's direction (in response, in 1719 the British government outright banned the emigration of skilled artisans like watchmakers).[25] Sully's factories then bought and melted down old gold and silver coins, keeping the precious metals in France by using them to make luxury watches. Buoyed by their success, in 1718 Law and Sully together even founded a *Société des Arts*.

Disaster struck in 1720, however, when Law discovered he had printed too much paper currency and tried to devalue the company's shares. Law's financial projects collapsed, and so did the *Société* when Law was sacked and fled the country. Sully, however, managed to profit from the disaster by persuading the British government to pay him to return with the other British watchmakers. It was on his return to London that Sully circulated his proposals for a society of arts. But the project found no takers: Britain had just seen its own financial crisis when the share prices of the South Sea Company collapsed. The South Sea Company had the monopoly on supplying African slaves to Spain's American colonies, and like the Mississippi Company had also been used to try and restructure the British government's debt.[26] With the 1720 stock market crashes in both Paris and London, the reputation of all publicly traded companies, or 'projects', was tarnished. Sully's scheme for a society of arts, promising easy profits to its subscribers like any other project, was a non-starter. Rejected, Sully went back to France and managed to refound the *Société des Arts* in 1728, though he died later that year.[27] The *Société* continued without him for about a decade, meeting privately in the apartments of a young aristocrat. Yet when the aristocrat lost interest and was called away to fight in a war, those involved became disaffected and all trace of the organisation disappeared.[28]

Despite the abortive attempts in London and Paris, Sully was not alone in trying to create a society of arts. In both Ireland and Scotland, the need for the diffusion of useful knowledge was all the more urgent. Many Scots believed that the economic gap between England and Scotland had only widened since the union of the two states in 1707. To remedy the situation, in 1723 in Edinburgh a group of major landowners with a few natural philosophers established a 'Society of Improvers in the Knowledge of Agriculture in Scotland', which collected and disseminated information on the best agricultural techniques. They began with agriculture because it was, in their view, 'not only a science, but the life and support of all arts and sciences'.[29] In 1727 some of its members also obtained government funding for a 'Board of Trustees for Improving Manufactures and Fisheries of North Britain', to oversee the development of Scotland's major industries (Scotland was often referred to as 'North Britain' well into the nineteenth century). The Board of Trustees lobbied for linen subsidies, sent spies to discover foreign techniques, encouraged foreign linen workers to immigrate, funded a few linen-related inventions, and established schools to teach spinning and the drawing of woven patterns. Edinburgh's Society of Improvers hoped that Scotland would replace continental Europe as the main source of linen imports to England.

Likewise, the natural philosophers and antiquarians meeting at Dublin's Philosophical Society complained that the economic gap between Ireland and England was widening. Many of the major landowners rarely set foot in Ireland, simply collecting their rents and spending the money in England or abroad. When an English aristocrat squandered the family money on luxuries, most of it was at least spent in London where it would stimulate English industries; but the profligacy of an Irish absentee landlord harmed both his family and his country. Even more gold and silver left Ireland to pay for English coal and other imports, leading to a general shortage of coin circulating in the economy. Dublin's scholars feared that Ireland would revert to a barter economy.[30] Their solution was to move beyond simply assigning blame, to instead applying useful knowledge in the service of Ireland's agriculture and industry. In 1731 they founded a 'Dublin Society for Improving Husbandry, Manufactures and other Useful Arts'. It collected information on best practices, printed and distributed the latest agricultural tracts, collected and displayed models of the latest agricultural machinery, and even purchased a botanical garden for its own experiments.[31] Just like its Scottish counterpart, the Dublin Society paid especial attention to promoting Ireland's linen industry.

By the 1740s some saw the need for a similar organisation in England, particularly as natural philosophy seemed to have failed to meet Bacon's promises of material improvement. As the Royal Society shifted away from practical applications, natural philosophy developed a reputation as mere 'idle and empty curiosity'.[32] In *Gulliver's Travels*, natural philosophers were lampooned as 'so taken up with intense speculations' that to bring them to their senses their servants had to periodically smack them with blown bladders fastened to sticks.[33] A popular play, *The Virtuoso*, had as its main character an aristocratic amateur scientist, Sir Nicholas Gimcrack (a gimcrack was a derogatory term for a useless invention), who tried to learn to swim on dry land by imitating a frog, transfused sheep's blood into a man, and went around the country bottling air. His problem was in considering practical application as 'base and mercenary, below the serene and quiet temper of a sedate philosopher'. 'I care not for the practice. I seldom bring any thing to use', boasted Gimcrack. Only 'knowledge is my ultimate end'.[34] Yet the Royal Society's founders had in fact warned of science's worsening reputation. They had stressed science's usefulness as a way to gain public support for their programme.[35] Looking to the distant past, it seemed as though only things that were widely considered useful were preserved from the ravages of time and barbarian invasion.[36] The best way to defend natural philosophy was thus to apply it to practical purposes.

In their own personal ways, some English natural philosophers devoted themselves to applying scientific theory to practice. Stephen Hales, a clergyman and fellow of the Royal Society, spent most of his scientific career investigating how sap flows through plants and how blood circulates in animals, as well as how both fluids interact with the air. When he reached his late sixties, he decided to put his findings and theories into practice. His brother had likely died in prison from typhus, a deadly fever believed to be caused by noxious air, and Hales was alarmed by a serious typhus epidemic among soldiers who were

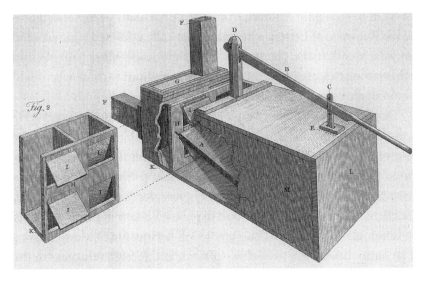

1.1. Stephen Hales's ventilator. The engraving was taken from a model in the Society's repository, which was donated by Thomas Yeoman. From a catalogue of the Society's machines assembled by the register, William Bailey, RSA/SC/EL/2/6–7.

cooped up in ships while awaiting passage abroad. So he applied his understanding of gases to invent the ventilator—a device for bringing fresh air into enclosed and stuffy spaces. It would improve health in mines, hospitals, prisons, and workhouses—anywhere that people had to endure cramped and damp conditions. Applied to ships, it would make sea-travel less deadly and thus encourage commerce. Although it did not in fact prevent typhus (which is usually transmitted by lice), the ventilator undoubtedly made life more bearable for seafarers. Its most lasting use, however, was in preserving various goods by keeping them dry: gunpowder, malt, hops, and particularly grain, which when damp attracted weevils.[37] For Hales, his invention of the ventilator was clear proof that 'the study of natural philosophy is not a mere trifling amusement'.[38]

Yet although Hales was not alone in demonstrating natural philosophy's uses, such efforts were undertaken by individuals, and only occasionally. England still lacked an organisation to encourage the application of science and other improvements systematically. The decisive impetus for change was to come from outside the Royal Society's elite circle of natural philosophers, from one of the many peripheral figures of the Republic of Letters who enthusiastically collected and recorded unusual fossils, rocks, plants, insects, antiquities, weather patterns, and other curiosities, communicating their observations to those who might better make sense of them.

This figure was William Shipley, a younger son of minor gentry. He was raised by his mother's family at Twyford Hall, in Hampshire, and allowed to train as an artist in London while his elder brother was educated for the clergy and later became a bishop. Shipley was briefly a member of the King's ceremonial bodyguard, the 'Honourable Band of Gentlemen Pensioners', but he quit to pursue his love of painting. While in London, he frequented Slaughter's Coffee House in St Martin's Lane, a favourite haunt of artists, chess-players, and foreign refugees (to the extent that some people even went there to learn French).[39] Shipley visited Slaughter's for his afternoon tea, but largely kept to himself, preferring to quietly read the newspapers, take notes on antiquarian curiosities, or sketch diagrams of inventions. He would place his sixpence on the bar, and leave silently. When he did speak, it was usually in monosyllables, both solemn and slow.

Shipley's introverted behaviour reportedly got him into trouble. Coffee houses were places to talk. Customers were expected to join the general company and engage in the debates and discussions, not sit quietly apart. In the late 1740s, many in Britain were also worried about a French-sponsored invasion by supporters of the deposed Catholic line of James II, the Jacobites. In 1745, a Jacobite invasion force had even landed in Scotland, and with the support of many Highlanders, had marched to Derby, right in the heart of England. Even though the invasion was quashed, people continued to suspect fresh plots. Dressed all in black, and barely saying a word in a coffee house well known for its French customers, Shipley appeared a likely foreign spy; his various notes and diagrams might in fact be coastal charts, to aid another French invasion. His fellow customers at Slaughter's reported him to a magistrate, who had Shipley hauled before him for questioning. Shipley was reportedly unable to say much to defend himself, but was rescued by a couple of friends who came to vouch for his patriotism and high standing as a gentleman—they promised that in future he would be coaxed to do a little more talking.[40]

One of Shipley's friends was Henry Baker, who had made a fortune as a speech therapist, treating the stutters and lisps of the wealthy after he discovered a method of teaching deaf children to speak and read. Baker was a member of both the Royal Society and the Society of Antiquaries, and became particularly famous for his use of the microscope. He collected and examined whatever he could get his hands on, including crystals, scorpion stings, maggots, animal blood, and diseased human skin. Baker tried to make natural philosophy popular and accessible, publishing bestselling books on how to use the microscope and composing a successful poem that extolled nature's glories. He was also, crucially, an active link between the Royal Society and men like Shipley, the amateur enthusiasts on the periphery of the Republic of Letters. Baker was both natural philosophy's distributor and its 'insatiable' gatherer.[41] 'I should be a very undeserving member of the Royal Society', Baker wrote, to not 'encourage or assist others in enquiries that tend to the same delightful purpose.'[42]

Shipley promised to transmit to Baker whatever observations or curiosities came his way when in 1747 he left London for Northampton. Preferring a rural life to the crowds of the capital, Shipley toured the countryside to paint perspective views of gentlemen's parks and estates, all the while recording and collecting for Baker.[43] He sent him fossils from quarries and mines, a design for an improved barometer, casts of carved ancient Roman gems and coins, the eggs of some microscopic water animals preserved in mud, and descriptions of the ancient stone circles at Stonehenge and Avebury. Shipley soon joined the local philosophical society, a group of about thirty gentlemen 'very much addicted to all manner of natural knowledge', and enlisted their help in collecting knowledge for Baker.[44] The members of the Northampton society transmitted to Baker their accounts of a minor earthquake, more fossils, and even a box of unusual-looking worms. When they stumbled upon something useful, Baker passed on their information to the Royal Society or the Society of Antiquaries. Shipley was not that original a natural philosopher in his own right, but he was always finding ways to help and encourage others, and his selflessness extended beyond natural philosophy and antiquarianism, to society in general.

Shipley, like many others in the mid-eighteenth century, was concerned that private, selfish interests were increasingly subverting the public good.[45] The problem seemed to pervade every level of society. At the top, the nobility and gentry had divided into self-serving factions, each political party seeking its own advantage at the expense of the nation. The upper classes also seemed to be 'dissipated in idle and expensive diversions', frittering their money away on gambling and foreign luxuries, and setting a bad example to the lower classes, who also seemed to be wracked with idleness and vice.[46] The gentry spent all their time in London on party politics and luxury, while neglecting their landed estates and leaving their tenants and labourers unemployed and hungry.

In the middle, too, manufacturers and merchants seemed to be profiting at the expense of the public, especially the poor. Manufacturers guarded their secrets closely, driving up prices and denying their competitors the opportunity to employ more people, leaving 'swarms of thieves and beggars throughout the kingdom'.[47] When manufacturers made improvements, they protected the most useful inventions with patents, again restricting competition and driving up prices, albeit temporarily. Merchant companies limited competition in international trade by acquiring government-sanctioned monopolies, and local retailers took advantage of any situation that allowed them to drive up prices and lessen quality. Merchants and manufacturers all seemed ready to conspire against the public.[48]

In Northampton in particular, Shipley noted that merchants hoarded wood and coal during the cold winters, selling it at high prices when it was most needed for fuel for heating. These 'engrossers' seemed to pursue personal profit by exploiting the poor. Yet Shipley's response was not to deplore the practice or to campaign to have it outlawed. Instead, he suggested a practical improvement: a fund to which members of the public could subscribe, which would buy wood and coal in the summer when they were cheap, and sell them for as little as possible during the winter. If successful, the scheme would undercut the engrossers and force them to lower their prices. Shipley's approach was not to change public opinion, but to appeal to public action. It worked. When he put some of his own money towards the scheme, the other gentlemen of Northampton followed suit.

Yet Shipley's vision did not stop with taking on the Northampton fuel engrossers. He soon developed a plan for the improvement of the entire nation: a fund that might be used to solve any and all of the public's problems. His solution was to turn the general problem on its head: instead of allowing the public good to be subverted by individual selfishness, Shipley suggested harnessing people's self-interest in order to serve the public.[49] It was simply a matter of incentives.

When Shipley moved to Northampton, he had been impressed by the town's horse fairs. Thousands of horses were brought in to be sold at each fair, attracting buyers from across the country and abroad. Shipley was thus able to see Britain's market for horses all gathered in one place. He was shocked that the demand for horses could be so large. Vast sums of money changed hands at each fair, and the horse breeders tried everything to improve the quality of the horses on offer, importing breeds from as far away as North Africa. Shipley discovered that the cause of the demand was the growing popularity of horse racing. Races were being established in county after county, with the public subscribing towards silver plates and cash prizes for the winners. The promise of either honour or riches for horse owners and their riders seemed to be 'two sharp spurs' driving on the improvement of the breeds, and the effects of the plates and prizes seemed to be out of all proportion to the rewards on offer. Shipley reasoned that similar prizes might be applied to loftier purposes.

Upon further research, it seemed to Shipley that the arts and sciences progressed in proportion to the rewards they received. Among the ancient Greeks and Romans, it was when the rulers had become patrons of the arts that the pinnacles of classical civilisation had been reached. There did not seem to be anything special about the ancients in terms of their natural abilities or locations—it was again just a matter of the right incentives. The reign of Rome's first emperor, Augustus, was particularly famous among the coffee-house antiquarians and literati for the influence of his cultural adviser, Gaius Cilnius Maecenas. Under Maecenas's patronage many of the greatest poets and authors of the age, such as Horace and Virgil, had flourished. In the early eighteenth century, with the printing press making literature accessible to new consumers, English literature was widely considered to be undergoing a new Augustan Age. The printing press allowed anyone, in their own way, to be a modern Maecenas. Supported by the wealth of a growing middle class, new writers, poets, and playwrights, such as Alexander Pope, Jonathan Swift, and Joseph Addison, each vied to be the modern Horace or Virgil.

Beyond literature, Shipley reasoned that the other aspects of civilisation might also be encouraged. Prizes, or 'premiums', might be used to promote the other arts and sciences. The Dublin Society since 1741 had offered premiums for agricultural improvements, and Irish landed estates in some cases had more than doubled in value—'incontestable proof' that premiums were beneficial to the country as a whole as well as to the rents of the nobility.[50] Irish success seemed to confirm Shipley's theory that the only thing that held back a nation was the lack of encouragement, not the climate or people. Some observers already wondered why premiums that were 'so evidently advantageous' had no equivalent in England.[51]

In stressing the potential of premiums, Shipley recognised the importance of self-interest. As Baker put it, 'whoever would lead mankind, even to their own good, must take advantage of their passions.'[52] But the premiums needed to be funded. Shipley's own experience of the Northampton fuel scheme suggested that much could be achieved through public subscription, and the experience of the Dublin Society confirmed this—their fund was raised through subscriptions and private donations. If there were enough 'generous and public-spirited persons' to fund the premiums in Ireland, then surely enough could be found in England too.[53] At first glance, there was a contradiction at the heart of Shipley's plan: that in order to exploit most people's selfishness, he would rely on other people's selflessness.

Shipley drew mostly upon a feeling of public-spiritedness that was already present—an affinity with the 'imagined community' of the nation.[54] By 'the public', Shipley had in mind first the nation, and then the wider world. Only scholars, the citizens of the Republic of Letters, tended to be interested in the good of all 'mankind'.[55] They might feel a closer affinity to distant foreigners who shared their interests in natural philosophy or antiquarianism than with their uninterested neighbours. They also hoped to uncover scientific laws that would be applicable anytime and anywhere, and often envisaged the practical uses of that knowledge in similarly universal terms—for the benefit of the entire world. For Shipley's plan to find enough backers, however, he had to appeal to more than just a few scholars. For everybody else in England, the rest of the population of English speakers was already a sufficiently broad group of strangers with whom to develop an affinity.

Serving the public interest was thus synonymous with patriotism—not necessarily a dislike of foreigners, nor even a belief that England was superior to its rivals, but an altruistic devotion to the very broadest group with whom most people in England felt some special bond. A subscriber to Shipley's fund would first and foremost be a 'patron of the nation'.[56] The fund might still encourage improvements that were of universal benefit, for example when it came to alleviating sickness or saving lives—nobody would begrudge such improvements to the rest of the human race. But these had to compete for attention with other, more local concerns. Practical improvements also had to be applied somewhere—that place would be where it was most convenient, at home. When it came down to it, on matters of security, trade, and industry, Shipley's fund in the service of 'the public' would always prioritise the interests of the English. It was 'for the good of mankind in general and of this nation in particular'.[57]

Yet serving the public by subscribing to the fund would not entirely be an act of selflessness. His plan was not contradictory after all. Shipley recognised that in demonstrating some self-sacrifice there was honour and social standing to be had. Public-spiritedness was widely considered a unique attribute of the nobility, 'which does honour to the eminence of their station, and dignifies the enjoyment of superior opulence and wealth'.[58] The nobility's vast riches and political power were deserved, the argument went, because they alone shouldered the responsibility of protecting the public interest. Their wealth gave them the independence to make decisions for the country, in theory making them too rich to be swayed by appeals to self-interest. But the division of the nobility into self-serving party factions had put this justification at risk. What Shipley offered was a new way to affirm their worth—a subscription fund whose sole purpose was serving the public. It would 'unite in one common band all real patriots', leading at least one well-wisher to hope it might even eventually 'utterly extirpate all party distinctions'.[59]

The appeal, however, also extended beyond the nobility, to the minor gentry and the emerging middle classes—the expanding group of merchants and artisans and their children and grandchildren, who had grown wealthy off trade and industry but who now sought the prestige to match it. For them, the ability to demonstrate public-spiritedness would allow them to justify their newly gained privileges and to prove that they, too, could be as noble as the nobility. Shipley's subscription fund would offer a clear proof of that public-spiritedness. He looked to Ireland, which thanks to the Dublin Society's fund could already 'boast her patriots unenobled by titles, and her heroes of a private station'.[60]

In collecting support for his fund, Shipley thus took advantage of self-interest—the human desire for social standing—because he framed it as an act of selflessness. Unlike Henry Sully's society of arts, a speculative project for private profit, Shipley's version was successful because he framed it as a service to the public alone. Whereas Sully's reputation was tarnished by his association with schemers like John Law, Shipley's public-spirited scheme to take on the Northampton fuel engrossers reassured potential subscribers that his proposals were both serious and selfless.

Shipley set out by calling upon Northamptonshire's local gentry, trying to persuade them to sign their names to a list of potential subscribers. If high-ranking aristocrats could be persuaded to sign the list, it would encourage the wealthy middle classes to add their names too. Shipley alone had limited success, but his friends knew of someone with the influence and connections to ensure the scheme's success: Stephen Hales.

By 1751, Hales was a high-ranking clergyman, a trustee of the colony of Georgia, and had recently been given direct access to the royal family as chaplain to the mother of the future King George III. He was the young prince's botany tutor. He thus had connections to the country's highest nobility, clergymen, and natural philosophers. He was also sympathetic to Shipley's aims. Hales, too, was worried about the subversion of the public good to private interests. 'I cannot keep useful secrets', he claimed, unlike the many artisans and manufacturers who denied the public the full advantages of their inventions.[61] Henry Baker knew Hales through the Royal Society, and the host of Northampton's philosophical society, Thomas Yeoman, was the engineer who built and fitted Hales's ventilators.[62] They both seem to have put Shipley in touch.

Hales recommended that Shipley move back to London, particularly in the winter to late spring, when many of the country's politicians and aristocrats would be in town because Parliament was in session. This time of year was known as the 'London season', or even the 'petitioning season', when the roads back to aristocrats' country seats were rendered difficult or impassable by coach or carriage, turned to soft mud by the rains. It meant a relatively captive audience of 'persons of high rank, large fortunes, and great minds'.[63] Hales introduced Shipley to his nephew's nephew-in-law, Robert Marsham, the 2nd Baron Romney, who had apparently been formulating his own plan for a similar organisation together with his brother-in-law, Jacob Bouverie, the 1st Viscount Folkestone. The two aristocrats saw in Shipley someone with the persistence to get it done. Crucially, they allowed him to use their names as he went from door to door trying to drum up support. Hales also facilitated an introduction to a fellow high-ranking clergyman, Isaac Maddox, the Bishop of Worcester, who likewise put his name to the plan.

Shipley now had the credibility he needed. He even managed to get a satirical newspaper to take a break from poking fun and to print his scheme in full: 'I shall make no apology to the lovers of mirth and humour', proclaimed its pseudonymous editor, 'for the seriousness and gravity of what is now laid before them'. Yet after spending December 1753 in the metropolis, Shipley's canvassing failed to yield any new recruits.[64] The London season dragged on without results, and the spring of 1754 approached—an impending closure of the window in which to get the fund started. Finally, on 22 March 1754, Shipley called a meeting of the plan's supporters at Rawthmell's Coffee House, on Henrietta Street in Covent Garden.

Ten others turned up. Shipley was joined by Folkestone and Romney, along with Hales and Baker, who dragged along some of their connections: a couple of other fellows of the Royal Society (a merchant and an instrument maker), and Hales's neighbour (a wax chandler and linen draper). Shipley persuaded one of his friends and his landlord, a surgeon, to show up, along with a jeweller-turned-porcelain maker named Nicholas Crisp. The Bishop of Worcester could not make it, but he paid his subscription. Over coffee, or perhaps something stronger, this small gathering of aristocrats, clergymen, scientists, merchants, artisans and others, declared themselves to be a 'Society for the Encouragement of Arts, Manufactures and Commerce'.

Over the following years it would be called a number of things, sometimes the Premium Society, occasionally the Society of Arts and Sciences. Yet it was most often known as simply the Society of Arts. The members of the new Society committed to pay at least two guineas a year into the fund—almost 3,800 pounds in today's money when compared to the average wage[65]—or twenty guineas to be members for life. Folkestone and Romney committed to cover the costs of the Society's premiums until more subscribers joined. The Society agreed to meet regularly on Wednesday evenings (the Society of Antiquaries and the Royal Society both met on Thursdays), and Shipley jotted down the minutes. The small group met wherever was most convenient, moving between coffee houses, a library, and Shipley's own rooms.

Growth was slow at first. In some early meetings only two or three subscribers were in attendance, and on one occasion Shipley waited around for two hours for someone else to turn up, before giving up and going home.[66] Yet within two years the list of subscribers had swelled to over two hundred, and in another two years to almost seven hundred. Shipley's persistence paid off. By 1758 the Society's fund was so large as to allow them to offer over a hundred separate premiums. Its subscribers included many of the country's top nobility and politicians: various dukes, the prime minister, the chancellor of the exchequer, most of the other cabinet ministers, and many other members of Parliament and government bureaucrats.[67]

The model of the Society of Arts was also quickly adopted elsewhere in Britain, and further afield too. In 1755 in Edinburgh, members of a debating club, the Select Society, founded a subsidiary body to award premiums: an Edinburgh Society for Encouraging Arts, Sciences, Manufactures, and Agriculture in Scotland (the Society of Improvers there had since faded away). And in Wales, at Brecon, a group of enthusiasts in 1755 set up the first of many county premium societies (it continues today as the Brecon County Show, making it the oldest surviving agricultural society in Britain). Other premium societies, often calling themselves 'economic' or 'patriotic' societies, sprung up throughout the 1750s and 60s across France, Germany, Switzerland, America, and even Russia, spurred on by the apparent success of both the Dublin Society and the Society of Arts in London.[68] By 1764, just ten years after the last-ditch attempt at Rawthmell's to get the fund off the ground, the Society of Arts had over two thousand subscribers and had spent over eight thousand pounds in premiums.[69]

The Society printed and circulated lists of its subscribers, mostly in alphabetical order (except that each letter started with the highest nobility, followed by the lords, then the knights, before alphabetically listing the names of the commoners). It seemed that Shipley's intuition was correct: hundreds of people were willing to pay to prove their patriotism (and have their names placed alongside those of the country's highest nobility).

Yet there was more to being a subscriber than just handing over money for appearances. Everyone who paid their two guineas also had an equal say in everything the Society did, whether they were a duke from an ancient lineage, or a merchant with some profits to spare for a patriotic cause. 'The greatest and the meanest are equally industrious in the same design', boasted Henry Baker to a friend, adding that 'all rank and distance is laid aside'.[70] It was a subscriber democracy, and directly democratic. Subscribers could be involved as members so long as they

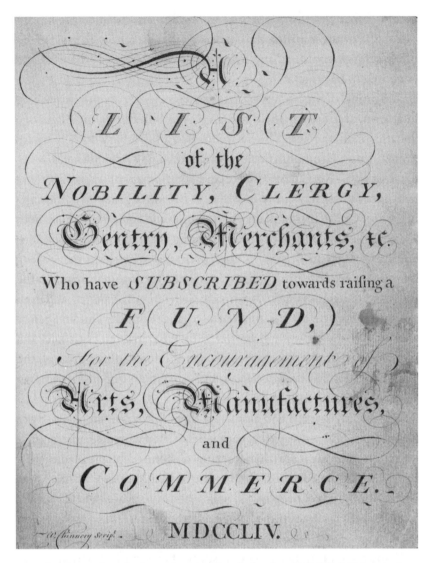

A LIST of the NOBILITY, CLERGY, Gentry, Merchants, &c. Who have SUBSCRIBED towards raising a FUND, For the Encouragement of Arts, Manufactures, and COMMERCE. MDCCLIV.

1.2. Frontispiece from the Society's original list of subscribers. RSA/AD/MA/900/16/1a.

turned up to the meetings, where everything was usually decided by just a show of hands.

The Society gradually adopted rules to formalise their proceedings, for example setting an order in which to discuss matters, requiring that each vote be confirmed at the following meeting, and only allowing the rules and orders to be changed at a quarterly general meeting. But for at least a century the organisation remained essentially flat. From 1755 it annually elected presidents—Folkestone was the first, upon his death succeeded by Romney—but their role was only to lend prestige to the meetings, ensure order, and if necessary cast a tie-breaking vote. A number of vice-presidents were also elected each year to stand in for the presidents when they were away. Beyond this, the sole privilege of these officials was that at the meetings they were the only ones allowed to wear their hats—probably 'cocked' tricorns, made of beaver felt.[71]

As it grew, the Society appointed committees to investigate detailed matters, such as which premiums to advertise and which submissions deserved prizes, but any member of the Society was allowed to attend, and their recommendations were only recommendations. The general membership of the Society always had the final say, voting on whether to accept the committee's recommendations, and often disagreeing. The members could reject a committee's report outright, or force it to reconsider and present fresh recommendations. In the early years the committees would meet throughout the week in coffee houses or taverns, or wherever else was convenient. Over time these committees became more established, and split into regular categories: correspondence, accounts, agriculture, chemistry, mechanics, manufactures, the polite arts, colonies and trade, and miscellaneous matters. As with the president and vice-presidents, the members annually elected committee chairs too.

Shipley had purposefully created a Society over which he had no control. His vote was worth just as much as anyone else's. (He had even originally proposed that the number of votes should be proportional to the amount paid, which would immediately have meant handing over control to the much wealthier aristocrats he had canvassed.) Instead, Shipley was content with serving the Society not as a leader, but as a functionary: he took the minutes, drew up the lists of subscribers and premiums, managed the Society's official correspondence, took care of all its effects, and chased existing members for their two guineas a year. At first he did much of this for free, but it soon became a paid role. The title that eventually stuck for the chief functionary was that of 'secretary', though as the subscription fund grew, so did the Society's activities and staff. Soon many of Shipley's original duties were split between the secretary, an assistant secretary, a collector to chase up the subscriptions, and a 'register', later called the housekeeper, to take care of the Society's rooms and effects.[72] As with all the other positions, however, the Society's principal staff were annually elected by the subscribers. Even their wages and bonuses were put to the vote.

The subscribers were thus more than just piggy banks; if they wanted to, they could turn up to the Society's meetings to exercise their democratic rights. And other than the subscription fee, albeit substantial, there were essentially no other barriers to entry. New members had to be proposed by an existing member and balloted for—at the end of the weekly meetings someone, at first the porter, later a pair of servant boys, would circulate the room with a balloting box, allowing each member to vote by placing a cork ball into a compartment either for or against.[73] But hardly anyone seems to have been turned away. The procedure kept out only known troublemakers—those who had already publicly insulted or libelled members—not those of lower rank or station.[74] Some savvy tradesmen and artisans realised that membership of the Society shortened the social distance between them and many of the wealthy upper classes: the furniture designer Thomas Chippendale, for example, found many future patrons among his fellow members. Over time the number of required proposers for a member increased from one, to two, to three, but with no discernible effect—the Society does not appear to have become more exclusive. If anything, the proportion of the members who were from the middle classes seems only to have increased. By the early nineteenth century one eminent scientist disparaged the members of the Society of Arts as mere 'tradesmen from the Strand'.[75]

Shipley's plan was that anyone and everyone should be allowed to become a modern Maecenas, at once both a patron of the nation and a patron of the arts. Unusually for the eighteenth century, this even extended to women: Shipley saw no reason why women would be any less patriotic or public-spirited than men. Whereas the Royal Society and the Society of Antiquaries admitted members based on perceived achievements in science and antiquarianism, fields from which women were almost entirely excluded, the Society of Arts accepted members based on their values alone. Their patriotism, regardless of gender, would itself be demonstrated by the fact that they chose to subscribe. This open approach meant that the Society of Arts had female members from the very beginning, whereas the much older Royal Society and Society of Antiquaries did not admit women until the 1940s, almost two hundred years later. Yet the Society of Arts was unusually open even when compared to other patriotic funds: its Irish precursor, the Dublin Society, did not admit women to full membership until 1921.

It is not clear just how involved the early female members were. As fully paid-up subscribers, they certainly had the right to attend and vote at meetings, yet there is no evidence that they actually did. Coffee houses had a reputation as raucous places for men to socialise with other men, where they might acquire 'a swagger in the gait, a drunken totter, a noisy riotous deportment, a volley of oaths, and a total want of what is called good-breeding'.[76] Although the establishments were often run by women, they were places men went to escape the company of their wives. The coffee-house culture seems to have stayed with the Society of Arts, even after it moved into more sedate venues. Its debates could become heated, full of 'strong expressions and shouting' as well as 'hissing and clapping'.[77]

A public assembly of men was considered an unsuitable place for women in polite society, even by some of the female members themselves. Elizabeth Montagu, who was a member of the Society of Arts for almost half a century, preferred to cultivate intelligent conversation more privately, over breakfast or tea in the home of an aristocrat. She was leader of the 'bluestockings', a social circle that actively encouraged female intellectuals in traditionally male-dominated spheres, particularly art and literature. Montagu promoted a public role for women, and gloried in the pursuit of fame, but it was to be done via art or the written word, not in person. Women, in her view, needed to protect an image of decorum and virtue so that their words and works could also be admired. If women engaged in heated debates in a public assembly, she feared they might instead appear impassioned instead of reasoned, factious instead of patriotic. She was disparaging of women who were overtly political, complaining that they adopted 'masculine opinions and masculine manners'.[78] Montagu and other female members still engaged in the politics of the Society—they voted in the annual elections of its officers and staff—but they did so behind the scenes, by proxy.[79] (It was only in 1807 that the Society explicitly stated that female members were allowed to attend and vote at all meetings and committees—the introduction of the rule suggests that women had been almost, if not entirely, absent.)

Although the Society's meetings could be raucous, the rules and procedures increasingly resembled those of Parliament. Members were to be seated, only rising one at a time to speak, and had to address the president or vice-president in the chair, much like a member of Parliament should address the Speaker of the House of Commons. The Society became 'a place where many persons chose to try, or to display, their oratorical abilities'—a less exclusive arena in which to gain experience of public speaking, especially for people who might not ever have had a chance of being elected to Parliament.[80] This may explain why so many of the coffee-house literati joined, such as the theatre actor David Garrick.

But the meetings could be intimidating. Oliver Goldsmith, an Irish novelist, playwright and poet, began a speech only to lose his train of thought and be 'obliged to sit down in confusion'. Samuel Johnson, famous for his dictionary, likewise complained how 'all my flowers of oratory forsook me', although on another occasion he is said to have 'excited general admiration' for his 'propriety, perspicuity, and energy' in a speech related to mechanics.[81] It was not all soaring oratory, however. One foreign observer, allowed to attend one of the Society's committee meetings, complained of 'long and vehement speeches' by certain members.[82] Anyone could pay to have their say—the droning bores as well as the eloquent wits.

Also like Parliament, as the Society grew in its prestige, its members felt that it deserved a suitably prestigious venue. There were practical reasons for a new venue too. The number of members hoping to have their say very soon outgrew the living rooms, libraries, and coffee-house booths that the Society had commandeered. It began to hire larger and larger spaces to serve as its 'Great Room'. In 1758, the architect William Chambers—partly responsible for bringing the neoclassical style to Britain—drew up ambitious plans for a building to permanently house the Society. It would be as grand as his later design for Somerset House. He envisaged the Society having halls for displaying models of machinery and works of art, numerous vestibules, living quarters for the staff, and a grand central corridor 'in the manner of an Egyptian hall', flanked by gardened courtyards, which led to a vast oval amphitheatre for the meetings.[83] It was, unsurprisingly, too expensive.

In the end, in 1759 the Society moved into more modest premises in Denmark Court, just off the Strand, though with a Great Room that could fit four hundred. Chambers had to content himself with designing the interior and furniture (the ornate chair he created for the Society's president survives to this day). Fluted Ionic columns decorated the walls, and 23-foot Corinthian pillars held up a 16-foot-high ceiling dome.[84] Yet even these expanded premises became too crowded. Within a year of moving in, the Great Room was so packed and stuffy that the Society considered installing one of Hales's ventilators.[85] The evaporated sweat from the packed-in bodies was condensing in the ceiling dome and dripping back down onto the members' heads.[86]

The Society's rapid growth also produced unpleasantness of a social kind. There was a risk that the Society might 'degenerate into cabal and corruption', a charge often levied at Parliament.[87] In the early days of the Society, sat around a coffee-house table, decisions were often reached unanimously. From this evolved the arrangement of members in a U-shape facing the president, who was flanked by the secretary and assistant secretary. This was unlike Parliament, divided by a wide aisle into two opposing benches—a layout that was immediately adversarial. The Society's somewhat semi-circular layout was instead, at least in theory, conducive to consensus.

The lofty promise of the Society was, after all, that it would unite Britain's middle and upper classes in a common patriotic cause, not descend into petty political factions. Chambers's proposed oval amphitheatre would have emphasised its consensus-building even further. Yet the Society was in this sense a victim of its own success. A larger and

1.3. The distribution of premiums at the Society of Arts. Note the horseshoe configuration of the benches in the Great Room. This is the oldest known depiction of the Society as it actually was. Drawn by Edward Pugh, engraved by Isaac Taylor, and published in 1804 by Richard Phillips to illustrate his *Modern London*.

larger group of members inevitably resulted in a greater diversity of opinions and interests, with members splitting into factions, each with their own ideas as to how the Society should spend its fund. At the same time, the increased size of the fund meant that there was an even larger prize potentially up for grabs. As we shall see, some unscrupulous individuals saw the potential to direct the fund to their own personal gain. So long as they could hoodwink the other members to vote in their favour, the Society's growing wealth provided opportunities for corruption.

It did not help that the Society's aims were so vague—a Society for the Encouragement of Arts, Manufactures, and Commerce covered a lot. Shipley's plan encompassed essentially anything and everything that might be encouraged with the use of premiums. His original proposals promised to 'embolden enterprise, to enlarge science, to refine art, to improve our manufactures, and extend our commerce'.[88] When he mentioned specifics, he covered everything from husbandry to painting, tapestry, architecture, education, and even poetry. Hales had chipped in with naval improvements—nothing could be more useful for a maritime nation—and Shipley had also mentioned ways to reduce unemployment and crime. Ultimately, it would be up to the Society's members to decide.[89]

The Society became popular because its wide remit allowed people to project their own ideas onto it; the control that members had over the Society gave them the chance to materially further each of their own pet projects. At least, if they could persuade enough of their fellow members. Some tried to use the fund to reward new advances in medicine and health. Hales after all had thought that combating disease was one of the clearest proofs of knowledge's usefulness. But for some reason, in the early years, the majority disagreed and premiums for cures were routinely rejected.[90] Others wanted the Society to encourage literature: one hopeful bookseller even proposed the Society be renamed the 'The British Society for the Encouragement of Letters, Arts, and Manufactures'. His hope was largely in vain, except for a 1758 premium for 'the best dissertation on the history of the arts of peace', which would enumerate 'the effects of those improvements on the morals and manners of the people'—several contenders were considered, but never rewarded. The same bookseller also proposed the Society be called 'The Philopatrian Society', because the word was new and distinctive, and alluded to 'the very motive and bond of our association, namely the love of our country'.[91] The original name has nonetheless stuck to the present, except for the 1908 addition of 'Royal', and all of the suggestions retained the breadth of Shipley's ambition: it was a Society to improve everything.

The breadth of Shipley's vision meant that the Society would offer premiums to encourage a staggering and seemingly incoherent variety of things. The Society was often prey to well-organised interest groups, as well as individual schemers. The painters and sculptors wanted it to encourage fine art; the amateur farmers proposed premiums for agriculture; the natural philosophers wanted it to encourage experiments and to collect and disseminate useful knowledge; some people just wanted money for their latest project. As we shall see, the Society was forced to develop ways to deal with corruption and to reduce the power of factions, gradually adding rules to obtain consensus and prevent private interests using the fund to benefit themselves.

Because the majority ruled, the Society often came to reflect the widely held opinions of London's elites, particularly the newly wealthy middle classes, who tended to turn up to vote at the meetings more often than the aristocrats. Subscribers paid to have their say, but they still had to convince enough of the others if they wanted to have their way. The Society's activities thus reveal the priorities of Britain's expanding elites over at least a century. They encouraged everything from sowing acorns, to improved hand-mills, to mechanical means of cleaning chimneys, to transporting fresh fish to London by land. Yet all had in common elements of Shipley's ambition: the redirection of private interests to the benefit of the public.

2

Exciting an Emulation

THERE WAS ONE THING that all members of the Society of Arts agreed upon: the need to encourage commerce. Trade in the eighteenth century was closely tied to the coercive power of the state. It was one of the principal sources of government revenue, both directly through the imposition of customs duties, and indirectly through excise taxes levied on the consumption of many valuable, imported goods such as sugar or tea. As the economic historians Ronald Findlay and Kevin H. O'Rourke have put it, power and plenty were two sides of the same coin: trade financed wars, and wars were used to take control of lucrative trades.

Trade was also seen as a tool for enriching a country at the expense of its neighbours. The prevailing belief among rulers and politicians across Europe was that it was essential to maximise a country's stock of specie—the amount of gold and silver that circulated in its economy. Insufficient specie would harm economic activity and consequently the state's tax revenues. Rivals should thus be made to pay for exports, while as little as possible should be spent on foreign imports. This attitude towards trade, which has since become known as mercantilism, had extraordinary repercussions for policy. Napoleon, for example, reacted to a poor British harvest in 1810 by increasing rather than decreasing France's exports of grain to Britain, taking advantage of the higher prices. That year, French imports supplied over a tenth of its enemy's demand for grain. Meanwhile, France tried to prevent British exports to the rest of continental Europe. Rather than attempting to starve

Britain of food, Napoleon believed the key to victory was to starve it of gold.[1]

Mercantilist attitudes had further geopolitical repercussions. A series of laws in force since the mid-seventeenth century, collectively known as the Navigation Acts, funnelled the lucrative exports of Britain's colonies in the New World and Asia exclusively to Britain, from where it could be re-exported at inflated prices to the rest of Europe. The more Britain could monopolise those trades, the more it could enrich itself and impoverish its rivals. Such monopolies, of course, could only be established and maintained through force. Throughout the seventeenth century, the British and Dutch East India Companies had fought over the control of a handful of islands that exclusively supplied cloves, nutmeg, and mace. The English and Dutch navies, as well as privateers, had likewise repeatedly preyed on each other's merchant shipping, with tensions occasionally spilling over into outright war. Mercantilist attitudes thus drove the acquisition of colonies and stoked European rivalries.

By the mid-eighteenth century, Britain's principal rival in both trade and war was France. To the west, they competed in North America for control of supplies of tobacco, fur, and cod, and in the Caribbean for sugar. In the east, they competed in India for control of supplies of tea and rice. Closer to home, too, British policymakers were concerned by the growing popularity of France's own exports. The French were deemed to have surpassed the British in the beauty of their designs, their exports capturing or creating high-end domestic markets in industry after industry: brightly patterned silk garments, stitched lace of astonishing fineness, ornamented coaches, and elaborate furniture.[2] A British addiction to imported foreign luxuries was thus being taken advantage of by their chief rival, the gold to pay for it flowing out of the country and into their age-old enemy's coffers. The concern with reducing Britain's imports motivated many, if not most, of the premiums offered by the Society of Arts for almost a century.

Apart from the strictly commercial considerations, however, the addiction to foreign luxury was a national embarrassment. Over the course of the early eighteenth century France had established a monopoly on fashion, of which Britain had become an enthralled follower. Luxury

had pervaded all levels of society, from the poorest aspirational consumers right up to the biggest spenders. Robert Walpole, who dominated
British politics for most of the early eighteenth century, in a single year
spent three thousand pounds on imported white wine and chocolate
alone—just under half a million pounds in today's money.[3] Perhaps
unsurprisingly, his indulgence, like that of so many of his peers, left him
with considerable debts. Such expenditure was not just lavish, it was
conspicuous. The aristocracy built vast houses in the country, which
they then stocked with expensive foreign artworks, and surrounded
with fashionable yet otherwise useless landscape gardens. Others abandoned the management of their country estates, spending more and
more of their time in London, where their expenditure on clothing,
food, and drink could have a wider audience.

Members of the Society of Arts wished to do something about Britain's addiction to luxury—the prosperity and pride of the nation was at
stake. Yet there were several potential solutions to the problem. One was
to eradicate the taste for luxury itself. It was considered by many to be
a vice, and in the context of paying the French for their manufactures,
it was almost treasonous. One member, the artist and satirist William
Hogarth, condemned it in his paintings and prints. His satires included
a 'viscount of Squanderfield', dressed to the point of absurdity in the
latest French fashion: red-heeled shoes, lace ruffles, richly embroidered
sleeves, a fake beauty spot on his chin, and a vast black bow in his hair.
Hogarth even depicted him with the mark of syphilis, a sexually transmitted disease, which many believed to be yet another import from
France.[4] Hogarth's warning was that foreign luxury was both morally
and physically debilitating.

An earlier group that attempted to solve the problem was an Association of Anti-Gallicans (from the Latin for anti-French), which in the
mid-1740s began to meet and dine in taverns, coffee houses and chocolate houses across London. They aimed to make the consumption of
France's exports unpopular, publicly refusing to drink French-
imported claret or to wear French-imported lace, which was often
used in men's elaborate shirt ruffles or in the lappets and ribbons that
adorned women's heads.[5]

Yet no amount of Hogarthian moralising, nor the attempt by the Anti-Gallicans to lead a consumer revolution, could stem the tide of imported indulgence. The alternative solution was for Britain's manufactures to out-compete the French. If the taste for luxury could not be eradicated, it might as well be fed from home. In the early 1750s the Anti-Gallican Association offered cash prizes to encourage English-made lace, aiming to replace the French imports. But the Anti-Gallicans split over whether it was a good idea. Some saw it as adding to the problem of luxury rather than solving it. The prizes were soon ended.

The Anti-Gallicans did not last long, but given their similarly patriotic aims, many of their members would find a new home in the Society of Arts. A satirical print in 1757, dedicated to both organisations, depicted French luxuries being unloaded in port, with 'swarms' of French valets, dressmakers, hairdressers, quacks, and disguised Catholic preachers in tow, apparently aiming to infiltrate and enfeeble the British population.[6] Unlike the Anti-Gallicans, however, the members of the Society of Arts recognised from the very beginning that people's taste for luxury was here to stay.

Instead of trying to eradicate luxury, the Society of Arts decided to harness it for the benefit of Britain's economy and society. As historians like John Brewer have argued, the eighteenth century saw the emergence of a new way of thinking about the finer things in life. Luxury could be respectable, with consumption often demonstrating intellect and sophistication, not just indulgence. For the growing middle class in cities like London, being able to show refinement was a key part of being able to rub shoulders with the aristocracy. It was not enough just to be rich; they had to show that they could spend their wealth with taste.[7] The need to demonstrate refinement might be used to benefit the economy, especially if consumers could be persuaded to buy from domestic manufacturers rather than from abroad. To meet the demand for luxury, the Society of Arts sought to encourage a supply that was British.

Out-competing the French, however, required a root-and-branch reform of every aspect of British art and industry, for which the Society's members developed an all-encompassing plan: they would foster the creativity to invent new designs, obtain the skills and materials with

which such designs could be executed, and, for Britain's industries, acquire the technology to apply those designs to manufactures. It was as
part of the contest with France that the Society promoted the 'polite
arts' of drawing, painting, and sculpture, as well as things more obviously applicable to industry.[8] Their plan even required cultivating the
tastes of British consumers, to provide demand for manufactures and
works of art of higher quality. They tried to develop a distinctly British
definition of what counted as tasteful. Rather than being a follower of
fashion, Britain was to be its font.

The Society's founding members started with some of the ingredients for artistic materials, especially colour. Red, for example, was typically obtained from the crushed and dried roots of the madder plant;
and a rich blue was obtained from cobalt ore, roasted into a pigment
called zaffre. Both materials, however, were entirely imported, requiring
the flow of British gold into the coffers of foreign rivals. To make matters
worse, there was a growing suspicion that the Dutch were abusing their
monopoly over madder by ramping up the prices and adulterating it.
British textile manufacturers could not hope to compete with the
French if they had to rely on dyes that were so degraded. The Society's
members believed that the imports of both pigments might be substi-
tuted domestically—there had once been a cobalt mine in Cornwall,
and madder had once been grown in England too. The Society accordingly advertised premiums for the greatest area cultivated with madder
and for the discovery of a new cobalt mine.

A vein of cobalt ore was soon discovered and mined, but within a few
years had been exhausted. More progress was made, however, in discovering the method of extracting the pigment from the ore. One of the
Society's founding members, the goldsmith-turned-potter Nicholas
Crisp, claimed a medal for the process, and Britain soon gained an industry—cobalt ore was by the 1760s being imported from Austria un-
processed, rather than being manufactured into the pigment abroad.

As for madder, the Society met with less success, but not for want
of trying. Its members successfully lobbied Parliament to change the
way madder was taxed, and they made a rare exception for the root in
the way they awarded premiums. Instead of offering a prize for the

most madder grown in a particular year, for a few years in the 1760s the Society offered a straightforward subsidy of five pounds for any and all acres of madder grown (about six hundred pounds in today's money). This proved to be expensive—the Society ended up subsidising almost three hundred acres, and so madder alone in those years cost the Society more than the rest of their agriculture-related premiums combined.[9]

Yet for all the time and money spent on the madder root, the Society would have little to show for it. Imports of madder decreased only in the short term, and the English growers quickly disappeared without a trace. By 1803, only a few decades after the scheme had ended, even the freshest madder available in England was imported from Holland.[10] The Society's members consoled themselves by claiming that the threat of competition from English-grown madder at least forced the Dutch to lower their prices, though it is unclear whether this was true.[11] British art and manufactures continued to rely almost exclusively on imported madder until it was supplanted in the late nineteenth century by synthetic dyes.

The Society also offered premiums for various other artistic and design materials in its competition against the French, from watercolours, to crayons, to sources of black chalk, as well as varnishes and new dyes for cloth.[12] The list goes on and on. One member proposed a premium for better kinds of paper, saying he was moved to do so 'as an Englishman': the finest and whitest papers, which could be used for printing engravings, were almost entirely imported from France.[13] The Society's members were even concerned by imports of artificial flowers, often made from fine painted paper, for which Britain apparently paid 'a sum that would appear almost incredible'.[14]

Yet the Society did more than just encourage the acquisition of materials and the manufacture of imported fashion items. From the very beginning, the Society also sought to encourage drawing, the artistic skill deemed most essential to the greatest number of trades and industries, as well as to art itself.[15] In encouraging skills, the Society would have more success. At the very first meeting at Rawthmell's coffee house, the eleven founder members decided to offer cash prizes for the best drawings by young boys and girls, to identify artistic talent as early as possible. By offering such prizes, they hoped that more young people would be encouraged to apply themselves to art for the first time, and that the already talented young people would be inspired into a healthy competitiveness, each trying to surpass the other. They hoped, they said, to 'excite an emulation'. Over time, the overall standard of young people's art and design would rise.

Shipley ran a drawing school for children while he was in London, and referred some of his pupils to the Society for the competition. For a time, his school and the Society even shared premises. For the youngest boys and girls, the drawings could be of any type, as the aim was to first identify talent in general—'dawning genius'.[16] For the slightly older boys and girls, the Society very early on encouraged the application of their talents to industry. They advertised prizes for designs that could be woven, embroidered, or printed, to aid Britain's textile industry in its competition with France. To these were soon added drawings for the use of cabinet-makers, coach-makers, potters, and the manufacturers of metal objects.[17]

As the Society became more popular, however, it could afford to encourage more than just drawing. Its advertised list of premiums soon included prizes for modelling in wax or clay, useful for designing medals, furniture, vases, and chandeliers. It also offered premiums for engraving, which would allow the best designs to be printed and thus more widely disseminated and adopted.[18] Embroidery, knitting, lace-stitching, and pattern-weaving were also essential if the superior designs were to be applied directly to textiles.[19] Yet the Society's encouragement of these skills inadvertently opened the door to a group that had its own, special interests. As a direct democracy, and with its broad aims, the Society was vulnerable to being taken over.

The vulnerability was almost immediately put to the test. To encourage artistic talent with its premiums, the Society required artists to act as judges. It approached some of the most eminent artists of the day, such as the sculptor Henry Cheere, the architect William Chambers, and the celebrated portrait painter Joshua Reynolds. They soon joined as members too. But the artists had their own ideas about how the

2.1. Ornamental design by John Bellingham, for which he was awarded
a premium by the Society in 1757. RSA/PR/AR/103/14/37.

Society ought to use its subscription fund. They were, in fact, an increasingly coordinated group, largely led by a painter named Francis Hayman. His 'jolly and facetious' manner smoothed over their frequent
bickering, allowing them to act in concert. When the artists began to
disagree on something, Hayman's favourite tactic was to 'drown their
heartburnings in bumpers of wine'.[20]

In the late 1750s, the artists waged a campaign to redirect the Society towards their own ends. For Hayman and his friends, Britain's slavish following of French style was not simply a matter of money, nor even of fashion, but of artistic prestige. It was embarrassing that a nation of Britain's military and economic might did not have its own correspondingly beautiful and unique artistic tradition. British victories were mentioned only in 'plain journals of facts', while even the most heinous of French crimes would be immortalised in art as glorious triumphs.[21] It was a matter of national ornament.

To compete with the French, however, the artists felt that the Society was wrong to encourage the application of art to design. If artistic skills were immediately applied to manufactures, they argued, the Society would merely encourage designs that inevitably followed what was already known to be profitable, and French. They believed that 'no taste can ever be formed in manufactures', as creating designs that were profitable would mean that people never risked creating something that was too new.[22] If they were to achieve a uniquely British style, they required images that were fresh and original. Hayman and his friends pushed instead for an exclusive focus on 'high', or 'fine' art.

If the Society wished to free Britain from its following of French fashion, the artists argued, then it would need to encourage painting (and to a lesser extent sculpture and architecture). This belief stemmed from the art theories of the Renaissance, of which painters like Joshua Reynolds were avid followers. There was, Reynolds argued, an 'intellectual dignity' that separated the painter from the 'mere mechanic'. Painting was not just about copying nature, skilfully reproducing everything in minute detail; at its best it was about improving nature, using the imagination to uncover a hidden essence or ideal of beauty. Skills like drawing were of course necessary, and the artists were content for the Society's premiums for drawing and engraving to continue, but these mechanical aspects of art were not enough. Unlike profit-led design, obliged to follow fickle fashions, painting at its purest could be timeless, universal. To reach greatness, Reynolds argued, painters had to separate themselves from what was merely trendy, and create something that would appeal to 'the people of every country and every age'.[23]

Achieving the universal ideal involved capturing the viewer's imagination and stimulating them intellectually, not merely delighting their senses. This belief implied a strict hierarchy: the more intellect involved, the higher the branch of painting. At the bottom were still lifes, followed by landscapes and scenes of everyday life. Higher still was portraiture, but highest of all was 'history painting'—a category that encompassed allegorical, mythological and religious scenes, as well as actual history.[24] It was here that 'genius is chiefly exerted': the artist needed to be inventive, arranging scenes that never were, and educated enough to choose symbols that could convey hidden meanings.[25] The artist needed to be intimately familiar with religious and classical references, and the same education was required of the viewer, too, who needed to be able to identify the allegories and appreciate their subtleties. A great history painter was on par with a great poet.

If painting, sculpture, and other forms of 'high' art were encouraged, argued Hayman and his friends, then they had no doubt that the 'inferior' artistic applications would inevitably benefit too. Their argument seems to have held some sway with the Society's other members. In 1759, the artists persuaded the Society to offer generous premiums for the best original history painting, open to painters of any age. Hayman and his friends began at the summit—with the highest of high art—and then worked their way down. A premium for landscape paintings soon followed. The painters' taste, they believed, insulated from having to consider vulgar profitability, would eventually trickle down to manufactures.[26]

The artists appealed to the rest of the Society on the basis of history painting's supposed effect on manufactures and commerce. Yet history painting was also about improving the nation's morals. The symbols and hidden meanings were not just clever puns; the images were supposed to be instructive, to inspire viewers to virtue. History painting illustrated the exploits of the great and the good—paragons of virtue—to set an example to others of integrity and public-spiritedness. This was yet another reason the production of high art had to be insulated from the dictates of the market: if it was to instil virtue, it could not simply follow demand. Most demand from private individuals for art was for their own portraits. The artists instead wished to impose moral messages on the public.[27]

Yet the rest of the Society apparently added their own, patriotic twist to the premiums for history painting.[28] According to academic art theorists, the subjects of history paintings were supposed to be taken from classical Greek or Roman history. Figures draped in togas who had been dead for over a thousand years were far removed from the drudgery of everyday modern life. They were uncontroversial and could thus be upheld as paragons of virtue in a way that more recent and local historical figures could not. Someone like Oliver Cromwell, who had died only a century earlier, was too divisive. Depending on the viewer's politics, he was either an ambitious and fanatical tyrant, or a selfless promoter of parliamentary liberties. Such difference of opinion got in the way of moral education.

Nonetheless, the other members of the Society stipulated that the subjects of the premium paintings should be taken from English history, not the Greek and Roman classics.[29] The symbols and allegories would thus be distinct from those found abroad. The artists gave way: it would, after all, be a key step in asserting Britain's artistic independence and developing an original, national style. British history painting would still try to instil virtue, and would remain uncontroversial, at least to the British. The first painting to win the prize was Robert Edge Pine's *Surrender of Calais to Edward III,* which depicted the French at the mercy of an English king.[30] It was perhaps uncontroversial to any staunch British patriot, but probably not to any viewers who were French.

Hayman and the artists were not content, however, with just adding premiums to the Society's advertised list. To truly insulate artists from the dictates of the market and enable them to produce great history painting, they believed they required state funding. British artists looked with envy at their counterparts in France: Louis XIV, whose opulence earned him the epithet the 'Sun King', had in 1648 founded a royal academy of painting and sculpture. High art in France had a permanent source of training and funding, and an institution to oversee the refinement of its national style.[31] With such an institution in Britain too, a

2.2. Drawing in chalk from a bust, by a Miss Augusta Hamlyn of Plymouth, 1824, for which she won the Society's silver palette medal. RSA/PR/AR/103/14/1025.

national style might be allowed to develop (not to mention the good it would do for artists' finances).

British artists had tried to set up an academy of arts throughout the early eighteenth century, but with limited success.[32] The exceptions were in Ireland and Scotland, where state subsidies found their way to art academies in Dublin and Edinburgh via other organisations.[33] In London, however, attempts to organise an academy tended to disintegrate into fractious splinter groups.[34] Teachers like William Shipley provided only basic training for children in the mechanics of drawing, for example getting them to repeatedly sketch parts of the face.[35] The very best pupils might then win a drawing premium from the Society of Arts, but those who wished to pursue art as a career had limited options. Some joined the St Martin's Lane academy where they could draw

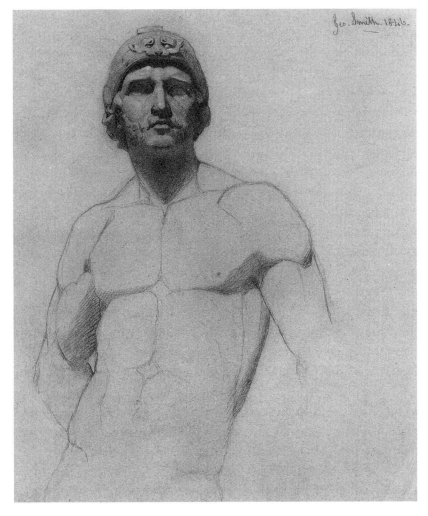

2.3. Drawing of a classical sculpture by a George Smith, 1846. RSA/PR/AR/103/14/561.

nude models, though the choice there was limited to just one male and one female.[36]

Young would-be artists tried to go abroad to widen their imaginations and intellects, particularly to Italy, where they could be exposed to the most celebrated art of ancient Rome and the Renaissance. From 1758, they were partly saved the trouble of travelling when the Duke of Richmond commissioned copies and plaster casts of many of the most famous sculptures for his private collection in London, allowing some artists to come and sketch them. He gave special access to young artists hoping to obtain the Society of Arts drawing premiums. Nonetheless, British artists were still at a disadvantage. A national academy on the French model would give more than just a few plaster casts to copy. It would provide comprehensive instruction in classics, history, philosophy, anatomy, and perspective—the academic skills needed to produce art that was intellectual, like history painting.[37]

Some British artists, however, vehemently opposed the idea of a French-style national academy. The painter and satirist William Hogarth, who ran the St Martin's Lane academy, worried that such an institution would inevitably reduce British artists to stifling conformity. He saw it as fundamentally un-English to have a top-down organisation imposing its ideas of what counted as superior or inferior. He was proud that the artists at his academy each had an equal and democratic say in how it was run, much like the subscriber democracy of the Society of Arts. The St Martin's Lane academy's artists were not dependent upon one another, divided into hierarchies of students and teachers, which was what a French-style academy would entail. Nonetheless, Hogarth was in the minority. Many artists saw in the Society of Arts their chance to acquire their national academy, particularly given its connection to Shipley's drawing school. In 1755, less than a year after the Society was founded, the artists had begun to lobby for its support.[38]

Hogarth's opposition, however, was not just ideological. He also opposed a national academy on more practical grounds. Despite being an early member of the Society of Arts, he quickly became disillusioned with its premiums for drawing. He worried that encouraging young people to become artists was actually cruel, as there was simply not enough demand for their work. The domestic market was simply too small to support more than a handful of contemporary British artists.[39] Those who managed to scrape a living tended to stick to profitable trades like portraiture, which satisfied individual vanities, not high-minded and preachy projects like history painting. Hogarth argued that training people to become artists, as would happen in a national academy, would leave artists unemployed and destitute. Over-supply of artists would lead them to undercut one another's wages, to the harm of them all.[40]

In the face of these problems, Hayman and his friends changed tactics. If Hogarth's objection could be removed—if demand for art in Britain could be demonstrated or even boosted—then nothing would stand in the way of the creation of their national art academy. But there were major obstacles to boosting demand. Abroad, artists could rely on the patronage of their monarchs. In France, artists lived off the opulent court at Versailles, which demanded ever-changing images and fashions. Louis XIV of France had achieved fame as 'the soul and spirit of all improvements in France, which make it the present envy of the world', and his successors had emulated him.[41] Britain, meanwhile, had George I and II—German kings more interested in hunting, cards, and minutely arranged military parades than in high-minded intellectual pursuits like art. Their era is often referred to as 'pudding time', connoting easy but unrefined indulgence.[42] (The only major exception was music. The first two Georges were patrons of the composer George Frederick Handel, though he was also a German import.)

Even below the monarch, among the aristocracy, the market for art in Britain was for the works of long-dead 'Old Masters', not contemporaries.[43] And when there was demand for art that was new, it was for the foreign, with the French and Italian artists widely considered superior. British aristocrats, to complete their education in taste, went on a 'Grand Tour' through France, to Italy. There they inspected the works of the ancient and Renaissance Italians while picking up French styles along the way.[44] As a result, Britain's self-styled connoisseurs tended to be collectors of antiquities abroad rather than patrons of the living at home. Hogarth once satirised them as a half-blind monkey outfitted in the dandiest French styles, inspecting and watering trees that had been dead for centuries.

One solution to the problem of demand was to inspire an appreciation of contemporary art in the patrons of the future. In 1757 the Society created a special class of drawing premiums specifically for young aristocrats. As befit 'persons of rank and condition', the prizes could not be in anything so vulgar as cash. They instead offered honorary medals. The

2.4. William Hogarth's satire of English connoisseurs, showing them as a half-blind monkey dressed as a dandy, inspecting and watering long-dead trees. The print appeared in the exhibition catalogue of the Society of Artists of Great Britain, 1761.

idea was that wealthy children, if they could be encouraged to develop their own skills as amateur artists, would learn to appreciate the superior skills of contemporary and native professionals. The medals encouraged young aristocrats to engage in art as active practitioners, and in their native land, to supplement their passive viewing and collection of the works of the ancients while abroad on the Grand Tour.

The children who won the Society's medals would be recognised for their 'elegant taste', allowing them to claim public acknowledgement as art connoisseurs.[45] Eventually, when they came into their inheritances or gained control of their incomes, they could confidently lavish their funds on contemporary artists without the risk that the rest of polite society would accuse them of being pretentious. The medals would be proof that the children of the aristocracy were sufficiently knowledgeable and discerning to be 'competent judges of the merit of artists'.[46] Whereas undertaking the Grand Tour allowed them to claim they were connoisseurs of classical and foreign culture, the medals were specifically focused on art that was both native and current. They also, significantly, cultivated an appreciation of contemporary British art while the aristocrats were still children, long before they came of age and departed for Italy. The Society got to them while they were young.

Probably unintentionally, the medals proved especially popular with girls. Young women could not go on the Grand Tour as easily as men— it was seen as unsuitable (in addition to classical art and architecture, the men often used the trip to gain experience of European brothels, or to conduct affairs). But women were equally entitled to the Society's premiums. When the Society had first offered its premiums for drawings by girls and boys, the category had been mixed. 'Several young ladies and girls', however, soon petitioned the Society for separate drawing prize categories for women—they wanted to increase their chances of winning, to not have to compete with boys who were often given more training. The Society accepted their request.[47] The Society's medals thus provided women, denied the opportunity of going on the Grand Tour, with a way to prove that they, too, could be connoisseurs. Indeed, most of the medals for the children of the nobility were won by girls.

The first winner, in 1758, was the daughter of an earl, and other young aristocrats followed her example.[48] The distribution of Society of Arts premiums soon became a place for young aristocrats to see and be seen: 'one of the most interesting scenes which the metropolis affords', said one popular London guidebook, where a polite audience could appreciate 'lovely diffidence of blooming beauty, tremblingly alive to the distinction, approaching to receive the honours which await her'.[49] Although the prizes were initially awarded as and when they were won, from 1788 the distribution of prizes became major annual events. Right up until the mid-nineteenth century the newspapers never failed to comment on how many elegantly dressed women were to be seen at them.[50] (Indeed, the Society once received a letter, signed 'Modestus', suggesting that as so many women were present at the ceremony, the 'pudenda' of a statue of Mars in the room should be covered with a lump of clay.[51]) The full impact of the Society's medals is impossible to measure, but by 1847 the demand for contemporary art had grown to such an extent that they were considered redundant and were discontinued: 'art now forms so considerable a portion of the education of all the upper classes, that it does not need any such stimulus'.[52]

For Hayman and the artists, however, this was only the beginning. It was all very well cultivating the art patrons of the future, but they wished to see demand boosted in the short term too. Some of them had visited France and been impressed by the ways it cultivated a market for art that was new. Since the late seventeenth century, the French academy had exhibited the work of contemporary artists in large halls, known as *salons*, exposing them to wider audiences of potential patrons. The salons were also an appropriate venue for art aimed at the public rather than individuals, creating the potential for an entirely new kind of market.[53] The nascent middle classes, who might not be able to afford private portraits, might be charged for a viewing of public history paintings. They might even be inspired to buy print copies. Given British monarchs seemed uninterested in funding art, perhaps British artists could pursue a bottom-up approach and organise similar such exhibitions themselves. The profits could then be used to fund a national academy.

There was reason to be optimistic about holding such an exhibition in Britain. The artists had the example of the Foundling Hospital, a charity set up in 1739 to support abandoned and orphaned children. Hogarth had been one of the founding governors and used his fame as a painter to make it London's most fashionable charity: he persuaded many of his contemporaries to donate and display their works there, alongside his own.[54] The popularity of the exhibits there persuaded many artists—some of whom became quite famous—that there might be demand in Britain for a dedicated exhibition, in which contemporary art would be the focus, not just the sideshow.

The obvious venue for a dedicated exhibition was the Society of Arts. By 1759, the Society had acquired a suitably large 'Great Room' on the Strand, which was used to showcase the works of the boys and girls who won its premiums for drawings. The Society was also already a widely respected institution, which by acting as host would allow the unfamiliar novelty of an exhibition to be seen as a reputable event rather than a potential scam.[55] And the artists were well-placed to use the Society to get what they wanted. Francis Hayman and his friends, initially involved as judges for the drawing prizes, by that stage dominated the Society's committee dealing with the polite arts. They had turned up in numbers to hijack a meeting of the chemistry committee, using it to instead push through the Society's premium for history painting.

But when the committee on history painting recommended that the prize-winning works be shown to the public at a special exhibition, the Society's other members shot the proposal down. The artists tried again the following week, extending the proposed exhibition to sculpture as well as paintings, but they were once again thwarted.[56] The artists decided they would have to be more coordinated to get the exhibition they wanted. Hayman and his friends met separately, at the Foundling Hospital, and put out the call for a general meeting of painters, sculptors, architects, engravers, and any other kinds of artists they could think of as potential allies. They would need all the help they could get if they were to outvote the other members of the Society of Arts.

This broad coalition of artists met at the Turk's Head Tavern, in Gerrard Street (the building survives, in what is now London's Chinatown). They elected a committee to represent them, with Hayman at its head.[57] Having thus secured an air of democratic legitimacy, with the help of the famed author Samuel Johnson they drafted a formal letter to the Society of Arts to request the use of its room for their exhibition. They then flooded the Society's meetings with their members. Hayman even sat on the special committee appointed to consider his own letter—after all, any subscriber to the Society was entitled to attend any committee they wished. In the face of such numbers, the Society was forced to agree to the artists' request.[58] The Society, a direct democracy, had seemingly been captured by a well-organised faction.

Finally, almost a century later than the French, in April 1760 the Society of Arts hosted England's first dedicated exhibition of contemporary art. The walls were crowded with 130 works, right up to the ceiling: a crammed hodgepodge of paintings, sculptures, wax models, drawings, and medallions. The artists exhibited for an audience that had never been assembled before, so each pursued experimental strategies to stand out. Some immediately aimed high, with moralistic history painting chock full of classical allusions that would only be familiar to the most discerning of connoisseurs. Others sought to flatter their hosts, for example with a portrait of William Shipley, or with a portrait of the wife of Viscount Folkestone. Quite a few artists decided the best way to grab attention would be to depict recognisable celebrities, particularly noted beauties and actors. There was more than one image of the actor David Garrick (who had also been an influential ally in persuading the Society to hold the exhibition). Some artists tried to combine the celebrity factor with an appeal to patriotic sentiment, particularly as the previous year Britain had won a string of seemingly miraculous victories during the Seven Years' War. Rival sculptors revealed their proposed designs for a tomb for Britain's latest military hero, General James Wolfe, who had died during the capture of Quebec.[59]

On the face of it, the exhibition was a success, pulling in an estimated crowd of twenty thousand. But from the perspective of Hayman and the artists, things had not quite gone to plan. Alongside the ordinary exhibits, the Society of Arts used the exhibition to display that year's premium-winning history paintings and landscapes, as well as the works of the children who won its drawing premiums. Adding the premium-winning works to the mix confused some visitors into thinking that any works without prizes attached to them were the competitions' also-rans. More than one artist bitterly complained of the imputed 'disgrace of having lost that which he never sought'.[60] The press coverage also failed to mention the new coalition of artists, instead giving all the credit to the Society of Arts as hosts.[61]

To make matters worse, the artists had also wanted to charge a shilling for entry, but were forced by the rest of the Society to make admission free. To raise any money from the venture, the artists instead had to print and sell catalogues for only half a shilling. This was not a matter of grubby profit, they argued, as they proposed that the funds would all be used for charitable purposes, to support artists who were too old or infirm to continue their profession. The real issue was that free entry attracted the wrong sort of people. The Society of Arts tried to exclude various undesirables, such as servants, foot soldiers, and women with children. They even banned smoking and drinking on the premises, and constables were present to eject any troublemakers.[62] Despite these efforts, however, the exhibition was beset by 'irregularities': windows were smashed, and the Society's porter, the unimaginatively named Morgan Morgan, was 'greatly abused and assaulted' when he tried to nudge a man out of the way of some ladies (Morgan promptly returned the punch, but no witnesses could be found to prosecute his attacker).[63]

The artists complained that the exhibition was 'crowded and incommoded by the intrusion of great numbers whose stations and education made them no proper judges of statuary or painting'.[64] They had originally planned to sell only a thousand catalogues, but the unexpectedly high numbers meant they ended up printing and selling over six times that number. The 'tumult and disorder', they grumbled, scared off the intended, more refined audience. Whereas they had hoped to attract wealthy potential patrons, they instead heard 'their works censured or approved by kitchen-maids and stable-boys'.[65] The artists believed a shilling for entry—worth almost ninety pounds today, and equivalent then to an ordinary seat at the theatre—would easily have prevented what they described as a 'prostitution of the polite arts'.[66]

Yet when Hayman and his friends asked the Society of Arts to host a second exhibition in 1761, their suggested improvements were flatly rejected.[67] The Society had not been totally captured. The other subscribers to the Society likely opposed entry fees because they might be seen as for the private benefit of artists, rather than for the public good. They also had good reason for suspecting the artists' motives, as the profits from the sale of catalogues from the first exhibition had not found their way to the old or infirm. Hayman's committee at the Turk's Head Tavern, when it totted up the profits, had instead immediately redirected the funds towards setting up their dreamed-of national academy.[68]

The artists tried a number of times to propose entry fees at the Society's meetings, but could never quite muster a decisive majority.[69] Although the artists had seen some initial success in capturing the subscriber democracy, the Society's leaders had found ways to prevent a determined faction from gaining total sway. They repeatedly postponed discussion whenever votes were likely to be too close, or when things became too heated (the minutes euphemistically describe entry fees as having been a 'matter of much debate', with artists 'expressing their dissatisfaction').[70] They also required every resolution of the Society to be confirmed at the following week's meeting. This rule, along with the postponements, meant that the artists had to turn up to meetings week after week and in sufficient numbers to get the results they wanted.

Such coordination proved beyond them; many of the artists simply gave up and left. In 1761, Hayman and his friends—particularly many of the famous painters, sculptors, and architects—held a separate exhibition just a few minutes' walk down the road at an auction house at Spring Gardens, where they charged for entry. They came to style themselves the Society of Artists of Great Britain (SAGB), to stress that their fees would go towards the patriotic ends of glorifying the nation (while also quietly dropping their previous promises of charity). The success of the first exhibition had buoyed confidence in their ability to attract an audience, and they were even briefly joined by William Hogarth, despite his vocal opposition to a national academy. Yet Hayman's splinter group became increasingly exclusive and elitist, emphasising the superiority of painting, sculpture, and architecture over fields like engraving. The painters in particular came to dominate, though their exhibitions gradually gained a reputation for high-quality history painting.[71]

Not all of the artists left with Hayman and his friends. Some continued to exhibit at the Society of Arts, where entry remained free, and where they made a point of actually giving their profits to various charitable causes. This group, who came to call themselves the 'Free Society of Artists' (FSA), was largely organised by the miniature painter and engraver John Finlayson, and a lawyer and amateur landscape painter named Jared Leigh. Their exhibitions at the Society of Arts continued to be popular. Worried about the crush of bodies, in 1762 they refitted the doors to the Great Room to open outwards.[72] That same year, possibly due to the strain of so many people, the room's supports even threatened collapse.

In 1764, however, the members of the FSA fell out spectacularly. Finlayson appears to have accused Leigh and his fellow FSA committee members of embezzling funds.[73] This caused some 'very warm debates till very late at night'.[74] Things must have become even more heated, as Finlayson was eventually expelled from the Society for 'having disturbed the peace'.[75] His name was struck off the list of members and he was forbidden entry to the premises. (Leigh would later turn out to have been corrupt in the judging of one of the artistic premiums, so Finlayson's accusations may well have been justified, and he was eventually allowed back in.[76]) Fed up with the infighting, the Society of Arts refused to host the FSA's exhibitions any longer. The FSA moved elsewhere.

Meanwhile, although Hayman's splinter group and its exhibitions continued to grow in popularity and prestige, within a few years it had also succumbed to infighting. Hayman and his friends, in their positions of leadership within the SAGB, were accused of abusing their authority by excluding the works of their younger rivals or otherwise displaying them in a bad light (sometimes, quite literally, up in the highest and darkest corners of the room). In 1768, the disaffected artists managed to eject Hayman from his position as president by a general vote, prompting many of his friends to resign in angry protest—the architect William Chambers reportedly railed against the young upstarts in an expletive-ridden tirade.[77]

Despite the repeated splits, public exhibitions of contemporary art very quickly became permanent fixtures of London's cultural scene. Londoners even had a choice of at least two or three exhibitions for the next few years, as the rival groups each vied to outdo the other. Yet success proved to be a double-edged sword. Although exhibitions exposed artists to a wider public of consumers, they also exposed them to criticism. Some of the more eminent artists, even Hogarth, were mercilessly criticised in the press for some of their exhibition performances, or found themselves upstaged by young new rivals. Hogarth in 1762 hit back against the idea of exhibitions with satire. He contributed to the exhibition of a fictional 'Society of Sign-Painters', which ridiculed Hayman and his friends for their pretended hierarchies of art, and purposefully duped the public into paying for something they could see for free out on the street.[78] It poked further fun at the SAGB's entry fees by pretending to have patriotic purposes while advertising that the proceeds were spent at the pub.[79]

The added risk to artists' reputations meanwhile did not always come with much cash attached, as exhibition audiences did not often choose to buy what they saw. Even when artists were lavished with praise, this did not necessarily bring them financial reward. Nonetheless, the exhibitions did have the desired effect of encouraging forms of art—particularly history painting—that otherwise suffered a lack of demand.[80] They also, finally, led to the realisation of the artists' long-standing dream: a national academy.

Although George II had been wholly uninterested in intellectual pursuits, the education of his grandson and successor in 1760, George III, had been replete with artistic training, including private lessons in architecture with William Chambers. Carefully cultivated to a love of the arts, George III was an active patron of architects, sculptors, and painters. He reputedly even displayed a landscape drawing at the first breakaway 1761 exhibition at Spring Gardens, under the name of his former perspective-drawing tutor.[81] In 1765 he granted the SAGB royally incorporated status, and in 1767 attended its exhibition and donated money.[82]

The exhibitions had thus done more than just demonstrate the potential new market for art; they had captured the imagination of the country's most important patron. Meanwhile, in 1764, Hogarth died—the academy's most influential opponent was gone. Hayman and his friends, when they were unceremoniously ejected from the SAGB, therefore had nothing to lose. Via Chambers's personal connection, they presented a petition to the king for the creation of a national academy. After decades of obstructive bickering among British artists, George III in December of 1768 established a Royal Academy of Arts.

The Royal Academy's exhibitions continue to this day, long outlasting those of the SAGB and the FSA, which limped on for only a few more years. Just as importantly, Britain gained an institution that provided artistic training on the French model. Yet the Royal Academy was more hierarchical than Hogarth could ever have imagined. It limited itself to a mere forty members when the already exclusive SAGB had had about two hundred. It was also focused on the 'high art' of painting, sculpture, and architecture, to the exclusion of most engravers, seal cutters, and other assorted artists.[83]

Over the following decades the Society of Arts and the Royal Academy settled into a new routine of coexistence, in which they divided the labour of encouraging British art. (Despite the animosity of the original split, the Society of Arts soon even started to take credit for the Royal Academy's founding, citing its support of the original exhibition.[84]) In terms of demand, the Society continued to foster future patrons with its medals for young aristocrats, while the Royal Academy exposed the works of contemporary artists to the already existing patrons at its annual exhibitions. In terms of supply, the Society continued to identify fresh young talent, rewarding boys and girls for their drawings, painting, and sculpture. They were often educated by their parents or at a number of small elementary art schools—sometimes even at Shipley's own. As they approached adulthood, however, the Royal Academy often admitted the very best of the boys to its school, which had absorbed the St Martin's Lane academy (quite literally by stealing its equipment).[85] There, young artists were provided with a more advanced education in art, taught by professors in subjects like anatomy and perspective as well as painting and architecture. The very best of these young men might then eventually be admitted to the Royal Academy's membership, as one of the select group of forty.

In the late eighteenth century almost half of the men who completed the tortuous path to being elected a full Royal Academician had earlier won awards from the Society of Arts. The Society often gave them their first public recognition. John Everett Millais, in 1838, aged only 9, was reportedly on a coach to London with his family when he sketched a slumbering Joseph Paxton (we shall later meet him as the designer of the Crystal Palace). Paxton awoke and was so impressed that he wrote him a letter of introduction to the Society of Arts. Millais, who trained at the art school of yet another former Society of Arts prize-winner,

Henry Sass, won its premiums for three years in a row, the first for a chalk drawing from a bust.[86] At Millais's first prize-giving, dressed smartly in a black-belted white tunic with a filled collar and bright necktie, his bare knees showing between frilled white shorts and white socks, he was so tiny that the Society's president, the Duke of Sussex, did not see him from behind his raised desk. 'A long time coming up', commented the duke, to which the secretary intervened by diplomatically pointing out 'he is here'.[87] A couple of years later, aged only 11, Millais became the youngest student ever to be admitted to the Royal Academy's school. There he met some like-minded artists and would eventually form the Pre-Raphaelite Brotherhood—an artistic movement that would overturn many of the Renaissance theories propounded by the Royal Academy's founders. Despite this radicalism, Millais would later spend the final few months of his life as the Royal Academy's president.

Yet another young painter who went from winning Society of Arts prizes to eventually becoming Royal Academy president was Thomas Lawrence—one of the leading portrait painters of the early nineteenth century. His start, however, was less fortunate. He submitted a drawing to the Society when he was 14, but the polite arts committee discovered that he had continued to draw beyond the allotted time. They disqualified him from the gold medal, though in recognition of his talent still awarded him a lesser medal and some cash.

Although the Society's awards featured in the early careers of many of the nineteenth century's most eminent British painters, its main impact was on British sculpture. In the mid-eighteenth century, Britain did not have many sculptors: only three were included among the thirty-six founding members of the Royal Academy, and the market was dominated by foreign-trained immigrants: Rijsbrack and Scheemakers from Flanders, Carlini from Italy, and especially the French-born Roubiliac. The Society saw a role for itself in helping to establish a pool of native-born talent.

One of Shipley's own drawing pupils, the sculptor Joseph Nollekens, was first brought to the attention of the public by the Society's awards—the first in 1759, when he was 18, for a drawing of a faun, along with a

number of later awards for sculpting in clay and on marble tablets in
bas-relief. Even at this early stage he stood out: on one occasion he was
reprimanded in front of the entire Society by the president, Viscount
Folkestone, for complaining about how the prize for clay models had
been judged.[88] On another occasion he was accused of having been
helped by a teacher. Nollekens was locked in a room alone for three
hours, and another four hours the following day, to prove to the judges
by the quality of his drawing that his work really was his own. They were
duly satisfied and impressed.[89] Nollekens used his prize-money to fund
a trip to Rome—then considered essential to the education of any great
sculptor, which allowed him to directly study the works the Renaissance, particularly Michelangelo, as well as to meet future patrons
among the young aristocrats on the Grand Tour. As luck would have it,
in Rome he was recognised by David Garrick, who remembered him
from the various controversial prize-givings and became his first patron.
Having been given this initial boost by the Society and one of its members, Nollekens rose swiftly in the British art world. He was soon elected
to the Royal Academy and become the country's most popular sculptor
of portrait busts.[90]

Another major sculptor whose career was aided by the Society of
Arts was John Bacon. Unlike Nollekens, however, Bacon never left England. He was proof that Britain could develop its own, native style. He
also thought the Society responsible for his success. The son of a poor
weaver, he had been apprenticed to one of the Society's eleven founders,
the porcelain maker Nicholas Crisp. Crisp had encouraged him to compete for the Society's premiums for clay models, and Bacon won again
and again. He soon came to the notice of the Royal Academy and then
the king. He owed it all, Bacon said, to the Society's encouragement:
the prizes allowed him 'to pursue those studies which a disadvantageous
situation had otherwise made difficult, if not impossible'. In gratitude,
he presented to the Society a life-size statue of Mars—the one with the
scandalous 'pudenda.'[91]

The Society of Arts divided the labour of encouraging British art with
the Royal Academy in other ways too. The Royal Academy schools did
not admit any women until the late nineteenth century (and apparently

only because the woman who applied for admittance, Laura Herford, masked her gender by signing her test drawing with only her initials). Although the Royal Academy counted two women in 1768 among its original founder-members, no further women were elected to join the select group until 1936. The Society of Arts, by contrast, since the very beginning allowed members of 'either sex' to win its premiums. Thus, it played a role in supporting some of the country's most prominent professional female artists. Although women were allowed to show their works at the Royal Academy's exhibitions, the Society of Arts was a place for them to first gain public notice.

Among the earliest of these women was Mary Moser. She won premiums in the late 1750s for her drawings of ornaments and paintings of flowers. Her second prize-winning work, executed when she was only 15, was considered so good that the Society had it 'handsomely framed and glazed' for display in the Great Room.[92] She exhibited it at the Society's first contemporary art exhibition in 1760, and was one of the two women among the Royal Academy's thirty-six founder-members.

The Society's relative openness thus meant that it encouraged the kinds of people who were excluded by the Royal Academy. Indeed, in 1845 it awarded a medal to an Indian, Nubboo Coomar Paul—although the Society's committee judged his sculpture to be an 'inferior work of art', they were impressed that he had executed it from an engraving and was entirely self-taught.[93]

The Society was also more open than the Royal Academy to different kinds of art. It awarded a silver medal, for example, for works of needlework by Mary Linwood—for an embroidered hare, a still life, and a portrait. An exhibition of her needlework, with copies of famous paintings and portraits, later became one of London's major tourist attractions. The Society also provided a source of prizes and public notice for engravers like William Finden or Thomas Bewick, at a time when engravers were excluded from becoming full Royal Academicians (with the exception of one founder-member, engravers were only admitted to 'associateship' until the 1850s). The same applied to die engravers and medallists (after all, the Society needed to produce lots of medals). Overall, between 1755 and 1849, the Society gave some three thousand awards for the polite arts, many of them to encourage people who would not otherwise have received recognition.

Nonetheless, the Society did not entirely give up on the promotion of history painting. In 1774, the Society moved to a new building designed by a few of its members, the Adam brothers, particularly Robert Adam, a Scottish pioneer of neoclassical architecture and one of William Chambers's major rivals. The new premises were part of Adam's redevelopment of a dilapidated part of central London, the old estate of Durham House, an area which had become a home for criminals and prostitutes. He had teamed up with his brothers to create a site that they named the Adelphi (ancient Greek for 'brothers', after themselves). The building that they created for the Society was a temple-like structure with a Great Room for meetings, a repository to display the various things that won premiums, along with some other, smaller rooms. The Society has remained there ever since.[94]

When it moved in, however, the walls of the Great Room were bare. One of the Society's most active members on the polite arts committee, an engraver named Valentine Green, thus suggested that it use the opportunity to promote history painting, perhaps even to reestablish its old links with the artists at the Royal Academy. The Great Room was a large and public space, and thus suitable for the kind of work that sought to address the public. The Society offered its walls to a group of prominent artists, many of them Royal Academicians, but they collectively refused. A few years later, however, one of the artists, James Barry, came back with a proposal of his own.

Born in Ireland, Barry had submitted a painting to the Society's Irish counterpart, the Dublin Society, and come to the notice of the politician Edmund Burke (now considered one of the founding fathers of conservatism, though he usually aligned with the Whigs, the forerunners of the Liberal Party). Burke, who was also briefly a member of the Society of Arts, brought Barry to London and arranged for him to go to France and Italy to develop his talents. Barry became obsessed with history painting. The work he sent back to Britain caused a sensation at the Royal Academy's exhibitions—upon his return, he was almost immediately elected an associate, and a few months later a full Royal

Academician. It was the 'fastest advancement of any painter in its history'.[95]

Barry believed that the problem with history painting in Britain was that there were too few public spaces for it. France and Italy both benefitted from having many richly decorated Catholic churches. London had a few ceilings with historical images here and there, but Anglican churches were mostly too afraid of appearing Catholic. Upon his election to the Royal Academy, one of Barry's first suggestions was to create a history painting in a prominent place. Were it allowed, he hoped, then other chapels and churches might soon follow. Artists like Joshua Reynolds, it turned out, had already approached St Paul's Cathedral. Yet anti-Catholic sentiment was too strong: 'I will never suffer the doors of the metropolitan church to be opened for the introduction of popery into it', was the Bishop of London's response.[96]

Thwarted, Barry eventually looked to the Society of Arts. He was among the initial invitees to fill the Great Room, but had that project been approved, he would have had to share the space with the paintings of others. What he had in mind, instead, was to paint the entire room himself. He approached the Society in 1777, asking only that it cover his expenses. In exchange, he asked that he be allowed to choose his own subjects. The Society agreed, making it an unprecedented contract: 'for the first time in the history of Western art', wrote the art historian William Pressly, 'the patron of a large, impressive interior turned over complete control to the artist commissioned to decorate it. Barry, and Barry alone, formulated the series' subject matter'.[97] The only wall-space denied to him, much to his chagrin, were two portraits of the Society's first presidents.

What Barry chose to do with all that space was to depict the progress of civilisation. The vast paintings, often called murals, though they are in fact on canvas, are the Society's greatest treasure. Displayed for the first time to the public in 1783, the cycle begins with the legendary poet Orpheus bringing culture to humanity in its savage state—around his feet as he strums a lyre sit near-naked men and women looking at their hands as though seeing them for the first time. Next, Barry shows a harvest festival, a fleeting paradise of music and dancing. Moving on, he depicts an ancient Greek procession, a crowning of the Olympic victors with laurels, followed by a personification of London—Father Thames—receiving the wares of all continents. Barry then depicted an idealised version of the Society of Arts prize-givings, before finally showing heaven and hell. Heaven, called Elysium, he filled with as many famous artists, scientists, explorers, writers and philosophers as he could think of, whereas in hell, or Tartarus, he showed allegories of the sins. Pride, violence, vanity, and lust, all sit there, though Barry also took pains to depict a writer of anonymous reviews—'that detestable species of mischief in which we so much abound'.[98]

Whole books have been written about the hidden meanings in Barry's murals, yet the immediate focus of the historical cycle—the vast painting that is immediately visible when entering the Great Room, both then and today—is the scene with the Olympic victors. He had the idea for it when still in Rome, long before he approached the Society of Arts, and it was originally intended to cover even more of the available space. Its focus is a legendary ancient sportsman, Diagoras of Rhodes, but instead of showing him in his athletic prime, he is an old man borne on the shoulders of his sons, who are in the process of winning their own victory laurels. Diagoras might be old, but Barry shows him at his most glorious, having succeeded in educating his sons to emulate him. Indeed, a man is shown grasping Diagoras's hand to whisper that he might as well die now, as only heaven itself could be more glorious. The focus of the painting is thus about the value of education—the inculcation of the highest standards of virtue. It is, in essence, a history painting about the value of history painting.[99]

Barry exhibited the paintings in 1783 and 1784, though he made little money from the proceeds. They have been there ever since (other than during the Second World War, when, having been evacuated to the country, they were almost destroyed in an ordinary house fire).[100] Barry was irascible and difficult—the only person ever to be expelled from the Royal Academy, essentially for publicly insulting its leaders. At one stage while painting, he reportedly even locked the Society's secretary out of the Great Room. Barry believed he was a misunderstood genius, and that such genius was necessary to inculcate the public with virtue. Yet he also believed that true geniuses would be martyred. He was often paranoid, believing that jealous artists were attempting to assassinate him.

Nonetheless, despite his irascibility, the Society eventually awarded him a bonus, a gold medal, life membership, and later even a pension (though he died just before receiving it). When he died, he was lain in state in the Great Room, and the Society arranged for him to be buried in St Paul's alongside Joshua Reynolds. Although Barry had been given control of the Great Room's walls, the overt message of the paintings was one that resonated with the Society's members. They, like him, were obsessed with making the nation more virtuous.

3

Peculiar Genius

SOME MEMBERS OF THE SOCIETY soon became frustrated at its emphasis on art. As early as 1759, one member wrote to a friend abroad that it increasingly resembled 'a mere Society of drawing, painting, and sculpture, and attends to little else'.[1] Yet the Society soon saw off the attempted takeover by the artists, and its members were able to direct its accumulated funds towards whatever they could persuade the other members to support. As with Barry's paintings in the Great Room, many of their projects had a moral purpose, even though they were tied up with considerations of the commerce and defence of the nation. After all, Shipley's aim in creating the Society had been to exploit people's self-interest, to redirect it to the benefit of the public.

One of the first considerations was the defence of the realm. Anti-French sentiment in Britain reached a fever pitch in 1756 when the two nations embarked on the Seven Years' War—the first truly global conflict, which spanned five continents and eventually cemented Britain's dominance of the oceans. The battles in North America are often known today as the French and Indian War, and in India as the Third Carnatic War, but these were just a few of the theatres in Britain's successful worldwide struggle with its ancient foe.

The Society's predecessors, the Association of Anti-Gallicans, reacted to the declaration of war with characteristic zealotry, paying for a merchant ship to be manned and armed with twenty-eight cannon and sixteen swivel-guns for privateering (officially sanctioned piracy on enemy shipping). They made sure that every aspect of their piracy was

English, right down to the biscuits and brandy for the sailors, although at least one member of the crew was Algerian (who won popularity by selling his mates gin at discounted prices). Off the coast of Portugal, the newly dubbed *Antigallican* seized a couple of French ships laden with coffee, sugar, cotton, and wine, as well as rescuing a handful of English prisoners. It even caused a minor diplomatic incident when it took a French ship in the waters of Spain, which at the time had been attempting to remain neutral.[2]

The Society of Arts, however, took a less direct tack. It used its premiums to try to secure essential materials for the waging of war, often complementing the efforts of the government. One of the reasons Britain was able to win a global struggle like the Seven Years' War was that its government had developed extraordinary abilities to raise money. Britain had a 'fiscal-military state', with wide-ranging powers to raise debt, impose taxes, and encourage any commerce or production that might support its war-making capabilities.[3] The Society of Arts, based in London and in close proximity to the centres of power, had many members who were in some manner connected with the growing British state, as officials and politicians, or as the merchants and manufacturers who benefitted from supplying it.[4] When it came to economic policy, the Society's members often shared the opinions of those in power.

In terms of the defence of the realm, of the utmost importance were Britain's warships, its 'wooden walls'.[5] Indeed, even before the Society had first met, Stephen Hales had suggested that naval improvements should be one of its priorities. A typical 74-gun warship, the Royal Navy's favoured tool, was extremely expensive, in 1780 costing ten times more to build than England's largest factory.[6] It also required massive amounts of timber—some three thousand trees.[7] This was not to mention the additional wood required for maintenance and repairs. White pine, which grows tall and straight, was especially suited to ship masts. Elm, pliant yet resistant to splitting, was suitable for the keel (the long spine at the bottom of the ship that required bending into shape). The ship's planks could be sawn from many different trees, usually oak, elm, beech, or fir. Such straight-growing trees were already difficult to acquire at the best of times, but the ship also required massive oak trees with rare curves or crooks to provide its ribs, the bent 'knees' supporting each deck, and the various curves at the bow and stern. They also needed to be strong enough to bear the weight of the rudder and anchor. These exceptional oaks, known as 'compass' timbers, needed to grow in isolation and be somehow coaxed into shape. Otherwise, the building of a ship might be delayed for years because a tree of a particular shape and size could not be found.[8]

Yet Britain had suffered continual deforestation for centuries, wood having also served as the principal source of fuel for heating and industry. By the late seventeenth century, timber supplies were already judged to be in crisis, and the situation had only worsened since then.[9] Timber increasingly had to be imported from the Baltic, which was considered a 'drain upon this nation' in terms of bullion flowing abroad to pay for it, as well as putting the country at the mercy of foreign powers.[10] Russia or Norway might restrict their timber exports for strategic reasons, or otherwise take advantage of Britain's shortages by raising prices. The shortage of timber was even a threat to Britain's independent existence. The worst-case scenario for the Royal Navy was that if the main fleet were destroyed, an enemy blockading the coast and stopping timber from arriving might leave Britain totally incapacitated, unable to repair its fleet or construct a new one—a worry that occasionally forced the fleet to disengage the enemy and retreat to safety.[11]

The problem was that trees had to compete for land with food crops, which were more immediately useful and profitable to farmers. Sowing and raising trees was by comparison an extremely long-term investment that only the wealthiest landowners could afford to undertake. And even then, no single individual could reasonably expect to live long enough to reap the profits.[12] Depending on the quality of the soil, oaks were not suitable for ship-building until they had been growing for at least 80 to 120 years.[13] Many of the trees that were already being grown were prematurely pruned or cut, and many were being stripped of all their branches for firewood by wood-stealers.[14]

One proposed solution was that the required long-term investments might be made by local authorities—especially parishes—which as corporate bodies outlived any single individual. By encouraging the parishes to plant forests, the profits from the timber and other by-products like acorns and chestnuts for feeding livestock might also be used to support the poor. By tying the profits to the local community, including the poorest among them, the idea was that stealing wood would become socially unacceptable. The added benefit to landowners would be to replace the poor rates—the tax levied in each parish to support the local poor.[15]

Parliament seems to have taken these proposals under consideration, reacting to the tree shortage at the beginning of the Seven Years' War by passing a law to allow land 'held in common'—woods or pastures that locals had various rights to use—to be compulsorily purchased and fenced off by landowners or parishes for the express purpose of raising timber. Their solution to the problem of wood-stealing was, however, more draconian. If individual culprits could not be caught, the owners of the newly enclosed forests could demand compensation from every-one living nearby.[16]

The Society's members considered offering a premium to parishes for using the new law to obtain, fence, and plant the most timber.[17] But they eventually decided that they would have the greatest impact if they targeted the nobility and gentry—there was a risk that the new law might not be properly implemented, and much of the already owned land could be used for raising timber.[18] Some members may also have been sceptical that parishes would be sufficiently competent custodians of Britain's trees. In any case, the landowners were the principal culprits for allowing the deforestation in the first place: more and more of them idly lived off their fortunes in London rather than overseeing their country estates.[19]

Just as foreign luxuries had enfeebled Britain's trade, the Society's members saw deforestation as yet another case of self-interest under-mining the public good. Aristocrats were thought to have deprived their lands of proper management and allowed their stewards and tenants, more interested in short-term profit, to prevail. The problem was one of esteem: by the 1750s it was apparently considered 'a shame' for gentlemen of fortune to be interested in matters like agriculture, husbandry, and forestry.[20]

The solution was to offer medals for planting and raising the most trees in a given year. The Society could not hope to incentivise the wealthiest of the wealthy with the usual cash sums, so the premiums on offer were honorary medals, much like those used to encourage their children and grandchildren to practise art.[21] The Society had to appeal to their image of themselves as sacred custodians of the land, stressing the project's patriotic aims and the selflessness of investing for the sole benefit of posterity. At the same time, the competition for each year's honorary medals channelled baser motives, tapping into people's desire to outclass their peers. Members of the minor gentry in particular had the chance to socially elevate themselves; winning the year's medal gave them something in common with even the grandest dukes and duchesses.[22]

The strategy worked. The Society awarded its first gold medal in 1758 for sowing acorns for raising oaks to the Duke of Beaufort, and over the following years its medals were claimed by various other dukes, duchesses, earls, viscounts, marquesses, bishops, and members of parliament, not to mention many more untitled members of the minor gentry. Viscount Newark, who before his ennoblement had served as a naval captain during the Seven Years' War, signalled his patriotic intent by naming his forest plantations after the British commanders of recent victories. Just as the Society had hoped, Newark described how he and his neighbours were engaged in a 'very laudable emulation', each vying to outdo one another in the extent and quality of their plantations.[23] In a similar vein, when one competitor said they intended to plant a million trees in a single year, another landowner responded by planting even more.[24]

The Society's approach to encouraging the planting of trees went beyond those that were directly useful, such as oak and elm. They offered premiums for the planting of larch, because its bark was used in tanning leather, and for planting willows and poplars.[25] These faster-growing trees were intended to lower the general price of wood, reducing the temptation to fell or strip the all-important oaks before they were ready.[26] Their other key feature was that they might actually be profitable, as they came to maturity more quickly—planting larch, willows, and poplars benefitted the planters as well as the public. It appealed to the poorer landowners as well as the wealthiest—those who might not be able to afford to plant solely for the prestige.

The overall result of the Society's efforts to plant trees was dramatic. Over the course of almost a century, the medal-winners altogether planted at least sixty million trees—a figure that fails to take into account the countless others who entered the annual competition and lost, as well as the broader and intended effect of making tree-planting fashionable.[27]

Rewarding the planting of trees, however, was only one kind of premium that the Society offered to support the war effort. It also sought to secure Britain's supply of hemp and flax, used for rope and sailcloth, much of it imported from the Baltic. In this regard, the Society looked initially to Britain's colonies in North America. To influential economic commentators in London, the point of the colonies was to support the home country. North America was seen as a place that could provide Britain with raw materials, such as hemp, iron ore, or raw silk, which might then be manufactured in Britain itself. Britain would purchase the materials by exporting its more expensive manufactures back to the colonies. The colonies were thus seen as both a cheap source of Britain's raw materials, and a captive market for its expensive manufactures.[28]

To some in North America, however, this policy was cause for dissatisfaction. Benjamin Franklin—politician, inventor, natural philosopher—increasingly felt that the colonies in North America should be allowed to develop their own manufactures, and perhaps even to export to countries other than Britain. In short, Franklin felt that North America should be treated as though it were a part of Britain itself, rather than an appendage to provide cheap raw materials. In 1756, his hopes were raised that someone in London might be doing something to change Britain's prevailing policy. William Shipley wrote to him, expressing the Society's 'desire to make Great Britain and her colonies mutually dear and serviceable to each other'. Shipley seemed to suggest that the Society might offer premiums to encourage manufactures in America, writing that when it came to colonial policy its members discarded 'all narrow-minded partiality and unreasonable jealousies'.[29]

Shipley invited Franklin to become a corresponding member. Franklin's response was instead to send twenty guineas, making himself a full member for life. He moved to London in 1757 and there became heavily involved in the Society, attending many of its committees—particularly those that discussed and decided upon the premiums to support the colonies. Franklin even stayed a while at Shipley's brother's home, Twyford House, where he began writing his autobiography. In the late 1760s, however, Franklin became increasingly disillusioned. Shipley had claimed in 1756 that the Society's members wished to treat the colonies without narrow-mindedness, but either that was untrue or new members with very different ideas had joined.

Despite Franklin's hopes, the members of the Society who were most interested in the colonies seemed only to care about using them for raw materials. The Society used its fund to subsidise imports of hemp from North America, supplementing another subsidy provided by the government. 'You want to suppress that manufacture and would do it by getting the raw material from us', Franklin complained, scribbling in the margins of a book. He accused the Society of using its subsidies for hemp to benefit Britain at the expense of its North American colonies, 'to quit a business profitable to ourselves and engage in one that shall be profitable to you'.[30] He was just as annoyed by its premiums to promote other raw materials in America, such as indigo and raw silk. By the late 1760s, Franklin had stopped attending the Society's committee dealing with the colonies, instead concentrating on those dealing with agriculture and mechanics. By 1775, when he left England on the eve of the American Revolution, he seems to have stopped attending entirely.

Although much of America soon became independent, the attitude of the Society's members towards Britain's colonies did not change. At the height of the Napoleonic Wars, it offered new premiums for the growth of hemp in Canada, which it soon extended to Scotland and eventually the whole of the United Kingdom—as the supply of hemp grew shorter, they tried to grow it anywhere.[31] The Society's priorities thus continued to reflect those of the politicians and officials among its members who ran the growing fiscal-military state.

The use of direct subsidies, however, was soon considered wasteful. The Society expended a lot of its funds in the 1760s simply paying people per acre of madder or hemp grown, with little to show for it. Indeed, some members suggested that their subsidies may have been doomed from the start: in the vast open spaces of America, what was in scarce supply was labour, meaning people there demanded higher wages and were less likely to engage in producing cheap raw materials. Activities like picking the petals of safflower, used for a yellow dye, were 'a less suitable matter to the colonies, where labour is dear'. 'Till the people are more numerous', some prominent members reasoned, many of the attempted premiums for raw materials in the colonies would simply never work.[32]

Indeed, the Society's members did much, in Britain itself, to try to lower wages. In order to compete with France, both economically and militarily, its members believed that Britain needed to expand its exports. One strategy to do so was to lower the costs of manufacturing them, which could be done by lowering wages. Yet to lower wages, they would need to make the cost of living cheaper. Many of the Society's premiums thus focused on cheapening 'the necessaries of life'.[33] If they could at the same time import fewer of those necessaries, all the better.[34]

Beeswax, for example, used in candles, was both imported and increasingly becoming an expensive luxury. The Society offered premiums for creating the greatest number of hives, but to little avail. It also offered premiums for discovering cheaper fibres for clothes, and for finding ways to make leather more cheaply for shoes.[35] It even tried to encourage the cultivation of a certain type of purple orchid: in the eighteenth century, a cheap alternative to tea and coffee was salep, or saloop, a drink made from the flour of dried orchid tubers, imported from Turkey (the word salep comes from Arabic and translates literally as 'fox's testicles', much like an older English term for orchids, dogstones). Many coffee houses served salep alongside coffee and gin. Indeed, the Society may have had its wish of cheapening the substance—by the 1820s salep had developed a reputation as the drink of the poor.

Yet another necessary of life was oil, for use in lamps, often derived from the blubber of whales. When a blacksmith named Abraham Staghold sent in an invention of a gun harpoon for whaling, in the 1770s the Society tried to persuade sailors to adopt it by paying a bounty for every whale caught using it. The Society also pursued a chemical solution to making whale oil cheaper by trying to find a way to purify the lower-grade kind, which was not used in lamps because it had a 'putrid smell' that 'rendered it very disgustful'.[36] The Society was sent an anonymous offer to reveal a method of treating the low-grade whale oil, to 'edulco-rate' it (to sweeten it, or make it less foetid), in exchange for a hundred pounds—a huge sum, worth almost two hundred thousand pounds today. The Society's chemistry committee conducted tests of the process at the height of summer, when the oil especially stank, and then recommended the award be given. Only then, however, was it revealed to the rest of the Society that the person who sent in the anonymous offer was the chemistry committee's chairman, Robert Dossie. Dossie was an active member and well liked, so the money was still awarded, but soon afterwards the Society introduced a rule that members were entitled only to win honorary medals, never cash.[37]

By far the most important necessary of life that the Society could make cheaper, however, was food. One of its major strategies to lower wages was to improve the productivity of agriculture. Indeed, the Society became especially obsessed with cheapening beef.[38] This was partly a matter of economic policy, but it was also a matter of pride. Hogarth's prints depicted the English as well-fed and happy, with a fat side of beef in hand, whereas the French were often depicted as thin and emaciated, subsisting on thin gruel, and having to resort to hunting tiny animals like frogs.[39] This may not have been the source of the stereotype, but Hogarth and later satirists reinforced it. It was a comment on political systems. Hogarth depicted French poverty as the result of the tyranny of Catholicism and an autocratic regime, whereas ordinary British people could grow fat and tall under parliamentary liberty. Having a cheap and steady supply of beef was, for the British, proof of their constitutional monarchy's superiority.

Almost all of the Society's early agricultural premiums, either directly or indirectly, focused on keeping cattle alive and healthy. If beef were cheaper, then they reasoned that other meats would be too. The problem, however, was the winter. When hay became scarce after a long frost, cattle required other kinds of feed. The Society thus began an international search for the ideal 'winter pabulum'—a crop that would grow in the winter or early spring and provide a ready supply of feed. The Society's members wrote to similar societies and natural philosophers all over the world, asking for seeds and suggestions, and offering premiums for agriculturists in Britain to experiment with everything from kohlrabi, kale, gorse, and colereed, to white Chinese vetch and Siberian medicago. The Society learned that lucerne, or alfalfa, was used as winter feed in Switzerland and Flanders, and that white clover was used in Holland. It offered premiums for experiments on both. Carrots, parsnips, and parsley were also all encouraged. Among the most successful feeds was burnet.[40]

The normal winter pabulum for cattle was the turnip. But in this case other problems needed solving. Turnips were increasingly affected by pests—some kind of 'fly'—so the Society offered a prize for eradicating them (apparently without much success). More successful, however, was a machine for slicing turnips, for which the Society had offered a premium. When turnips were small, cattle frequently choked on them, which meant that many farmers had to cut them by hand to prevent this from happening. In the process, however, many labourers cut themselves by accident. Hence, a machine to do the job instead. The Society's members were especially enthusiastic when they received a model that worked.[41] In the late 1760s the Society's propagandists pointed to the invention of the turnip cutter as a key example of the organisation's usefulness, having brought the concept of such a machine to the public's attention via its advertised premium.

Apart from cheapening daily life, the Society's other means of lowering wages in manufacturing was to boost the labour supply. Idleness, for example, was something that had to be stamped out both for the good of the people who were idle, and for the good of the national economy. The Society promoted workhouses for the poor that would produce textiles to be sold. It also advertised premiums for textile machinery that would be suitable for children in orphanages, to make them more pro-

3.1. Turnip cutter. The image is taken from a catalogue of the Society's
machines assembled by the register, William Bailey, RSA/SC/EL/2/6–7.

ductive and to ensure that their growth was not stunted by the process.[42] The Society wished to make women and children 'profitable to
the public, and moral in their conduct, instead of being burdensome, or
loose in their way of life'. By calling for improved spinning wheels, the
Society planned to set 'idle hands to spinning'.[43]

The Society's concern with promoting industriousness also extended
to prostitutes. One member, a merchant named Jonas Hanway, became
especially distressed at the number of prostitutes in London. Hanway
had travelled widely, to Russia and Persia, and had made a fortune. He
became famous as the first man in London to carry an umbrella (which
was considered effeminate—it had been exclusively used by women in
Britain for decades). Much of Hanway's fame, however, came from his
actions as a philanthropist. He campaigned against ill-treatment of children, persuading Parliament to pass an act in 1762 that required all parishes to record the deaths of children who died in their care. In 1756 he
founded the Marine Society, a charity to clothe and prepare young men
and boys for service in the Royal Navy. In the case of prostitutes, however, he first tried to use the Society of Arts.

In 1758, Hanway persuaded the Society to offer a gold medal for the
best plan for a 'Magdalen Hospital for Penitent Prostitutes'. Prostitutes,

the Society's advertisement read, 'raise compassion and horror in every humane mind'. It asked for a charity house that would serve as a refuge to prostitutes 'as are desirous to forsake their evil courses', though it would also employ them in 'useful industry' so that they might be rehabilitated to society. The Society did not award the premium, but Hanway and some other members did open the Magdalen Hospital themselves. Inmates were organised into wards based on behaviour, and were only known by their first names. They wore a uniform and their correspondence was inspected by the matrons. It lasted until the 1930s.[44]

In combating idleness, the Society tried to improve the morals of the poor. With its medals for planting trees, it tried to coax the aristocracy to act in the public interest. Indeed, serving the wider public interest lay behind almost all of its premiums—even those that might otherwise, on the face of it, seem mundane. In the late 1750s, for example, the Society offered a premium for improvements to hand-mills, for grinding corn. The premium was not just about improvement for its own sake, but because the Society's members feared that poor people in the country were being 'abused by the millers', who were often effectively local monopolists.[45] If the poor had nowhere else nearby to go to grind their grain, then millers could get away with adulterating the flour. By offering a premium for a cheap and effective hand-mill, the Society wished to break the millers' monopoly.

In the 1760s, too, the Society spent thousands of pounds on a scheme to bring fish to London from other English ports via land. The aim was to undercut the monopoly of the London fishmongers, who were not best pleased.[46] At one point, they sent a letter to the Society 'containing an indecent expression', which the subscribers ordered to be ceremonially burned by the porter (in the summer, when there was no fire, such letters were torn up and thrown under the table in the centre of the Great Room).[47] The fish land-carriage scheme did not end well, however, and may even have damaged the Society's reputation. Its members could not decide whether the Society had made a grant or a loan to the person who oversaw the scheme, Captain John Blake. He had many supporters among the Society's ranks, but others accused him of financial misconduct. Irate members at one point even debated the matter until as late as 3 am.[48] Nonetheless, although Blake was accused by some of corruption, the fish land-carriage scheme was yet another example of the Society attempting to serve the public good.

Historians of the Society since the late nineteenth century have criticised it for not having encouraged some of the Industrial Revolution's most significant inventors. James Watt, for example, an important improver of the steam engine, does not feature in the Society's history. Even those members of the Society who did achieve fame, such as Edmund Cartwright, the inventor of the power loom, did not submit their most famous inventions for premiums. The Society's premiums have even been contrasted with the patent system, to show that prizes were not as effective as intellectual property rights at promoting invention.[49] But these criticisms miss the point. The Society of Arts was never supposed to compete with the patent system, nor even to promote great inventions. It was supposed to encourage things that would not otherwise have been done. It operated at the margins, and only at the margins. It did so on purpose.

Very early on, in the early 1760s, the Society decided not to give its premiums to inventions that had received patents.[50] It was, after all, about revealing information and undercutting monopolies rather than entrenching them. Even before this, however, in cases where a patent had already been granted for a process the Society had been considering giving a premium for, it purposefully backed down—not because it would cause people to infringe on the patent, but because its encouragement was no longer necessary.[51] Patents were expensive in the eighteenth century, so a patent for a process suggested that it might already be profitable—that, at least, was the way the Society's members saw it. Instead, the Society actively tried to promote things that would not otherwise have been profitable. In other words, its premiums cannot be directly compared with the patent system because it actively avoided competing with it.[52]

Although the Society published its own lists of suggested premiums, which set out precise terms by which to win a prize, it also rewarded unsolicited inventions. Such unsolicited awards were often referred to as bounties rather than premiums. Indeed, by the early nineteenth century, most of the Society's awards were for bounties. Because of its rule against patented inventions, however, the kinds of inventions that were submitted for bounties were very similar to the kinds that were advertised in premiums. A few of the inventions that received bounties were simply not profitable enough to need patents, which is why famous inventors like Edmund Cartwright still submitted some of their less well-known improvements for prizes. He received medals from the Society for an improved plough, for example, and for his experiments on manures.

Inventors also often sent the Society the kinds of improvements that they may not have otherwise been able to commercialise. These included, for example, systems of communicating at a distance, then usually referred to as telegraphs, but now more often known as semaphores. Many naval officers and concerned members of the public devised these systems, each involving their own vocabularies of signs and symbols, conveyed by flags, shutters, or wooden poles. One system, invented by Lieutenant James Spratt, involved tying a single white handkerchief in various configurations around a person's arms. Spratt called his invention the 'homograph', because it made 'every man a signal tower'. The Society awarded him its silver medal. The system sent to the Society by an admiral, Sir Home Riggs Popham, was more widely adopted. These pre-electric telegraphs were often useful to the Royal Navy, but could not be made profitable. The Society thus provided the outlet for them to be made public, and for the inventors to gain recognition, cash, or both.

For the same reason, the Society often awarded bounties and premiums for inventions that saved lives—once again, improvements that were useful to the public, but not always profitable. It awarded a bounty of fifty guineas and a gold medal to an inventor of lifeboats, Henry Greathead. The Society also awarded a bounty of fifty guineas to a sergeant of the Royal Artillery, John Bell, for a method of firing a rope and grapple by mortar from a ship to the shore, to save the persons on board from shipwreck in a storm. A gold medal was awarded some years later to another inventor for a device that did the opposite, firing from shore to ship.

3.2. Lieutenant James Spratt's 'homograph' signalling system, as illustrated in his
pamphlet *The Homograph, or every man a signal tower*, RSA/SC/EL/1/157.

The Society also received many inventions related to making work
safer. A schoolmaster in Sheffield, John Hessey Abraham, won a medal
in 1822 for a magnet apparatus to prevent metal dust getting into the eyes
and lungs of workmen employed in grinding the points of needles.
Abraham did not invent the device for profit—in fact, he toured the
country's manufacturing towns to demonstrate and donate the apparatus to workers.[53] The Society provided a platform for him to spread the
use of his invention and to gain a little glory. Likewise, in 1767 the Society awarded a bounty to a clockmaker, Christopher Pinchbeck, for a
crane. Cranes at the time were like gigantic hamster wheels, in which

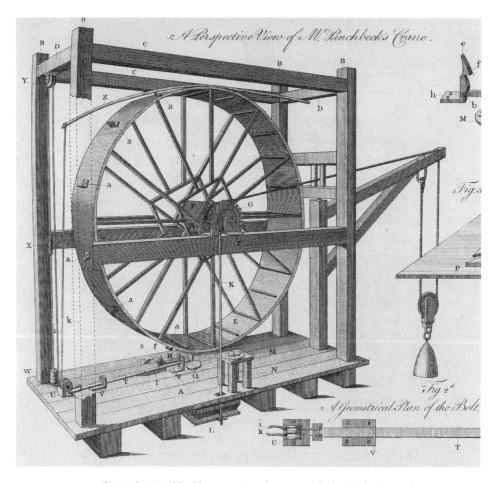

3.3. Christopher Pinchbeck's pneumatic safety crane, which won the Society's
gold medal in 1767. The image is taken from a catalogue of the Society's
machines assembled by the register, William Bailey, RSA/SC/EL/2/6–7.

a man or number of men walked to lift a load. When lines snapped,
however, fatal accidents were common. Pinchbeck added a pneumatic
braking mechanism that prevented the accidents from occurring. To test
it, the Society even set one up on a London quay.[54] Such inventions
could have been patented because they were mechanical, but more often
than not the inventors struggled to persuade manufacturers to adopt
them. They were not profitable in the short term.

One of the Society's most significant campaigns to promote the invention and adoption of a technology came in 1796, when it offered a

premium for a mechanical means of cleaning chimneys. The Society's aim in this was to abolish the employment of children, sometimes as young as 4, who were forced to climb up inside chimneys in order to clean them. These children were sometimes abducted by the master chimney sweeps, and frequently perished in horrific accidents or of soot-induced cancers. The idea was that if a technological replacement could be found, then the case for outright abolition could be made— it was a concerted effort to get machines to steal children's jobs.

The Society played its role with the offer of a premium, but it took place alongside another campaign run by some of its members, who ran the snappily titled 'Society for Superseding the Necessity of Climbing Boys, by Encouraging a New Method of Sweeping Chimnies, and for Improving the Condition of Children and Others Employed by Chimney Sweepers' (SSNCB), founded in 1803 at the London Coffee-House on Ludgate Hill. The movement to abolish climbing boys had much older roots. Jonas Hanway had, decades earlier, also campaigned to abolish the 'peculiar disgrace of England'.[55] But the 1803 campaign was to prove more successful, and drew on wider political support. The SSNCB's key members included William Wilberforce, who later became famous for his zeal in abolishing the slave trade.

The Society of Arts' premium was won in 1805 by George Smart, a timber merchant and engineer. His tool, the 'scandiscope', could be operated from the fireplace, was cheap, effective on all but the bendiest of flues, and weighed 'no more than a musket'. The brushes, if wetted, could be used to put out fires in the flue—a task that otherwise fell to the climbing boy equipped with a damp cloth, putting him in extraordinary danger. Yet the existence of an effective invention was not enough to abolish the use of climbing boys. The master chimney sweeps opposed it.

At first, the SSNCB's campaigners tried to cooperate with the sweeps, offering prizes for the number of flues swept using the scandiscope, subsidising their purchase of the machines, and advertising the reliable sweeps who used them. But the sweeps took advantage of this generosity, purposefully misusing the scandiscopes in an effort to turn customers against them. By 1809, the campaigners had had enough. Emboldened by the success of the abolition of the slave trade in 1807, their

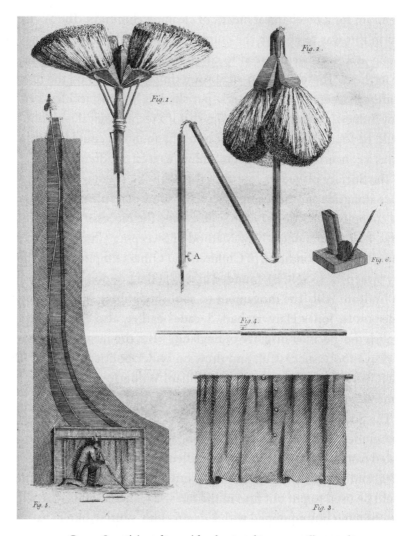

3.4. George Smart's 'scandiscope' for cleaning chimneys, as illustrated in
the Society's *Transactions*, Volume 23, plate 5.

strategy changed from cooperation to outright disruption. They encouraged brand new entrants into the sweeping trade, extolling the modest
profits that might be made by using the machines. They also encouraged
the owners of larger homes to buy their own machines (to be used by
domestic servants), so as to actively remove customers from the market.
If the master sweeps complained about this disruption, argued the

SSNCB, then it was their own fault: 'they are exclusively indebted to themselves, as the Society for years took uncommon pains to give them that preference which they pertinaciously refused'.[56]

The campaign eventually met with success. The scandiscopes were gradually brought into use, in London as well as further afield, and the lot of the climbing boys improved. Crucially, the scandiscope made laws banning the use of climbing boys possible, although this took decades of more campaigning as well as further improvements to Smart's machine. In 1834 Parliament banned the use of boys under 14 years old, extended in 1840 to 21. But the climbing boys would have to wait until 1875 for a law that had sufficient teeth for enforcement.

The Society of Arts thus attracted the kind of inventions that were not otherwise served by the patent system. Over the course of a century it awarded over two thousand premiums and bounties for inventions, nearly all of them with humanitarian or patriotic aims. It rewarded means of preventing accidents on horse-drawn carriages, the reduction of smoke from steam engines, ways to prevent steam locomotive accidents, the reduction of noxious fumes from industrial processes, extendable fire-escape ladders, and safety apparatus for use in mines. As the Society was a direct democracy, the premium list reflected the concerns of its members. John Howard, for example, an eighteenth-century prison reformer, in 1775 persuaded the Society to offer a premium for improvements to Hales's ventilator, specifically to improve the sanitary conditions in prisons. He had apparently not been much involved in the Society before this date, other than winning a premium for some experiments on potatoes. Yet he stood up before the assembled subscribers, made his case, and then attended the relevant committee to help draw up the premium advertisement.[57] Howard's experience was typical—people could use the Society to support their humanitarian pet projects.

Some members also devised ways to combat slavery in the West Indies, though in its early years some of the Society's premiums had done the opposite. In the 1760s, it had offered a premium for the production in England of glass beads, to be exported to Africa in exchange for slaves as part of the triangular trade across the Atlantic. It had also offered a

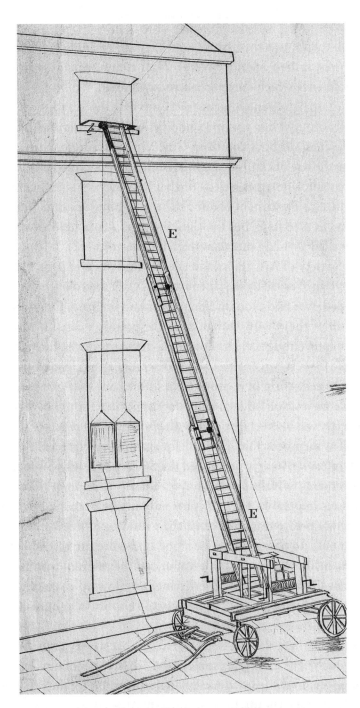

3.5. Drawing of an extendable fire escape ladder, invented by
a John Davies of Spitalfields and awarded a premium of 50
guineas by the Society in 1810. RSA/PR/MC/101/19/04.

premium for transplanting the mango tree from Goa to the West Indies, intended as a cheap and high-energy food with which to feed the slave population. In 1777, for exactly the same reasons, it had offered a premium for transplanting breadfruit trees from Tahiti in the South Pacific. The first major attempt to transplant breadfruit trees, by Captain William Bligh in command of HMS *Bounty*, was stopped when his crew mutinied. Bligh and a small group of loyalists were cut adrift in just the ship's launch, but managed to navigate over 3,500 miles back to safety. Bligh succeeded on his second attempt in command of HMS *Providence*, however, for which in 1793 he was awarded the Society's gold medal. (In the end, however, the breadfruits were neither as cheap nor as tasty as plantain.)

Although the British slave trade was famously abolished in 1807, slavery continued to exist in much of the British Empire until a series of acts of Parliament in the 1830s and 40s. In the early nineteenth century, the attitude of the Society's members towards slaves in the West Indies changed to one of sympathy, although they did not pursue outright abolition. As a direct democracy, its intentions were only as noble as the majority of its members. In 1823, the Society offered a premium for 'diminishing the labour of persons employed in the cultivation of sugar, cotton, and coffee in the West Indian Colonies, by the substitution or by the use of cattle'. The premium was specifically aimed at reducing slaves' hard physical burdens, to demonstrate to slave-owners that it was in their self-interest to make life easier for their slaves: 'that the interest of the master is inseparably connected with the content and ease of his bondsmen'.[58] The Society awarded the premium in 1829 to Josias Booker for introducing the use of oxen for the hard labour on his cotton plantation in Demerara (present-day Guyana). As one slave reportedly commented, 'these oxen are our negroes now'.[59] But though Booker's improvement may well have eased the burden on his slaves, he still remained a slave-owner.

As well as catering to particular kinds of invention, the Society of Arts also catered to the kinds of people who might not otherwise use patents. Its cash prizes were often attractive to people who were too poor to afford patents, while its honorary medals were attractive to aristocrats for whom making a profit from patents seemed too vulgar. It also catered to other people who were generally excluded from making improvements.[60] In 1758, for example, it instructed the people who awarded its premiums in the American colonies to accept submissions from Native Americans.[61] It also allowed women to claim premiums, just as it allowed them to be members. Ann Williams, for instance, a postmistress at Gravesend, in Kent, won twenty guineas from the Society in 1778 for her observations on the feeding and rearing of silkworms. She kept them in one of the post office pigeon-holes, referring to them affectionately as 'my little family' of 'innocent reptiles'. She sent in many different ideas to the Society on other subjects too. As she put it in one of her letters: 'Sir, curiosity is inherent to all the daughters of Eve.'[62]

The Society also recognised inventors who its members felt had been neglected or forgotten. In the late 1810s, the story of a German immigrant to London, Alois Senefelder, reached the ears of the Society's members. Senefelder was an unsuccessful actor and playwright, who in 1796 had invented a new process of printing. He could not afford to print his plays using the traditional methods, and therefore tried using cheaper materials like stone. When carrying out one of his experiments, Senefelder's mother reportedly entered his room, asking him to write down a laundry list. Finding no paper, Senefelder wrote his mother's commands on one of the stones. Curiosity then pushed him to treat the stone with chemicals, and he found that he could print what he had written. The process he invented, lithography, eliminated the need to engrave designs onto copper plates. It allowed artists to obtain perfect copies of original pencil-drawn designs.

Senefelder was aware of the importance of his invention and tried to keep it a secret. Intending to patent it, he travelled to London in 1800, where he stayed with his agent, Philip André. He was kept in seclusion for more than seven months for fear of the secret being revealed—it was so well kept, that the invention remained unnoticed for eighteen years. When Senefelder left London, André tried to take all the credit while still keeping the method secret. Eventually, however, Senefelder published a full explanation of the process, which finally allowed British printers and artists to adopt it. The Society awarded Senefelder its gold medal, to recognise him as the true inventor, and offered premiums for further development of the process. Indeed, thanks to the Society's encouragement of lithography, a young artist named Edward Lear, later famous for his nonsense poems like *The Owl and the Pussycat*, used the process to produce a book of forty-two masterfully executed and hand-painted prints of parrots. His book, *Illustrations of the Family of Psittacidae, or Parrots*, by the twentieth century was considered one of the greatest series of illustrations of natural history (the nature broadcaster David Attenborough became an avid collector of the prints). Lear presented sets of the prints to the Society of Arts, as thanks for its role in making the process more widely known.[63] Lear's own lithographic printer, Charles Hullmandel, won one of the Society's silver medals for his improvements to the process.

The Society thus operated at the margins, encouraging the kinds of inventions that might not otherwise have been created, and catering to the kinds of inventors who might not otherwise have been recognised. By the late 1780s it had settled into a routine, continuing to advertise specific premiums while mostly bestowing bounties. The inventions it rewarded could be viewed by the public in a repository—one of the conditions for winning a premium was to present the Society with a working model. In 1761 the Society opened its repository to a public exhibition of the machines, alongside the one it hosted for contemporary British artists (though the public seem to have been overenthusiastic—a few years later its mechanics committee warned that the machines were in danger 'of being broke to pieces' from over-use).[64] In the 1760s the Society also began to publish descriptions and catalogues of some of its inventions, sometimes with perspective drawings, and from 1783 it published a regular series of *Transactions* to serve as a means of exchanging information about inventions and improvements.

Its members had decided that the most cost-effective approach to serving the public was to reward the discovery of techniques, the invention of new machines, or the transfer of plants from one part of the colonies to another, where they might be more effective. It became focused on the spread and diffusion of knowledge, rather than using its fund to directly subsidise particular activities as it had in the 1760s with madder, hemp, and fish. Over time, it saw those activities as wasteful, or 'little'.[65] Its members decided it could do the most good by spreading information on *how* to serve the public good, rather than undertaking the schemes itself. The Society thus became a clearing house for useful information. For some inventors the Society 'was the most suitable medium' to communicate discoveries 'to those who are commercially interested'.[66]

As a result, the Society soon gained expertise in a range of industries. The person who held the position of secretary, in addition to taking minutes of the meetings and managing the other staff, was increasingly expected to be an expert in a number of different fields. Samuel More, who was secretary in the final decades of the eighteenth century, knew many of the most famous inventors of his day, including the group surrounding Matthew Boulton, Erasmus Darwin, and James Watt—the Birmingham Lunar Society. More was also a close friend of the celebrated potter Josiah Wedgwood, and persuaded him and some others in the Birmingham circle to join the Society as members. More's expertise of dealing with so many different fields meant that he and his successors were sometimes called upon to advise the government on its industry and trade policies, and to give expert evidence in court in cases dealing with patents.[67] One of his successors, Arthur Aikin, also instituted lectures on science and invention. The Society was increasingly relied upon as a repository of information on the arts.

Having gained expertise in lots of different fields, the Society soon began to combine them. By the late 1810s, its active members included some of the country's best artists, engravers, printers, mechanics, and inventors. It made it the ideal organisation to seek solutions to problems that required more than one specialism. Thus, when 1,400 invading French troops landed in Wales in 1797, the Society was well placed to respond to the ensuing crisis.

The French troops were easily defeated, but rumours of an invasion caused panic. People rushed to their local country banks to convert their paper banknotes into gold coin. To avoid the rapid depletion of Britain's gold reserves, the government suspended convertibility. British banknotes before 1797 had not circulated widely. They were generally printed in denominations of £10 and upwards—almost £1000 in today's money—so they exchanged hands infrequently and noticeably.[68] Forgery was very rare. But when the Bank of England suspended gold convertibility it replaced the coinage with tens of millions of notes in denominations as low as £1 and £2. With so many notes entering circulation, it became impossible for shopkeepers to keep track. This, together with the poor design of the notes, made forgery both easy and common.

The Bank of England reacted to the growing number of forgeries by dispensing death. The punishment for forgery, or paying with a forged note, was hanging. In 1801, the bank even criminalised possession, to be punished by being transported to Australia. The bank's lawyers pressured people into pleading guilty to possession, in exchange for avoiding the death penalty: it was one of the first systematic uses of the plea bargain.[69] But by 1818 the bank's own inspectors were reportedly unable to distinguish some fake notes from the real ones. If even the experts could not tell them apart, how could the public? People began to wonder if many of the growing numbers being sent to their deaths were in fact innocents, simply caught up by accident in the bank's attempt to set an example. Many believed the bank was itself to blame for making its notes so easy to copy.[70] A technical solution was needed.

Solving the problem of forgery required the combination of art and industry in the service of the public—the ideal project for the Society of Arts. On the urging of John Thomas Barber Beaumont, a painter-turned-soldier-turned-managing-director of a fire insurance office, in 1818 the Society put out the call for solutions. Some, like Beaumont himself, argued that banknotes should be engraved by only the very best artists. The idea was that true talent was difficult to reproduce. Yet finer art would also require the latest engraving technology. The Bank of England used copper plates to print its notes, which quickly wore out and needed to be re-engraved many times every day by hand. To solve this, the Society recommended a method of engraving steel, recently developed in America by the inventor Jacob Perkins, which could be used twenty to thirty more times than copper.[71]

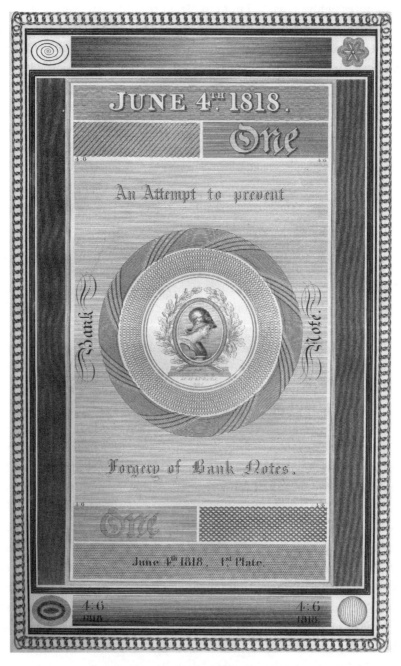

3.6A.–C. Specimen banknote designs, from the Society's report on preventing the forgery of banknotes, 1819, RSA/SC/EL/5/314.

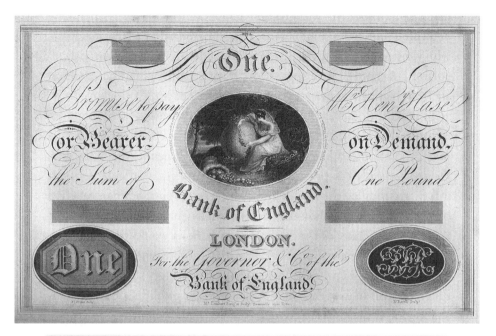

3.6A.–C. (*continued*)

Another suggestion was to engrave by machine: the rose engine could etch intricate geometrical patterns, impossibly complicated for anyone to reproduce by hand. Even if the forger could obtain access to exactly the same machine, it would be difficult for them to work out which settings had been used. Many of the Society's members had already been working on developing such engines, including the engineer Joseph Clement, who had just won the Society's gold medal for a machine that could draw circles and ellipses, as well as parallel, radiating and spiral lines. (Clement is most remembered today as the mechanic who worked on Charles Babbage's difference engine, a mechanical calculator.) A more bizarre suggestion, from another would-be inventor, was to integrate real peacock feathers into the paper.[72]

In 1819 the Society printed its report, recommending a combination of proposals. But the report fell upon deaf ears—the bank pursued a perfect solution at the expense of useful improvements. And in the end, the crisis simply disappeared: in 1821 the bank restored gold convertibility and recalled the low-denomination notes (but not before it had prosecuted over two thousand people for forgery, many of whom lost their lives).[73] Many of the Society's suggestions would eventually become standard elements of modern banknote design. Although its campaign did not immediately bear fruit, the Society's combination of different areas of expertise in the service of the public good was a foreshadowing of what was to come.

4

Jack of All Trades

IN 1754 THE SOCIETY'S FOUNDERS had largely been aristocrats, clergymen, and natural philosophers, with the middle classes overwhelmingly represented by well-off merchants and artisans—people who ran small workshops, often from their own homes, or whose businesses consisted of small partnerships of family and friends. Over the century, however, the middle classes were transformed in the wake of new technology. Human tasks were increasingly replaced or aided by machines, which in turn became larger and more efficient. Dexterous fingers were replaced by unfailingly precise mechanism, and muscled limbs were superseded by the power of wind, water, animals, and eventually steam. Scientific advances also spawned new industries, as scientists and inventors discovered new fuels, alloys, and chemical compounds. They applied electricity to communications and discovered the principles of photography. Artisans soon gave way to industrialists—the people bold enough to adopt the new technologies early, and savvy enough to make it profitable. They formed a new and wealthy upper class, sometimes accumulating even more wealth than the landed aristocracy.

At the same time emerged a class of ever more specialised professionals: civil engineers to construct the infrastructure that provided access to raw materials and markets; mechanical engineers to design the latest machines; mechanics to service and repair them; chemists to implement or advise on the latest scientific advances; and retailers to sell the products. The machinery became concentrated into factories, operated by many different hands at once, and thereby requiring new forms of employment too. As industry after industry was automated, hourly wages for employees gradually replaced the payment-by-results of the individual artisan. With this new kind of work came yet more specialised professionals—a host of foremen and managers to coordinate the workers' tasks and ensure discipline. The membership of the Society changed accordingly. Whereas the members of the mid-eighteenth century included millwrights, drapers, and apothecaries, that of the mid-nineteenth included mechanical engineers, the foremen of textile factories, and industrial chemists.

As inventions changed Britain, even the process of invention became specialised. Professional inventors could concentrate their efforts on making improvements, without having to then make money from the products of their new machines and techniques. So long as inventors could find someone to fund their patent, they could sell it or license it to a manufacturer and move on to inventing something else. 'Inventor seeks capitalist' was a common advertisement in the pages of nineteenth-century newspapers, though many also worked as consultants or employees. In the wake of professional inventors emerged patent agents—specialists in navigating the bureaucracy and legal requirements of obtaining a patent.[1]

Natural philosophers also increasingly specialised. As the sheer mass of what was known expanded, the labour of expanding it further became increasingly divided. The number of people interested in science also grew, partly due to the efforts of associations like the Society of Arts to both collect and spread knowledge. As their numbers grew, people gravitated towards those who shared their particular interests. Those interested in chemistry might increasingly only read the section of the *Transactions* devoted to chemical improvements, or only attend the lectures on chemical topics, while ignoring those to do with agriculture, mechanics, or manufactures. In an organisation with a broad remit like the Society of Arts, a person specialising in chemistry might be frustrated when lectures or discussions did not go into the detail they craved, with non-specialists either unable or unwilling to debate minutiae. The specialists might meet informally after the Society's lectures, before meeting more regularly on their own and founding their own independent organisations. Arthur Aikin, when he retired as secretary of the Society, helped found the Chemical Society of London. He even negotiated a cheap rate for it to hold its meetings in the rooms of the Society of Arts.

Specialist groups proliferated, many of them born of the Society itself. They gave attention to every field imaginable, holding their own meetings and lectures, and often printing their own publications. Some even offered medals and cash prizes, in a few cases fulfilling the same ends as the Society of Arts premiums. For members of the Society of Arts, there were ever more groups competing for their time, attention, and subscription fees. There were only so many evenings in a week to be spent going to discussions and committee meetings, and only so much money that could be laid aside for useful causes. When it came to improving any particular field, the specialist spin-offs often seemed the more useful; the Society of Arts by contrast seemed a jack of all trades and a master of none.

Faced with the competition of so many specialist groups, in the 1830s the Society of Arts attracted fewer and fewer new members. The remaining active members dwindled away through either death or indifference, and with them went their two-guinea subscription fees. Bankruptcy loomed. From the shrinking pool of members, fewer people could be found to volunteer their time and effort to committees, or to sit through meetings dealing with administration. Wealthy aristocrats and prominent politicians did continue to lend their prestige to the Society as honorary vice-presidents, but they were rarely present. In the early 1840s, general meetings regularly had to be postponed because too few people had turned up.[2] For a direct democracy like the Society of Arts to function, it had to have some voters.

But with crisis came opportunity. The members who remained came largely from the emerging professional classes: patent agents, industrial chemists, civil and mechanical engineers. They saw new potential in the Society as a means of sharing knowledge across the boundaries of their narrowing professions, and to stimulate improvements from the combination of different disciplines. In some fields of activity, the Society still lacked competition.[3] There were few rival societies that rewarded mechanical inventions, improvements to manufactures, or the opening up of new trades with the colonies. It was in combining disciplines, however, that the Society could be of most use—its status as a jack of all trades was potentially its greatest asset. The Chemical Society might be left to specialise in chemistry alone, but the 1839 announcement of the invention of photography showed new ways that chemistry could be applied to art. New research into electricity held the same promise, for example with the discovery that passing electrical current through a solution could be used to create exact metal copies of any treated surface (a process now known as electrotyping).[4] Some of the older members of the Society might also have recalled the combination of mechanics and art to find a solution to banknote forgery. Even in agriculture there was room to find useful applications of the Society's other disciplines. It had become one of the least popular premiums due to competition from first the Board of Agriculture and then the Royal Agricultural Society, but many agricultural tasks were yet to be mechanised. In the late 1830s, too, some people began to apply their chemical knowledge to agriculture in order to produce artificial fertilisers.[5]

The combination that would perhaps be most useful, however, was to apply fine art to manufactures. Due to its head-start in industrialisation, Britain could manufacture goods in the greatest quantities, for the cheapest prices, and of the most consistent quality. By 1850, Britain produced half of the world's iron, half of its textiles, two thirds of its coal, and made almost all of the new, efficient machinery.[6] In industry after industry, British manufactures found their way abroad, supplanting foreign producers from even their own domestic markets. Except, that is, when it came to design. Despite the early British lead in automation, its age-old rival France still managed to dominate the European market for many luxury goods. Its woven silks, Savonnerie carpets, and Sèvres porcelain had few competitors, and it seemed 'decidedly in advance' of Britain when it came to enamelling, bronze-work, vibrant textile dyes, printed paper-hangings, and certain kinds of pottery. It had a reputation for high-quality furniture, famed for achieving intricate patterns of different woods and veneers (parquetry and marquetry), as well as in using papier-mâché to create ornamented ceilings and walls. What French industry lacked in consistency or cheapness, it made up for in beauty. France produced things that looked good, and which people wanted to buy, even if to the British they sometimes appeared structurally defective or poorly fitted.[7]

What was alarming, however, was that the French authorities had made a slow but concerted effort to improve the efficiency of their machines and the quality of production.[8] If France was able to catch up with Britain in cost and quality, while also retaining its lead in beauty, then British manufactures would be seriously threatened. In some respects, particularly when it came to developing new dyes or alloys, France seemed to be shooting ahead.[9] Something had to be done before it was too late, and the Society of Arts had the potential to do it. No other group could draw simultaneously upon expertise in the fine arts, manufactures, mechanics, and chemistry.

But first, the Society of Arts needed to be saved from imminent dissolution. The man who led the rescue mission was a member of the new professional classes: Thomas Webster, a newly qualified barrister who specialised in patent law. The son of a vicar, he had graduated from Cambridge with a high score in mathematics, and had spent a few years as secretary to one of the many new professional societies, the Institution of Civil Engineers. He was a lawyer and an administrator, but also a scientist and an engineer—he had written a physics textbook and made his own experiments on the properties of steam. He was only a recent member of the Society of Arts, having joined in 1838. But in late 1841, when the Society's accounts committee sounded the alarm of looming bankruptcy, Webster convened a special rescue committee.

He and his allies on the committee—mostly other lawyers, engineers, and industrialists—proposed that the Society live up to its potential as an organisation to bridge specialisms. They argued that its premiums should be refocused on the application of art to industry, and it should otherwise become a place for the new professional classes to communicate the latest developments in their respective disciplines. Instead of just approving the committee reports and dealing with other administrative business, the focus of the Society's weekly Wednesday meetings should be lectures and presentations on the arts, manufactures, and inventions—'illustrations', as they called them, to be followed by discussion. The Society should also hold more enticing and entertaining events, then called 'conversazioni', in which the members and presenters could mingle informally.

Lectures and conversazioni had already been pioneered for some years by Arthur Aikin during his tenure as secretary, but they had only been occasional additions. Aikin initially used his platform to add context to an invention during a prize-giving, and from 1828 a few evenings were set aside for a lecture on the history of a particular industry. Other members soon also presented on their own specialist subjects. The lectures and illustrations were often entertaining, involving images and working models—a welcome break from the usual discussion of committee reports, rules, and accounts. To these he soon added the conversazioni.[10] To save the Society, and for it to do the most good, Webster and his allies wanted to make these lectures, illustrations, and associated social gatherings the Society's focus.

Yet to make the lectures and illustrations really popular, the Society would have to lift its prohibition on inventions that were patented. For almost a century, no invention had been allowed to receive the Society's premiums if it had been patented. The ban eventually extended to any discussion of patented inventions by the Society.[11] When the ban had originally been introduced, the idea was to prevent the Society from rewarding things that would already be profitable. It was its way of ensuring that premiums only went to something that would not otherwise be done. Patents were also distrusted for being monopolistic, albeit temporarily—one of the many ways in which private interests acted at the expense the public.

But to Webster and his allies this seemed outdated. Many of them held their own patents, or otherwise regularly dealt with patentees in the course of their business. They did not see patents as harmful, but rather as a necessary and temporary recompense for revealing useful secrets to the public. The deal, as they saw it, was that they got a temporary monopoly on the use of their invention, in exchange for which they had only a few months to provide a detailed description of their invention with drawings—a specification.[12] The specification allowed anyone to adopt the invention once the patent expired, and in the meantime could be used by someone else to make their own further improvements. Patents did not hide useful inventions; in fact, they revealed them.[13]

The Society's early members might once have been forgiven for being sceptical of this argument. Back in the 1760s, specifications were hard to get unless you lived in London and had both time and money. People had to apply to the Court of Chancery where specifications were kept, and pay a fee to obtain a copy. The Society occasionally sent its secretary to obtain copies of specifications, to check that its premiums did not contravene them. But from the mid-1790s enterprising publishers were printing the most useful-looking specifications in monthly journals.[14] By the 1840s, the latest British patent specifications were being reproduced in journals all over the world. The argument that patents revealed useful information was much more justifiable. And patenting was much more common than it had been. In the 1760s only a couple of hundred inventions had been patented; in the 1830s the number of inventions patented had risen to over twelve times that number.[15] Dropping the ban on patents would greatly expand the range of things that could be discussed at the Wednesday meetings, and thereby increase the Society's scope for promoting new combinations of art, science, and manufactures.

Webster and his allies faced resistance. Many other members objected to their proposed emergency cost-cutting measures, particularly a proposal to sack the elderly assistant secretary, who was less and less able to carry out his duties, but who had faithfully served the Society for almost four decades. A recently hired secretary also resigned when he discovered that his job might be abolished, or that at the very least his wages and benefits would be cut.[16] So in 1842 Webster and his allies went on a membership recruitment spree.[17] If they could get enough of their friends to join, then the Society's revenue would improve and they would also have the votes to push through their reforms. With his background in science, engineering, and the law, Webster and his allies had access to a wide range of like-minded people. Within a few years the Society's membership had swelled by over a third; within a decade it had doubled.[18] Their recruits included people like the railway engineer Robert Stephenson, and the co-inventor of the electric telegraph William Fothergill Cooke, along with many more of the country's most prominent engineers and inventors.[19] Webster and his allies rebuilt the Society in their own image.

In the meantime, the old Society of Arts was dying—often quite literally. In 1843 the Duke of Sussex, its president for almost three decades, passed away (though not before having Webster's proposed reforms read out to him, so that he could approve them clause by clause). The following year the Society lost Ann Birch Cockings, who had looked after its rooms and effects for forty-two years, and whose father had done the same since 1765. Cockings had been a continuous part of the Society since birth—she was born soon after her father got the job— and was among the first ever residents of its Adelphi building. Art historians could rely on her to share reminiscences of the irascible James Barry, or to 'perfectly' recollect the childhood prize-giving of a given famous artist.[20] She had been a pillar of the Society's administration. When a member demanded to see the secretary, she ostensibly replied that 'one old woman ought to do as well as another'.[21] The death of Cockings in 1844 severed a living link with almost the entirety of the Society's history.

Cockings would not have recognised the Society that emerged from Webster's reforms. In 1845, Webster's committee was voted so many extra powers that it became a committee of management, the Council. The Society of Arts, which had been a direct democracy for almost a century, became a representative democracy. Members still voted for most of the people who sat on the Council, and changes to rules and regulations would still need to be approved by a general vote, but the day-to-day running of the Society was from then on in the hands of a representative body.

Handing over all these powers to the Council freed up the regular Wednesday meetings from any discussion of accounts and rules. Meetings could now be focused entirely on lectures and illustrations, which would be interesting and attractive to new members, and would allow the Society to explore new areas. And having taken on so much control,

the Council could take action without the onerous democratic procedures and barriers—the votes one week rescinded by votes the following week—that had previously stood in Webster's way. In 1847, having
completed much of their rescue mission, Webster and his allies obtained
for the Society a royal charter. The Society of Arts thus became an officially incorporated body, a signal of its prestige and permanence.
(From then on, it would occasionally be called the Royal Society of Arts
in the press,[22] but its official name remained unchanged—the 'Royal'
was only officially added to the name in 1908.) In the early 1840s the
world had forgotten about the Society of Arts—one newspaper even
derided it as an institution that had become so stale, it existed merely
to look after the Barry paintings.[23] The royal charter was a signal that it
was ready to be useful again. It represented a new beginning.

Among the recruits to the Society, Webster found a like-minded civil
engineer named Francis Whishaw to be the new secretary. Whishaw
specialised in building railways, and was something of an enthusiast—
he had even published a bestselling book about Britain's railways for
which he had undertaken a 7,000-mile 'trip' for research. He was constantly coming up with schemes to expand Britain's railway network
further, believing the technology to be 'one of the greatest blessings ever
conferred on the human race'. It benefitted 'the prince, the peer, and the
peasant' alike.[24] Whishaw had also invented a 'hydraulic telegraph'—
a means of communicating messages by raising or lowering water in
pipes (though it was quickly superseded by the invention of the electric
telegraph). As secretary of the Society of Arts, Whishaw devoted much
of his energy to managing the recruitment drive, and delivered many of
his own lectures and illustrations. Through Whishaw, the vision of the
Society of Arts as an organisation that combined fields to create entirely
new ones quickly bore fruit.

At one of his illustrations Whishaw presented some samples of gutta
percha, a naturally occurring latex from the sap of a tree found in
Malaysia, which had been sent to the Society by one of its correspondents in Singapore. The samples were examined by the combined committees for chemistry and colonies and trade. They found that gutta
percha could be moulded when heated—it was a thermoplastic—and

at Whishaw's lecture he demonstrated how it could be used to make both a hard pipe and an elastic band. As well as its uses in manufactures, gutta percha had potential uses in art, for example in casting medals. At the lecture, one enterprising member induced a firm to immediately start importing the stuff.[25] And the 22-year-old German engineer Carl Wilhelm Siemens got the idea that its waterproof and insulating qualities might be useful. A few years later, Siemens and his brothers were using gutta percha to insulate underwater electric telegraph cables, providing near-instantaneous communications between Britain and France, eventually expanding to Russia, India, and North America.

But Whishaw's greatest contribution to the Society was to introduce the idea of holding industrial exhibitions. Exhibitions of machinery and manufactures were widely seen as the reason for France's rapid catch-up with Britain. They were also considered a means by which France had seemingly spread its internationally renowned design skills, once limited to only its most prominent luxury manufacturers, to all of its workers. Every few years since 1798, the French government had held an exhibition of its national industries in Paris. The state paid for everything—a grand temporary building, as well as all the expenses of the exhibitors—and the head of state himself awarded medals and cash prizes for the best works on display. Some of the very best exhibitors were admitted to the *Légion d'honneur*, France's highest order of merit. The benefits to exhibitors were so high that essentially every manufacturer wished to take part. In the days before GDP statistics, the exhibitions were thus an effective means of getting a detailed snapshot of the nation's manufacturing capabilities. It was the nation's industrial audit.

Armed with the knowledge of the condition of its industry, every few years the French state had been able to identify ways to improve it. Following the second exhibition in 1801, it had seen the need to establish a French version of the Society of Arts, the *Société d'encouragement pour l'industrie nationale*—an organisation that could reward improvements immediately, without having to wait some years for the next exhibition. In later years, the French state used its exhibitions to determine where to focus its subsidies for particular industries, or which subjects to prioritise in schools. Yet the exhibitions themselves were more than just a means of measuring industry—they were themselves a tool for improvement. Motivated by the prizes on offer, manufacturers would try to outdo one another each year, as well as to outdo their previous performances. The exhibitions thus 'excited an emulation', while revealing to manufacturers the latest technology and most fashionable designs. The juries for deciding the exhibition's prizes also explicitly rewarded inventions and manufactures that might best help France compete with Britain. From 1801 the juries prioritised the application of art to industry; in 1839 they paid special attention to items that could be mass-produced cheaply.[26] The exhibition prizes were a tool of the French government's industrial strategy—a means of directing the efforts of industrialists toward solving particular problems.

The exhibitions also harnessed the visiting public—the mass of potential consumers. When consumers were uninformed, manufacturers could easily become complacent, finding that people bought their wares even when their products were not very good. They could continue to manufacture their sub-standard wares, with no incentive to improve. Exhibitions shattered this complacency. They showed consumers what was possible, educating them in taste and forcing the manufacturers to cater to their heightened demands. This was how the exhibitions spread good design. Once the paying public had been exposed to the best, they would settle for nothing less.

But the exhibitions also became a way for France's rivals to keep an eye on its industrial development and keep up. Exhibitions of industry were soon copied abroad. 1844 alone saw exhibitions in Berlin, Milan, and even Archangel in Russia. They were regularly taking place in New York, and the following year would see national exhibitions in Madrid and Vienna too. The 1844 Paris exhibition in particular set alarm bells ringing in Britain. France appeared to be catching up in terms of mechanisation and mass production, and in some respects it was pulling ahead. France's scientists were taking the lead in applying the latest chemical advances to industry, and it continued to secure its already existing dominance of design and fashion. Britain, by contrast, had not undertaken a comparable industrial audit. Without a national exhibition of its own, it could not be sure that it would remain competitive.

Many of Britain's principal manufacturing towns—Sheffield, Derby, Manchester, Birmingham—had held exhibitions of their local industries in the late 1830s and early 1840s.[27] The 1840 exhibition in Leeds even attracted two hundred thousand visitors. And a few exhibitions were held in London, though they were only small and short-lived.[28] Britain in 1844 had still not had an exhibition that was national—something on a scale to rival the French one, and able to produce the same results. It was Francis Whishaw who saw the potential of the Society of Arts to hold one.

Through exhibitions, Whishaw also saw a new way to boost the Society's popularity. More and more commentators had been criticising the Society's old method of awarding premiums, noting how few of them had actually been brought into use, instead gathering dust in the repository, their inventors forgotten. The Society's annual *Transactions* and prize-givings did little to expose the work of new inventors to the wider public. Even the weekly lectures were limited, fleeting, and soon forgotten. An exhibition would amplify the effects of the Society's premiums, combining entertainment with the diffusion of knowledge. A truly national event would give the premium-winners the exposure they deserved.

The Society was still recovering from its financial difficulties, so in November 1844 Whishaw persuaded his friend Joseph Woods—a civil engineer—to independently offer three hundred pounds in prizes for paintings and recent inventions, including fifty pounds or a silver goblet for the best design of a building 'suitable for a grand annual exhibition of the products of national industry'.[29] Whishaw managed the competition in a private capacity, and planned for the prize-winning entries to form the nucleus of the exhibition. But the press mangled their reporting of the conditions, which they labelled 'exceedingly absurd'.[30] Whishaw tried to clear up the misunderstandings, but the damage was done. Within a few months he had received some twenty plans for an exhibition building, but no inventions or paintings to put in it.[31] He continued to advertise in the papers for a couple of months, but in the end let the matter drop.

In the meantime, however, Whishaw was keen to make the Society's occasional evening conversazioni more entertaining. On 6 December

1844 he held an event in his private capacity in the Society's rooms, introducing exhibits for the guests to peruse while they socialised. Whishaw covered the tables with examples of science's application to the arts, and demonstrated some of the latest inventions, including a patented method of quickly producing ice on a warm summer's day. It was a trial run for the concept of an exhibition—a means to build support for the idea among the Society's members by showing them what was possible. Contrary to some historians, who have mistakenly portrayed this evening *soirée* as some kind of failed early national exhibition, Whishaw's evening was an overwhelming success.[32] 'We have never witnessed a more successful attempt to combine intellectual pleasures with social enjoyment', one journalist gushed, concluding that the evening was 'one of the pleasantest and most profitable we have ever passed'.[33]

This first of Whishaw's new and improved conversazioni attracted 150 people, mostly members of the Society of Arts and their wives (very few women were members themselves). The event had not been widely publicised, and seems to have been thrown together at the last minute.[34] But Whishaw's reputation as an entertaining and attentive host was immediately secured. The following month, this time with a little funding from the Society's vice-presidents, he outdid himself.

On 28 January 1845, Whishaw had the Great Room specially lit to better show off the Barry paintings. He served refreshments. He made sure there was music, allowing an inventor to show off his improvements to the piano.[35] Inventions vied with natural history specimens, samples of manufactures, rare books of engravings, and works of art. He had his friend William Fothergill Cooke demonstrate his new two-needle electric telegraph, sending messages back and forth with an assistant responding from across the room.[36] Cooke was the latest celebrity inventor, his infant invention having made headlines just a few weeks earlier when it was used to catch a murderer. The killer, dressed very soberly to resemble a Quaker, had attempted to flee the scene of his crime by boarding a train from Slough to London. The two-needle telegraph had no letter 'Q', so the message sent up the railway line had warned of a 'Kwaker', but he was caught nonetheless. Cooke's presence was a hit—he captured the audience's imagination when he told them they might one day instantaneously conduct long-distance games of chess.

Whishaw knew the value of celebrity. At an earlier event he had introduced as a guest 'General Tom Thumb', real name Charles Sherwood Stratton—a 6-year-old dwarf who was touring with the famous circus pioneer P. T. Barnum. Stratton's routine of singing, dancing, mimes, and impressions of famous people was causing a sensation in America and Europe. Somehow, Whishaw had managed to interest him in a presentation on bee hives.[37] So for his January conversazione, he introduced another guest who would get people's attention: a young Māori man in his traditional garb, who was visiting London to receive an English education. Overall, with celebrities, refreshments, music, inventions, and art, Whishaw's second trial exhibition was a success. People continued to arrive until 11 pm, at which point the Society's rooms were packed—an estimated eight hundred to a thousand people attended throughout the night (today, the maximum safe standing capacity of the Great Room is only two hundred).[38]

The potential benefits of a larger exhibition were now obvious. For the next few months, the idea of holding a national exhibition of industry became the talk of the Society of Arts. Cooke in particular seems to have seen the value of his friend's suggestion—the evening event had brought him press attention and allowed him to promote his new scheme for a London-to-Liverpool telegraph. The words that had been sent across the Great Room that night had been 'Adelphi' and 'Liverpool'. So Whishaw had no difficulty in persuading Cooke to suggest to the Society that it formally begin to look into a national exhibition.[39] The Society would not be able to pay for the event from its own coffers, unaided, but they might raise a special subscription fund, to which Cooke himself offered a loan of five hundred pounds. Given the success of Whishaw's conversazioni, there was no doubt that such an event would be profitable and the loan repaid. Others offered more, including one thousand pounds from Robert Stephenson.

A national exhibition for Britain would have to be bigger and better than that of any other country. After all, Britain was the world's economic superpower. The Society began setting up committees in all the manufacturing towns in Britain. They discussed holding the exhibition in Hyde Park, and looked into the likely costs of a vast, temporary building. At the Society's annual distribution of prizes Whishaw announced his plans. He also used the opportunity to corner a major celebrity, Prince Albert, the husband of Queen Victoria. When the Duke of Sussex died in 1843 and left the Society's presidency vacant, the Society had managed to get Albert to replace him. Albert only really turned up to lend some star power to the proceedings. But he was popular with the professional classes who had come to dominate the Society—the likes of Webster, Cooke, and Whishaw. As one engineer put it, Albert could talk 'to an engineer as an engineer; to a painter as a painter . . . and so on through all the branches of engineering, architecture, art and science'.[40] He shared their interests, or at least appeared to. They saw in Albert a potential champion—someone who was trying to make his wife's monarchy relevant to the growing ranks of workers and self-made industrialists, rather than just the old inherited aristocracy.

Whishaw had already tried to get Albert's support for his exhibition scheme about six months earlier when he was promoting the three-hundred-pound prize fund, but with no success. Buoyed by the popularity of his conversazioni and the support of other members of the Society, Whishaw tried again. Albert remained reluctant, but he expressed just enough interest for Whishaw to use. The prince requested— 'commanded' him, exaggerated Whishaw—that he present him with a plan for a national exhibition when it was more matured.[41] In the space of just half a year, Whishaw had built up extraordinary momentum for his scheme. It seemed as though the preparations for a British national exhibition of industry were imminent.

And then, nothing happened. Just over a month after receiving Albert's 'command', Francis Whishaw resigned. Perhaps he thought the scheme's success was assured, that he had done enough.[42] He found a replacement as secretary—a Scottish engineer named John Scott Russell, who was on the sub-committee for organising the exhibition. Russell was one of Webster's new recruits. He had run a steam-powered coach service between Glasgow and Paisley (though the heavy steam coaches were attacked for ruining the roads, and one overturned and exploded, killing several passengers). He had also made a major discovery concerning the properties of waves, allowing him to design more efficient ships. He was a talented scientist and engineer, and would in the 1850s build Isambard Kingdom Brunel's gigantic iron steamship, the SS *Great Eastern*, the largest ship that had ever been made. With Russell, Whishaw left a like-minded friend in charge.

Whishaw asked to stay on as a sort of honorary secretary, and continued to build support for a national exhibition, but he left London to pursue his other great love, the extension of Britain's railway system.[43] Without Whishaw there to single-mindedly push the project along, however, nothing was done. His decision to abandon the exhibition scheme would later haunt him, as others took all the credit for his work.

Russell was in favour of the national exhibition, but was soon inundated with the Society's many other concerns. Webster's administrative reforms were ongoing, and the threat of bankruptcy had not been fully put to rest. Russell had funding-drives to manage, as well as the creation of the Council, the acquisition of the Society's royal charter, and even a major refurbishment of its rooms.[44] A year after Whishaw's triumph had seemed so assured, some members began to ask for their membership subscriptions to be paid out of what they had already contributed towards the exhibition, rather than having to pay anything extra.[45] In the summer of 1846, Whishaw tried in vain to resurrect the project—he claimed to have been setting up committees of support in many of the main manufacturing towns throughout the country. He called a meeting of the original supporters at the Society of Arts, but only Cooke turned up on time, and soon left.[46] Without support at the Society of Arts, his dream of a national exhibition of industry was quietly dropped.

Yet even without an exhibition of national industry, it seemed obvious to many, including Russell, that British design in manufactures was inferior to the French. As early as 1837 the British government had begun to fund schools of design in London and some of the major manufacturing towns. But the designers who graduated from the schools were rarely employed by British manufacturers, who instead preferred to hire designers from abroad.[47] A national exhibition of industry might have gone a long way to solving the problem, particularly if it raised consumer taste and thereby forced manufacturers to improve their standards. Yet something might still be done on a more limited scale. Given the Society's limited funds, it was at least worth trialling the idea of educating manufacturers and the public.

In December of 1845, Russell offered fifty pounds of his own money to fund a new, special set of premiums. These would be for 'art manufactures'—examples of fine art applied to mechanical production. He persuaded William Fothergill Cooke and then the Society's Council to match his donations. From the prize-winners, they would be able to assemble a collection of 'select specimens'—the best designs for workers and manufacturers to copy. Yet Russell and the Society's members—by now mostly engineers and industrialists, with hardly any artists left—knew very little about what constituted good design. They hardly even knew what kind of objects deserved to be rewarded, let alone how to judge them. They needed someone to guide the way. It was thus, inadvertently, that Russell unleashed on the Society one of its most energetic, overbearing, and zealous reformers, who would come to dominate the organisation for decades: Henry Cole.

5

The Greatest Beauty for
the Greatest Number

BORN IN BATH, the son of an army officer, Henry Cole was a small, bespectacled man, with an untidy mane of curly hair and side-burns, and a usually dishevelled appearance. He was a middle-ranking civil servant with a lucrative sideline as a journalist, and was heavily influenced by the ideas of the philosopher Jeremy Bentham, the founder of modern utilitarianism. Cole was to become the conduit for utilitarianism into the Society of Arts. When Bentham had formulated his ideas, it had been from a frustration that England's laws seemed so ad hoc and messy, full of inconsistencies and omissions. It seemed irrational and incoherent; it was not a system. Bentham's proposed alternative was to base everything on a fundamental guiding principle: to achieve the greatest happiness for the greatest number of people. Utilitarian reformers inspired by Bentham introduced reforms for the benefit of 'the masses' or 'the People'. And in maximising their happiness, the ends always justified the means. For Bentham, and thus for Cole, it was the results that mattered, not the way they were achieved.[1]

Henry Cole was from a second generation of utilitarians, most heavily influenced by Bentham's protégé, John Stuart Mill. Mill was the son of Bentham's secretary, and had been brought up under his close guidance—he was raised to be the perfect rational being. But the intense intellectual regime had eventually brought on an emotional crisis. John Stuart Mill remained a major proponent of Bentham's utilitarian system,

5.1. Henry Cole. This photograph of him was discovered in a
bookshop in Hampshire in the 1980s. It is attributed to Julia Margaret
Cameron. The original is in the collection of A. J. Stirling.

but he softened it, finding room for beauty and poetry. Not everything
had to be rational; there was room for feeling. Cole was only a couple
of years younger than Mill, and a staunch devotee. They met frequently,
and went on long Sunday walks around London. Cole was not a deep
philosophical thinker; he often confided in his diary that he felt himself

out of his depth when engaged in academic discussions with the other young utilitarians.[2] But he was a man of action. His major goal was to see utilitarian principles applied. In all things—his career, his campaigns, and in life in general—Cole sought to create rational, comprehensive systems that would maximise good for the greatest number of people. And he would stop at nothing to achieve his ends. Perhaps because of his utilitarian influences, or perhaps because he simply had an abrasive personality, Cole ignored criticism and rode roughshod over opposition.

One of Henry Cole's first jobs had been as a lowly clerk for the Record Commission—a body tasked with investigating how the government's records were kept. At first, he simply got on with the job of transcribing and collating the records. But when his boss refused to pay him properly for some extra work, his utilitarian reforming zeal was unleashed. Cole wrote anonymous articles in the press arguing for easier and cheaper access to the records, while accusing his boss of giving jobs to his friends and family—a very common practice called 'jobbery'. Cole's employment dispute was frustrating to him personally, but he used the language of utilitarianism to deride the entire Record Commission as an irrational and expensive mess. In the midst of the dispute Cole was fired. But he persisted in his press campaign, portraying himself as a public-spirited whistle-blower. With the help of a politician who was in Mill's utilitarian circle, Cole was eventually re-hired and promoted.[3] Soon afterwards, in response to some of his criticisms, a law was even passed to reorganise the government's records into a centralised Public Record Office.

Cole's first campaign was personal. He does not seem to have minded jobbery unless it was to his own detriment, as he soon found jobs in government for his brother and cousin. But his second campaign was genuinely public-spirited. In 1838 Cole assisted in the project of another utilitarian reformer, Rowland Hill, who was trying to create a national prepaid postage system. Up until then, the cost of sending a letter depended on the distance it was sent and the number of sheets it contained, varying widely from region to region. Mail had to be both sent and collected from the local post offices, and was paid for by the receiver, not the sender. Only the royal family, aristocrats, and members of parliament had the privilege of 'franking' their mail with a signature, allowing it to be received free of charge. Poor people got their friends to deliver letters by hand, or found ways around the system. One approach was to hide coded messages on the outside of the letter so that the news could be transmitted by a glance at the address; the recipient could see the message and then decline payment. The postal system was complicated, incoherent, and favoured only the rich and powerful.[4] Hill's scheme was to replace the mess with a flat rate, so that any letter weighing under an ounce might be sent to anywhere in the country, from anywhere else in the country, for just a penny. Letters would be prepaid by the senders, as shown by a stamp, and the charges would be so cheap that nobody would have to cheat the system. It would allow the masses to communicate. Hill promised it would be profitable too.

Henry Cole's major contribution to the campaign for universal penny postage was to marshal public opinion in its favour, and against the system it sought to replace. He created and edited *The Post Circular*, a weekly broadsheet that would help circulate petitions and other pro-reform propaganda. Cole made sure the broadsheet included just enough news to be classed as a newspaper, meaning it could be distributed free of charge by the Post Office. He thus exploited one of the very privileges that the reform was trying to eliminate: in true utilitarian fashion, the ends justified the means. On another occasion, he highlighted the irrationality of a rule that, so long as the letter weighed under an ounce, a single sheet of paper was always cheaper than two sheets. He sent an assistant to the post office with an extremely thick single sheet, which was duly marked as being 'single' by a postal official. The assistant then produced an extremely thin two-sheet letter, only a fifth the weight of the first. The postal official 'turned crimson, became furious, and cursed a little', but was forced to mark it 'double', to the laughter of an assembled crowd. Cole proudly turned the Post Office's own system against itself.[5] Eventually, Cole managed to collect over 260,000 signatures—almost a third of the total number of votes cast at the previous general election.[6] The government gave way and introduced Rowland Hill's universal postage system.

Hill was put in charge of implementing his vision, with Henry Cole as his assistant. Their next step was to design ways to prove that a letter had been prepaid. One method they settled upon was to use a specially printed envelope, the other was to affix a small adhesive postage stamp. For the postage stamp they settled for a simple profile of Queen Victoria, now famous as the 'Penny Black'. For the envelopes, Cole consulted the president of the Royal Academy before commissioning an elaborate design from the Irish-born genre painter William Mulready: Britannia sending messenger angels forth to the furthest corners of the world. The idea of the design being distributed throughout the country captured Cole's imagination: 'such an opportunity of spreading models of beauty over the whole face of the country (we might almost say the world), and among all classes of people, has never occurred before in the history of mankind'.[7] Here was a chance to use the postal system to spread beauty to the masses—the greatest happiness for the greatest number. It was utilitarianism applied to aesthetics. The Mulready envelopes turned out to be a flop—they were widely satirised, and it was soon noticed that one of the angels was missing a leg. Yet for Hill and Cole, this simply showed that the public had a 'disregard and even distaste for beauty'.[8] Cole would continue in his efforts to help the masses communicate, as he did with postal reform and later campaigns, but for the rest of his life his over-riding project would be to improve the public's taste.

Cole's one-man crusade to improve the taste of the masses took many different forms. Under a fake name, Felix Summerly, he published guides to art galleries and museums, and wrote up a series of day-long 'pleasure excursions' in a newspaper called *The Railway Chronicle*. With more and more people able to travel on the expanding railway system, Cole's guides called attention to the beautiful art and architecture that lay dotted around the country, reachable for the first time in a matter of hours rather than days. Cole believed that good taste could only be taught through exposure to beauty; as with the thinking behind the French exhibitions of national industry, people would not know what they wanted until they had seen it. Yet museum and excursion guides relied on people deciding for themselves to seek beauty during their precious leisure hours. To increase the exposure, Cole had to bring beauty into the home.

One of Cole's solutions was to publish a series of illustrated children's books—Felix Summerly's *Home Treasury*. The series mostly just recycled old stories and nursery rhymes, but Cole took the illustrations from prints and drawings available in museums, or commissioned them from a growing group of professional artists he had befriended through Mulready. One of Cole's illustrated children's books, *An Alphabet of Quadrupeds*, took its rabbits from Albrecht Dürer, and its lions from Rembrandt. Many of the other books were illustrated by some of the country's greatest living artists, and Cole made sure to use the latest techniques in lithography. He prioritised the illustrations, but Cole also eliminated any moralising in the stories he published—a children's book was supposed to be fun, not a lecture.[9] Unsurprisingly, the books were popular. Cole even created toy sets for children to develop their taste for ornament and architecture—brightly coloured clay tiles to be arranged into geometric patterns, and terracotta bricks to assemble miniature buildings. To these he added a children's guide to 'the art of seeing', to train them to appreciate visual beauty.[10]

Cole also tried again to use the universal postage system as a means of disseminating beauty. In 1843 he published the first commercial Christmas card—a work of art to be sent to everyone he knew. It showed a large family at dinner making a toast, flanked by scenes of food and clothing being given to the poor. Cole commissioned the design from one of Mulready's protégés, the painter John Callcott Horsley (who also illustrated Cole's version of *Beauty and the Beast*). He sold about a thousand copies, but the effort was not repeated.

Finally, Cole was introduced to the Society of Arts by John Scott Russell, his editor at *The Railway Chronicle*. When Russell created the special premiums for applying art to manufactures, it was to Cole, as the newspaper's design expert, that he turned for advice. One December evening over tea, Russell visited Cole to draw up the list of prizes for the competition. For Cole, here was a chance to bring beauty into the home by applying it to everyday objects. The premiums they drew up were for mugs, tea urns, and even a complete tea service of teapot, basin, milk jug, cup and saucer, and plate. That would cover everyday eating and drinking. The next was for a washstand, basin, and ewer. That would cover everyday washing. To these they added geometric patterns for carpets and for tiled or mosaic floors. The manufacturer of Cole's clay toys, Herbert Minton, was one of a group of potters leading a revival of brightly patterned medieval encaustic tiles, developing new ways to produce the colours cheaply (the most famous of Minton's tiles adorn the hallways of the Houses of Parliament). Minton-like designs would bring the beauty of medieval abbeys into the hallways and staircases of the home. Last, Cole suggested that the Society reward designs for bible covers, and for a watercolour drawing of the Holy Family. Cole adhered to the Church of England, but he had no qualms about exploiting people's religiosity to infiltrate their homes with beauty. Many of his utilitarian friends were among the country's most prominent atheists. The ends justified the means.[11]

Henry Cole saw in the Society of Arts the ideal tool for his agenda. Here was an organisation with expertise in mechanics and manufactures, a connection with royalty, and a record of encouraging the arts. The things he was interested in—ceramics for encaustic tiles, and the latest advances in lithography for his book illustrations and Christmas cards—were the kinds of things presented and discussed at the Society's Wednesday evening meetings. A month after his meeting with Russell, he joined as a member. Over the next few years, however, he took control.

In April 1846 Cole got himself elected to the fine arts committee (by now renamed from the original 'polite arts'). In pursuit of the special art-manufactures premiums he had helped to draw up, Cole also submitted his own designs. He studied some Etruscan pots in the British Museum and applied elements of their designs to the nineteenth-century English tea service—as with so many of his artistic ventures, he took art out of the museum and into the home. The tops of the handles were sculpted with animal heads and limbs, the teapot's spout was a lion's mouth and its lid handle was the head of a ram. He had it manufactured by his friend Herbert Minton. But Cole submitted the tea service under his old pseudonym, Felix Summerly; as a result, he actually sat on the committee that decided to award him the Society's silver medal.[12]

5.2. The tea service designed by 'Felix Summerly', aka Henry Cole, for which
he won the Society's prize in 1846. Illustration from Cole's autobiography,
Fifty Years of Public Work, RSA/SC/EL/1/211.

It was only at the 1846 annual distribution of the Society's premiums
that Felix Summerly's true identity was revealed. It is unclear how the
rest of the fine arts committee reacted to Cole's deception, but he
pressed on regardless. The tea service became popular, and would be
produced by Minton for decades. It also gave Cole the opportunity to
forge a personal connection with Prince Albert. In August 1846, Cole
persuaded Russell to arrange a private meeting in which he could formally present his tea service.[13] Cole was now, after all, a prize-winner.
Yet what could have been a mere formality he turned to his personal
advantage by suggesting he send the prince any new examples of British
art applied to manufactures. Albert reportedly once said that 'if he
wanted to pack the greatest quantity into the smallest space', he would
send for Cole.[14] Their short meeting was no exception, as he hurriedly
convinced Albert of the need to improve the nation's taste.

The commercial success of Cole's tea service fully persuaded him that
professional artists, not just amateurs like himself, ought to be employed
as designers by manufacturers. He wished to reproduce his own relationship with Herbert Minton, but for better artists like his friends

William Mulready or John Callcott Horsley (by now head of the government's School of Design). Cole privately started a business to forge such connections and take on the responsibility of marketing and promotion, all under the name of his alter-ego Felix Summerly. He already knew many of Britain's greatest artists, and the Society of Arts now provided him with connections to manufacturers. Cole appealed to artists by invoking the old master painters: Raphael had designed crockery, he claimed, and Holbein had designed brooches and salt-cellars. Prestigious living artists like Mulready would set an example by reviving the practice of design for manufactures, though with a modern twist: they would apply their skills to everyday objects, not just the luxuries of the aristocracy. The greatest beauty for the greatest number. As for the manufacturers, Cole promised commercial success. And if they became used to employing the top artists, they might also employ more of the younger designers graduating from the government's design schools. His art-manufactures eventually included ornamented inkstands, intricately carved wooden breadboards (he was particularly proud of this one), and even a matchbox shaped like a crusader's tomb.[15]

In the meantime, Cole began to refashion the Society of Arts to meet his own objectives. The art-manufactures premiums that Cole and Russell had offered for 1846 did not receive many entries that they considered of high quality—certainly not enough to form the hoped-for collection of 'select specimens' that might inspire manufacturers. But Cole's interview with Prince Albert in August 1846 brought on a dramatic change in the Society as a whole. The list of the Society's premiums for the following year was prefaced by an extended manifesto on the importance of applying art to industry. 'Of high art in this country there is abundance, of mechanical industry and invention an unparalleled profusion; the thing still remaining to be done, is to effect the combination of the two, to wed high art with mechanical skill'.[16] It was pure Cole. And with Russell's help, the premiums themselves were almost all refashioned towards achieving his personal goal: in the fine arts, the Society asked for the best designs for clocks for chimney mantlepieces, for geometrical patterns on window blinds, and for cheap inkstands and candlesticks; in chemistry, they asked for cheap ways to produce vibrant colours in glass for decorating everyday objects—turquoise, crimson, ruby, and deep green; in manufactures, they called for glass vases and coloured porcelains, for designs for earthenware baths, and for the most elegant designs for wool table-covers. Even the premiums for agriculture were affected—they asked only for flax adapted to lace-making. Only mechanics seems to have escaped Cole's refashioning of the premiums, but then again he was not yet even a member of the Society's Council.

Cole's refashioning even affected the way the Society itself looked. Cole persuaded Herbert Minton to join as a member, who as part of the 1846 refurbishments donated a geometrically patterned mosaic floor for the Society's hallway and stairs—it is still used today. It also seems no coincidence that when preparing for the refurbishment, David Ramsay Hay, an artist Cole admired and later proposed for membership, offered to repaint the Great Room for no extra charge. The simple white ceilings were repainted to resemble a Gothic mosaic of interlocking geometric shapes and shields of gold, red, and blue; the frieze beneath it was painted an 'Etruscan brown'; and the beige walls around the Barry paintings were covered with purple cloth.[17] The Society itself began to resemble Cole's attitude to beauty—the more decoration, the better.

To consolidate the Society's changes, Cole tried to persuade artists to join as members. They were initially uninterested, unable to see what an institution dominated by engineers and industrialists had to offer.[18] His solution, proposed at the end of 1846, was for the Society to hold an exhibition each year devoted to the works of a particular living artist. Exhibitions of this kind would demonstrate the Society's commitment to applying high art. By celebrating people's work while they were still alive, they would actually be able to appreciate the honour. As a utilitarian, Cole cared about increasing happiness; the dead felt nothing. The exhibitions would have a permanent effect too. In the course of writing his guides for museums and art galleries, Cole had discovered that the National Gallery, founded in 1824, lacked modern works. Cole admired its collection of medieval art, but felt that a truly national repository of British art ought to cover all ages, right up to the present. He proposed that the Society use the proceeds from annual exhibitions in honour of living artists to either commission or purchase their principal works for the nation. He hoped the National Gallery would accept the works, but failing that there would at least be the nucleus of a superior collection of British art—art purchased by the public, for the public. Cole suggested they offer cheaper ticket prices for the working classes, both maximising the exposure of art to the masses, and allowing the masses to have a claim to be patrons of the arts themselves.[19]

With the first of these exhibitions, Cole wanted to honour his close friend William Mulready. But he quashed potential charges of favouritism by first approaching (and even prematurely announcing) an exhibition of one of the best-known British artists at the time, the animal painter Edwin Landseer. Landseer had been a child prodigy—from the age of 4 or 5 he had drawn cows in the fields near his home, and the lions at the Tower of London. In 1813, aged only 11, he had won a medal from the Society of Arts for his drawings of animals. He won even more over the following years for drawings and paintings of horses and dogs. As someone whose first public exposure as an artist had been via the Society, he must have seemed a safe bet to take part in the new exhibitions. One of his drawings of a dog is in the Society's archive. When Cole invited him to exhibit, he had just unveiled his most famous work—a portrait of a stag, *Monarch of the Glen*, which has come to adorn countless Scottish biscuit tins and whisky labels. But Landseer did not give his consent to hold the exhibition in his honour—he was flattered, of course, but worried it would seem indecently self-congratulatory.

The Society's first exhibition in honour of a living British artist would instead go, as Cole had always desired, to William Mulready—also a former Society of Arts premium winner. Despite the setback of Landseer's rejection, the announcement of the exhibition in early 1847 had an immediate effect on membership. Cole was able to bring artists—and thus supporters of his focus on art-manufactures—into the Society in droves. It probably helped that many of them had been childhood winners of the Society's premiums: John Callcott Horsley, the artist Cole had commissioned for his Christmas card; and Charles Eastlake, who later that year would become the director of the National Gallery

5.3. Drawing of a dog by Edwin Landseer. He won a premium from the Society in 1813 for his drawings of animals, aged only 11 (a note below the drawing mistakenly says he was 10). The sketch was made for the Society's judges, to prove that his submissions for the prize were his own. From the Society's archive.

and a few years after that the president of the Royal Academy.[20] Cole brought them back into the fold.

The exhibitions of British living artists helped Cole to infuse the Society's membership with his supporters. Yet his main focus was on another kind of exhibition. Cole and Russell hoped that the Society of Arts premiums, now so focused on promoting the application of high art to manufactures, would enable them to create a collection of 'select specimens' worth showing off to the public—the sort of collection that would enable consumers to demand more of manufacturers, and for manufacturers themselves to improve the quality of their wares. Manufacturers complained 'that the public prefer the vulgar, the gaudy, the ugly even, to the beautiful and perfect'. Cole and Russell hoped that the exhibition would remove that complaint by educating the public in taste. The exhibition would likewise educate the manufacturers. The exhibits would be items 'at the very summit of that perfection which has already been attained'.[21] The chemists would then know what colours had already been achieved, and thus where to direct their labours in inventing new ones. The artists would be educated as to the processes and materials now available to them. The manufacturers would know how better to decorate their wares.

The first exhibition of 'select specimens' of manufactures took place in March 1847. Cole and Russell did not get as many entries for the prizes as they had hoped, so they hurriedly dashed around London in horse-drawn cabs to try and persuade their friends and acquaintances to send something in. Many of them were the manufacturers Cole partnered with to produce the Felix Summerly art-manufactures. They then added the prize-winning entries from the previous year, including Cole's own Minton-made tea service. At this early stage it was important to demonstrate the popularity of the project, so entry to the exhibition was free. And it was, after all, about spreading beauty to the masses. Cole supplemented this with his talent for building public support. Prince Albert was persuaded to make an appearance, and Cole organised a special evening viewing for people he judged to be particularly influential—politicians who represented Britain's industrial centres, the presidents of various other societies, the senior officials of museums and design schools, and a few celebrities like Charles Dickens and Rowland Hill.[22] The exhibition was a hit. Some twenty thousand people turned up to view over two hundred specimens: pottery from the sixteenth century up to the present, to show its development; works made possible by advances in mechanically carving wood and marble; papier-mâché-ornamented furniture; enamelled glass; bronze lamps and chandeliers; samples of the latest advances in colour printing. Following this success, Cole and a few of his friends—utilitarians and artists—were elected to the Society's Council.

Cole repeated the exhibition of manufactures in 1848—a bigger and better event than the one before. On entering, visitors were struck by a gigantic papier-mâché sofa, adorned with mother-of-pearl flowers, birds, and butterflies. 'A room thus furnished would be dazzling', wrote one journalist, but overall the exhibition showed 'the combination of the useful and the graceful'. Over the chimney-piece in the Great Room was a marvel of mechanics applied to art—a carved wooden panel of some game animals, displaying such 'a softness in the fur, a flutter in the feathers', that visitors were amazed to learn it had all been done by machine. And among painted pottery, mosaics, and stained glass, a group of artists were keen to show off the latest improvements to photography.

'These ingenious gentlemen have actually caught a sunbeam', one newspaper exclaimed, noting that even a fast-moving cloud in a high wind could now be captured clearly, without blurring.[23] The technology still required long exposure times, but it was becoming noticeably more rapid and accurate. Cole himself displayed samples of the art-manufactures he was selling as Felix Summerly. He seems to have had no qualms about making a bit of money from his efforts on behalf of the Society of Arts.

The 1848 exhibition of art-manufactures drew in seventy thousand visitors, over three times the previous year's number. A few months later, the Society held its exhibition in honour of William Mulready, which caused a minor sensation in the art world (helped along by the fact that Cole anonymously wrote favourable reviews for some major newspapers). Rarely, perhaps never before, had a single British artist been so singled out and honoured by a public exhibition.[24] Overall, the exhibitions were gaining momentum.

Buoyed by this initial success, Cole now sought to revive Francis Whishaw's dream of a much larger, national exhibition of industry. Utilitarian logic dictated that Cole should pursue whatever would produce the most beauty for the most people, and an event on a national scale would be able to achieve so much more than he had hitherto been able to do using smaller exhibitions, travel guides, Christmas cards, art-manufactures, and illustrated children's books. Cole appealed to Prince Albert for support, pointing to the success of the initial exhibitions. Yet the prince was reluctant, even more so than he had been with Francis Whishaw a few years earlier—he told Cole there was no support among the senior ministers in the government. The French national exhibitions of industry were entirely state-funded, but British politicians were unwilling to commit taxpayers' money.[25] The British state essentially spent its money on two things: war, and paying off the debt from previous wars. Even its subsidies for trade directly supported military might. Bounties for importing Canadian hemp supplied the sailcloth for warships. The state's spending on things like art, even education, went little beyond its limited subsidies for schools of design, a few museums, and limited grants to voluntary organisations to build new schools. The central government was not suddenly about to spend a vast amount of taxpayers' money on a one-off exhibition of national industry.

Yet Cole had other options. If support would not come from the top, he would build it from the bottom. He used all means at his disposal. Through his work as a civil servant, and as a campaigner for postal reform, Cole had many contacts throughout government. His reputation as an able administrator interested in design even led to him being asked in 1848 to help reform the government's central School of Design in London, which had been riven with infighting. His proposals came to little, but the body that funded the School of Design was the Board of Trade—also the body most likely to support a national exhibition of industry. Cole built on that association and received assurances that his national exhibition would gain official approval, even if they could not promise any funding. Meanwhile he consolidated his association with another useful politician—the Chief Commissioner of Woods and Forests, George Howard, the Viscount Morpeth (who later that year became the 7th Earl of Carlisle).

Although the name suggests an obscure and limited role, the Commissioner of Woods and Forests was in fact responsible for the use of all state-owned land—his full title also included 'Land Revenues, Works, and Buildings'. Cole did not know Morpeth well, but had already found a way to secure the connection. In 1847 Cole had arranged for him to preside over the general meeting of a campaign to create a monument to William Caxton, the person who had introduced the printing press to England in the late fifteenth century. After all, a public monument would require Morpeth's permission, which he heartily gave—he had sympathies with the utilitarian cause of aiding 'the masses and the many'.[26] The meeting took place in the Great Room of the Society of Arts, and the person chosen at the meeting to be secretary to the campaign was, predictably, Henry Cole himself. The campaign came to nothing, but it reinforced Cole's connection with Morpeth—he won a promise that the government would provide a site large and central enough to hold a national exhibition. Cole had Trafalgar Square in mind, but Morpeth insisted on the courtyard of Somerset House. The details did not matter at this stage—what mattered was that Morpeth agreed in principle. By mid-1848, Cole had successfully circumvented senior ministers and obtained from the government promises of official recognition and a suitable site.[27]

But there was still the question of funding. The government had made its position clear, and Cole's connections could not promise funds. The Society of Arts, still recovering from its near-bankruptcy a few years earlier, would certainly not be able to afford an exhibition on the necessary scale. The only option was to raise a public subscription fund. The exhibition was intended for the masses after all—they might pay for it too. To make this work, Cole would have to draw upon his experience as a publicist. The Society's 1849 exhibition of art-manufactures provided a crucial boost. An estimated seventy to a hundred thousand people visited, despite the fact the Society introduced entry fees—for the first time the event generated a small surplus.[28] It suggested that an even larger and more impressive exhibition might be both popular and able to support itself financially. Cole now had evidence of demand; and the supply of exhibits had also increased. Back in 1847, Cole and Russell had been forced to run around London begging manufacturers for something to display; now they were swamped with potential exhibits, turning many away. They could afford to be selective, leading to an increase in the perceived quality of the exhibits. Cole used this as evidence that exhibitions actually worked—that they caused an improvement in manufactures. Visitors to the 1849 exhibition were even greeted by a silver centrepiece designed by Prince Albert himself.[29] Cole capitalised on the publicity generated by the exhibition to announce plans for a national exhibition, to be held in 1851. Through a member of Parliament who was a member of the Society of Arts, the Society submitted a petition to the House of Commons formally requesting the use of public land.[30] The time was now right for Cole's private agreements with the Board of Trade and the Commissioner of Woods and Forests to be confirmed publicly.[31]

Cole meanwhile established a mouthpiece for his exhibition propaganda, much like he had during the campaign for postal reform—a newspaper called the *Journal of Design*. He used it to contrast the apparent success of the Society of Arts exhibitions with the perceived failures of the government's School of Design.[32] It was not enough for the exhibitions to demonstrate an improvement in the quality of design, as few others shared Cole's obsession with spreading beauty to the masses. The exhibitions also had to fill a perceived need, to remedy an existing failure. The administrative chaos at the School of Design in London fitted the bill. National exhibitions would help to reform it, he argued. They would provide a collection of high-quality designs from which students at the school could learn. And by promoting the union of art with manufactures, they would encourage manufacturers to employ the school's pupils rather than relying on foreign designers.[33] It was the kind of argument that might appeal to policymakers. But the *Journal of Design* was targeted at people already interested in the subject. It was not a paper with mass appeal. To raise support throughout the country, to attract enough subscriptions to fund a national exhibition, Cole would have to draw upon a preexisting mass movement. There was no better candidate than the campaign for free trade.

6

For the Masses, by the Masses

SINCE THE FOUNDING of the Society of Arts in 1754, it had predominantly operated on the assumption that what was most important for an economy was the amount of gold and silver it was able to obtain from its rivals—a belief about economic policy that has since become known as mercantilism.[1] As we have seen in previous chapters, the Society encouraged industries that would replace foreign imports, and rewarded improvements that boosted exports. The more exports a country sold, the more gold and silver it acquired. The Society promoted exports and replaced imports through its private subscription fund, but the state maintained the mercantilist system with force. Over the centuries the British state had acquired colonies to provide raw materials, used tariffs to restrict foreign imports, and allowed a few merchants to monopolise trades. Tariffs provided the state with income, and it maintained monopolies in exchange for a cut of the trade. The same principle had for centuries extended to city guilds too.

A number of people in the eighteenth century criticised the system of monopolies, arguing that it allowed a handful of merchants to raise prices for consumers. Monopolies allowed the few to benefit at the expense of everyone else. As we have seen, when it came to London's fishmongers or to country millers, the Society of Arts had tried to undercut the monopolists of domestic industries. William Shipley had taken on Northampton's fuel merchants in the years before he founded the Society. Writers like Josiah Tucker also criticised organisations like the East India Company, which monopolised various foreign trades. He argued that such monopolies counteracted the aim of boosting exports. Other writers, since at least the seventeenth century, had also begun to question whether economic policy should stress the acquisition of gold and silver for its own sake. They still favoured the boosting of exports and the replacement of imports, but many argued that these were a means to an end—a way of increasing domestic employment.[2] In 1776, however, the entire mercantilist approach to economic policy came under attack. A Scottish moral philosopher, Adam Smith, published his monumental treatise, *An Enquiry into the Nature and Causes of the Wealth of Nations*.[3]

Smith was not the first person to question mercantilist beliefs, but he was by far the most influential. Instead of being preoccupied with restricting imports, he argued, policymakers should focus only on expanding the market for Britain's exports. The wealth of a nation was not to be found in its quantities of gold and silver, but in the productive capacity of its people. There was no point worrying about trade deficits—when a country paid more for imports than it earned in exports—because the whole point of that production was to pay for consumption. Wealth only mattered in so far as it could buy something, and if people wanted to pay for imports from the fruits of their labour, then that was perfectly reasonable. Normal exchange took place between two parties acting prudently, to their mutual benefit. Where there was injustice, it was from a handful of producers actively using monopolies, tariffs, and other restrictions on trade to drive up prices. These 'mercantile interests' used the state to 'engage in a conspiracy against the public'. The economic system should not be geared towards a handful of producers, Smith argued, but should instead benefit the mass of consumers. Tariffs and monopolies benefitted a few merchants at the expense of the many.

To support this, Smith explored economic fundamentals. His treatise looked in detail at every aspect of how the economy worked. He used every stage of his analysis to demonstrate that mercantilist policy was not just unjust; it was stupid. Smith showed how the productive capacity of any group of people was expanded through the division of labour, which allowed them to specialise in what they each did best. The overall result was that they produced more than if they had not specialised, and everyone involved benefitted. When a person bought something, say a wool coat, they paid the wages of everyone who had a hand in its production, from the shepherd who looked after the sheep, to the person who sheared it, right down to the spinner, the weaver, and the person who sold it at market. Importantly, the extent to which labour could be divided—and the wealth thus shared—depended on the extent of the market. The larger the mass of consumers for goods, the greater the possible specialisation.

The benefits of the division of labour were perhaps uncontroversial when it came to a particular factory, an industry, or a country's domestic trade. But Smith argued that the principle applied to international trade too. Tariffs and other protectionist policies restricted the markets for exports, as other countries retaliated with their own trade barriers. Overall, countries pursuing mercantilism restricted the size of the market, and thus the extent to which the division of labour could occur. By failing to pursue openness, nations did not just beggar their neighbours; they beggared themselves. Smith's alternative was to liberate the system of mercantilist restrictions, to achieve free trade.

For many years the impact of Smith's *The Wealth of Nations* was limited—a few changes to policy here and there, but nothing like the wholesale tearing down of trade barriers that it recommended. When he came to London in 1775 to promote the book, Adam Smith had briefly joined the Society of Arts, presumably because it gave him access to his intended audience of largely mercantilist policymakers.[4] The publication of his work seemingly failed to affect the Society's premiums, which still tried to replace imports with reference to the annual sums of gold and silver sent abroad to pay for them.

The breakthrough for the popularity of Smith's ideas instead occurred after 1815, with the end of the Napoleonic Wars. With the increase in European trade following the war, Britain was flooded with cheap grain, which threatened the interests of the landholders. Lower grain prices forced them to charge lower rents. Parliament at the time was overwhelmingly dominated by major landholders, who voted to impose a ban on foreign grain until prices reached a certain level—the Corn Laws. To some, it was a clear example of what Smith had attacked: the few using protectionism to benefit at the expense of the many. Whereas Smith had directed most of his criticism at merchants and manufacturers, proponents of free trade now attacked the ultimate villains—the landed aristocracy. Wealthy landlords seemed to be lining their pockets by forcing the masses to either pay more or go hungry. *The Wealth of Nations* provided the intellectual ammunition for a political attack on the landed aristocracy.

Free trade was soon adopted by a few radical politicians, many of whom were also influenced by Bentham's utilitarianism. Both schools of thought sought to help the masses rather than the few. And both movements became closely associated with the campaign for political reform.[5] Parliament in the eighteenth century was dominated by aristocratic landlords: eldest sons inherited titles and sat in the House of Lords, and their younger brothers were often elected to the House of Commons. In order to be a voter, a person had to own sufficiently valuable property. To make matters worse, the number of voters in different parliamentary constituencies was highly unequal. Cities like Manchester, Leeds, Birmingham, and Sheffield had grown in population due to industrialisation. Yet they were hardly represented. Manchester and many of the surrounding major manufacturing towns were represented by the single constituency of Lancashire, which had only ten to fifteen thousand voters from a population of over a million. Meanwhile, Dunwich, in Suffolk, with a population of barely over two hundred, had a mere thirty-three voters who elected two MPs.[6] It was no wonder that Parliament legislated in favour of landlords while paying little mind to the interests of the rest of the country.

The situation particularly annoyed the new professional classes who gradually came to dominate the Society of Arts in the early nineteenth century—the engineers, factory foremen, industrialists, and inventors, many of whom came from the major industrial hubs in the North and Midlands. The Corn Laws raised the price of food, particularly for the poorer class of workers, and many of the new professionals saw themselves as a part of that class. The professional classes were better paid, and sometimes able to invest some of their savings in owning the businesses they worked for, but they were often the sons of miners, factory workers, and shop-floor mechanics. They saw themselves as workers too, albeit ones who had lifted themselves to higher rates of pay though hard work and education. And those who ascended to the heights of captaining industry were employers. Higher food prices due to the Corn Laws meant they had to raise wages, which squeezed profits. When business was bad, they were forced to lay their workers off. Workers and industrialists thus forged an alliance in opposition to both the Corn Laws and the landed aristocracy that had created them. They might be able to repeal the Corn Laws, they reasoned, if they could extend the franchise and get proper representation for the major manufacturing towns in Parliament.

Seeing a threat in the alliance of the working and professional classes, the landowner-dominated Parliament of the late 1810s and the 1820s resorted to the repression of the peaceful actions of campaigners like John Cartwright, a veteran of the radical movement. He was the elder brother of Edmund Cartwright, the inventor of the power loom. Both brothers were members of the Society of Arts. Although John Cartwright was from the landed gentry, since the late 1770s he had consistently argued for parliamentary reform: equal electoral districts, annual elections, a secret ballot, and the extension of the vote to all men (something that would not be achieved until 1918). Yet Cartwright found he was most persuasive only in the late 1810s, due to widespread dissatisfaction with the Corn Laws. By 1817, at which time he was 77 years old, he had set up almost 150 societies across the country—called 'Hampden Clubs'—in which the disenfranchised workers and professionals of the major manufacturing towns discussed and agitated for reform. When these clubs met in London and sent a polite petition to the House of Commons, however, they immediately panicked the government. The government feared imminent violent revolution, of the sort that France had seen in 1789. In early 1817, Parliament suspended the right to trial by jury, and even passed a Seditious Meetings Act, making it illegal to hold public meetings or lectures without the approval of a magistrate.

The act banned the Hampden Clubs, along with gatherings of the even more radical Spencean Philanthropists, who argued for redistribution of the land. The government, however, in its suppressive zeal, gave too much discretion to the magistrates in interpreting the law—they accidentally banned various scientific and literary debating societies, not just their political targets. The City Philosophical Society, a scientific society run by Michael Faraday and his friends, had its licence refused; many of its members ended up joining the Society of Arts instead.[7] The Seditious Meetings Act might even have affected the Society of Arts too, which was not technically exempt—it did not then have a royal charter. Some prominent members of the Society were well-known radicals, like the lawyer William Tooke, and the MP Francis Burdett, one of a tiny minority who opposed the act in Parliament as an unprovoked attack on ancient English liberties. Tooke and the radicals moved that the Society should take a stand and declare to the prime minister, Lord Liverpool, that it would rather shut down than 'submit to the degrading alternative' of applying to a magistrate for a licence.[8] But at the next week's meeting, when the motion needed to be confirmed, it seems that the radicals were outnumbered; the motion was rescinded and the entire matter was dropped. The non-radical majority of the Society likely considered itself sufficiently respectable for the law to not apply to them, and with good reason—the prime minister was himself one of the Society's long-standing vice-presidents.

Meanwhile, the government's repression grew. In 1819, at St Peter's Field in Manchester, cavalry charged into a crowd peacefully protesting in favour of both parliamentary reform and the repeal of the Corn Laws. The exact number of casualties is unknown, but perhaps as many as fifteen people were killed, and many more were injured. The event became known as the Peterloo Massacre—an inglorious contrast with the battle of Waterloo that had ended the Napoleonic Wars only a few years before. Yet the movement saw some limited gains—the Corn Laws were slightly weakened in the late 1820s, and the Great Reform Act of 1832 gave many of the major industrial towns better representation while slightly extending the franchise. With greater sway for industry in Parliament, the total repeal of the Corn Laws seemed imminent.

Despite the promise of the Great Reform Act, however, the Corn Laws remained, and in the late 1830s the free trade movement again gathered support. New leaders came to the fore, such as John Bright and

Richard Cobden—both Lancashire-based manufacturers. In 1839 they set up the Anti-Corn Law League to agitate for reform, and organised speeches across the country. Indeed, Cobden asked Henry Cole to be secretary of the league's London branch due to his success agitating for postal reform.[9] Cole declined, but the league issued an *Anti-Corn Law Circular,* very much based on Cole's *Postal Reform Circular.* Cole also put Cobden in touch with William Makepeace Thackeray, the talented novelist (author of *Vanity Fair*), who created cartoons for the campaign.

The Anti-Corn Law campaign popularised Smith's *Wealth of Nations,* while its leaders added a spin of their own. Their propaganda portrayed the struggle as between a massive productive class—the combined working and professional classes—and a tiny group of aristocratic parasites. They framed the productive class as a group that was both independent and 'manly'. Many of the industrialists, some of whom had become wealthier than most aristocrats, seemed to have risen to their position through their own hard work. Indeed, many of them had risen from non-conformist religious backgrounds, which meant they had been excluded from the traditional centres of power—the clergy, politics, and even the universities of Oxford and Cambridge (restrictions that had mostly only been abolished in the late 1820s).[10] Likewise, the workers on the shop floor saw for themselves a new route to self-improvement: one based on merit. They might improve their own prospects through hard work or education, obtain better-paid professional work, perhaps save up enough to buy their own share in the capital of a business and eventually become captains of industry.

Many industrialists had also supported themselves rather than relying on high birth or aristocratic patronage—something they were proud of. Patronage now seemed patronising. Indeed, it was important to stress that the working classes could be self-sufficient, because it strengthened the case for political reform. The ability of the working classes to rise to wealth and property would prove that they were deserving of the vote—especially if they were able to do so independently. The landowning classes had traditionally been seen as uniquely able to act disinterestedly in favour of the national good because they were independently wealthy. They were beholden to nobody. The introduction of the Corn Laws showed them up for what they had always been—a faction that was just as self-interested as any other. If the working classes were able to show that they could better themselves—to improve their lot through the pooling of their own savings, without any charity from the aristocrats—then they would prove themselves to be more capable of disinterestedly favouring the common good. Workers, with some support from members of the new professional classes, set up libraries, established news-rooms, and created 'mechanics' institutions' (sometimes 'institutes')—organisations that paid for lecturers to come and deliver courses in the evenings after work. The same period saw the creation of 'friendly societies', groups of working men who pooled their savings so that they could support themselves and each other in times of ill health. Crucially, the productive classes were proud that all such institutions were 'self-supporting'.

Bright and Cobden framed the productive classes as 'manly' in another sense too. Support for free trade showed a willingness to face challenges head-on, rather than hiding behind protection like the aristocrats had done with the Corn Laws.[11] The productive classes essentially said 'bring it on'—their industry would stand or fall based on merit alone, not outside help. The aristocrats' use of protection was, by contrast, cowardly.

For Henry Cole, these were all themes that he could build on in raising support for a national exhibition of industry. In fact, the Anti-Corn Law League had already attempted to hold just such an exhibition. Cobden had called for a collection of the products of national industry, to have 'proof of what the unguarded, the unaided, the unprotected skill of England can do', without the help of aristocratic patronage.[12] Accordingly, in May 1845 at the Covent Garden Theatre, the free traders held an Anti-Corn Law League Bazaar. It was intended as a celebration of the productive classes—a publicity stunt to enable the free traders to ask why the hands that made such articles should be made to go hungry or forced to be unemployed. It came at the peak of the league's activity—indeed, the following year, partly due to the pressures of the Great Irish Famine, the Corn Laws were finally repealed. The bazaar was effective propaganda, and was so popular that it made a profit. Yet as a national exhibition of industry, it was a failure. It was more like an exhibition of handicraft. Many of the productive classes, reportedly mainly Quakers, had sent in all sorts of articles they made in their spare time. The local league association from the Lancashire town of Bury, famous for its Simnel cakes, even brought a gigantic plum pudding weighing 280 pounds.[13] Yet to call the bazaar an exhibition worthy of the nation, wrote one newspaper, would be 'a satire upon the industrious classes'.[14]

Cole saw the potential for something better, which would draw upon the same groups who had been involved in the bazaar. The national exhibition of industry could be a celebration of the productive classes, paid for by the productive classes—especially if the government were not willing to put up the money. Indeed, this would help ensure its success, giving the masses a sense of ownership over the project, rather than having it imposed upon them by being paid for through taxation. The exhibition would meet the ideal of being self-supporting. And in drumming up this support, the Society of Arts would be an effective tool.

The Society's members were largely drawn from the new professional classes, with connections throughout the country. Many of them had also been free traders. Even some of the older members—those who had been there since well before Thomas Webster's reforms in the 1840s—were champions of the radical movement. The radical lawyer William Tooke, who in 1817 had wanted the Society to take a stand against the Seditious Meetings Act, was by the 1840s a well-regarded champion of the people (he later used his skills as a solicitor to get the Society its royal charter in 1847, and in 1862, after the death of Prince Albert, would briefly replace him as the Society's president). The Society had already made some limited moves towards involving the working classes more closely in its operations, from 1835 offering mechanics' institutions outside London a copy of the *Transactions* and a ticket to its meetings and model repository that could be used by any of the institution's members, all for just the price of an ordinary subscription to the Society.[15] The Society had also often emphasised the fact that it was itself self-supporting, funded almost entirely by its members' subscriptions, and with no help from government.[16]

The Society thus had the potential to appeal to the masses. The next step was to create a sense of urgency. Fortunately for Cole, when in 1849 he began to make the plans for a national exhibition of industry public, the French held a new exhibition of their own. Whereas the French exhibition of 1844 had prompted Francis Whishaw's initial attempts to hold something similar in Britain, for Cole the exhibition of 1849 became an important source of propaganda. It allowed him to play upon fears of international competition—the worry that France was catching up with Britain in terms of machinery, while retaining its lead in fashion and design. Cole himself attended the French exhibition of 1849, along with his collaborator Herbert Minton and another member of the Society of Arts in favour of an exhibition, a land surveyor named Francis Fuller. The Society produced an official report: if things continued on the current trajectory, it warned, then France would soon push Britain out of markets it had long considered its own. Britain needed to be jolted out of complacency.[17]

Henry Cole does not seem to have personally been concerned about the French catching up. But he knew that it would worry others. He played upon their fears so that his own project—that of spreading art to the masses—would also gain support. For Cole, the reasons people might have for supporting his proposed exhibition of 1851 did not matter. In typical utilitarian fashion, what mattered was that he got results. As propaganda, the 1849 exhibition in Paris was perfect.

More importantly, however, it was a source of inspiration. For a while, some French officials had been floating the idea that their exhibition should be about more than just the products of French industry. They proposed an exhibition of the industry of *all* nations. Cole seized on the idea. If his proposed exhibition were international, it would appeal to the free trade movement and thus win popular backing. Cobden, Bright, and the movement's other leaders had argued that free trade would bring an end to war. The productive classes of rival nations competed peacefully, they argued, simply by trying to outdo one another in the quality and quantity of what they produced. It was the landed aristocrats who let the competition become violent, feeding their pride by causing the destruction of what the productive classes made. With free trade, the argument went, the consumers of one nation would buy more from the producers of another, so they would think twice before causing a war and cutting off the supplies of their favourite imports. Likewise, exporters would think twice before severing ties with their consumers abroad. With free trade would come interdependence, raising the cost of war and thus making it less likely.

Holding a grand exhibition of the products of all nations—a Great Exhibition, as it came to be known—would be free trade in physical form. Nations would compete openly and peacefully, creating new connections and mutual understanding between their peoples. An international exhibition would thus be a start on the road to world peace— a 'competition of arts, and not of arms'.[18] Paradoxically, Cole could also appeal to national pride. Hosting such an exhibition would demonstrate Britain's unique generosity—its ability to set age-old jealousies aside and compete without the barriers of protectionism or secrecy. It would lead the way towards a new, peaceful, and more enlightened age. Britain already claimed to be 'the asylum of the outcast and unfortunate', where people of all political persuasions went into exile from the civil wars or revolutions of continental Europe. It had also recently opened its ports to free trade in grain, and had seen no war with a major European power since the defeat of Napoleon in 1815: 'what office so proper to London', the exhibition's supporters asked, as 'the reconciliation and improvement of the civilized world'?[19]

On his return from France in June 1849, Cole had no trouble convincing people of this vision. Prince Albert immediately agreed to the idea, perhaps partly because it would bring so much prestige to Britain, and partly because Cole sold it as a celebration of the works of the productive classes. The same classes had, the previous year, overthrown the French king and replaced him with the nephew and heir of Napoleon as president of a second republic (a few years later, he would become Emperor Napoleon III). Indeed, 1848 had seen attempted revolutions across Europe, and Karl Marx and Friedrich Engels had sought to take advantage of the disorder with their publication of a Communist manifesto. Britain had been spared the unrest of that year, but it was not obvious that it would remain immune. If Albert were to lend his support to the Great Exhibition, it would put him and his wife's monarchy firmly on the side of the masses. A modern monarchy needed to remain popular.

Albert and Cole chose a site for the Great Exhibition that would be in keeping with these aims. Cole had already been promised something like Somerset House, but this would be far too small for an exhibition on an international scale; they instead chose a vacant plot of land in Hyde Park. Crucially, access would be equally easy to both 'high and low, rich and poor'.[20] The poor could get to it from horse-drawn omnibuses as easily as the rich could get to it in their private carriages. Hyde Park was also a royal park rather than public land, so it would be easier to get permission.[21] They also set about creating a Royal Commission— an official organisation that would oversee the administration of the Great Exhibition. Royal Commissions were typically used to investigate contentious matters of policy. They were, at least in theory, bodies independent of the government, whose members were impartial experts. The advantage of having a Royal Commission for the Great Exhibition of 1851 would be to put potentially controversial aspects of its organisation above reproach, such as the allocation of exhibition space, the choice of a building, and the choice of a jury to decide exhibition prizes. Albert himself, in his official capacity as president of the Society of Arts, petitioned the government to appoint one.

Not content to wait around for the government's approval, however, Cole and his collaborators formed themselves into an executive committee. One of them, Francis Fuller, even managed to find a contractor for the building, the firm of Messrs James and George Munday, who agreed to front the money and even the cash for a prize fund, in exchange for a share of the expected ticket fees (Cole was careful to insert a clause allowing a future Royal Commission to cancel the contract, with some compensation). Although the exhibition would be paid for by a subscription fund, Cole and the rest of the executive committee worried that this would take too long to collect. The contract proved that the Society of Arts was serious about holding the Great Exhibition. They had committed. The contract was occasionally criticised—the fact that a private company might profit from a share of the ticket pro-

ceeds seemed to contradict the idea that the exhibition would be both
by and for the masses. But the exhibition's supporters lauded the Mun-
days for being the only people willing to risk their capital for the endeavour, and for being so public-spirited as to accept a clause that
would cancel it.[22] When the Royal Commission was finally appointed
in January 1850 it made the popular move to cancel the contract and
declare that the Great Exhibition would be funded entirely by public
subscriptions. As Cole had always intended, the Great Exhibition
would be entirely self-supporting.

The Royal Commission could be so confident of the public's support
because Cole, Fuller, and another Society member, the architect Matthew Digby Wyatt, had spent half of 1849 touring Britain's towns and
cities, collecting promises of support at public meetings. They took with
them a signed diploma from Albert, authorising them to 'collect opinions'. In raising support and publicity, Cole now did what he did best,
though at times he got carried away. At one meeting he announced a
five-thousand-pound prize for the best exhibitors; no prizes had actually
been decided upon. At another meeting in Dublin he said that the exhibition's international scope had all been Prince Albert's idea—'his
own spontaneous act, irrespective of external influences'—which was
both in direct contravention of Albert's wishes and untrue. Cole correctly judged that Albert's celebrity status would bring the exhibition
more attention. He apologised to the annoyed prince, and complained
that he could not stop the press misreporting his words. At yet another
meeting, however, Fuller reportedly hinted that Queen Victoria herself
might present the exhibition's prizes. Cole had to apologise again, but
otherwise pressed on with his pursuit of publicity.

Everywhere they went, Cole and his fellow 'missionaries' for the
Great Exhibition found unanimous support (or at least, that was what
they reported). Cole was able to find arguments that would appeal to
everyone. The Great Exhibition would be a grand audit of the world's
major industrial economies. To supporters of free trade, it would be an
event where 'England may learn as much as she can teach', with every
country offering to show off their advantages: 'England her mechanical
ingenuity, America her boldness of invention, France her unequalled

delicacy and novelty of taste, and even the least and lowest nation its traditionary crafts and household lore.'[23] Industrialists of all nations would be able to see who was behind and who was ahead, and exactly what they needed to do to catch up. To the radicals and reformists, the Great Exhibition would be a celebration of the works of the productive classes of every country, placing their machinery and wares alongside one another for direct comparison—a 'festival of the working man and the working woman.'[24]

To consumers, the Great Exhibition would be a chance to compare the products on offer both at home and abroad. They would clamour for new imports and for lower tariffs on them, while forcing domestic producers to improve their quality to compete. Even to the self-interested British manufacturers, they would have a chance to show Britain's consumers that they were capable of producing things of equal or higher quality than what was currently imported. Glaswegian cotton-printers were apparently confident that the exhibition would have the effect of 'letting the ladies of Great Britain see that English manufacturers could produce as good articles as the French.'[25] Cole mentioned that consumers might develop a taste for the grain of Ireland when it was directly compared with that of California, England, and the Baltic. The Great Exhibition would even give Britain the chance to forge closer commercial links with its empire: it received promises of support from the East India Company and the Hudson's Bay Company, who saw the chance to show British manufacturers the unexploited raw materials available to be imported from their territories in India and Canada.

The message of world peace resonated with many, including clergymen. At one event in London, even the Archbishop of Canterbury spoke in favour of the exhibition. Most people did not expect results overnight: 'we do not imagine that a Chinaman, or a Mexican, or a Swede . . . will rise up . . . and exclaim, "Ha! A sudden thought strikes me—let us all swear eternal friendship!"'[26] But people did think that the exhibition would create new opportunities for international cooperation. Even the prime minister, Lord John Russell, noted the universal aims of the exhibition, describing it as a celebration of how to produce better and cheaper clothing, furnish houses, and improve communication—the kinds of improvements that would benefit all, not just the British. Radical campaigners like William Tooke confidently asserted that it would be 'one of the most important proceedings of the century'.[27]

To the assembled merchants of London, Cole pointed out how many extra visitors would come to the metropolis—tourists, merchants, and scientists too. Some of these arguments even found resonance abroad. While Cole, Fuller and Wyatt toured Britain, John Scott Russell went to Germany, where he canvassed the opinions of foreign manufacturers and politicians. After all, if the exhibition were to be international, it would need exhibits to be sent in from other countries. Foreigners saw many advantages to be had from the Great Exhibition. It would assemble the merchants of all nations, making it easier for them to forge new business partnerships and find new markets for their exports.

As support for the Great Exhibition grew, however, Cole's position of control came under threat. As it looked ever more likely to be a great success, people began to position themselves to take the credit. Even today, it is difficult to untangle all the spin and outright fabrications. The contributions of people like Francis Whishaw are often undeservedly relegated to the footnotes, or else over-emphasised by later revisionists. Cole was careful from the very beginning to document his own involvement in key decisions, or else to give credit to Prince Albert—a figure whose contributions were least likely to be questioned. Indeed, he and Russell compiled an official version of events that was published by the Society of Arts. Francis Fuller would later complain that his role had been neglected, as did John Scott Russell himself. Indeed, towards the end of 1849 Cole and Russell's friendship began to sour.[28] Cole wanted to be hired as secretary to the Royal Commission for the Great Exhibition. But when the commission was finally appointed in January 1850, Russell beat him to the post, accepting a lower salary and resigning his position at the Society of Arts.

A further threat to Cole's position came from the Royal Commission itself. The commissioners were mostly high-profile gentlemen and aristocrats, appointed to lend the exhibition their credibility and prestige. Albert acted as president, with the other commissioners including the prime minister, the leader of the opposition, and the former prime minister Sir Robert Peel, who had been responsible for the repeal of the Corn Laws. It also included the free trade leader Richard Cobden, as well as a few other MPs, industrialists, bankers, merchants, and artists, and the presidents of the Royal Society, the Royal Academy, the Geological Society, and the Institution of Civil Engineers. The members of the Society of Arts executive committee for the exhibition then became the Royal Commission's own executive committee, with Robert Stephenson as chairman and the architect Matthew Digby Wyatt as its secretary. Although the Society of Arts ceased to be involved as a corporate body, its members thus continued to be heavily involved. Yet Henry Cole now found himself sidelined—he was now a mere ordinary member of the executive committee, without any official excuse to have the private ear of Prince Albert. To make matters worse, the Royal Commission also began to sideline the entire executive committee—they refused to admit them to meetings, and essentially prevented them from taking any further action.[29]

At this point even Henry Cole's position at the Society of Arts came under threat. Cole had very rapidly swayed the Society's focus towards his personal mission of spreading beauty to the masses. Yet by concentrating the Society's efforts on the decorative arts, Cole had alienated the likes of Thomas Webster and Francis Whishaw—the new professionals who had rescued the Society from imminent dissolution only a few years earlier. As engineers, industrialists, chemists, and patent agents, they worried that the Society was neglecting the work of improving other fields, particularly mechanics, chemistry, and agriculture. The application of art to industry had certainly been a part of their vision of a reformed Society of Arts—one that would explore new combinations of increasingly specialised fields—but the particular combination of art to industry was supposed to be only one among many.

In 1845, when Russell had created the special premiums for art-manufactures, another donor had simultaneously created a special 105-pound premium to find a substitute for potatoes during the Great Irish Famine, which had been brought on by potato blight. This was the kind of activity that the Society's members were more used to, and which they hoped to continue: a joint committee of agriculture and chemistry spent a day taste-testing thirty-two different breads and biscuits, most of them including American maize and cornmeal, which had been secretly purchased by the government on the orders of the prime minister Robert Peel in an effort to stem the rising hunger (few people knew how to prepare the maize, however, and it soon caused bowel complaints, earning the nickname 'Peel's brimstone'). The Society's committee did not record the effects of the breads on their bowels, but they did note that the submissions of a certain baker that included Irish moss, a kind of algae, ranged in taste from 'very unpalatable', to 'more unpalatable', 'most unpalatable', 'worse', and finally 'vile'. (In the end, the Society did not award the cash prize, as none of the solutions were particularly original or effective. But it did award a gold medal to a Dublin baker named Timothy O'Brien, who produced a 'palatable' cornmeal bread in large quantities, and whose persistence overcame an initial aversion of the Irish population to the strange, yellow loaves.)[30]

To Webster and Whishaw, the Society's activities seemed to have narrowed to the exclusion of such work. They began to complain. Cole tried to smooth things over a little by noting that the Society could not do everything at once: 'the Council have postponed the mechanics—not lost sight of them', he argued.[31] In the winter of 1848–49, perhaps to appease the grumblers, the Society even began to hold exhibitions of the latest mechanical inventions. Yet this did not fully eliminate their concerns. Thomas Webster had taken great pains to rescue the Society from bankruptcy a few years earlier, and began to worry that as the exhibitions of art-manufactures became larger and larger, they were also getting riskier. Webster did not want to see all of his hard work undone by Cole expanding the exhibition programme too rapidly and thus over-extending the Society financially. The 1849 exhibition of art-manufactures had been a success, and Cole had used it to build support for the Great Exhibition. The first exhibition in honour of living artists—the one in 1848 for William Mulready—was mildly profitable. Yet the second exhibition for a living artist was a disaster.

Cole had hoped to honour the landscape painter J.M.W. Turner—yet another prominent artist who had once won premiums from the Society of Arts.[32] But Turner was too ill, and the Society instead settled for the York-born painter William Etty (for a change, not a former premium winner). Etty was an extraordinarily prolific artist. He produced an estimated two thousand paintings and drawings over the course of his career, though was infamous for an obsession with painting nudes. He complained that he had been ignored or misunderstood—perhaps the nudes were a bit much for increasingly prudish Victorians. For Etty, to be honoured with an exhibition was a much-appreciated sign of public recognition. On seeing his most prominent works assembled together in the Society's Great Room, he broke down in tears of joy.[33] He died a few months later, a happy man, at the end exclaiming 'wonderful, wonderful, this death'.[34] For the Society of Arts, however, the exhibition produced a large deficit. The exhibitions in honour of individual living artists would not be repeated, and provided an opportunity for Cole's rivals.[35]

In 1850, the Society of Arts also held an exhibition of ancient and medieval art, to give potential exhibitors at the Great Exhibition some models of great works from which they could copy or adapt designs. They could come and view a rosary by Holbein alongside twelfth-century enamels, a locket that had belonged to Mary Queen of Scots, and a silver-gilt sword from the collection of the queen herself.[36] Yet with the Society holding art exhibition after art exhibition, Webster began to worry that Cole was being reckless. The failure of the Etty exhibition gave Webster and Whishaw the excuse they needed to try and put a stop to his emphasis on applied art. Francis Whishaw of course favoured the Great Exhibition—holding a national exhibition of industry had been his idea in the first place—but he objected to the annual exhibitions of art-manufactures and the works of living artists. He and Webster tried to take back control.

Cole and his supporters argued that the exhibitions as a whole had been a success—in the cases where they had charged for entry, they had usually made a profit, and in general they had increased the visibility and prestige of the Society, attracting new members. Yet Webster outmanoeuvred them. He used his greater knowledge of the Society's post-1845 constitution, which he had written, to get a change in the bye-laws that seriously diminished the power of the pro-exhibition party. Cole and his allies were forced to take drastic countermeasures: they collectively resigned from the Council, triggering an election. On 3 April 1850, after a hurried and desperate canvassing of supportive members—the artists, manufacturers, and utilitarians he had been introducing to the Society over the previous few years—Cole and his friends won in a landslide.[37] Having seen off the challenge from Webster and Whishaw, Henry Cole's reign over the Society of Arts was from then on supreme.

Using similar tactics, Cole tried to see off the challenge to his control of the Great Exhibition. He and his allies signed letters of resignation from the executive committee, to try and force the Royal Commission's hand. But in this case the plan backfired. The committee's chairman, the railway engineer Robert Stephenson, withdrew his resignation in return for a seat on the Royal Commission. Cole was eventually persuaded to withdraw his resignation in exchange for nothing. The executive committee was also appointed with a new chairman, Colonel William Reid—he was not a member of the Society of Arts like the rest of the committee he headed, and had not been involved with exhibitions at all. He was a seasoned soldier from the Royal Engineers and was content to wait for orders from the Royal Commission, which rarely came. Reid also shared a concern with some of the aristocrats on the Royal Commission that too much activity or publicity would lead to 'a great agitation of the working classes', which would increase the threat of revolution. Cole tried to organise a Working Class Committee to help popularise the exhibition, which included the author Charles Dickens and a number of pro-reform radicals, but it met only a couple of times at the Society of Arts before disbanding itself because the Royal Commission refused to recognise it.[38] The very thing that Cole had seized upon to make the Great Exhibition popular—a preexisting mass movement—was what Reid and the commissioners refused to use.[39]

The only person to call Reid out on the inaction was John Scott Russell, who had become the joint secretary of the Royal Commission. But in the process Russell made enemies of some of the commissioners. He was accused of prioritising his shipbuilding business over his role as joint secretary, and one commissioner apparently found Russell so insolent that he refused to sit in the same room as him. Russell's rivalry with Cole had also intensified, especially as Cole tried to force him out of his rooms at the Society of Arts to make way for his successor as secretary. Cole found his hands tied, unable to actually do anything to help the Great Exhibition along. He chafed at the bit, his initiatives often quashed by Colonel Reid. He became increasingly despondent, and repeatedly considered resigning.[40]

In the summer of 1850, however, Henry Cole found new opportunities to take back control. On 22 June the Royal Commission published its design for the Great Exhibition's building—a brick edifice with slate roofs and a vast, iron-covered dome, designed by the famous civil engineer Isambard Kingdom Brunel. But the public found it ugly, and a campaign began to stop it being built in Hyde Park. The campaigners especially opposed the tearing down of any of the park's great elm trees—any building for the exhibition would have to be erected around them. It was the first major opposition to the Great Exhibition. Prince Albert was aghast.

Yet in the meantime, a professional gardener named Joseph Paxton had called on the executive committee's offices with a proposal for a different kind of building—one that would be mostly made of glass. Paxton was chief gardener to the Duke of Devonshire, with charge of the vast estate of Chatsworth House. By title a gardener, in practice he was also a seasoned inventor. He had even won a silver medal from the Society of Arts back in 1840 for a machine that allowed him to construct the window sash-bars for large glasshouses.[41] Paxton's suggestion was well past the deadline for any suggestions for building designs, but Henry Cole nonetheless found a way to push it through on a technicality. Cole was responsible for persuading builders to tender for the project, and if Paxton's design were considered an 'improvement' made by the contractors to the Royal Commission's official design, it might still be approved. Cole found a contractor ready to go along with his scheme: the construction engineering company of Fox, Henderson & Co, with a factory at Smethwick, near Birmingham. They hurriedly turned Paxton's idea for a glass building into proper plans for tender. They then got very lucky—on the train to London to submit the detailed plans, Paxton bumped into Robert Stephenson, who by now was both a Royal Commissioner and sat on the Great Exhibition's building committee. Paxton showed him the design. Stephenson loved it.[42]

The building committee prevaricated. Brunel was not happy about his design being usurped. But Cole or one of his co-conspirators forced the committee's hand by leaking an artist's impression of Paxton's design to the press. The public seemed to like it. Paxton's design was approved. Instead of Brunel's vast iron dome, the Great Exhibition would be housed in a greenhouse-like structure of wood, iron, and glass, which has since become iconic. Much of the construction took place in the factories, each piece fitting together in modular fashion so that it could simply be assembled onsite. The result was that its skeleton seemed to rise from Hyde Park in near-silence, punctuated only by the occasional chink of the parts being secured together.[43] One newspaper recommended visiting the construction site just before a mealtime—the dinner bell would set hundreds of workmen skipping across girders and slipping down columns 'seemingly careless of the danger, but with a certain air of order and regularity'.[44] As a gigantic greenhouse, the structure perfectly accommodated Hyde Park's elm trees, which were seized on as a symbol of British liberty—'standing proof of the attention which the government paid to the will of the people' (though Cole later admitted to having a few of the younger trees cut down).[45]

Covering nineteen acres, when the building was completed it was the largest enclosed structure that had ever been built, made of three hundred thousand of the largest panes of glass ever produced. Glass was a rare construction material—a heavy tax on glass manufacture had only been removed in the late 1840s, and the government had long taxed glass windows in an attempt to make the wealthy pay more.[46] Set against the blackened, soot-stained buildings of London, many of them with windows bricked up to avoid the tax, the Great Exhibition's massive glass edifice gleamed. At night, when the wood-shavings from the construction work were thrown onto bonfires, the whole building was illuminated by dancing flame.[47] It was soon dubbed The Crystal Palace.

7

A System to Force down the General Throat

THE GREAT EXHIBITION opened on 1 May 1851, and soon surpassed all expectations. Over the course of five and a half months, the exhibition attracted six million visitors—an estimated two million people, almost a tenth of the entire population of Great Britain, most of them returning again and again.[1] The crowd was 'a restless sea of human beings, agitated by the strong impulses of curiosity', exclaimed one newspaper. 'There is a majesty about "the million" thus collected to survey their own peaceful triumphs'.[2] In a single day, up to one hundred thousand people would pass through the Crystal Palace's doors, a number larger than the entire population at the time of Newcastle-upon-Tyne, a major city in England's industrial North.[3] (On one particularly crowded day, the Duke of Wellington—war hero of the Napoleonic Wars—happened to visit and was cheered. The noise was misinterpreted as a cry that the building was falling, which caused a stampede. Fortunately, only a stand of French plates was harmed.[4]) The exhibition even impressed Queen Victoria, who wrote that she was 'bewildered from the myriads of beautiful and wonderful things'.[5]

It was a triumph, particularly for Henry Cole. Since the summer of 1850 he had managed to make himself indispensable to the Great Exhibition's organisation, accumulating responsibilities that allowed him to gradually reassert control. Despite opposition from Colonel Reid, Cole became responsible for the arrangement of the exhibits, negotiating the space allowed to manufacturers from all over the world. Cole found himself in de facto command of a contingent of soldiers, seconded from the corps of the Royal Engineers (Reid's own corps) and the Royal Sappers and Miners.[6] Cole directed them in demarcating the different spaces for exhibitors, moving around the exhibits, standing duty as firemen, and even sweeping the floors in the mornings.[7] At the opening ceremony, they held back the crowds eager for a glimpse of the queen.[8]

Cole even had a hand in securing the Great Exhibition's finances. At a chance meeting in the street, he persuaded one of the wealthier Royal Commissioners, the member of Parliament and railway contractor Samuel Morton Peto, to promise the vast sum of fifty thousand pounds as a guarantee in case the exhibition failed to break even. The guarantee fund was needed to back a loan to pay for the construction work, and with the contributions of others it soon rose to 350,000 pounds. Fortunately for the guarantors—Cole himself promised five hundred pounds—the promises never needed to be called in. The Great Exhibition instead produced a huge surplus.

With that surplus, and with the exhibition's general popularity, came opportunity for Henry Cole and the Society of Arts. Alongside the artists and manufacturers Cole had introduced to the Society in the late 1840s, he had also brought in many utilitarians—reformers who wished to do the greatest good for the greatest number of people, by any means necessary. Instead of the piecemeal approach of the Society's premiums—a medal or cash prize to help solve a specific problem—reformers like Cole now saw the Society's potential as a platform for changing entire systems. Its members had expertise in both art and invention, and with the success of the Great Exhibition and with Prince Albert as president, the Society's prestige had reached a new high. To the reformers, all of those useful features were most 'urgently needed in the development of enlarged generalisations and comprehensive measures'.

The utilitarians were relatively few, yet they came to exercise an extraordinary influence over the Society.[9] Their names feature most prominently among the people who proposed initiatives for reform, forming and often heading committees of the Society to see those reforms through. They took support for their reforms wherever they could find it, packing committees with their close friends and forming coalitions with other groups with whom they shared common ground, usually radicals, free traders, and other liberals. When it suited them, they appealed to special interests too. Crucially, they also took upon themselves the nitty-gritty work of writing the committees' reports and drafting proposed legislation. Utilitarian reformers like Cole thus made sure that they had a final say in almost everything the Society did, successfully transforming the organisation into a platform for changing systems.

The first system that required reform was that of rewarding inventions. In this, they exploited the Great Exhibition before it had even opened. Instead of awarding cash or medals to inventions that would not otherwise be profitable, as the Society had done for almost a hundred years with its premiums, Cole and his allies decided to reform the entire system of protecting intellectual property. The issue became particularly urgent with the approach of the Great Exhibition. Cole worried that inventors and manufacturers would be dissuaded from exhibiting their latest creations. They did not have enough time to obtain patents for them, and unprotected items shown at the exhibition might easily be ripped off. The underlying problem was that obtaining a patent in Britain was notoriously expensive and time-consuming. Inventors could not always afford to obtain a patent themselves; they often needed the help of a wealthy investor.

Cole drew up a complete list of the bureaucratic hoops that an inventor had to jump through in order to obtain a patent. He identified thirty-five separate stages, including repeated visits to a host of seemingly random officials, from the attorney-general and master in Chancery, right down to the more obscure clerk of the hanaper and deputy chaff-wax. It was only after all this that the specification for the invention was lodged, and there was no easy way to search old specifications. One might look to a few magazines to find drawings or descriptions of newly patented inventions, but their coverage was incomplete. There was not even an index to help locate old patents. The result was that inventions might easily have been independently reinvented by someone else after a few decades, without anyone really noticing. Many inventors discovered they had wasted their efforts reinventing something that already existed. To a utilitarian like Cole, this system made no sense. It was not built for the purpose of encouraging invention, but had instead slowly evolved from the ancient monopolies granted by monarchs. The laws seemed 'so antiquated that the origin of them is lost in the obscurity of past centuries—so empty and frivolous, that common sense revolts at them'.[10] It was time to sweep the inefficiencies away and create a system that was rational.

The campaign for patent reform was perhaps one of the Society's most successful lobbying efforts ever. Things did not proceed quite as quickly as planned—Cole had hoped to have the reforms through Parliament before the Great Exhibition—but a stop-gap law was passed in 1850 to give all exhibitors patent protection if they simply registered their inventions, thus bypassing the usual system. Then, to bring about a more permanent change, Cole used his talent for publicity. He enlisted the help of Charles Dickens, perhaps the most celebrated author of the Victorian era, who was interested in intellectual property. Dickens's own published works had often been ripped off. Cole and Dickens had known each other since the early 1840s, and Dickens became a member of the Society in 1849 (he was proposed by the old radical campaigner William Tooke). He soon joined the Society's committee on patent reform, and in 1850 was even elected one of the Society's vice-presidents.

Dickens took the draft of Cole's dry list of thirty-five stages and transformed it into a short story, 'A poor man's tale of a patent', which appeared in his weekly magazine *Household Words*. He satirised each step and then succinctly summarised the campaign's aims: 'if the laws of this country were as honest as they ought to be, you would have come to London, registered an exact description and drawing of your invention, paid half-a-crown or so for doing of it, and therein and thereby have got your patent'. As for the old system, 'the whole gang of Hanapers and Chaff-waxers must be done away with', he declared: 'England has been chaffed and waxed sufficient'.[11] In Dickens, Cole had found an effective propagandist.

The Society's committee on patent reform—Cole, Dickens, a few radical politicians, and some inventors and patent agents—drafted a bill for Parliament.[12] In 1852, they got most of what they wanted—a law that completely overhauled the patent system. Inventors would now be able to go to a single, centralised Patent Office to hand in all the paperwork. The fees were also considerably lowered.[13] Before 1852, a patent covering the entire United Kingdom might cost at least 380 pounds—almost 300,000 pounds in today's money.[14] After the act of 1852, it cost only 25 pounds—just under 20,000 pounds in today's money—followed by higher fees if the patent needed to be extended after a few years.[15] The effect was almost immediate. In 1853, British inventors patented almost five times as many inventions as they had in 1851.[16] Cole and the Society would return to the issue of patents in the decades to come, but only to try and modify the system slightly. The key change for the Society of Arts, however, was one of approach. It more or less ceased to spend its money rewarding particular inventions that were not otherwise worth patenting; it instead lobbied to lower the cost to all inventors of obtaining their own rewards.

The Society did the same for another form of intellectual property: copyright for works of art. The campaign for artistic copyright was the result of two of Cole's social circles coming together in the Society of Arts, namely the artists and the reformers. The Society's committee on the matter was chaired by Charles Eastlake, a childhood winner of the Society's art premiums, who had been reintroduced to the Society by Cole in the late 1840s. By the time he involved himself in artistic copyright, Eastlake was president of the Royal Academy. Cole and Eastlake sought to remedy an omission in Britain's copyright laws: the people who painted, drew, or photographed an image did not have exclusive rights to that image. Copyright applied only to engravings and lithographs—specific kinds of copy. But painters could not stop someone creating an identical painting. The same applied to drawings. As for photographers, the technology was so new that no law applied. Meanwhile, writers had all sorts of protections: 'if a man expressed an idea in black marks with a pen and ink upon paper, the law gave him a copyright, but if he expressed the same idea in colours upon canvass he had no copyright'.[17]

To a utilitarian like Cole, it was yet another example where the law was irrational, in need of a coherent system. To artists and art-collectors, it was a matter of self-interest. Extending copyright would protect and extend their sources of income. Unsurprisingly, the campaign received support from every artist Cole knew, including Edwin Landseer, William Mulready, and John Callcott Horsley.[18] From 1857 the Society of Arts lobbied for a law that would give a consistent set of rights to all kinds of artists, for all kinds of copies of their work. They did not quite get the all-encompassing change they wanted, but in 1862, after a few failed attempts, some of their proposals finally became law.[19] Artistic copyright was extended to painting, drawing, and photography.[20] Once again, instead of offering artists individual premiums, the Society now lobbied to change the way all artists were rewarded.

Reforms to intellectual property were only the beginning. The Society of Arts became obsessed with the creation of new systems in every field imaginable—not just those relating to its age-old concerns with invention and art. Charles Dickens modelled one of his characters, the school inspector in *Hard Times*, directly on Henry Cole—'always with a system to force down the general throat'.[21] Next on the agenda, as a direct result of the Great Exhibition, was to do something about public sanitation. The Crystal Palace's six million visitors needed somewhere to relieve themselves.

In mid-nineteenth-century London, the options for going to the toilet were limited. There were only a few facilities available to the public. Wealthy people might buy a small item from a shop, and ask to use the shop's toilet. For women, the favoured establishments were corset-makers, bonnet-makers, and milliners; the men preferred hairdressers, tailors, cigar shops, and taverns.[22] Most people, however, just relieved themselves in alleyways, doorways, and on walls. The owners of the walls took measures against it, for example by affixing special deflectors designed to splash the urine back onto a person's shoes. To the reformers in the Society of Arts, it was obvious that there needed to be a system of public toilets. With the expected influx of people for the Great Exhibition, the campaign gained a sense of urgency. Without some kind of action, they worried that London's streets would flow with urine.[23]

The Society of Arts addressed an open letter to the city's sanitation authorities, pressing for the creation of a system. But the authorities replied that of 154 planned urinals, only four or five had actually been constructed; property owners were unwilling to volunteer their walls. This was not good enough. And besides, urinals were useless to women—half the population. The Society suggested 'a general system' of what became known, euphemistically, as 'public conveniences'. Ideally, the authorities would hire the use of ground-floor toilets in houses or shops on the main streets. Short of this, they might at least establish a network of home-owners and shop-owners willing to charge a cheap rate for the use of their toilets, who would clearly signpost their facilities, and who could then be registered and advertised publicly. If the public conveniences proved profitable to the owners, the authorities might eventually be able to raise standards of hygiene by being able to threaten to remove sub-par conveniences from the advertised lists. The system would be self-sustaining. The Society's suggestion was supported by many of Cole's collaborators on the exhibition, as well as his artist friends and even Charles Dickens.[24]

The suggestion was ignored, but this did not stop Henry Cole. He reasoned that the exhibition itself might help 'reconcile the public to the use of a convenience'.[25] Exposing the public to novelties was, after all, one of the Great Exhibition's main purposes. They simply did not know they wanted them, Cole decided, because the concept was so unfamiliar. He arranged for the Crystal Palace to have its own toilets, for which entry was charged at a halfpenny or penny, depending on the services required. Over the course of the Great Exhibition these 'waiting rooms' were visited by over 700,000 women and 820,000 men.[26] The figures did not even include the use of urinals, which were free. For Cole and the reformers, this was evidence that their suggested system of public conveniences for London might be self-supporting.

With funding from Samuel Morton Peto, whom Cole had persuaded to start off the Great Exhibition's guarantee fund, in 1852 the Society persuaded a couple of shop-owners on London's busiest thoroughfares to make their ground floors available for a trial. A gentlemen's waiting room was opened in a pub on Fleet Street, the Old Bell Tavern, which is still there. A ladies' version was opened in a failing dairy shop on Bedford Street, just off the Strand, across the road from the Society of Arts itself. Cole's friend Herbert Minton, the pottery manufacturer, provided the urinals and some tiles (it seems Cole could not resist this fresh chance to show off beautiful design to the masses).[27] The Society also actively publicised the conveniences. It advertised them repeatedly in the newspapers and distributed fifty thousand pamphlets. Yet the conveniences were a costly failure. After six months the toilets had cost almost five hundred pounds and brought in only fifteen pounds. Hardly anyone had used them, and the project was abandoned. Ironically, the Society's campaign to create a system of public conveniences had the opposite effect. Its failure convinced many of London's sanitation authorities that there was simply no demand—the experience became a barrier to future reform.

Public conveniences, however, were of lesser importance to Henry Cole—one of the systems he tried to create along the way, when the opportunity presented itself while organising the exhibition. His main goal was still to spread artistic beauty to the masses. It is impossible to say whether the Great Exhibition itself had the effects Cole desired, of cultivating the taste of British consumers and encouraging manufacturers to improve their designs. Taste is difficult to measure, not to mention subjective. But the exhibition itself was a dazzling display. The Crystal Palace—'the blazing arch of lucid glass with the hot sun flaming on its polished ribs'—seemed to be filled with every object imaginable.[28] Walking down the central aisle, visitors admired colossal statues, a gigantic telescope, fountains, and pillars of granite, coal, and other raw minerals. Vials of spermaceti oil, from the heads of sperm whales, vied for attention with models of bridges and lighthouses, and even a huge diamond, the Koh-i-Noor, which had been presented to Queen Victoria after the British conquest of Punjab a few years earlier (the public queued up to see it, but were apparently disappointed—it was smaller and less shiny than the hype had promised, reportedly looking like 'a piece of common glass').[29] One section of the exhibition showed the latest steam-powered machinery, clunking away; other stalls advertised the manufactures of different countries—Belgian furniture, Italian vases, Indian patterned cloths, and vast French bronzes. Charles Dickens was overwhelmed: 'there's too much. I have only been twice, so many things bewilder one'.[30]

But Cole worried that the exhibition would be a one-off display, a fleeting amusement that would soon be forgotten. Before the exhibition had even closed, he raced to secure its legacy. The most obvious way was to organise more exhibitions. An audit of the world's industries would need to be updated every few years, and future exhibitions would reinforce new ties of trade and peace. Fortunately for Cole, international jealousy did most of the work for him. Both New York and Dublin announced their intentions to hold international exhibitions in 1853. France also announced that it would hold an international exhibition, an *exposition universelle,* in Paris in 1855. 'We have a revenge to take on the Exhibition of London', said one French newspaper.[31] The French complained that the Great Exhibition had been too biased towards British industry, that British manufacturers had had the advantages of competing on their home ground, that France and the rest of Europe had still been recovering from the 1848 revolutions, and besides, that Britain had appointed the juries that decided the exhibition's prizes. Paris in 1855 would be France's chance to reclaim its glory, under fairer conditions. As one newspaper noted, international exhibitions were becoming modern versions of 'the great fairs and chivalric gatherings of the middle ages'. Instead of 'fierce encounters with lance and shield', however, they involved 'bloodless contentions of skilled labour'.[32]

Over the following decades, right up to the present, country after country has hosted its own international exhibitions. The Great Exhibition of 1851 was the first of what are now known as the world's fairs or world expos. Many of them even featured their own versions of the Crystal Palace, and the Society of Arts continued to play a role in their organisation. It hosted the London office for the organisers of Dublin's exhibition of 1853, and Henry Cole was put in charge of the British section at the Paris exhibition of 1855. He was responsible for persuading manufacturers to send their exhibits, oversaw their passage to France, and arranged the exhibits at the stands. Later officials of the Society would continue to play such roles. Its secretary in the last decades of the nineteenth century, Henry Trueman Wood, organised the British sections at the Paris exhibition of 1889 and the Chicago exhibition of 1893.[33] Wood and his assistant were reportedly among the first foreigners to climb the specially built entrance arch to the 1889 Paris exhibition, the Eiffel Tower, before it was officially opened to the public. They only made it as far as the second storey, as the lifts were not yet working. The French newspapers the next day mistakenly reported that two disgruntled workmen had been seen ascending the tower intending to sabotage it.[34]

The Society of Arts also organised the next international exhibition in London. This was almost entirely the project of Henry Cole—Prince Albert was initially reluctant, much like he had been before 1851. Cole had always intended the Great Exhibition to be a regular event, and planned for a repeat in 1861, on its tenth anniversary. But events on the international stage intervened. In 1859, France joined the Kingdom of Sardinia in a war with Austria, now known as the Second Italian War of Independence. War introduced potential diplomatic problems when inviting exhibitors and allocating their space at the exhibition, as well as simply distracting all press attention. It was difficult to raise subscription funds when everyone was paying attention to the war. Although it ended within just a few months, unexpectedly early, the organisation of the exhibition had already been delayed by a year—a delay that would prove almost fatal to the exhibition's popularity.[35]

The International Exhibition of 1862 was in fact larger than the Great Exhibition of 1851. It had slightly more visitors, a greater variety of exhibits, and included more countries. Even the building was larger. But it was mostly forgotten. For a start, the outbreak of the American Civil War in 1861 distracted attention. The Confederacy also tried to force Britain into the war on its side by stopping its exports of slave-grown raw cotton.[36] The lack of raw cotton caused a depression in the cotton-manufacturing industry, usually known as the Lancashire Cotton Famine, which in turn led to mass unemployment in many of England's northern manufacturing towns. The working classes could not be expected to attend an exhibition in London when they could not find work. And it did not help that the building was considered ugly. It involved too many plain brick walls, said the critics, who fondly remembered the shining glass of the Crystal Palace. Whereas the exhibition of 1851 had stood out in Hyde Park, the 1862 exhibition was nestled

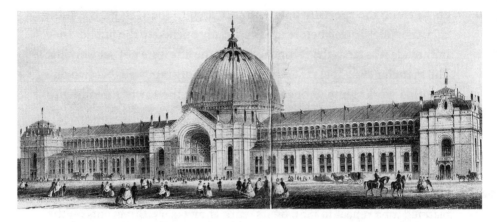

7.1. The International Exhibition of 1862, engraved from drawings by W.H. Prior. From *Views of the International Exhibition of the Industry of All Nations*, T. Nelson and Sons, London, 1862.

between streets, built around the gardens of the Horticultural Society at South Kensington. Perhaps the biggest blow to the exhibition's popularity, however, was Prince Albert's death towards the end of 1861, aged only 42. As one of the event's chief organisers, so fondly remembered for the Great Exhibition, his death cast a shadow over the whole event. Deep in mourning, Queen Victoria did not open the exhibition. She did not publicly visit it at all.

Yet the main activity of the Society of Arts was not in helping to organise the world's fairs; it was in taking advantage of them. The Great Exhibition had, after all, built much of its support upon the movements for free trade and world peace. It seemed an effective means of achieving those ends, if it could be exploited correctly. For Henry Cole and his allies at the Society of Arts, the exhibitions provided an opportunity to reform things on an even larger and all-encompassing scale: to create systems that were international.

As a member of the Great Exhibition's executive committee, Cole had been involved in assembling a panel of experts—the most eminent scientists, manufacturers, artists, inventors, and merchants from around the world—to decide who should receive prizes for the best exhibits. In the process, Cole had consulted his utilitarian mentor, John Stuart Mill, who advised that every jury should be international.[37] On a practical level, this lent the prizes legitimacy, ensuring that nobody could complain of nationalist partiality. More importantly, the world's experts would be forced into conversation with one another. They would note the annoying inconsistencies in the laws that governed them, Cole argued, and seek to impose some rational order. There was no reason the utilitarian reformers should limit themselves to reforming just their own nations; they could create systems for the entire world.

The Great Exhibition was the perfect opportunity to start such conversations. When it was over, the Society of Arts, as an organisation that was permanent, would keep the conversations going. All the foreign commissioners for the exhibition—the people who organised their respective countries' exhibits—were offered corresponding memberships of the Society, along with the use of its rooms for meetings.[38] The Society thus created an international network of experts to push for international reforms. One of their first initiatives was a campaign to create an international postage system. The plan was to standardise the various rates imposed by different countries on sending letters abroad, and to try to lower them in general. Each country would become a part of a postal union, in which they all agreed to forward foreign mail for free. Only the sending country's postal authority would keep the money for sending mail internationally. Such a system would allow people to send letters easily from anywhere in the world, to anywhere in the world. As things stood, unless there happened to be a direct delivery route between two countries, the sender had to pay someone in every country the mail travelled through, so that it could be forwarded across every border. An international postal union would thus make international communication both uniform and cheap, which would further enable both free trade and peace. The proposed system would be, in essence, an international version of Rowland Hill's reforms in Britain, which Cole had done so much to promote. It would be an 'Ocean Penny Postage'.

The Society of Arts played host to the campaign—an 'Association to Promote a Cheap and Uniform System of Colonial and International Postage'. The association included Cole and many of his usual utilitarian, radical and free trade allies, but its driving force was the Great

Exhibition's commissioner for Spain, Manuel de Ysasi.[39] Ysasi toured the world, obtaining interviews with the relevant government officials of country after country, all of whom expressed their approval for the plan. In 1853, he and the Society successfully persuaded the British government to establish a uniform postal system for its colonies, though it was not as cheap as they had hoped. Yet for a global system, the problem was coordination—getting everyone in the same place at the same time so that they could thrash out the system's details. This was an opportunity provided by the series of world's fairs: Ysasi urged that while many of the relevant dignitaries were in Paris for its exhibition in 1855, they should also hold a postal congress. Before the event could take place, however, Ysasi died in a shipwreck off the coast of Canada. Some countries came to their own deals—notably Britain and France used the 1855 Paris exhibition to come to an agreement—but it was not until 1874, with the creation of the Universal Postal Union, that Ysasi's dream became reality.[40]

The Society's reformers soon also turned their attention to parcel postage and telegrams, as well as to international travel. Henry Cole hoped that the conversations begun at the Great Exhibition, and continued at its successors, would lead to the abolition of passports and the harmonisation of customs administrations and quarantine laws. In the late 1860s the Society briefly sought ways to improve the quality and comfort of London's horse-drawn cabs, partly prompted by complaints by foreign visitors to the 1862 International Exhibition.[41] Cole claimed London had 'the meanest cabs in the world'.[42] The Society also sought to improve the 22-mile steam ferry crossing to France—an aspect of international travel that Cole found personally annoying. Cole frequently crossed the Channel to visit the various exhibitions at Paris, a journey he described as 'barbarous and cruel', particularly for women, children, and the sick. Passengers had to choose between being packed into the cabin, 'detestably close and stinking, filled with human beings senselessly prostrate and sick', or being battered by 'hail, rain, snow, and cold' out on the open deck.[43]

In 1869 the Society offered medals for technological solutions. Although none of the submissions were deemed sufficiently effective, a few years later the inventor Henry Bessemer, who was famous for developing a process of mass-manufacturing steel, launched a new steamer with a swinging saloon. The idea was that the passengers inside a spacious and lavish saloon would always remain level while the hull tilted from side to side around them. Bessemer hoped it would solve the problem of seasickness. He even named it the SS *Bessemer*. But it was far too large for Calais harbour and difficult to steer; it twice lurched out of control and wrecked the pier. The ship was immediately scrapped, without actually having tested the swinging saloon.[44] (The saloon became a billiard room and then a lecture hall at Swanley Agricultural College but was unfortunately destroyed by a bomb in the Second World War.) Nonetheless, in the meantime a series of minor improvements to the older ferries, such as coverings for the deck and better ventilation of the cabins, made them markedly more bearable.[45]

Beyond Cole's gripes about international communications and travel, he and his utilitarian allies in the Society of Arts proposed the standardisation of the world's commercial laws, as well as its weights, measures and coinage. The Society campaigned in the early 1850s for Britain to adopt the metric and decimal systems, though some of the proposed measurements would be unrecognisable today: one proposal was for ten feet to become a decot, a hundred a centot, and for ten pints to become a decim, a hundred a centim.[46] The campaign was unsuccessful—the British government only began concerted moves towards decimalisation over a hundred years later, in the 1960s. But the Society did not stop there. The world's knowledge might also be standardised. Cole and his allies proposed that the countries of the world compile and exchange the records of all the books in their libraries, as well as all their patents and copyrights. A universal catalogue of such knowledge would help to prevent wasteful duplication.[47]

Underlying all these reform efforts was another project, to remake the state along utilitarian lines. In Dickens's satire of Henry Cole in *Hard Times*, the utilitarian school inspector 'had it in charge from high authority to bring about the great public-office Millennium, when commissioners should reign upon earth'. The satire was accurate. Cole believed that the Great Exhibition's prize jury—its assembly of

7.2. To reflect the Society's promotion of international standardisation, in 1856 it changed its official seal to show a serpent ('of wisdom') encircling the globe. It was used as the Society's logo until the early twentieth century, when it was replaced by less ominous-looking depictions of the Society's house at the Adelphi, and then by just the letters RSA. The serpent and globe remained as the official seal, however, until 1966.

international experts—was an unprecedented gathering in the history of the world. They were perhaps the largest ever collection of the greatest minds of the age, united in the service of world civilisation. Cole believed they would demonstrate how easily peaceful agreements and rational reforms could be reached, so long as the right people were in charge. International questions 'should be settled by the voices of merchants and manufacturers', he hoped, 'rather than by the correspondence of diplomats, or by the thunder of artillery'. 'The men of art, science, and commerce' would show 'their brethren of politics, law, and war' how it was done.[48] The way to world peace and universal happiness would be shown by the technocrats.

The state's major preoccupations in the early nineteenth century were public order and the defence of the realm, which was why the 'brethren of politics, law, and war' had been in charge in the first place. For utilitarians like Cole, however, the state was also a potential tool to promote other useful ends: science, design, education, health. In this, they again found common ground with radicals and the supporters of free trade and world peace. Yet convincing the state to take on new roles was a drawn-out struggle. Limited grants for building new schools had been the result of campaigns since the 1820s by a handful of utilitarian and radical members of Parliament like William Ewart.[49] Art and education in Ireland and Scotland received some funding—the Royal Dublin Society had received state subsidies since the 1740s—but there was little of the kind in England. Reformers in 1836 managed to get the government to create schools of design, yet these were limited in their scope, as Cole discovered in the late 1840s when he tried to improve them. When it came to the state's support of science, design, education, and health, by 1851 there was certainly not anything that might be called a system.

Laws regarding the arts and education were often merely permissive. Ewart had helped pass the Museums Act of 1845, but it simply allowed local authorities to slightly raise local taxes to pay for their own, local museums. His next attempt, the Public Libraries Act of 1850, was much the same. If locals wanted education, they would have to pay for it themselves. And the proposals of Ewart and his allies were heavily watered down to make it into law. Other politicians insisted upon limitations that made it difficult for local authorities to make use of their new abilities. Raising local taxes for public libraries, for example, could not simply be done by the resolution of a town council; it had to be approved with a two-thirds majority in a local referendum.

But a whole new opportunity for reform was provided by the Great Exhibition due to its role as an audit of the world's industries. The Great Exhibition, as well as the later world's fairs, gave some indication of how Britain stood relative to rival nations, especially France, Prussia, and the United States, in terms of machinery, design, and manufactures. Some people saw the Great Exhibition as a clear mark of Britain's superiority, but for would-be reformers it was a chance to expose worrying weaknesses. The Society of Arts held a series of lectures on the exhibition's implications, giving the reformers a platform. Cole and his allies thus exacerbated fears of Britain's impending decline, giving them the excuse to create the systems they desired. 'Are we to relapse into the old jog-trot systems', they asked, or would Britain grasp the opportunity to reform itself before it was too late?[50]

The reformers identified two areas of worry: science and design. Britain of course had many eminent scientists and artists—some of the best in the world—but it needed to diffuse science and design more widely throughout its population. French manufacturers of all kinds seemed to have superior taste; many of their working classes were provided with scientific training. At the same time, the discoveries on display at the

Great Exhibition revealed how the application of science was 'found influencing production to an extent never before dreamt of'.[51] Visitors to the exhibition had marvelled at the recent inventions of artificial dyes, a method of processing beetroot sugar, and the latest improvements to photography and the electric telegraph. If Britain were to keep up, it would need to promote the greater dissemination of science, particularly to the workforce as a whole. It would have to do the same when it came to design. Countries that educated their workers produced designs with 'manifest superiority to our own, in which every rule of sound taste, every law of congruity and harmony between material and design, was recklessly and abundantly violated'.[52] Whereas the French took a top-down approach, using the state to support industrial education, the British government was content to rely on a patchwork of private, voluntary institutions across the country: self-supporting libraries funded by the mechanics who used them, or schools supported by charity. If Britain was to remain competitive, argued the reformers, it would require 'an entire revolution in her education system'.[53] Their major ally in this project was Prince Albert.

Following the Great Exhibition, Albert found himself in a unique position to bring about reforms. He was more popular than ever, had the prestige of royalty, was president of the Society of Arts, and was chairman of the Royal Commission that had overseen the exhibition. When it came to lobbying the government to do more for science and art education, his word carried weight. In 1854, when the country was in the middle of the expensive Crimean War with Russia, it was Albert's personal intervention that persuaded the government to fund the British section for the 1855 international exhibition in Paris. 'As we were spending so much in destruction', Albert pointed out, 'we ought to spend in construction'.[54] His hope, like Cole's, was that the experts of art, science, and industry would show the politicians and generals how it was done.

Albert's position as chairman of the Royal Commission also allowed him to secure the exhibition's legacy. The Great Exhibition had produced a huge surplus of 213,305 pounds—in today's money approximately 167 million pounds.[55] People began to suggest how that fund should be spent, and by whom. There were calls in the press for the fund to be handed over to the Society of Arts.[56] After all, Royal Commissions were supposed to be only temporary, whereas the Society had been around for almost a century. And had the Society not started the Great Exhibition in the first place? The Society had the most experience of organising exhibitions and had collected and displayed premium-winning designs and inventions for its entire history. As Cole dominated the Society's Council, such a move would probably have suited him. In the end, however, Albert had his own plans.

Albert envisioned a permanent educational institution to promote the application of science and art to industry—a centre from which to create the country's system of industrial education. He wanted to bring all of London's cultural and educational institutions together. London had at least a hundred learned societies, each doing something to promote science and the arts or to apply them to industry. It seemed so inefficient for them all to be separate, wasting money by each paying for their own accommodation and other administrative expenses. Many of them seemed to have inadequate space. If they could all be brought together, the money saved could be put to better use.[57] Albert's institution also needed ways to spread the knowledge of the experts to the masses. One method would be to host actual classes, perhaps by acquiring the government's existing School of Mines and its School of Design. Yet they could only have so many pupils at a time, and hiring teachers was expensive. The other, more cost-effective method of education was to use museums—in other words, to make the Great Exhibition permanent.

Albert believed that working people should be able to visit a permanent collection, in which they might study raw materials, the processes and machinery used to transform them into manufactures, and the art used to beautify them. When it came to design, working people would thus have a set of model designs they could come back to again and again, from which to study the principles of taste and beauty. When it came to science, they would be able to access a similar collection of materials, instruments, and machinery. This project began during the Great Exhibition itself. Some suggested that the exhibitors at the

Crystal Palace be asked to donate their exhibits to a special museum of manufactures, or 'trade museum'.[58]

In this respect, Henry Cole was quickest to the mark, even though Albert had initially tried to keep his plans for an industrial education institution from him. Albert perhaps feared that if Cole got involved, he would inevitably seize control. Those fears were justified, though Albert conceded that if something needed to be done, Cole was the man to do it: 'When we want steam, we must get Cole', he quipped.[59] Cole persuaded the Royal Commission to purchase some of the exhibits, to form the nucleus for a trade museum under his own control. He also persuaded the government, before its enthusiasm for the Great Exhibition could wane, to fund another collection for use at the School of Design. Cole had received much of the credit for the exhibition's organisation (and even a handsome cash bonus), and was made a Companion of the Bath, a standard honour for public servants. His standing was higher than ever, and he capitalised on the Great Exhibition's success while it was still freshly remembered.[60]

In early 1852 the government created an entirely new department: the Department of Practical Art. Henry Cole was put in charge, though he was asked to share leadership with an old friend, the artist Richard Redgrave. Redgrave was one of Cole's principal allies on the Council of the Society of Arts—he had helped redirect the organisation towards promoting art-manufactures—and was headmaster of the School of Design, having initially lectured on the application of botany to art. He was Cole's model artist—someone who had applied his talents to manufactures. Redgrave's first job had been as a draughtsman in his father's factory, and he had collaborated with Cole in illustrating his children's books and decorating Felix Summerly's art-manufactures. Much of Redgrave's art also called attention to the conditions of the working poor. Like Cole, he was concerned for the masses. Perhaps most importantly, however, Redgrave was willing to work with Cole, whose reputation for being obstinate and dictatorial was by now very well established. Redgrave was content to sit back and allow Cole to take on the main responsibilities.[61]

Cole's new department controlled the government's central School of Design in London, as well as nineteen other design schools across the country. It also controlled the models he had been collecting for the use of the schools: the nucleus for a museum of art-manufactures that would educate the wider public in taste. He expanded the collection with new examples of art and ornament, using any excuse he could think of to acquire more items. The museum was opened in 1852, initially at Marlborough House, between Pall Mall and St James's Park in London. With the government's design schools and a museum at his command, Cole began to create a new, comprehensive system of design education: the ultimate tool in spreading beauty to the masses. To maintain the government's support, he tried to make the system as cheap as possible. When he had charge of the British section at the 1855 international exhibition in Paris, he told government ministers he might deliver it on only two thirds the allocated budget (in the end, he delivered it on just under four fifths—not quite as efficient as he had hoped, but still well under budget).[62] Cole also strove to make his system self-supporting. He had the design schools open their doors to the middle and upper classes in the mornings, so that their higher fees could subsidise the lower fees paid by artisans when they took their classes in the evenings after they finished work. The more independent the system was from the government's funding decisions—his political masters might change with an election and could also be capricious—the more secure the system would be. When he first took charge of the department, he idealistically told his allies that within a few years the entire project might be self-funding. They wisely talked him out of making such a rash promise public.[63]

Meanwhile, the Society of Arts continued to be one of the principal tools for Cole's agenda. Some of the items in the Society's repository, particularly the 'select specimens' for the art-manufactures exhibitions, eventually found their way to his museum. Cole also arranged for the Society to offer a premium for a box of watercolours with brushes, to be sold at retail for only a shilling, as well as a premium for a cheap set of drawing implements: compasses, a triangle, and a ruler. Cole's aim with these premiums was to make basic design tools more affordable, both for his design schools and for the working classes in general. The Society even promised to purchase at least a thousand of the shilling paint boxes, though there was little need. Over the next couple of decades, the winner of the premium, Joshua Rogers, sold over seven million.[64] In 1852 the Society also published a couple of textbooks for use in drawing and design schools. One was called, straightforwardly, *Directions for Introducing the First Steps of Elementary Drawing in Schools and among Workmen*. Cole's aim with these textbooks was to simplify instruction to such an extent that even teachers who could not themselves draw would, at least in principle, be able to teach drawing.[65]

The Society's textbooks also reflected a new development in Cole's overall project. His aim had expanded from simply spreading beauty to the masses; he now wanted to ensure that their taste conformed to his increasingly specific ideas of what was correct. Cole and Redgrave drew up principles of what counted as good taste, which were issued as edicts by the department, and hung up in the schools of design.[66] The Society's textbooks conformed to these principles too. The Department of Practical Art's museum even had a room dedicated to manufactures that broke their rules—examples of bad taste. It soon became known as Cole's 'chamber of horrors', and was satirised in Charles Dickens's magazine, *Household Words*: it described a gentleman who had visited the exhibition, was horrified to see his own patterned trousers on show, and was now 'haunted by the most horrid shapes. . . . When I went home I found that I had been living among horrors up to that hour. The paper in my parlour contains four kinds of birds of paradise, besides bridges and pagodas'. Unsurprisingly, the manufacturers of the 'horrors' also complained at having been so publicly embarrassed. That part of the museum was eventually changed.[67]

Although Cole was content to focus on art and design, Albert's vision encompassed all forms of industrial education, especially science. Only a year after Cole had taken charge of his department, in 1853 Albert persuaded the government to expand it. Cole now found himself in charge of a new Department of Science and Art. He had to share leadership with a scientist, Lyon Playfair, as well as with his artist friend Richard Redgrave. Playfair was yet another Council member of the Society of Arts, and had been an early supporter of the Great Exhibition. After Cole's work in 1849 to build support throughout the country, Playfair had consolidated it with a nationwide lecture series. He had also come up with the classification system for arranging the exhibits, which Cole had put into action. With the addition of science to his department, Cole found himself in control of the government's School of Mines as well as its School of Design; he had control of a museum of geology as well as his museum of manufactures. He even found himself responsible for the Royal Dublin Society, the state-funded Irish ancestor of the Society of Arts.

It was all part of Prince Albert's wider plan. With the management of the state's science and design institutions consolidated under a single department, it was time to bring many of them together physically—to realise Albert's vision of a centre for industrial education. They needed a site. Albert had initially hoped to use the Crystal Palace itself, envisioning it as a permanent fixture in Hyde Park. But he was thwarted; Parliament refused to give permission. The building was dismantled and then rebuilt in Sydenham, in south London (it burnt down in 1936, but the area is still known as Crystal Palace). Instead, under Albert's direction, the Royal Commission began to buy land in Brompton, just south of the Great Exhibition's site in Hyde Park. Although royal commissions were supposed to be temporary, Albert made this one permanent. The Royal Commission of the Exhibition of 1851 still exists today. Albert was even able to persuade the government to aid with the purchases of land. The site would soon be nicknamed 'Albertopolis'.

It was not long before Cole had the Department of Science and Art moved to the Royal Commission's Brompton site, along with most of the museum collections and schools under his control. Cole even considered getting the Society of Arts to make the move too, though it ended up staying put at the Adelphi.[68] But Brompton was an unfashionable part of town, and when a large iron structure was erected to house the various museums and educational institutions, it was widely considered ugly—it soon became known as the 'Brompton Boilers'. It was an unsuitable name for Albert's high-minded vision of a centre for the cultivation of art and science. When the museum of manufactures moved into a new site on the grounds in 1857, Cole renamed it the South Kensington Museum. Kensington was a much more aristocratic area nearby, though it had no 'south' at the time. The rebrand stuck, however, and ended up applying to the entire district: the surrounding area is still known as South Kensington, even though the museum was renamed the Victoria and Albert Museum.[69]

Although Cole was initially forced to share power at the Department of Science and Art, by the mid-1850s he had come out on top. Redgrave and Playfair continued as inspectors of the government's artistic and scientific schools, while Cole remained at South Kensington to run the department as a whole. He went through a number of titles, including Superintendent of General Management, Joint Secretary, and even Inspector-General. But it was simply as sole Secretary that he enjoyed the most control. Throughout, he continued to expand the collection of institutions under his control.

Cole and Albert both tried, unsuccessfully, to bring the National Gallery to South Kensington. Yet they had more success with other institutions, managing to realise much of Albert's vision of a cultural and scientific hub. The School of Design was soon moved there, and renamed the National Art Training School. In 1896 it was reconstituted as the Royal College of Art. In 1872, the Royal School of Mines and the Royal College of Chemistry moved there too. After a series of mergers with other institutions over the years, they became parts of what is now Imperial College London. South Kensington also became the home of the Patent Office Museum—a collection of inventions that evolved into the Science Museum.[70] Eventually, after some lobbying from Cole, the Patent Office handed control of the museum over to the Department of Science and Art. The headquarters of the Royal Horticultural Society soon found their way to the site too, and Cole persuaded them to plant a garden there. When other museums found themselves pressed for space, South Kensington became their natural destination—often with a little help from Cole. When the British Museum's natural history section became overcrowded, it relocated to South Kensington to become London's Natural History Museum.

As mentioned above, South Kensington was also used as the site of the International Exhibition of 1862, which Cole organised through the Society of Arts. Like its predecessor of 1851, it was entirely funded by public subscriptions. Cole was unable to prevent its building being demolished after the exhibition had ended, but many of the parts were re-used to build Alexandra Palace, a north-London counterpart to the Crystal Palace at Sydenham, often referred to as 'Ally Pally'. In 1871, on the twentieth anniversary of the Great Exhibition, Cole also used South Kensington to hold an annual series of specialist exhibitions instead of a single international exhibition. The Society of Arts was this time only marginally involved. Cole was concerned that the international exhibitions had been getting ever larger and more expensive—the 1867 exhibition in Paris had over fifteen million visitors, more than twice that of the Great Exhibition of 1851—so he tried a new format that was cheaper and easier to manage, lest other countries be put off holding new ones.[71] In the end, however, his annual exhibitions between 1871 and 1874 were disappointingly unpopular—only a million people turned up in 1871, and fewer thereafter.

Cole and Albert often used the Society of Arts to help fill in their system's gaps. When it came to South Kensington's collection of raw materials, Albert planned for the minerals to be provided by the Museum of Practical Geology, which the Department of Science and Art controlled (in the end, its collection was not brought to South Kensington until 1935). Yet there was no comparable collection of animal products—wool, silk, skins, horns, furs, feathers, wax, shells, and animal oils—to be shown alongside the things they could be turned into. So Albert and Cole had the Society of Arts put the collection together.[72] The collection even included samples of manure, along with various other chemicals produced from animal waste. A selection was exhibited in the Society's repository before it made its way to South Kensington. The Society also continued to hold its own exhibitions, usually on specific topics such as the products of India, or on educational apparatus and textbooks. When the exhibitions were over, the Department of Science and Art often purchased the exhibits for its permanent collections.

In general, whenever government bureaucracy or political decision-making got in the way of Cole's vision, his tool to get around them was the Society of Arts. When the government would not commit to buying a particular collection for his museum, Cole used the Society to send public petitions.[73] He used it to campaign for the use of gas lighting in museums, so that they could be opened in the evenings, making it easier for the working classes to visit. The South Kensington Museum was the first museum in the world to be lit with gas, but it took a campaign to get the principle extended to museums beyond Cole's personal control. As a result of the Society's lobbying, a government commission of scientists, including the chemist Michael Faraday, showed that the lights did not damage old paintings. Cole also used the Society to lobby other museums to share their treasures. When items were not on display, he argued, such 'superfluous specimens' should be sent to other museums throughout the country. The same should be done for library collections. He wanted a system that would do the most good for the most people, which meant spreading it throughout the country rather than confining it to South Kensington. In general, Cole's approach was to maximise accessibility. His museum collections were carefully labelled so that visitors would not need to purchase catalogues. He even persuaded the local buses to stop at South Kensington.[74]

Cole also used the Society of Arts to campaign for more museums to be set up throughout the country, with funding from the government. Much of the collection of animal products that the Society had assembled for use at South Kensington found its way to a new museum in Bethnal Green, an especially poor area of East London (today, the building houses the V&A Museum of Childhood).[75] Some other collections, originally taken from the Society's exhibitions, also made their way there. The Bethnal Green Museum, opened by the Department of Science and Art, but with much of the funding raised by the Society of Arts, was intended to show how the so-called superfluous specimens might be circulated between museums. It was also intended to set an example to the government and to local authorities, to encourage them to set up more museums. In the late 1860s, at a time when the government was trying to cut spending, Cole and his allies emphasised the museum's value for money by recycling the iron skeleton of the 'Brompton Boilers', beautifying it with some brick and decorative mosaics. When it opened in 1872, they noted that the museum attracted seven hundred thousand visitors in only its first three months. And contrary to the expectations of its opponents, it was not damaged by the 'rough people' of the neighbourhood.[76] 'I trusted the poor', said Cole. A modern government, Cole argued, was one that provided what the people wanted. The masses turned up to his museums and proved that they wished to be educated. It was up to the government, he argued, to provide more: 'as people become intelligent and free, so are they likely to demand public education'.[77]

Cole and the Society of Arts also pursued another ambitious strategy to persuade the government to spend more on the arts, sciences, and education, despite funding cuts in the late 1860s. In 1868, the government embarked on far-reaching reforms to the military. The Crimean War, fought against Russia in 1853–56, seemed to have revealed worrying problems, which after a decade had still not been resolved. The quality of new recruits seemed to have declined, which in turn led to low-quality officers. Reformers called for the army to reflect the class make-up of Britain as a whole—instead of a 'a purely aristocratic institution, the British army will become emphatically a popular army'.[78] Practices like being able to buy ranks were abolished; the army became meritocratic.

One of the solutions to the question of military reform was to improve the quality of the raw recruits. From 1859, with the government's backing, would-be reformers had set up volunteer corps throughout the country. They swore oaths of allegiance and trained part-time, funding their own arms and equipment. The patriotic public had begun to form itself into an army. The reformers even arranged for children to practise military drill in some schools. They argued that military drill taught self-discipline, leading to better attention, readiness, obedience, and unity of purpose. These were useful traits in factory workers, civil servants, accountants, and even churchmen, not just soldiers. As one reformer noted, approvingly, drill made children 'gentle' like cattle.[79] Drill also promoted physical fitness. As the ancient saying went, 'healthy body, healthy mind'.[80] One proponent, Edwin Chadwick, argued that military drills were so physically exhausting that pupils would be too tired to be boisterous in the evenings. When a government minister noted that he had done some drill at school and had still had energy in the evenings to be unruly, Chadwick responded that this was simply evidence he had not been drilled enough.[81] Chadwick also recommended drill for British people who went to India, so that they would be more likely to survive its tropical climes.[82] Military drill was even considered beneficial for girls, ostensibly training them to have elegant 'upright figures'.[83]

For Henry Cole, however, the debate over military drill in schools provided an opportunity to push his own agenda. If everyone in Britain were trained in military drill, and if some of them were trained to be a militia, he argued, then the government would no longer need to pay for a standing army. For a government trying to cut back, this would save an estimated seven million pounds every year, allowing it to spend more on 'national objects more productive than war, such as the education of the people, and the promotion of those things that advance arts, manufactures and commerce'.[84] The saving, Cole argued, would allow the government to create a national education system, more colleges, more universities, more museums, and more telegraph lines. It would be able to abolish pauperism, and cut taxes on transport, production, and communications. Cole's suggestion was, paradoxically, to make the population more martial so that the government could concern itself more with the arts of peace. It was an ambitious part of his plan to re-make the state.

Cole's main instrument to promote military drill in schools was, once again, the Society of Arts. In 1869 it convened many influential headmasters to discuss the practice, and in 1870 began to organise drill reviews. The events, they hoped, would popularise the practice and demonstrate to the government the practicality of making military drill compulsory in all schools. The reviews, like exhibitions, were intended to educate policymakers and the public through simple demonstration. Members of the Society's Council themselves reported 'deep impressions of the importance of the system, far deeper than any they had before entertained, or could have conceived, of the effects of the bodily training, without having witnessed them'.[85]

The Society's first drill review took place in 1870 on the cricket grounds of the rebuilt Crystal Palace at Sydenham—almost three thousand boys, drawn from schools throughout London, marched up and down before some of the country's most prominent military leaders, a few members of the royal family, and a large audience. Most of the boys were from the poorest of backgrounds, taught in industrial schools or on training ships. A couple of hundred boys, known as 'The Homeless Boys of London', lived and received their education on a repurposed 52-gun frigate, the HMS *Chichester*. The newspaper coverage singled them out as 'manly youths', who 'formed a well-trained and excellently-drilled ship's company'. A few boys from each school competed in swimming and gymnastics, and some took part in a marching band, after which they were all rewarded with some cake. The Society of Arts rewarded the best-drilled schools with banners.[86] The Society continued to hold the drill reviews for a few years, often at South Kensington. But its efforts to get military drill adopted in every school in the country failed; Britain continued to have a standing army.[87] Cole was thwarted in his ambitious plan to free up state funds for the arts and education.

In the decades following the Great Exhibition, Cole used the Society of Arts so often to build his stronghold at South Kensington that the Society and his department were often confused.[88] The Society was occasionally derided as 'King Cole's Parliament'.[89] South Kensington became the favoured site of many of the Society's events, including its conversazioni—the large informal gatherings of members and recent lecturers, which had been pioneered in the 1840s by Francis Whishaw. But the Society of Arts was more than just an appendage of the top-down system emanating from South Kensington. While Albert and Cole campaigned to remake the state, other reformers used the Society to build Britain's education system from the bottom up.

8

An Education for the
Whole People

HENRY COLE AND PRINCE ALBERT were keen to create a top-down system of industrial education, as seen in countries like France. Paradoxically, however, the French system had been inspired by the education on offer in Britain. From around 1800 in Glasgow, a Yorkshire-born Quaker doctor, George Birkbeck, had delivered free Saturday evening lectures on mechanics to members of the working class. When Birkbeck left for another town, many of the workers, brought together by his lectures, had eventually pooled their own money to hire other teachers. They created a self-supporting institution for their own education, holding lectures in the evenings after they finished work. Over the course of the 1820s these worker-run 'mechanics' institutions' were established in industrial towns across Britain, often with the support of Birkbeck and his friends (the London Mechanics' Institute, founded in 1823, has since evolved into a university, Birkbeck College, which still teaches its classes in the evenings). Some of them added libraries, news-rooms, and even museums. They were careful to preserve the principle of self-support—if the masses educated themselves without the patronage of the aristocracy, then they would prove themselves beyond any doubt to be worthy of political power. Even George Birkbeck himself, who was of the middle class, was criticised by some working-class radicals for giving too much support to the movement he had helped start. The radicals wanted to preserve workers' claims to independence.[1]

The movement to create mechanics' institutions impressed a French scientist, Charles Dupin, who in the late 1810s had visited Britain to spy on its military and industrial capabilities. Dupin believed that Britain's early lead in machinery and manufactures was the result of the education that its workers obtained for themselves. That early lead, in turn, seemed to have been a key cause of Britain's victory in the Napoleonic Wars. If France could catch up in terms of its industry, military might would surely follow. He persuaded the French government to fund free technical education for workers in subjects like perspective, geometry, and mechanics, to encourage science's application to industry and its diffusion among the masses. The same approach was adopted for drawing and design. Thanks to Dupin, Britain's fragmentary and bottom-up movement for workers' education was replicated in France, but with the top-down creation of a comprehensive state system.[2]

As we have seen, Henry Cole sought to align the Great Exhibition with the movement for working-class self-sufficiency. The fact that the exhibition was funded by public subscription was a key part of its appeal. He had pitched it as an event both for the masses, and by the masses. But after the exhibition, the approach of Prince Albert and Henry Cole had been to impose a top-down system similar to that in France. They were happy to create a system that was for the masses, but by any means necessary. When Cole had needed the support of the public, he had appealed to the popular principle of self-support. Yet once he had charge of his own government department, with government funding at his disposal, he had no qualms about using the levers of state.

Cole's system almost immediately clashed with the classes taught at the mechanics' institutions. In 1852 he tried to use the Society of Arts to set up new drawing schools for artisans in towns where there was not already a government school of design. Cole and the Society decided to focus first on Bradford, a major wool-manufacturing town in Yorkshire. But they had not done their research. Although Bradford lacked a school funded by the state, when Cole turned up to give a speech there, he immediately discovered that the local mechanics' institution already ran its own drawing school.[3] The working classes had already provided for themselves.

Yet the mechanics' institutions were mostly in decline. Their membership dwindled in the late 1840s, and the quality of the education they offered also declined. As part of an effort to salvage their popularity, their lectures were increasingly entertaining rather than instructive. Some mechanics' institutions hired ventriloquists or held concerts. As a result, many of the institutions became clubs to entertain the wealthier middle classes, rather than sources of serious instruction for workers.[4] Some of the institutions tried to preserve their working-class roots, but they faced problems of their own. It was difficult to judge whether the lecturers they hired were any good, and they could often only offer a few sporadic classes rather than systematic courses of instruction. It was difficult to attract teachers to some areas, especially those that were especially industrial or poor: 'I once saw Wigan from the railway', one lecturer reportedly explained, 'but I have no desire for a closer acquaintance'.[5] The subjects on offer varied widely. A typical mechanics' institution might offer courses in only reading and writing in one year, but drawing, shorthand, and arithmetic the next. To try to solve these issues, some of the mechanics' institutions began to form associations— unions of institutions—to pool their resources. The unions of institutions bought books and other educational equipment in bulk, or shared information about lecturers who were visiting the area.[6] But the unions could not do enough to prevent the decline—they simply lacked the means. They would need some help.

In late 1851, a civil servant named Harry Chester wrote to the Society of Arts with a suggestion, imploring it to aid the mechanics' institutions. Chester was not a member of the Society. He was not even working-class. But he had found himself on the frontline of educational reform. Chester was born into the minor gentry, and had been educated at some of the most prestigious schools in the country, Charterhouse and Westminster. He had attended Trinity College, Cambridge, but left without a degree, which was common in those days, to become a clerk at a seemingly obscure branch of government—the Privy Council Office. The

Privy Council was, and still is, a group of formal advisers to the queen; Chester was one of a handful of clerks who served it. But in 1839, partly due to the campaigning of utilitarian reformers, the Privy Council became responsible for the state's funding of schools.[7] The government appointed a Committee of the Privy Council on Education, which was served by three clerks. Harry Chester was one of them. He found himself administering the beginnings of England's state-funded primary education system, organising school inspections, grants for school buildings, and the training of teachers. He became obsessed with improving education, even inventing a slow-burning stove designed to make sure classrooms would already be warm when pupils arrived on cold mornings.[8]

Chester was alarmed by how many children were forced to leave school at an early age, sometimes as young as 10 or 12, so that they could enter employment and begin to aid their families financially. He could do little to prevent it, but bemoaned the consequences: 'when I see men or women unable to read and write, I feel pained as if I saw that the poor creatures were maimed, or blind, or dumb'. He saw in the mechanics' institutions a way for adults to recover the educations they had been so cruelly denied. Chester hoped for 'an improved education for the whole people, rich and poor, adult and child'. He had been impressed by the Great Exhibition, particularly as it had drawn attention to the state of Britain's education in science and art. He saw in the Society of Arts an organisation that might aid the mechanics' institutions.[9]

Chester suggested the creation of a new union of institutions—one that would be national. The Society of Arts had the prestige and the means. It had also indicated its interest in educating the masses. The Society acted on his suggestion, inviting delegates from mechanics' institutions around the country to a meeting at Freemasons' Hall (the choice of venue seems to have been one of simple convenience—the Earl of Carlisle, who spoke at the conference, joked that he feared the walls of the hall would tumble down upon him when he admitted he was not a mason). On 18 May 1852, the delegates announced themselves to be the Institutions in Union (sometimes called the Union of

Institutions). 'A vast system of local organization for purposes of adult instruction', which *The Times* described as perhaps one of the Great Exhibition's 'most important fruits'.[10]

The Society of Arts would not interfere in the internal workings of the various institutions it took into the union. It would, however, agree to serve the union in any way it could, with its administrative costs covered by fees from the institutions. It would get lecturers and class teachers for the institutions more cheaply, and be able to check their quality. It would try to find more lecturers in subjects that were lacking, and encourage systematic courses. Wherever the lecturers could not go, it would circulate lecture transcripts. It would even lend books, works of art, drawings, diagrams, photographs, and models of inventions, for use in classes or to form the basis of local exhibitions. As well as assisting the institutions throughout the country, the Society of Arts would encourage the institutions to assist each other. Any member of an institution in the union would be entitled to attend the exhibitions, lectures, and libraries of any other institution in the union. Chester hoped the union would provide a 'well-organized system, whereby industrial knowledge may be cheaply and conveniently diffused'.[11]

Harry Chester himself soon rose rapidly in the Society. He became a member in early 1852. The following year he was elected the chairman of the Council, thus making him chairman on the Society's first centenary. At Chester's urging, the Society took further action to aid the Institutions in Union. It purchased and distributed its premium-winning shilling paint boxes and drawing sets, and later offered a similar prize for a cheap classroom microscope, so that the institutions might offer courses in natural history.[12] It also, in 1854, held an international exhibition of educational appliances: textbooks, maps, easels, scientific instruments, mechanical models, blackboards, globes, and instructional charts, collected from all over the world. The idea was that it would be a Great Exhibition, but for education. The Institutions in Union were encouraged to send their teachers to it, while the Society's house at the Adelphi was temporarily offered as a sort of hostel, at least for those teachers coming from outside London.[13] It was, however, not particularly popular and made a loss. People had been intrigued to see the products of the industry of all nations, which had been set alongside curiosities like the Koh-i-Noor, but they were not so keen to see an exhibition of textbooks. Many of the exhibits ended up, predictably, at Henry Cole's South Kensington Museum.[14]

Trying to aid the Institutions in Union, the Society also offered a prize for the best essay on the causes of their troubles, as well as asking for suggestions about how they might be improved. The winning essay came from one of the key movers in the West Riding of Yorkshire Union of Institutions, a man named James Hole. He was, himself, a beneficiary of the mechanics' institutions: a former worker in a cotton mill who had attended evening classes to become a clerk. He became well known in socialist circles, but though he favoured the use of the state in some circumstances, more than anything else he promoted working people collaborating and cooperating for the common good. He subscribed to a philosophy of 'associationism', and was involved with various efforts to found cooperatives and other self-supporting working-class institutions.[15]

In his premium-winning essay on the mechanics' institutions, Hole identified a number of potential causes of their decline, the first being that many of the people who the institutions were intended for were illiterate.[16] If they could not read, how could they be expected to follow lectures on science, art, or anything else? This, however, was an issue already being gradually dealt with by the Committee of the Privy Council on Education. It was also contentious. Most schools were controlled and funded by religious organisations, but they were split between the established Anglican church and dissenters. When the government first became involved in education, it had been bitterly opposed by many dissenters as they feared that their children might become indoctrinated to Anglicanism. A proposed compromise, however, of teaching no religion in schools, was unacceptable to everyone. Schools were crucial, the groups believed, to keeping religion alive.[17] The Society had no wish to get involved in the religious debate about schools, but there was no contention when it came to the education of adults. Proposals for the improvement of the mechanics' institutions would have to focus on the institutions themselves.

The next potential problem identified by James Hole was that the institutions had become too middle-class, that it was the wealthier and relatively educated middle classes who exerted pressure on the institutions to become places of entertainment rather than study. This argument, however, was not one that appealed to reformers like Chester. Before becoming involved with the Society, he had in fact founded his own literary and scientific institution in Highgate. He saw the institutions as a way to bring the classes together, to promote social harmony: 'here all classes may meet, without annoyance to any, and therefore with advantage to all'.[18]

He was not alone in thinking this. The Society itself had been used in this regard in the mid-eighteenth century, as a place where the upper and middle classes could collaborate for the public good, where 'all rank and distance is laid aside'. The Institutions in Union had expanded, by 1855, to 368 mechanics' institutions,[19] with a combined membership of some fifty thousand people.[20] The Society used those connections to try to promote social harmony. Trade unions had been decriminalised in 1824–25, such that workers were for the first time able to openly defy employers and demand better working conditions and higher wages, though strikes were still banned. In early 1853, a wave of strikes hit the cotton industry in Lancashire; centred on Preston, factories were brought to a standstill as spinners and weavers demanded higher wages. With its connection to the mechanics' institutions, many of whose members were also prominent trade unionists, the Society felt it might do something about it. The utilitarians among its leaders, it seems, believed that the problem was one of misunderstanding or miscommunication, and that through rational discourse the situation might be resolved.[21]

The Society invited representatives of the industrialists and of the workers to a conference, along with assorted radicals, political economists, and others. By convening the disparate interests, the Society hoped that it might, if not reconcile the opposing camps, then at the very least ensure that the two camps had full knowledge of each other's dilemmas. Unfortunately, however, the employers refused to cooperate—they sent hardly any representatives, and those that did attend

Plate 1. Portrait of William Shipley, by his former pupil and Society of Arts prize-winner, Richard Cosway. It was displayed at the Society's first exhibition of contemporary art in 1760, and donated by the artist in 1785.

Plate 2. The distribution of premiums at the Society of Arts. It shows the horseshoe configuration of the benches in the Great Room, as well as the many women who attended the event each year. Drawn by Augustus Charles Pugin and Thomas Rowlandson, aquatinted by a J. Black, and published in 1809 by Rudolph Ackermann to illustrate his *Microcosm of London*.

Plate 3. Samuel Johnson, between two noble ladies, points towards Elizabeth Montagu as an example of intellectual 'female excellence'. Montagu has her arm around a young girl with a drawing, who looks jealously at another young girl who has won the Society's gold medal. Detail taken from James Barry's series of history paintings in the Society's Great Room.

Plate 4. The Society's original gold medal, from among the first that were struck and awarded in 1758. It shows Minerva and Mercury presenting themselves to Britannia—a device that more or less became the Society's logo until the mid-nineteenth century. This particular medal was given to Lord Romney, 'for eminent services' as the Society's first vice-president. Design by James 'Athenian' Stuart, die cut by Thomas Pingo.

Plate 5. Textile design submitted to the Society for an award. By William Pether, c.1757. RSA/PR/AR/103/14/56.

Plate 6. Ornamental flower design submitted to the Society. By William Chinnery, c.1757. RSA/ PR/AR/103/14/64.

Within the painting: *Mary Moſer 1759*   *Claſs 63 firſt Premium*

Plate 7. Painting of flowers by Mary Moser, for which she won the Society's first prize of five guineas and a silver medal in 1759. The Society had it 'handsomely framed and glazed' for display in the Great Room. She was only 15 at the time. It was then displayed at the 1760 exhibition of contemporary art. RSA/PR/AR/103/19/119.

Plate 8. Diagoras of Rhodes, the legendary ancient athlete, on the shoulders of his sons—the central focus of James Barry's vast history paintings adorning the Society's Great Room, first displayed to the public in 1783.

Plate 9. Drawing of the front of the Society's building at the Adelphi—a temple to the arts and commerce—which it has inhabited since 1774. Statues were later added to the roof in the 1990s, in keeping with the original plans of the Adam brothers. By David Gentleman, 1990.

MACROCERCUS ARARAUNA.

Blue & Yellow Macaw

½ Nat. Size

Plate 10. Hand-coloured lithograph of a parrot by Edward Lear, donated to the Society in the early 1830s as thanks for its role in promoting the art of lithography. The lithographs were later bound together as a book, *Illustrations of the Family of Psittacidae, or Parrots*.

Plate 11. The Crystal Palace at Hyde Park. From *Dickinson's Comprehensive Pictures of the Great Exhibition of 1851*, Dickinson Brothers, London, 1854.

Plate 12. The central aisle of the Great Exhibition of 1851. Note how the barrel-vaulted ceiling accommodated Hyde Park's elm trees. From *Dickinson's Comprehensive Pictures of the Great Exhibition of 1851*, Dickinson Brothers, London, 1854.

Plate 13. The kind of Indian design that caused a sensation at the Great Exhibition of 1851, in this case an embroidery on crimson silk. Image from plate 88 of Matthew Digby Wyatt's *Industrial Arts of the Nineteenth Century*, which illustrated the exhibition's 'choicest specimens'. RSA/SC/EX/1/98.

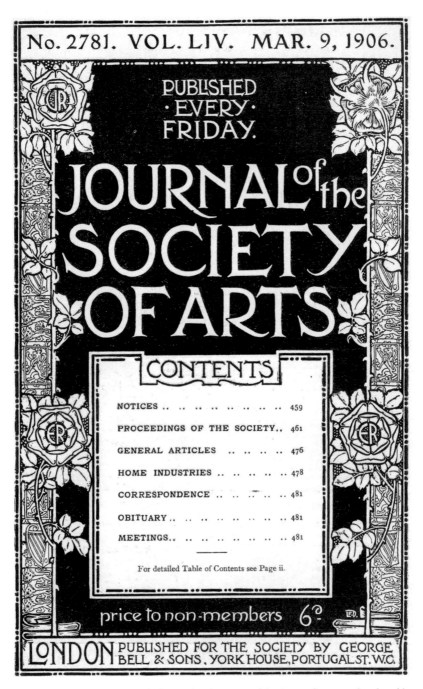

No. 2781. VOL. LIV. MAR. 9, 1906.

PUBLISHED ·EVERY· FRIDAY.

JOURNAL of the SOCIETY OF ARTS

CONTENTS

For detailed Table of Contents see Page ii.

price to non-members 6ᵈ

LONDON PUBLISHED FOR THE SOCIETY BY GEORGE BELL & SONS, YORK HOUSE, PORTUGAL ST. W.C.

Plate 14. Lewis Foreman Day's design for the cover of the Society's *Journal*, bordered by Tudor roses and heraldic devices, and harking back to a lost age of craftsmanship.

Plate 15. The preserved village of West Wycombe, illustrated for a Christmas card issued by the Society in 1979. By Brian Batsford, whose designs for book covers had, since the 1930s, helped to popularise the campaign to preserve England's beauty, © Brian Cook Batsford Estate.

Plate 16. The 'WEEE Man', commissioned by the Society to draw attention to the waste of electrical and electronic equipment. Sculpture designed by Paul Bonomini. Photograph by David Ramkalawon, © David Ramkalawon.

hardly spoke. Their attitude was that it was just a matter of time before the workers ran out of money and returned to work. Negotiation was futile. Indeed, the conference may have had the opposite effect to the one intended: the press that catered to the middle and upper classes denounced the Society for giving a platform to radical agitators, while the radical working-class press denounced the Society for being a middle-class sham. At the conference itself, a radical lawyer and journalist, Ernest Jones, went off-topic and launched into a heated rant about the inherent incompatibility of labour and capital. When the chairman tried to cut him off, Jones 'with increased warmth' denounced the meeting, took his hat, and 'hastily quitted the room'.[22] Unsurprisingly, Jones's radical newspaper was among those that denounced the Society the following day.[23]

Yet the entire conference seems to have also been intended for another purpose—to persuade the different interests to sign up to a more long-lasting solution to the problem of industrial disputes. When Jones stormed out, the speaker who followed him was Robert Slaney, a politician, who had formulated a plan to reconcile the classes. Indeed, two of the four topics that the conference was supposed to discuss were devoted to his idea, and the conference voted on a resolution to support it, revealing unanimous support. Slaney's plan was to change the law governing business partnerships, to expand access to limited liability.[24]

In the early 1850s the law stipulated that all partners in a business were fully liable for all of the debts that it might incur. The only exceptions were companies that received special dispensation from Parliament or the monarch. In the vast majority of cases, if a business went bust, then the partners were expected to pay. It put them at risk of personal bankruptcy.[25] For reformers like Slaney, this seemed unjust. It meant that only the very wealthiest people would ever risk investing in a company. The law, he said, benefitted only the 'great bankers, great capitalists . . . anchored and bound down to their present moorings by the weight of wealth they stand on'.[26] It also meant that the millions of workers who had savings were not putting those savings to use. There were a few 'penny banks', which accepted small deposits, but otherwise banking was out of the reach of many.[27] Workers saved up money for a rainy day, but their capital rarely earned interest. Their savings were not used for investment.

Slaney argued that the law should be changed to allow anyone to invest in a business, but not be liable for its debts beyond the stated value of their shares. Liability, he argued, should be limited. This would have an economic benefit, in that the small savings of millions of workers would suddenly be unleashed on the economy—a surge of investment from the working classes. Some argued that nobody would lend to such a company if they knew that the investors did not take personal responsibility for its debts, but Slaney did not wish to force companies to have limited liability. His proposals were merely permissive. If it were at least allowed, then it would be up to creditors to decide whether or not to lend. Indeed, other countries had begun to experiment with forms of limited liability. In France, it was called a *commandite* partnership. It had also been used with apparent success in the Netherlands and the United States.

The reason Slaney presented his proposal to the Society's conference on strikes, however, was because he saw it as a solution to the growing divide between industrialists and their employees. Making limited liability general would allow workers to invest in companies, making them, in effect, part-industrialists themselves. As shareholders, their interests would become more closely aligned with those of their employers. Some of the workers' representatives at the conference were sceptical of this argument, but they did see the benefit of acquiring information about businesses—as shareholders, they would be entitled to see a company's accounts, allowing them to judge whether their wages were being suppressed out of commercial necessity, as employers often argued, or simply out of greed. As for the employers, Slaney argued that they would be able to reward some of their more loyal workers by bringing them into small partnerships—it would provide a new strategy to improve industrial relations. Still others, like John Stuart Mill, saw the potential of general limited liability to reform the morals and manners of workers.[28]

Indeed, Slaney's proposal was to benefit more than just for-profit businesses. It would aid mechanics' institutions too, which otherwise found it difficult to become corporate entities. They were often unable to buy their own premises, for example, without the aid of wealthy patrons. With general limited liability, workers themselves would be able to pool their savings to create many more mechanics' institutions, libraries, reading rooms, and even schools.[29] Harry Chester, Henry Cole, and others at the Society took up Slaney's cause.[30] A law was ushered through Parliament by some of the Society's members. In 1855 limited liability was made general, and made even easier to obtain the following year. Indeed, despite the fears of its detractors, corporations with limited liability became the norm. (Slaney did not live long to see his reform's effects. At the opening of the Society's International Exhibition of 1862 he injured himself when he slipped through a gap in the floor, contracted gangrene, and died.)

The Society thus preferred to reconcile the interests of working men with their employers, not to separate them. And in any case, James Hole's premium-winning essay on the reasons for the decline of the mechanics' institutions' problems argued that the principal problem was neither poor literacy nor a takeover by the middle classes. The problem, Hole argued, was one of incentives. It was all very well to supply lectures and classes, but the kind of people who applied themselves to acquiring knowledge for its own sake were extremely rare. As Chester put it, 'such youths are not abundant in any class of society'. The self-educating young person was 'a hero of no mean order'. Most people needed some extra inducement.[31]

Workers might be told that self-education would give them opportunities for professional enhancement, but that was difficult to prove. Indeed, even if they did spend months educating themselves in the finer points of art and science, they might not be able to convince their bosses or potential employers. There was no simple, easy way to prove their skill and understanding. What the mechanics' institutions needed, Hole argued, were examinations. Most people would only pursue courses of study if they could then obtain a testimony to their abilities—especially one that would be taken seriously by employers. If the skills of the nation were to be improved, its workers needed an incentive. Examinations would also be better, he argued, than prizes for the best performances, which would 'breed ill-feeling among the pupils'. To be effective incentives for everyone, examinations would have to be based on attaining a certain standard, not on relative merit.[32]

The idea of using examinations was especially appealing to utilitarians. It had been espoused by Jeremy Bentham himself. He had decried the irrationality of Britain's system of hiring civil servants. Instead of the best connected or highest born, he had argued, the country should be run by the most able. Bentham had called for the creation of a complicated national examination system, open to all, from which the prime minister would then be able to select the highest-ranking candidates to run the country.[33] In the 1850s, Bentham's dream had already begun to become reality. In 1853, reformers had introduced competitive examinations of candidates for the bureaucracy of the East India Company. The practice was introduced to the British civil service later that year. The civil service, at least in theory, became more meritocratic. Harry Chester's bosses at the Committee of the Privy Council on Education had in the late 1840s implemented examinations for state-trained school teachers. And Henry Cole, at his department, in 1853 implemented examinations to qualify as art teachers at the government's schools of design.[34]

Yet these examinations were about entry to particular institutions. They were internal, not intended as qualifications to be used in general, as proof of skill or aptitude for all employers. The only thing approaching such qualifications were those used to enter and graduate from universities. Since the 1830s, for example, many people sat entrance examinations for the University of London so that they could simply qualify to enter—matriculation. They often had no intention of actually studying there, only wanting the matriculation certificate as proof of their abilities. As for the examinations to graduate, these were available to only a tiny proportion of the population. Getting into a university was usually available to only the richest or best connected. People had to be able to afford to go all the way to Oxford or Cambridge just to sit the matriculation exams, let alone afford to study there.[35]

What was needed, said some, was a system of purposefully public, or external examinations. The principal proponent of such a system was a utilitarian vicar, James Booth. Booth had been born near Carrick-on-Shannon, County Leitrim, a rural part of Ireland. He had been educated at Trinity College, Dublin, which had involved an especially rigorous series of examinations. He had moved to England and become a vicar, but his over-riding endeavour was to improve the education of the nation. He was involved in attempts to set up schools and colleges in Bristol, Liverpool, and Wandsworth. Indeed, in Benthamite fashion, he saw education as the solution to many of the country's woes, and one that should be undertaken by the state. State-led education would benefit the economy and would even prevent crime. The state, he said, 'claims the exclusive privilege of punishment of crime; why then shrink from and repudiate the nobler one of preventing it?'[36]

For Booth, the way to increase education was through examinations. By incentivising people to study—giving them a useful qualification to work towards—Booth argued that examinations would introduce habits of persistence and self-discipline. Indeed, Booth cared little about whether students retained their knowledge. The purpose of examinations was to inculcate 'habits of self-instruction'. Even if they forgot facts, people who had studied for examinations would still remember how to learn.[37] Indeed, examinations would increase the demand for courses of study, as well as for the people to teach them. Examinations would boost the demand for education among the people, calling forth its supply.

In 1847, Booth had called for the government to create an examinations system for children leaving schools. Examinations, he argued, would get around the disputes about teaching religion, which stood in the way of the government running and funding schools. The state would provide and fund examinations, boosting demand for schooling, while leaving the schools themselves in the hands of the fractious religious groups. Examinations were Booth's strategy to break the deadlock and create a state education system. Indeed, the subjects that were examined would determine what was taught. Teachers would teach to the test. By controlling the examination syllabus, the state would determine schools' curricula, providing the incentive to teach subjects to a certain level while leaving them free to teach religion or whatever else in any way they thought fit.[38]

Booth's proposals, however, did not result in any immediate action from the government. Following the creation of the Institutions in

Union, he decided that the Society of Arts might be a suitable vehicle for his proposed reforms. If he were able to use the Society to create an examinations system, thereby demonstrating that the system worked, then he might be able to persuade the government to adopt it.

To be taken seriously, however, Booth first had to find a way into the Society. Like Chester with his proposal for the Institutions in Union, Booth did it by proposing a good idea. In 1852 he suggested the creation of a new journal of the Society, to be the mouthpiece of its Council, and a medium through which the mechanics' institutions could communicate with one another. The Society's *Transactions* had become less frequent following its near-bankruptcy in the 1840s, and had only been replaced with a few weekly records of its proceedings. What Booth proposed was instead to create a repository of all that occurred in the country with regard to reform and education. It would, he said, register 'the progress of the mind of the nation'.[39] The Council was convinced. *The Journal of the Society of Arts and of the Institutions in Union* began in late November 1852. It has continued to this day, though it has been rebranded a number of times. It has, however, always been called the Society's *Journal*.

Off the back of his proposal, Booth rose through the ranks of the Society as rapidly as Chester. Within a year of joining, Booth was elected to the Council. In 1853 he began to put his plans for a national examinations system into motion. He persuaded the Society to create a committee to investigate the 'industrial instruction' of the working classes, using its report to make the case for examinations. The schoolchildren, he argued, would particularly benefit from such a system, as well as the mechanics' institutions. James Hole's essay strengthened his case. Booth did not convince the Society that it needed to implement a system that was national and for the benefit of schools, but Chester soon proposed the creation of examinations for the benefit of the Institutions in Union. The Society's Council agreed.[40]

Booth took charge of the project. In 1854 the Society announced that it would be holding its first examination in March 1855, writing to the various members of the Institutions in Union to ask them how many candidates to expect. In the meantime, it set to work recruiting a prestigious board of examiners—some of the most eminent men in their fields. The examiners included fellows of the Royal Society, university professors, and high-ranking clergymen. Yet with only a month to go until the proposed examination, they had only received notice of one candidate—a Mr Medcraft, who wished to be examined in mathematics. (In some accounts, he is described as a chimney sweep. I have found no evidence to support this.[41]) The examination was cancelled, and Booth wrote to Medcraft to let him know.

Despite this false start, Booth reconstituted the examinations the following year. He was, by this stage, chairman of the Society's Council. The problem, he realised, was that the mechanics' institutions had not had enough time to prepare their students, while the syllabus had been too vague. If the institutions were to teach to the test, they required more detail about what would be in the test, as well as more time. He and Chester had also not had much success persuading employers to commit to taking the examinations seriously. If the qualifications were to provide an incentive to candidates, they had to be confident that employers would accept them. Over the year, they collected signatures of support and widely publicised the names of the expert examination board too. Their names and status lent confidence to the Society's proposed qualifications. In 1856, fifty-two candidates were examined at the Society's House, most of them coming from London, Lancashire, and Yorkshire. They sat three-hour-long papers, writing down their answers before facing the eminent examiners for an oral examination. Some of the candidates sat as many as four or five papers, all over the course of three intense days. Albeit limited to the members of the Institutions in Union, it seems to have been the country's first purposefully external examination.[42]

Although Booth had not persuaded the Society to provide examinations for schools, the success of 1856 directly led to their provision by other bodies. One of the Society's examiners in English History and English Literature, a state inspector of schools named Frederick Temple, was so impressed that he persuaded the University of Oxford to hold examinations for school-leavers throughout the country.[43] Cambridge soon followed. Instead of forcing candidates to travel to the universities to take entrance examinations, with the creation of local examination boards the universities came to them. Successful candidates did not gain admission to the universities, but they did get qualifications with their associated prestige. Those who passed Oxford's examinations could call themselves an 'Associate in Arts'. Although Booth had envisaged his national examinations system being created by the state, from their first local examinations in 1858, both universities began to create it instead. As Temple put it, the universities were 'made to feel that they have an interest in the education of all England'.[44] Their local examinations were the direct ancestors of today's General Certificates of Secondary Education (usually known as GCSEs, and once known as O-Levels).[45]

In the meantime, Booth tried to expand the Society's examinations system. In its second year they were held at both the Adelphi and in Huddersfield, accommodating 220 candidates, though Booth had pushed for many more sites. He also insisted on retaining the oral element—he feared that without it, students would simply cram. Without some questioning and discernment on the part of the examiners, he feared that there was no other way to check that candidates had properly understood a subject. The board of examiners agreed. Booth also believed that the opportunity to meet such famous experts in person was an important draw for potential candidates, especially while the Society's qualifications remained relatively untested in terms of helping people acquire jobs and promotions. (To move this along, the Society nominated some of the particularly distinguished candidates for vacancies at the civil service, some of whom were hired as clerks.) Yet the rest of the Council resisted. The Society bore the cost, and sending eminent examiners all over the country by rail was expensive. It would be easier, Chester asserted, to send out written examinations, to be supervised by trustworthy locals. He argued that written examinations would allow a much more rapid and cost-effective expansion of the system.[46]

Impatient, Booth took a step too far. Soon after re-election as the Society's chairman, and with the support of the board of examiners, he proposed that the board be managed separately, also taking sole control of the subscriptions paid by the Institutions in Union. The rest of the Council were outraged—it seemed as though Booth was trying to split the examination board into an entirely separate entity, while taking the Institutions in Union with it. At a meeting of Council, Booth's proposal was labelled a violation of the Society's constitution. He was outvoted nine to one. Henry Cole then stuck in the knife: he moved that Booth be forced to resign as chairman, which was carried.[47] Booth was never involved with the Society again. He spent his remaining years out in the country, experimenting with using sewage as a fertiliser.[48]

The examinations expanded without Booth, mostly under the direction of Harry Chester—using written papers instead of oral examiners, they were soon held cheaply in centres across the country. Yet the examinations did end up being used to create the system that Booth had desired: public examinations, funded and controlled by the state. This was due to the intervention of the Department of Science and Art. Cole and Playfair formulated a plan to accelerate the adoption of examinations. Once again, it came down to incentives. In 1856 they implemented the department's own examinations for drawing, and from 1860 for science. These might have suffered from competition with the Society's examinations, except that Playfair had an idea to make his more popular: he paid the teachers based on the results of their students.[49] Whereas qualifications gave pupils the incentive to learn a subject, payment-by-results gave teachers the incentive to teach them. The effect was dramatic. In chemistry, the most popular of the Society's science subjects, the number of candidates each year rarely exceeded a hundred—until 1862 there were never more than forty. The Department of Science and Art's examinations, backed by payments to teachers, immediately drew in candidates by the hundreds, and after a few years the thousands. Having led the way and shown that examinations for drawing and science worked, the Society eventually dropped those subjects, handing them over to the department entirely.[50]

Payment-by-results soon became the government's favoured tactic for creating the state education system, especially as it required no new legislation. In 1862, the minister responsible for schools, Robert Lowe, was tasked with improving them as rapidly as possible while also doing so cheaply. Following a suggestion from Cole, Lowe introduced payment-by-results in schools for reading, writing, and arithmetic.

Booth's original plan to create the state education system thus proceeded without him. And like he had, those involved also saw it as a
strategy to circumvent religious disputes about control of the schools
themselves. Indeed, Cole and his collaborators even saw payment-by-
results as a means of making the schools more secular: when applied to
science, they were a blow 'against parsonic influence'.[51]

As the government took on the examination of particular subjects,
the Society dropped those and moved onto new ones. The international
exhibitions that followed the Great Exhibition of 1851 provided an opportunity to find out what was being done abroad, and thus work out
which subjects needed to be encouraged next. The Society arranged for
British artisans to visit the exhibitions in Paris, so that they might learn
from what was on show. They found them cheap travel fares, accommodation, and English-speaking guides.[52] They even persuaded the
government to grant the artisans passports free of charge.[53] The artisans'
reports, alongside reports by other official visitors, were then exploited
to push for new reforms.

Lyon Playfair, for example, raised the alarm after the 1867 Paris exhibition about Britain's lack of technical training. The French and other
rivals, he said, were pulling ahead of Britain because they educated their
workers in specific, practical skills such as how to manufacture silk textiles, dye wool, or build carriages. It was another case where the Society
might lead the way, filling in the education system's gaps before another
organisation stepped in. At the suggestion of Playfair's successor at the
Department of Science and Art, John Donnelly, in 1873 the Society
began to hold examinations in technical subjects.[54]

This time, however, the Society's examinations were not taken up by
the government. Instead, payment-by-results came from a private
source: the ancient guilds and livery companies of the City of London.
The guilds had been formed hundreds of years earlier as monopolies on
the city's trades. They had kept out competition while, at least in theory,
maintaining the quality of their products. Over the centuries, however,
the power of London's guilds had weakened. By the 1870s they no longer
regulated anything, but had nonetheless survived on huge endowments.
Their members rarely had much to do with the trades that the guilds

supposedly represented, and were attacked by politicians and the press for frittering their funds on lavish dinners.[55] Some of their funds went towards charitable causes, but they came under increasing pressure to do something more useful, especially if it could serve their ancient supposed aims of improving the quality of Britain's trades. Education, railed the press, was 'a matter of far greater interest than the quality of turtle and venison'.[56]

In 1878, the Society's technical examinations received funding from the Worshipful Company of Clothworkers. It was a trial run. The livery company provided payment-by-results at a rate that matched those of the Department of Science and Art, and teachers leapt at the chance to earn some extra money. The number of candidates for the technical examinations that year increased by over three times, from 68 to 218.[57] Having conducted this trial, some of the Society's members then reported to the guilds on the demand for such examinations throughout the country. A report for the guilds was drawn up by Henry Cole's son-in-law, George Bartley, who was also assistant director at the Department of Science and Art. Later that year, sixteen of the guilds and the City of London together formed a City and Guilds of London Institute (CGLI), which in 1879 took over the Society's technical examinations. The Society's assistant secretary, Henry Trueman Wood, oversaw the handover and was even offered the job of leading the new institute, but turned it down to become the Society's secretary instead.[58] John Donnelly, in the 1880s, even coaxed the new institute to South Kensington (Cole by that point had died). By 1890, the CGLI offered forty-nine technical subjects, taught thousands at its classes, and offered payment-by-results across the country. The organisation still provides technical qualifications today.

Having handed over the technical examinations, the Society attempted to withdraw from examinations altogether. It had tried to do so a number of times, but had given way to the demands of the Institutions in Union. By this stage, the examinations offered by the Society were in commercial subjects, aimed at the kinds of skills needed by merchants and clerks, for example foreign languages, book-keeping, or shorthand.[59] By 1880, however, the cost seemed too great. It was persuaded to keep them, but instead of providing examinations for free, in 1882 the Society began to charge a fee per candidate, also opening them to the public at large. The decision would have huge unintended consequences for the Society in the years that followed, as we shall see in later chapters, though the most immediate consequence was that many mechanics' institutions gradually left the union. Their teachers were, in any case, by that stage receiving much of their funding from the government and the guilds. By 1908, the number of Institutions in Union had halved, to 150. Five years after that, there were only 14.[60]

In the meantime, however, the Society sought to promote other kinds of education, not just the acquisition of skills. Its members hoped to use education to impart habits to the people, to meet many of their own agendas for reform. One of these reformers was Edwin Chadwick, a prominent utilitarian sanitary reformer of the 1840s, who as a young man had been secretary to Jeremy Bentham himself. He had been introduced to the Society by Henry Cole. By the mid-1850s, however, Chadwick had fallen out of favour with the government and was forced out of his role as commissioner of the General Board of Health. He instead used the Society to pursue his obsession with sanitary reform. At the Paris International Exhibition of 1855 he even, as part of the Society's deputation, met Napoleon III of France. Chadwick told him to emulate the first emperor of Rome, Augustus, who boasted that he had found it a city of brick, but left it a city of marble. In this case, however, Chadwick urged the emperor to be able to claim that he 'found Paris stinking and that he left it sweet'. The emperor was reportedly 'a good deal tickled' at this.[61]

For the duration of Chadwick's involvement in the Society, right up until his death in 1890, he had it explore the issue of sewage. Chadwick was especially interested in the possibility of converting human waste into fertiliser for agriculture (which may be why Booth retired from the Society to make his own experiments). In pursuit of his pet project, the Society held conferences on sewage treatments, the pollution of rivers, and the best methods of drainage.[62] It even tried its age-old method of offering a cash prize for the best sanitary pan for 'for collecting pure excreta' ready for use, though nobody seems to have won. A lot of the debate was about whether sewage should be disposed of via water-pipes or dry.[63]

Yet there was also a role in Chadwick's project for education. One of the major problems of public health, believed many of the reformers, was that people did not know better—especially the poor: 'The question of health was very much a question of education.' For example, in the opinion of reformers, many people foolishly kept their windows shut and failed to ventilate the 'foul air' from their homes.[64] The Society attempted to use its examinations and exhibitions to impart better habits.

Another of the major driving forces behind this was Thomas Twining, a relative of the famous tea merchants, who wished to 'promote health, comfort and economy among the industrial classes'. Health was connected with domestic economy—the management of households. At the Paris exhibition of 1855, Twining was given permission to select many of the cheapest yet highest-quality articles on display to form a special 'economic' section. It was a display of the items with the highest value for money for the poor. Upon his return to Britain, Twining created a more permanent display for the Society, which in 1857 was donated to South Kensington (it eventually became the Food Museum, later absorbed by the London Science Museum).[65]

A few years later, the Society also formed a committee to investigate the 'Food of the People', to prevent malnutrition among the working classes. The reformers were particularly worried about the spread of foot-and-mouth disease in cattle. Cows died, and so the price of meat and milk rose. The committee investigated ways to solve the problem, for example by importing meat from Australia, where cows were plentiful and killed mostly for leather, their meat and milk wasted.[66] Imports of food from so far afield were increasingly achieved using new techniques like refrigeration, but the Society's role was educational. It had the various preserved foods displayed at exhibitions, to get the public more accustomed to these alternative sources of nutrition.

It was in cooking, however, that the Society was most active. The reformers feared that the fault of malnutrition largely lay with the people preparing it. It was a matter of ignorance: poor cooking was, they felt, 'one of the greatest evils of the day'. Indeed, one proposal to the Food of the People Committee was for the meals of the poor to be cooked in giant kitchens and then sent for delivery on carts (the idea was ahead of its time but was ignored).[67] Instead, the Society tried to educate. From 1860 it included domestic economy among the subjects for examination, and in 1873 it aided the Royal Commission for the Great Exhibition of 1851 in launching a lecture series on cooking, billed as a 'School of Popular Cookery', at that year's International Exhibition at South Kensington. Queen Victoria herself attended a lecture on how to prepare an omelette.[68] The Society helped raise funds to turn it into a more permanent National Training School for Cookery. The Society established scholarships to train female teachers at the new school, and added cookery as yet another subject in its examinations. (The National Training School for Cookery lasted until 1962.)[69]

Otherwise, the Society's educational initiatives were about filling in perceived gaps. Anything felt to be lacking from the state's growing system, the Society tried to provide. Much of the attention towards education, for example, had been focused on boys and men. Yet in 1870 this began to change. That year, at the urging of utilitarian reformers, Parliament passed an act requiring local authorities to provide enough schools in their areas to cover the entire population. The Society had played a role in building support for the law, commissioning Cole's son-in-law, George Bartley, to conduct a survey of schools in an especially poor area of East London. The report that he produced shocked its readers: two thirds of the children in the area had received no schooling. The Society commissioned further reports on other parts of London. With the backing of this kind of propaganda, the law had gained public support and been passed, despite the misgivings of the religious associations. The 1870 Elementary Education Act stipulated the creation of elected local educational boards, tasked with ensuring that every child in the area had access to a school, even enabling them to raise local taxes. The law also created an especially powerful elected body, the London School Board, which had an unusual feature: women could stand and vote in its elections.[70]

Cole and the Society took an interest in who won. They collected and disseminated information about the candidates, hoping that the London School Board could be yet another body to take up the Society's projects (the hope was justified, as it later took over the Society's reviews of military drill). The election also introduced them to a prominent campaigner for equal education for girls, Maria Grey. She was frustrated that state funds and private endowments for secondary schooling went, disproportionately, to the education of boys. In England and Wales, of over 1,300 endowed schools, girls were taught at only 14. When the London School Board elections were announced in 1870, Grey was approached about standing for election. She had declined, feeling it was too unusual a thing for a woman to do. But later, when listening to a Sunday sermon in church, she had reportedly become ashamed of her cowardice and decided to enter the fray. A position on the London School Board would, after all, provide an opportunity to promote secondary schooling for girls.[71]

She lost, narrowly. But Grey's election campaign had a much wider impact. It introduced her to both Bartley and Cole, who encouraged her to present her ideas to the Society. It was, after all, the place to address the education system's gaps. She wrote a formal letter to the Society requesting its help, which Cole appears to have presented to the Council—Cole's wife, Marian, was a signatory. He persuaded the Society to appoint a 'Ladies Committee'.[72] It invited Grey to give a lecture to the Society, and within a few weeks of that, the Society gave her its support: although the education of boys 'is far from satisfactory', it announced, 'that of girls is still more defective'.[73] Something had to be done. Grey's case for girls' education was presented to the annual conference of the Institutions in Union, at which were also present the newly elected representatives of the local educational boards. Many of them were supportive.

Grey and the Ladies Committee thus felt emboldened, on 25 August 1871, to announce in the Society's *Journal* the impending creation of a National Union for the Improvement of the Education of Women of All Classes (later shortened to the Women's Education Union). It was inaugurated at the Society later that year. Its aims were to fight 'the indifference of parents and the ignorance and apathy of the general public', and to combine the country's isolated campaigns for female education into a cohesive push for reform.[74] The Society allowed Grey to hold the National Union's committee meetings in its rooms, though it refused to take control of the campaign. The Society felt it had done enough.[75] It was up to Grey to continue. She toured the country, delivering lectures to drum up support. But the problem, she found, was that it was 'hopeless to persuade hard-hearted men to contribute to the establishment of really good public schools for the opposite sex'.[76] If they would not endow girls' schools for charity, then perhaps they would do it for profit instead. In 1872 the National Union announced the creation of a limited liability company to create schools for girls: The Girls' Public Day School Company. Sold at five pounds a share, its profit came from tuition fees at the schools it built. Over the next twenty-five years it opened thirty-eight schools, by 1900 preparing over seven thousand girls each year for the local examinations run by Oxford and Cambridge. The company's schools taught many of the early entrants to the first women's university colleges, as well as training many celebrated headmistresses. (The organisation continues to this day, though in 1905 it was converted to a charitable trust.)[77]

Thus, Maria Grey's campaign for girls' education took advantage of many of the other systems that the Society had helped to create, including limited liability, public examinations, and the Institutions in Union. It even took advantage of Cole's Department of Science and Art, which provided some funding. Indeed, the Girls' Public Day School Company launched at the Royal Albert Hall, a building that Cole had created to cater to yet another of the Society's educational projects: improving the standard of Britain's music.

In the mid-nineteenth century, Britain's musicians were widely considered to be mediocre. Cole, for example, believed that music had been in decline since the Reformation,[78] perhaps with the exception of George Frederick Handel, who in any case had been an immigrant from Germany and had died about a century previously. Music was ever more popular with the people, but many felt that this simply worsened the situation: the increasing demand allowed even the most mediocre of musicians to thrive. There was no impetus to improve. The problem was with Britain's musical education, which was widely considered to be of such poor quality as to 'render further neglect of the art impossible'. Although a Royal Academy of Music had existed since 1822, it was barely able to support itself financially. Nor was it very good. As one critic unabashedly put it, by 1859 'not one single artist, capable of doing England, or the Academy, or music, credit before the public, has issued thence'.[79] Lacking high-quality musicians to emulate, the rest of the population also followed suit. Although Britain had a popular tradition of public singing, it was apparently without much tune: 'the people roar and scream, because they have heard nothing but roaring and screaming'.[80]

English musicians who wished to master their art were forced to train abroad. This, at least, was the experience of John Hullah, who had been trained at the Royal Academy of Music, and had consequently been unsuccessful as a composer. A trip to Paris, however, changed everything. He paid attention to foreign teaching methods, which he then brought back to England. In 1840, to demonstrate the foreign methods, Hullah taught some boys from the workhouses near Battersea to sing. Clad in green uniforms, the boys astonished audiences and gained national fame as 'Hullah's Greenbirds'. Hullah soon taught pupils and music teachers across the country, although his success was more down to his natural enthusiasm and charm, rather than the method he used (later shown to be technically deficient). Hullah's teaching, along with the methods developed by his imitators and rivals, began a Victorian craze for singing.

As the country's most famous teacher of music, Hullah was appointed to the Society's committee to oversee its 1854 exhibition of educational appliances.[81] In fact, the exhibition was held at a music hall he had built, St Martin's Hall (it no longer exists). Later that year he became a member of the Society.[82] It was also on Hullah's urging that the Society looked into ways to improve the country's provision of musical education. Singing had once been considered a potential vice of the working classes—an activity that took place most often in the pub, making it a route to laziness and diversion.[83] Hullah used his platform at the Society of Arts to explode this notion. Learning music, he claimed, did the very opposite: it required and cultivated intellectual discipline, much like learning the grammar of a foreign language. More than a foreign tongue, music was a language that was universal, understood and appreciated by 'every people and every age'. It was a great unifier. Mastering it, particularly the ability to read music or 'hear with one's eyes', required patience, temperance, attention, obedience, and punctuality—all of the morally healthy virtues of Victorian self-denial. Instead of encouraging the working classes to the pub, a greater appreciation of singing drew them to the churches. Singing was a gateway to religious faith.[84]

With this moralising mission, it was essential that musical education be extended as far as possible. Hullah was its 'chief apostle', and captured the imaginations of both Harry Chester and Henry Cole. Indeed, Chester noted that music was an effective way of persuading local authorities to fund schools in their areas: when a school in Liverpool had been threatened with closure, it sent a marching band through the town. It 'excited quite a furore of admiration and interest, and the school was saved'.[85] Music was effective propaganda in the reformers' mission to expand education. It made education more visible, and audible, to the people who controlled it.

Hullah lectured for free at many of the Society's Institutions in Union, and in 1859 persuaded the Society to offer an examination in musical theory. Naturally, Hullah was appointed the Society's examiner. Of the different ways to make music, singing was the one to promote first. It was the most accessible to the masses as there was no need to buy expensive instruments. Some people of course possessed better natural ability than others, but Hullah believed that almost everyone might be taught to sing to a standard 'to give no offence to their neighbours'.

Singing was just the start—a basis from which the playing of musical instruments might also then be improved. But teaching and improving music still faced a major technological obstacle: musical instruments were not all made to a standard pitch.[86] The note 'A', for example, might be much higher on one instrument than on another—when played, the vibration of the particles of air might be faster. Within a single country, perhaps on a single street, the pitches of even the same kinds of instruments could vary widely depending on their makers. There was no problem when it came to singing without instruments—the singer could simply choose a pitch with which they were comfortable. But singing accompanied, or playing instruments in concert, introduced major challenges. How was a singer supposed to learn to pitch a note from written music, to 'hear with their eyes', when the instruments could be so different? Music was supposed to be a universal language, but in practice the composition of one country would sound rather different abroad.

In the eighteenth century, when Handel had composed his music, his note 'A' had a pitch of about 422 vibrations per second (a unit now called Hertz, abbreviated as Hz). By the mid-nineteenth century, however, the pitch usually adopted by orchestras had risen to 435 Hz. There was a widespread perception that pitch was gradually rising—a change that was easy to make to instruments, but not to voices. Singers complained that they were being forced to sing at ever higher registers, thereby straining their vocal chords. To stop the pitch inflation, in 1859 the French government decreed that the note 'A' would correspond to 435 Hz. A tuning fork set to 435 Hz was duly deposited in the Paris Conservatory for future reference.

Having heard of these reforms abroad, Harry Chester suggested that the Society of Arts investigate whether a standard pitch might also be adopted in Britain.[87] Standardisation in any case appealed to utilitarians. Agreeing upon a standard, however, would involve a unique combination of science and art—the kind of problem that the Society of Arts was well suited to solve. And it would involve politics. There was no preeminent musical authority in Britain, particularly given the weaknesses of the Royal Academy of Music, and adopting a standard would mean reconciling a wide range of interests. The kind of pitch favoured at the opera, set high to show off the impressive vocal ranges of the singers, would undoubtedly strain the voices of everybody else. But lowering the pitch of military bands and church organs would involve significant cost in changing or replacing the instruments. As a relative outsider to the world of music, and with the prestige to assemble all of the relevant parties round the table, the Society of Arts seemed a suitable organisation to oversee the negotiations. Everybody agreed that there should be a universal pitch. The question was, which one?

The assembled parties in 1860 settled on 'A' at a pitch of 440 Hz.[88] The Society had tuning forks made, and musical instrument makers thereafter sold copies. Yet its recommended pitch was not widely adopted, and some years later it rescinded its recommendation, instead resolving that it would be better to conform to French pitch for the purposes of international standardisation. Nonetheless, the Society's original 1860 recommendation had been ahead of its time: in the mid-twentieth century, 'A' at 440 Hz was adopted as the world's standard pitch.

With its new-found involvement in music, the Society soon became the target of other would-be musical reformers. For years, Henry Cole had been trying to bring the Royal Academy of Music to South Kensington. He had a personal love of music, almost as great as his love of art: his most memorable present was a black ebony flute with silver keys, which had been given to him by his father when he was 13. As a young man Cole held musical parties at his house, and was a huge fan of choirs. He had campaigned since the 1850s for there to be a music hall at South Kensington, eventually getting his way with the building of the Royal Albert Hall. In the mid-1860s Cole even formed a committee at the Society of Arts to again look into the issue of acquiring the Royal Academy of Music for South Kensington, but he could not get the funds.[89]

Foiled, Cole decided to set up his own institution. In 1873 he had the Society campaign for the establishment of a National Training School for Music. Cole opened a public subscription to endow musical scholarships at the school, and organised fundraising concerts at the recently opened Royal Albert Hall. The concerts, however, made a loss, and Cole was unable to raise the cash for even a hundred endowed scholarships—less than a third of his target. Nonetheless, he eventually found a benefactor for the scheme in one of his neighbours, a building developer named Charles Freake. Freake agreed to erect the building for the school in exchange for the underlying land, owned by the Royal Commission for the Great Exhibition of 1851. It agreed. (Some years later, Freake gifted the land back to the nation, for which he was made a baronet.) And in typical Cole fashion it was his son, H. H. Cole, who designed the building. The National Training School for Music opened in 1876, its first principal the composer Arthur Sullivan (one half of the comic opera duo Gilbert and Sullivan, who together wrote *H.M.S. Pinafore*, *The Pirates of Penzance*, and *The Mikado*). It did not last long, however, due to lack of funds—the subscription money had all gone towards scholarships, and even these were insufficient. 'My hand was always in my pocket to help some poor student get daily food', Sullivan complained. In 1882, the school was subsumed into a newly chartered Royal College of Music, an organisation with far more funding and official support.[90]

Overall, due to the influence of the Great Exhibition of 1851, the Society became the tool of educational reformers. Although it had begun by offering support for a bottom-up movement for education, this soon came into conflict with the plans of utilitarian reformers like James Booth, Edwin Chadwick, and Henry Cole, who created a top-down, state-led system. They used the Society to fill in the gaps as they emerged—in domestic economy, the education of girls, and in music. Yet the influence of the Great Exhibition did not stop there. While reformers like Cole built systems to spread beauty to the masses, the exhibition changed the way people thought about how beauty was made.

9

A Society against Ugliness

THE GREAT EXHIBITION OF 1851 had another major effect. As an industrial audit of the world, it included exhibits from Britain's empire, as well as from foreign nations. The East India Company, a private company which at that point exercised control over almost all of the Indian subcontinent, provided displays of the products of India and further afield. The aim was to reveal to merchants and manufacturers in Britain the kinds of raw materials that might be imported, 'furnishing materials for Englishmen to work upon'.[1]

India's own manufactures, such as woven cotton, which had once been popular in Britain, had been displaced by the machinery of the British Industrial Revolution. Over the course of the early nineteenth century, cheap British machine-spun and machine-woven cloths gradually replaced Indian manufactures from their age-old export markets in Britain and the rest of Europe. Indian hand-loom weavers, although they were paid very little, could not compete with Britain's more efficient water- and then steam-driven machines. Wages could only go so low. By the 1850s, British machine-made cloths were being sold in India itself, displacing even its domestic market for manufactures. Indian workers left manufacturing and instead went into the production of raw materials, which were increasingly profitable due to the need to fuel Britain's industries.

One of the purposes of the Great Exhibition was to enable Britain to economically evaluate its empire: in the words of Henry Cole, to gain 'the best practical notion of the value of our East Indian possessions'.[2]

The exhibition revealed various unfamiliar plant fibres, saps, vegetable oils, ores, and animal hairs which might find a market in Britain.[3] This kind of activity—bringing the products of Britain's colonies to the attention of merchants and manufacturers in Britain itself—was an extension of the Society's activities over the previous century. Instead of awarding premiums for exploiting new resources, however, it now focused on the spread of information.

It encouraged people throughout the empire to create local versions of the Society of Arts, to keep up the exchange of information. The only one known to survive to the present day is a Society for the Encouragement of Arts, Manufactures and Commerce in Malta—one that was directly connected to the Great Exhibition itself. It was founded in 1852 by William Reid, who had been the chairman of the exhibition's executive committee and thus Henry Cole's boss. As a result of his services to the exhibition, in 1851 Reid had been knighted and appointed Malta's governor. Members of these colonial versions of the Society of Arts were given the same membership rights when they visited London, and were encouraged to give lectures.

The Society also began to attract a membership outside of Britain—a former prime minister of Canada, R. B. Bennett, was briefly its president. In 1939, the Society even had an Indian chairman of Council, Atul Chatterjee (earlier, in 1896, he had been the first Indian to beat all British competitors in the examinations for the Indian Civil Service, and was the second Indian to be High Commissioner for India—the country's representative in London).[4] Many Indians joined the Society in the 1860s, including Dadabhai Naoroji, who came to be known as the Grand Old Man of India.[5] Naoroji became a member in 1861, was a financial guarantor for the Society's International Exhibition of 1862, and in the 1870s gave a number of lectures to the Society on the Indian economy, in which he criticised the British policy of encouraging India to produce only raw materials. (Naoroji would later become Britain's first properly elected Indian member of Parliament, and was a key figure in India's path to independence.)[6] Black Africans also joined the Society as members from at least the late 1860s, and often took part in discussions.[7]

With its increasingly diverse membership, the Society became one of the main places in London to hear lectures about the colonies. It was also a place where the ensuing discussion would be conducted by more than just experts on colonial affairs. They were joined by scientists, inventors, manufacturers, artists, civil servants, and politicians, as well as anyone else who happened to be interested. One of the most popular lectures at the Society was on the discovery, in 1851, of new deposits of gold in Australia—the gold rush began at the same time as the Great Exhibition.[8] Visitors might otherwise come to the Society to hear a discussion of Indian timbers or the agricultural industries of Jamaica. The Society's *Journal*, as its main conduit for information, could in a single bulletin mention Alberta's wheat crop, Australian trade statistics, Nigerian tin-mining, New Zealand's milk cooperatives, and South African sugar plantations.[9]

As well as the colonies' raw materials, the Society also later explored social movements, policies, and culture. The Society aimed, at least in theory, to make people in Britain feel a part of the wider empire (and later the Commonwealth). Many of the Society's members were involved in a 'Colonial and Indian Exhibition', held in 1886 at South Kensington. They also raised some of the money for the Imperial Institute—an organisation, founded in 1888, to hold further colonial exhibitions and act as a clearing house for information about the empire (it soon joined the complex of cultural institutions at South Kensington). In the twentieth century, too, the Society offered prizes for contributions to the cultural and economic progress of the empire, as well as prizes for journalism and documentary films in the Commonwealth. The Society of Arts continued its discussions of the Commonwealth right up until 1988. Yet it was just one arena among many. Already by the early twentieth century, it had to compete with a Royal Empire Society, a Victoria League, an Overseas League, an Imperial Relations Trust, a League of Empire, and even a British Empire League, not to mention countless other societies specialising in the discussion of particular regions.[10]

Yet the impact of the Great Exhibition's Indian exhibits went far beyond just the sharing of information about raw materials. It was India's manufactures, not its raw materials, that caused the greatest sensation.

Visitors to the Crystal Palace in 1851 marvelled at the beauty of Indian design, especially 'the general feeling for art which may be found in the humblest classes of workmen.'[11] *The Times* raved that the Indian section was the Great Exhibition's most beautiful and interesting section. Even an eminent visitor from France—French designs were widely considered to be the best in Europe—exclaimed that Indians must be 'the Frenchmen of the East'. The revelation of Indian design was, said the Frenchman, 'a revolution.'[12] To reformers like Henry Cole and his colleague Richard Redgrave, the beauty of Indian designs to European eyes suggested that aesthetics were not peculiar to particular peoples or countries, but might in fact be universal. There might, they thought, be 'true principles of design'—universal laws, much like in the sciences, which might govern what was beautiful and what was not.

To discover the universal principles of design, however, they would need to get their hands on many more designs from around the world. While the Great Exhibition was still in progress, Cole put in motion plans for a colonial exhibition, to be held in London in 1853. The Society also set to work collecting designs from China and Japan. They even managed to obtain the loan, from a Dutch museum, of a map of Japan. This was especially rare, as exporting a map of Japan from the country was punishable by death. But the exhibition did not happen—the Society lacked the funds and a site. Instead, on Albert's suggestion, the Society sent the oriental collections to the 1853 international exhibition in Dublin, where they might receive a wider audience—over a million visitors, it turned out, though this was fewer than expected. They caused a sensation: the exhibits from Japan, reported one newspaper, 'indicate a degree of civilization there on some matters which is truly surprising.'[13]

Indian design particularly impressed one of the people who had been responsible for decorating the Great Exhibition: an artist named Owen Jones. He, like Cole and Redgrave, began to investigate the true 'principles of design'. Jones felt that European design was often, by comparison, gaudy and over-ornamented. Indian craftsmen were able to masterfully abstract from natural objects or devise attractive patterns in a way that Europeans seemingly could not. The problem, Jones surmised, was

9.1. One of the Indian designs that so impressed visitors to the Great Exhibition of 1851, in this case an embroidery in white silk on black net. Image from plate 56 of Matthew Digby Wyatt's *Industrial Arts of the Nineteenth Century*, which illustrated the exhibition's 'choicest specimens'. RSA/SC/EX/1/98.

that British manufacturers had become separated from their tradition of making things themselves. By relying on machinery, unlike in India, where most things were produced by hand, British manufacturers had ceased to be craftsmen. Indeed, the high quality of English medieval designs seemed to confirm this. What ancient England and mid-nineteenth-century India had in common was that they had not become industrialised.

Jones was not the first to note this, but his writings on the subject placed a century of assumptions on their head: the high art of painting and sculpture did not simply trickle down to manufacturers, as people like Joshua Reynolds had insisted in the 1760s; instead, good design often came from below, from the slowly accumulated traditions of un-educated craftsmen. It was essential that the people who designed things were also the people who made them. Mechanised factories, by contrast, separated the makers from their creations—they lost their feel for materials, their subtle, tacit understanding of processes that could only emerge through years of practice, if not decades of tradition passed down from generation to generation. It was no wonder, thought Jones, that British design had become 'decadent' and over-stylised. Because of industrialisation, Britain had lost its tradition of craftsmanship. Cole, Redgrave, and other reformers agreed, as did art critics like John Ruskin, who had already noticed the apparent superiority of ancient English craftsmanship.[14] Ruskin's writings, in turn, heavily influenced a young William Morris, who was to become an intellectual founder of the movement to reverse the decline: Arts and Crafts.

Morris reportedly attended the Great Exhibition himself: aged 17, he had got as far as the door and refused to go any further, finding its con-tents 'wonderfully ugly'.[15] Yet he later exhibited items from his own workshop at the Society's 1862 International Exhibition, winning two gold medals and a special citation from the prize jury for the colour and design of his stained glass. Applying his belief in the value of craftsman-ship, Morris's workshop established a reputation for furniture, jewellery, tiles, metalware, and especially wallpapers. Most significantly, however, Morris preached what he practised, influencing many others through his speeches and writings.

The Society of Arts, too, played its role. In 1863, it aided the Society of Wood Carvers by holding an exhibition in its rooms, offering some money and a medal for the exhibition's prizes. Soon, the Society began to offer prizes for art-workmanship, which lasted until 1870. After Owen Jones died, too, a prize was established in 1878 in his name, distributed by the Society to the best students trained by the Department of Science and Art. In the same year, with the aid of a grant from one of the guilds, the Drapers' Company, the Society even helped establish a School of Art Wood-Carving (it eventually made its way to South Kensington, but in the early twentieth century failed due to lack of funding).[16] Whereas Cole had once tried to persuade professional artists to apply their talents to manufactures, he and his allies now wished to encourage workers themselves to develop their talents as craftsmen.

The art-workmanship prizes and exhibitions were revived in the 1880s at the instigation of Cole.[17] William Morris himself was occasionally a judge of the prizes, though apparently an unreliable one—he rarely turned up to meetings and often turned down invitations. Nonetheless, the Society was gradually drawn into the orbit of the movement he had inspired. In 1889 the Society collaborated on an exhibition with the Arts and Crafts Exhibition Society, founded by an artist and book illustrator, Walter Crane. The exhibition was discontinued the following year, and the Society's activities shifted almost entirely to hosting lectures on the subject, but people like Crane remained involved. By the early twentieth century, many of the Society's most active members were adherents to Morris's Arts and Crafts philosophy.

Morris's influence extended beyond the kinds of things he produced in his workshops, to buildings too: in 1877 he and a friend, the architect Philip Webb, founded a Society for the Protection of Ancient Buildings. They issued a manifesto, decrying what they saw as the 'strange and most fatal idea' of restoration. Old buildings, they claimed, were being ruined by people who sought to repair them. Restorers perpetrated a 'forgery' by attempting to reproduce the techniques and styles of bygone ages, in the process often damaging or ruining the buildings themselves. To Morris and Webb, modern people could not create a medieval building, or even recreate one, because they did not draw upon the same traditions of craftsmanship, nor the same beliefs. A modern person might have the same tools, or even more efficient tools, but Morris and Webb believed that what mattered was the worker's heart, not just his hands. 'Modern art', they argued, 'cannot meddle without destroying'.

Morris and Webb instead called for preservation, keeping old buildings as they were, staving off decay through daily care. If repairs were necessary—a prop for a sagging wall here, or a covering for a leaky roof there—then they should be done without the pretence of making them look older than they really were. Instead of making old buildings look like they had been in the past, preservation entailed keeping them useful and clearly defining what had been added. If old buildings could not be preserved, they argued, then they should be torn down and replaced with something new and better rather than attempt to ape the old. Restoration was an ugly insult to the past, they argued, not flattery.[18]

Morris and Webb were not the first, however, to seek to preserve old buildings. When they wrote their manifesto, the Society of Arts was already trying to persuade the owners of old buildings to preserve them. In 1866, George Bartley proposed that the Society begin a scheme to place small signs on buildings in London, describing the name and dates of a famous person who had once lived there. Bartley seems to have been inspired by the suggestion of William Ewart, the utilitarian Member of Parliament who had secured for local authorities the ability to raise taxes to pay for libraries. Ewart had proposed the idea of memorial signs as a way to celebrate people who had done much for the arts, sciences, and culture. Military generals, after all, already received statues.[19] For Bartley, however, directing people's attention to the historical associations of a building would serve another agenda. It would, he hoped, make them value the building more, making them think twice before tearing it down. London, Bartley feared, was quickly becoming uglier. The old buildings needed to be 'preserved from the ruthless hands of modern destroyers and improvers'.[20]

The Society took up Bartley's suggestion. The company of Cole's old friend, the potter Herbert Minton, produced two blue, round, ceramic plaques, one to indicate the birthplace of the poet Lord Byron in Holles Street, and the other the one-time residence of the French emperor,

Napoleon III, which in 1867 were affixed to the buildings' facades. The Society then proceeded to create more plaques, arranging with the owners to allow them to be affixed, while also publishing a long list of other historical residences that they thought might deserve them.[21] The idea was that individuals and other organisations would also commission their own memorial plaques for their buildings. Although a few shopowners put up their own signs, there was little response.[22] The Society affixed thirty-five memorial plaques, until in 1901 it persuaded London County Council to take on the scheme. Most of its plaques were by then a chocolate brown, as the blue was too expensive, but the plaques have since become well-known as the Blue Plaques, run since 1986 by English Heritage. At the time of writing there are over nine hundred blue plaques dotted across London. Despite their eventual popularity, however, the plaques only rarely preserved old London from the 'ruthless hands of modern destroyers' as Bartley had intended. The building with the very first blue plaque, for Byron, was demolished twenty-two years later (Napoleon III's at 1C King Street, Westminster, is now the oldest surviving). Indeed, almost half of the buildings that received the Society's plaques were destroyed.[23]

The preservationists needed to take more active measures. The Society for the Protection of Ancient Buildings was only one of many initiatives that emerged in the late nineteenth century, along with the National Trust, founded in 1895 to purchase old buildings that were in danger of destruction. Parliament also occasionally legislated to protect certain structures, starting in 1882 with prehistoric sites. Yet the pace of change to technology and the economy in the early twentieth century threatened further destruction. In the 1920s, the Society of Arts became a new focal point of the movement to preserve.

Many of the early efforts were successful when it came to preserving monuments, mills, and other large buildings, but in 1920 the architect Alfred Hoare Powell lectured at the Society of Arts on the need to preserve old cottages, some dating from the fourteenth century. They were, he said, 'the very gist of English country', and had been a comforting and encouraging memory to soldiers during the terrors and upheaval of the First World War. England's ancient cottages, he asserted, were monuments to a long-lost democratic age of medieval community. Yet they were threatened with development, especially the introduction of laws in the late nineteenth century to demolish unsanitary houses and replace them with new ones. With the Public Health Act of 1904, too, it became illegal for landlords to let properties below sanitary standards. Most of the oldest cottages, which, had been lived in for centuries, were partitioned into cramped, small rooms, and did not have proper drainage or plumbing. The original craftsmen in the fourteenth century had usually not even built foundations, so the buildings were slowly disappearing. Nonetheless, pleaded Powell, their beautiful exteriors might still be preserved while their interiors were made sanitary: 'no old cottage need be condemned to destruction that has its outer shell still in fair condition.'[24]

The problem was finding the money to pay for it. The secretary of the Society for the Protection of Ancient Buildings was in the room, and spoke of a particular case in need of preservation, but said he lacked the funds for it. Within a month, however, an anonymous benefactor promised him five hundred pounds.[25] The Society of Arts, it seemed, had provided a platform for action. A few years later, in 1926, the situation had only worsened, and so a group of campaigners called upon the Society to do something about it. Sanitation laws were one thing, but roads were also now being widened to make way for the motor car, leading to the destruction of many old homes. Even the Society's own building had been affected: the widening of the Strand had revealed the Adelphi's bare-brick behind, so they beautified it with some pilasters and statues so that it looked more like the front.[26]

The campaign was led by another devotee of William Morris, the architect Frank Baines. He was head of Her Majesty's Office of Works, essentially the government's architect-in-chief, responsible for the upkeep of ancient monuments as well as the development of new buildings. He had overseen the construction of state-owned terraced houses in the Arts and Crafts style as well as leading preservation work on many of the country's most famous churches, abbeys, cathedrals, and palaces. But the law did not allow him to do anything about inhabited dwellings. Ancient cottages were private property, so it was up to the landlords to preserve them. For Baines to preserve ancient cottages, he needed to educate the landlords. For that, he needed a popular campaign. His platform was the Society of Arts.

'The movement for preservation', as Baines called it, was to create a fund for the preservation of ancient cottages, which would undertake its own preservation work to serve as an example to others. The Society would act as convenor, using its prestige to assemble everyone with an interest in preservation, to draw on its connections with potential donors, and to use the *Journal* to collect and disseminate information. At the beginning of 1927, the fund was inaugurated: the prime minister himself, Stanley Baldwin, gave the opening address. Baines wrote it for him.[27] Thus, Baldwin decried the architecture of industrialisation— 'those abortions of red brick and slate which have arisen with such alacrity'.[28] Preservation, however, was not only a cause for Baldwin's Conservative Party. At the first meeting of the subscribers to the new fund, the opening address was given by Baldwin's rival, the Labour leader Ramsay MacDonald. Both of them used their platforms to quote William Morris. Preservation was popular.

The Society's fund undertook its own preservation work across the country. One well-wishing landlady donated a cottage in Hertfordshire, which she lacked the means to preserve. A couple more were bequeathed. In a few other cases the Society used the fund to purchase small groups of cottages—three here, a row there—saving them from being condemned. In 1929, the Society took a further step to make the campaign more visible. Instead of preserving isolated cottages, it decided to purchase an entire village, or at least as much as it could acquire. It was a publicity statement, but an effective one. The Society purchased and preserved almost the entire village of West Wycombe, in Buckinghamshire—about fifty cottages, some of them from Tudor times, but a few condemned by the sanitary inspectors, along with a fifteenth-century 'church loft' and two inns. Much of the money came from American donors, keen to preserve an idyllic vision of their ancestral country.

Yet the Society's main achievement was not to do the actual preservation work, but rather to initiate a mass movement. Baines had to resign from the campaign in 1928 due to ill health (or perhaps due to the pressure of living a double life—he had a secret wife and child who knew nothing about his real identity until he died). The person who took over, however, another Arts and Crafts architect named P. Morley Horder, travelled the country, negotiating with local authorities to prevent cottage demolitions, and speaking at impassioned local gatherings. His interventions saved over thirty cottages near Shrewsbury, and the Society's *Journal* soon teemed with new reports.

In 1931, it reported that John Maynard Keynes, the famous economist, in his capacity as bursar of King's College, Cambridge, had handed over a large tract of land in Ruislip to a residents' association for preservation. In another case, one member of the Society, Alfred Bossom, engaged in public correspondence on behalf of the Society with the Minister of Transport, having him publicly condemn any suggestion of a new road being built through West Wycombe—in his correspondence Bossom cited support for the campaign from Baldwin, MacDonald, and even the queen. (Bossom became an MP later that year and would later become a chairman of the Society's Council too. In the 1950s he became a political mentor to a young Conservative activist named Margaret Roberts, and walked her down the aisle for her marriage to Denis Thatcher.)

The campaign soon expanded beyond preservation of ancient cottages—the Society's work to preserve an entire village had people writing to the *Journal* to deplore all manner of new assaults on the beauty of the English countryside. They attacked the spread of roadside advertisement billboards, 'shouting customer's wares across the peaceful fields of England', along with unsightly petrol stations (then known as motor spirit stations).[29] At a conference in Oxford, one especially passionate activist for the Society of Arts even called for citizens to pull down disfiguring advertisements themselves, 'chancing the long arm of the law'. He said he had seen it done in America. Morley Horder called the activist's inflammatory comments 'eloquent and wise'.[30]

The movement coincided with another that had been founded in 1926, the Council for the Preservation of Rural England, which lent its support while condemning urban sprawl (the CPRE still exists, though the words in the acronym have changed slightly). Stanley Baldwin even expressed anxiety about the proliferation of separate societies dealing with the preservation of England's beauty—he called for a single 'Royal Society of England' to educate the public and prevent fresh ugliness.[31] The satirical magazine *Punch* recommended a 'Society for the Exhibition of Ugliness'.[32]

The campaign to preserve ancient cottages eventually subsided. In 1934, when the work was complete, the Society handed West Wycombe over to the National Trust. The various other cottages it preserved were likewise donated to appropriate organisations that would maintain them. Yet the campaign to preserve England's beauty was only a part of the Society's campaign against ugliness. It also sought to create beauty that was new.

At Powell's first talk in 1920, one of the discussants had been the Irish playwright and socialist George Bernard Shaw. Like much of the rest of the Society, Shaw had been heavily influenced by the writings of William Morris. Yet instead of preserving ancient buildings, he recommended their enforced demolition every twenty years. The problem, Shaw argued, was not that the old buildings were being destroyed, but that the new buildings were so ugly. Preservation, counter-intuitively, was 'one of the reasons why so much of our building work was bad', adding that Britain 'had got into the habit of sponging off the past'. Were craftsmen actually competent, Shaw argued, the country would have no reason to fear demolition.

Making craftsmen competent, however, was difficult. The nineteenth century had seen industrialisation, which had already been criticised for separating the makers from their creations. The early twentieth century saw mass production on an even greater scale. Yet in responding to this challenge, the Arts and Crafts movement were split. Some, like Walter Crane, were purists—they believed that craftsmanship could never be reconciled with the tools of modern industry. The world industrialised around them, so the only hope was to keep the traditions of craftsmanship alive.

Another of Morris's disciples, however, Lewis Foreman Day, took a more pragmatic approach. Like Crane, Day was heavily involved with the Society. He was one of the examiners at the Department of Science and Art, and became a long-standing member of the Society's Council. He even designed the *Journal*'s front cover from 1904 to 1911. Unlike Crane, however, Day argued that industry was here to stay, and so they had a duty to ensure its products were beautiful. Although he died in 1910, Day's more pragmatic approach to industry was the one that would prove more influential in the Society.[33] The Society was, after all, an organisation that included industrialists, inventors, and manufacturers, as well as artists.

An opportunity to put Day's thoughts into action soon presented itself. The Department of Science and Art had merged, in 1899, with the Committee of the Privy Council on Education, to form the first Board of Education (later the Department of Education). In 1915, the board decided to cancel its annual competition for the best design students at its schools of art, which meant that the Society's Owen Jones prizes could not be awarded. It was a silk manufacturer, Frank Warner, who stepped in to save them. Warner was heavily influenced by the Arts and Crafts movement. His father, whom he eulogised in the same breath as William Morris, had employed both Owen Jones and Walter Crane to execute some textile designs.[34] He agreed with Day that the age of mass manufacture deserved to be beautiful. Machinery, he pointed out, could 'produce the most beautiful designs as easily as the most detestable'. In fact, he believed Morris and Crane had gone too far. They had created a prejudice among art teachers towards machine-made goods, which meant they discouraged students from applying their talents to industry. It was no wonder, said Warner, that machinery produced a 'mass of gaudy, cheap, horrible rubbish'.[35]

In 1917, Warner persuaded the Society of Arts to save the Owen Jones prizes, which continued in association with the Victoria and Albert Museum (the successor to the South Kensington Museum). The judge from the V&A was Henry Cole's son, Alan Summerly Cole, who managed its textiles. Given Warner's own profession, the reconstituted prizes were initially only for the best textiles by design students, but by 1920 had expanded to other subjects too. In 1923, Warner had the Society reconstitute the prizes entirely, as annual competitions of industrial design. Rather than just using the remaining money from the Owen Jones trust, the Society raised funds from manufacturers. Warner hoped to create an enduring connection between industry and the country's design students. 'Industry', he said, 'had an insatiable appetite for design'.[36]

The Society's competitions of industrial design sought to beautify everything and anything, including the things the preservationists hated. The Society offered prizes for the best designs for advertisements, for example, and even, in 1928, for petrol pumps. The competitions were briefly stopped for a few years due to the Great Depression, and again during the Second World War, but otherwise continued to this day, going through various names and permutations. For many years they were the Design Bursaries, and most recently the Student Design Awards.

For much of the mid-twentieth century the award was for a bursary to travel and study design abroad. One design student, Bill Moggridge, in the 1960s won a bursary for some plastic consumer goods—a needlework box and shopping trolley. He said it 'made me think for the first time that perhaps I would be able to do this design thing'.[37] Some years later he would design one of the first laptop computers, the GRiD Compass. The awards later also aided another pioneer of computer design, Jonny Ive; he won the award twice in the late 1980s for the designs of a futuristic landline phone and an automated teller machine. With the money, he embarked on a three-month study trip to California, and from the connections he made there he later ended up designing the iMac for Apple, paving the way for the iPod, iPhone, and iPad. Overall, since 1924, the awards have provided tens of thousands of connections between student designers and industry.

The awards had the effect of making the students of art and design colleges aware of industry's demands for their talents. The manufacturers usually funded the prizes they offered, and were often keen to hire from among the winners. At the very beginning of the prize scheme two major chocolate manufacturers—J. S. Fry and Cadbury—even paid to create the prize category of chocolate box designs. Other confectioners soon followed.[38] Yet something more was needed to encourage art students to develop an interest in industry. Money and opportunity were one thing, but since the eighteenth century the Society had also appealed to prestige.

It was one of Warner's friends, John Alexander Milne, who took the next step. Milne was a furniture-maker but had met Warner during the First World War, when he chaired a government committee on textiles. He soon became involved with the Society's competitions of industrial design. When Warner died in 1930, Milne continued his emphasis at the Society on industrial design.[39] As chairman of the Society's Council in the early 1930s, Milne decided that more might be done to raise the image of designers for industry. The problem, he surmised, was that manufacturers sometimes considered design students unsuitable. Students had been taught some art or craftsmanship, the manufacturers complained, but not the technical requirements of mass manufacture. Likewise, art and design students often neglected industry as a career, thinking it beneath them. Walter Crane's purist approach to Arts and Crafts had not fully given way to Lewis Foreman Day's pragmatism.

To raise the status of industrial design, Milne decided to collaborate with the Royal Academy. As the preeminent society of artists in the country, it might lend industrial design some of its prestige. The Society and the Royal Academy co-hosted an exhibition of Art in Industry, held in 1935 at the academy's premises in Burlington House. Like the Great Exhibition, it was meant to educate the British public in taste, to stress 'the importance of beauty in the articles they purchase'. Yet the principal targets were artists and manufacturers themselves. Milne wished to show them the best that designers could do, to dispel any reservations about industry being an unsuitable career for an artist, or about artists not knowing how to reconcile beauty with the products of industry.[40]

In this regard, Milne judged the event a success. It supposedly even prompted the government to assemble a group of expert designers to advise it on how to improve the designs of British products: the Council for Art and Industry.[41] Certainly, industrial designers involved with the Society played a role in creating the group's successor, the Council of Industrial Design, now known as the Design Council. Despite this impact, however, the exhibition of Art in Industry was a financial disaster. The Society was forced to call upon its guarantors, many of whom had

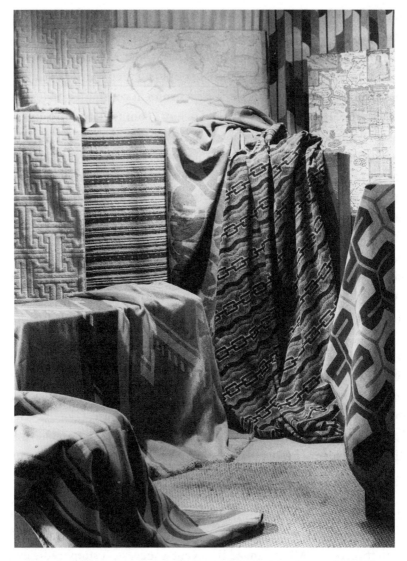

9.2. Some exhibits at the 1935 Art and Industry exhibition. The photograph, by Gilbert Cousland, shows fabrics manufactured by Messrs. Donald Bros. RSA/PR/AR/101/19/22.

been promised it would be profitable. Some of them apparently refused to pay.[42]

Nonetheless, the following year Milne capitalised on the publicity generated by the exhibition to further raise the status of industrial designers. He noted that Royal Academicians were distinguished by the use of the letters RA after their names, and that their prestige stemmed from their exclusivity. He decided that industrial designers should have a similarly coveted distinction. In 1936, Milne persuaded the Society of Arts to create a new distinction, of Designers for Industry.[43] The Society then chose a few industrial designers to receive it. In 1937 they obtained permission to call themselves the Royal Designers for Industry—they later became a 'faculty', with a Master and rules for selection to ensure their exclusivity. The faculty of RDIs exists to this day (and was administered by the Society until 2018). The RDIs often helped judge the annual competitions for student designers, lending their prestige to the awards. Due to their close association, the Society was also able to draw upon the advice and services of some of the most prestigious designers in the country, if not the world, for an honorary distinction was created for foreign designers. Over the years, the RDIs have included the fashion designer Vivienne Westwood, the engineering designer James Dyson, and the illustrator Quentin Blake. Some of them were originally winners of the annual competitions of industrial design, such as Jonny Ive.

The creation of the distinction, however, was one of only a few areas in which the Society tried to raise prestige. In the case of the RDIs, it served a purpose. Yet in the late nineteenth and early twentieth centuries, the Society developed a sometimes debilitating obsession with its own status.

10

'Society of Snobs'

WHEN THE SOCIETY OF ARTS began in 1754, William Shipley had benefitted from the aid of its first two presidents, Viscount Folkestone and Lord Romney—they had lent their names so that others would take Shipley's vision seriously, providing both attention and money. The Society had also, since the 1850s, capitalised on the credit it got for initiating the Great Exhibition, using that reputation to push for reforms. Prestige had often been a useful tool. But over the course of the late nineteenth and early twentieth centuries, the Society began to accumulate prestige for its own sake. Some of its actions introduced confusion about its aims and identity, which then took decades of reform to undo.

The trend began slowly. After the death of Prince Albert, one of the ways the Society's Council decided to commemorate him was by rewarding an 'Albert Medal', to be given to people who over the course of their careers had done much to aid arts, manufactures, and commerce.[1] The first recipient of the Albert Medal, in 1864, was Henry Cole's old colleague in the campaign to create the Penny Postage system, Rowland Hill. It was supposed to accord honour. But it became, in practice, a way for the Society to draw honour to itself. In just its second year, Henry Cole forced the Society to award the Albert Medal to France's emperor, Napoleon III, for in 1861 abolishing the need for passports when visiting France. The move had led many other countries to follow suit. For Cole, it was an important step in his vision of greater international ties leading eventually to world peace. (Passports were only brought back in many

countries in 1914, at the start of the First World War, to help catch foreign spies. They have remained ever since.)

Yet the rest of the Society's Council would have preferred to award
the medal to someone else, probably the scientist Michael Faraday (he
received it the following year). So Cole lied to the British ambassador
in France, telling him that the Council had decided to give the Albert
Medal to the emperor, and wished to him to enquire whether he would
accept it. The Council had not, in fact, even begun its deliberations.
Before they could back out, however, the Society was told that Napoleon III had agreed to accept the medal. The rest of the Council was too
embarrassed to back out. Cole somehow got away with it, dismissing
the Council's complaints as mere 'fussiness'. He himself received the
medal a few years later, in 1871.[2]

Having a medal to award each year allowed the Society to associate
itself with household names, or simply to recognise its own activists—
people like Henry Cole or John Alexander Milne. Over the years the
Albert Medal went to members of the royal family, famous politicians
like Winston Churchill and Franklin Delano Roosevelt, and scientists
like Marie Curie (for her work on radioactivity—a term she coined),
Alexander Fleming and Howard Florey (for their work on penicillin),
and more recently to Stephen Hawking (for making science more accessible) and Tim Berners-Lee (for his invention of the World Wide
Web). The Albert Medal's recipients were listed on the Society's staircase to its Great Room, giving the impression that the likes of Churchill
had been active members. Yet most of the recipients were never much
involved—for many, the ceremony to award the medal, if they even
turned up, was their first and only contact with the Society of Arts. Most
recipients were not members, and few became involved after receiving
it. Some had probably never heard of the Society. In general, most people were unaware that the Albert Medal existed.

In the 1950s the Society created even more medals. To commemorate
its two-hundredth anniversary in 1954, the Society began awarding an
annual Bicentenary Medal, to recognise people who promote good design, but not as designers. And since 1956, as part of an effort to attract

a membership in the United States, the Society awarded a Benjamin Franklin Medal for the promotion of Anglo-American understanding—its creation marked the bicentenary of Franklin becoming a member.[3] The use of his name reinforced historical associations that appealed to twentieth-century Americans. The Society's old model repository, which in the mid-nineteenth century had become its library, was later renamed the Benjamin Franklin Room—a name it still has at the time of writing. (In a recent redecoration it even acquired lights inspired by his invention of bifocals.)[4] Up until the 1950s, the Society's reach in North America had mostly been restricted to Canada. Its lectures and discussions on the colonies and later the Commonwealth, printed in full in the *Journal*, were popular there. Within a decade of it promoting its association with Benjamin Franklin, however, the Society's membership in the United States had more than doubled, from around three hundred to over seven hundred (there are currently over nine hundred).

The Albert, Bicentenary, and Benjamin Franklin Medals were a departure from the Society's age-old practice of awarding medals as part of its premiums. The premium medals had been won through competition. They were awarded for the greatest number of trees planted, or as recognition for revealing the details of an invention to the public. The prestige that the premium medals conveyed was determined by the strength of the other contestants, not just the status of the group that gave the awards. Premium medals were sought after, and thus had value to the seekers. But the commemorative medals, essentially given for lifetime achievement, were entirely unsolicited. They conveyed little in the way of prestige.

When the Albert Medal was first instituted, some members of the Society hoped that it would become as prestigious as some of the medals given, for example, by the Royal Society. Its Copley Medal is among the most prestigious awards a scientist can get.[5] A more famous and similar kind of medal might now be the Nobel Prize. But the commemorative medals of the Society of Arts could never hope to achieve that kind of status. The Royal Society is exclusive by design, only admitting people to its fellowship for their achievements in science—that exclusivity makes its medals for lifetime achievement valuable. Its Copley Medal is awarded for scientific achievement, by scientific achievers. Even among the other distinctions instituted by the Society of Arts, such as the Royal Designers for Industry, it was the fact that its faculty was a small group of prestigious designers who had to agree to admit a newcomer to their number that made it a distinction worth pursuing. It depended on exclusivity.

Yet the Society of Arts was never truly exclusive. The whole point of William Shipley's vision—the reason the Society had, for example, admitted women as members since the very start—was that membership has always been contingent on intentions, not achievements. Membership of the Society of Arts was open to anyone willing to subscribe. Its Albert Medal and Benjamin Franklin Medal simply associated the Society with already recognised high achievers, without conferring honour of their own. Later additions, like the short-lived Hartnett Medal— essentially, the Albert Medal, but for Australia—suffered the same flaw.[6] The exception, perhaps, was the Bicentenary Medal, which, because its terms were sufficiently limited, might have been appreciated as a sign of recognition within a small community of people interested in design.

Nonetheless, the Society of Arts took even more steps to enhance its status. Its members regularly compared it with the Royal Society and the other, newer learned societies. After all, over the course of the late nineteenth century, the Society of Arts increasingly resembled them. In its first century, meetings of the Society of Arts had been democratic deliberations about who deserved to receive a portion of the membership subscription fund. But one of the reforms to rescue the Society in the 1840s had been to make the meetings instructive and entertaining. Instead of a series of committees, the Society's meetings were purposefully made to resemble those of the learned societies. The impression that the Society of Arts was itself a learned society only strengthened. One might attend meetings at either the Royal Society or the Society of Arts to hear lectures or papers being presented. The *Journal* of the Society of Arts, just like the journals of the learned societies, published the lecture transcripts—it was even more comprehensive than most, because it also printed the ensuing discussions. The Society of Arts simply covered a wider range of subjects, from colonial matters, to applied chemistry, to new inventions, to art and architecture. One satirical magazine, *Punch*, reported that the Society's forthcoming programme of events would probably include lectures on 'Polygamy, Vingt-et-un, The Advantages of Early Rising, Rinks and Rinking, Double Acrostics (the Lord Mayor and Sheriffs to preside at the distribution of prizes), Night Lights, Hair Dyes (with practical illustrations), Mineral Waters, Second-hand Clothes, Pickles and Preserves, and Torpedoes (with experiments), and Bicycling'.[7] The satire was not far from the mark: a typical year of the Society's lectures might actually include lectures entitled 'Recent Improvements in Decorators' Materials', 'The Economic Importance of a Study of Insect Life', 'War Balloons', 'Old Age Pensions', and 'The Role of France in West Africa'.[8]

Some of the lectures were especially popular. In 1854, the Scottish chemist John Stenhouse demonstrated the properties of charcoal as an air filter, which he applied to respirators, by revealing tubs with the putrid three-month-old corpses of a cat and two rats, covered in charcoal—the audience were amazed at the lack of any odour.[9] The Society also hosted lectures on the long-distance radio by its inventor, Guglielmo Marconi,[10] and an early demonstration of the telephone by Alexander Graham Bell.[11] A few attendees were able to try out a telephone connecting the Society's Council room with the Adelphi Hotel across the street, and with a building about a mile down the road. The technology was still very much in its infancy; the longer connection only worked well in the evenings, when the telegraph wires alongside it did not interfere with the signal. Bell's presentation of his telephone was so 'filled to overflowing', he was persuaded to repeat the lecture at a larger venue.[12] The Society's Great Room also hosted the first public demonstrations in England of Thomas Edison's incandescent light bulbs, powered by his electric generators (though Edison was not there in person). And in 1920 it hosted the first public demonstration of teleprinting by wireless, with apparatus lent by its inventor, Frederick G. Creed—at the agreed time, a message was sent from the Eiffel Tower in Paris and printed in the Society's Great Room.[13]

10.1. As the Society concerned itself more and more with holding lectures, the
Great Room changed. By the mid-1860s the horseshoe configuration of benches,
ideal for debate in a direct democracy, had instead been rearranged as a lecture
theatre. Ink drawing by Howard Penton, 1885. RSA/AD/MA/300/14/1.

By the late nineteenth century, the most visible of the Society's activities had become the lectures. It continued to run its examinations well
into the late twentieth century, but the examination board was increasingly managed separately, by specialists. Members of the Society only
tended to notice the examinations in so far as they subsidised the lectures. Although the Society of Arts continued to award some premiums
(it still occasionally offered a cash prize or medal for new inventions),
from 1850 it mostly simply awarded medals each year to the more popular lecturers, as tokens of appreciation. The Society's members could use
a library and reading room—another privilege often associated with
other learned societies. Even the Society's own leaders began to refer to
it as a learned society, a label that stuck right into the late twentieth
century.[14]

It was not just any learned society, it seemed to be a 'mother of societ-ies'. Many of the more specialist royally chartered societies had had their first meetings in the Society's rooms at the Adelphi, or had received some initial encouragement from its members. The Society's obscure lecture topics attracted specialists, who eventually splintered off to form their own dedicated societies. The trend had begun in the early nine-teenth century—it was a key cause of the Society's declining popularity in the 1840s—and it has continued ever since. With the Society's post-1840s emphasis on giving lectures, the trend accelerated. Although the Royal Society and the Society of Antiquaries were older, the breadth of the Society of Arts made it an especially useful place to start organisa-tions in new fields, like photography or aeronautics. The Society's mis-sion—the 'encouragement of arts, manufactures, and commerce'—was sufficiently broad to include anything and everything.

In the case of photography, the discovery had been first announced in 1839. In its early years, most photography involved capturing the image directly onto silver-plated copper sheets, although an English gentleman-inventor, William Henry Fox Talbot, had discovered a method of capturing faint images onto paper, which could then be chemically developed into a fully visible image. Talbot, however, had patented his method in the early 1840s, which restricted further devel-opment of the process. The Society of Arts invited demonstrations and lectures by some of photography's earliest improvers, and photographs were a highlight of its 1848 exhibition of art-manufactures, as well as the Great Exhibition of 1851. Inspired by the specimens on show at the Great Exhibition, a few amateur photographers in London began to meet at one another's houses. In 1852, they began to lobby Talbot to relax the terms of his patent. Many of them also joined the Society of Arts, using it to help gather signatures for a petition.[15] Talbot was eventually per-suaded—he allowed anyone to practise his method, so long as they stayed out of the lucrative trade of taking portraits. The photographers seized on their chance, later that year persuading the Society of Arts to host an exhibition of photographs. Just like the artists who had lobbied the Society back in the 1760s, the photographers in the 1850s saw the Society as the best means of helping them establish their profession.

10.2. The Society's photographic exhibition in the Great Room, 1853. Originally from the *London Illustrated News*, 1 January 1853. RSA/AD/MA/300/19/04.

The Society's exhibition, held in December 1852 to January 1853, was the world's first major public exhibition devoted solely to photography. Almost eight hundred photographs and examples of equipment were displayed, and they were a hit with the public, causing the exhibition to be extended by a few weeks. One newspaper described some of the images as 'indescribably beautiful', while waxing lyrical about how photography would transform art and exact scientific observation, much like the invention of printing had transformed literature.[16] While the exhibition was still in progress, the photographers decided to formalise their group. A few wished to become a part of the Society of Arts— a devoted 'section' for the lectures and discussions of photography, which would have the advantage of funds, a free room, the *Journal*, and the ability to leverage the Society's influence.[17] But the photographers instead resolved to be separate. They declared themselves the Photographic Society, which has since become the Royal Photographic Society. They probably only hastened the inevitable.[18] The Society of Arts hosted the first few meetings and provided some further assistance,[19] but the splintering was typical: for over seventy years it also hosted the Aeronautical Society (now the Royal Aeronautical Society).[20]

In other cases, the Society of Arts stopped giving lectures in areas where it felt other societies had appeared: in the late 1880s, for example, the Society's 'section' for organising lectures on industrial applications for chemistry and physics was disbanded because of the formation of the Society of Chemical Industry, alongside an Institute for Chemistry, and an even older Chemical Society. The splintering of the specialisms seemed to be accelerating. As one member joked, 'I feel the day may come when there will be an institute for the civil engineering of piers, another for lighthouses, a third for docks, and a fourth for iron girder bridges'.[21] The Society of Arts began to act as a coordinator for the other learned societies, even when they were not its splinter groups, by advertising in its *Journal* many of the various societies' lectures and exhibitions. It provided a near-comprehensive weekly list of London's intellectual entertainment. It did not matter that the Society of Arts had not given birth to a particular learned society it supported; it would mother them all the same.

The Society's sense of its own importance grew. Histories of the Society were published in 1913, 1935, and 1954—useful books, but all of them written by the Society's secretary at the time, each of whom had been in the post for at least a decade. Henry Trueman Wood, the author of the first, had been an employee of the Society for over forty years.[22] These histories often read as advertisements, describing some of the Society's activities as 'useful' without explaining how. The Society had always exploited its achievements—reformers like Henry Cole or Harry Chester used the hype generated by the Great Exhibition to spur further reforms. But as these achievements receded into the past, they were used by some future leaders of the Society as sources of self-congratulation. The Society's long history became a way to elevate its status, even during periods of inactivity. The published histories reinforced the image of the Society of Arts as a prestigious and exclusive learned society, even though in practice it remained as inclusive as ever.

Some of the Society's social events could be huge. Its informal gatherings of members and recent lecturers, the conversazioni that had been pioneered by Francis Whishaw in the 1840s, could attract thousands of attendees. One conversazione, held at the South Kensington Museum in 1869, had a crowd of 4,400. Members of the royal family or other celebrities might be spotted among the mass, but the crowd were instructed not to mob them, to let the celebrities walk around 'like any private person'. Nonetheless, members still seem to have found ways to be obsequious. One attendee at the conversazione, Karl Marx's daughter Jenny, complained that many members of the Society were 'much given to tuft hunting'—they were obsessed with status. The Society of Arts, she declared, was a 'Society of Snobs'.[23] An American journalist agreed: the Society's conversazioni, she claimed, were 'unspeakably dull', an endless promenade of old-fashioned 'fossilized' ladies.[24]

The Society as a whole engaged in tuft hunting. Following the deaths of its first two presidents, Viscount Folkestone and Lord Romney, the Society had made it an unofficial rule to elect its highest ranking member of the aristocracy to the position. This had meant the Duke of Norfolk following Romney's death in 1794, and then the Duke of Sussex from 1816. With the election of the Duke of Sussex, the Society established a direct link to the royal family. Sussex was a younger son of George III, a younger brother to George IV and William IV, and an uncle to Queen Victoria. Since his election, other than a handful of temporary non-royal stand-ins, the Society has always had a member of the royal family as its president, including a few future monarchs (whenever they succeeded to the throne, they had to be replaced). Sussex was succeeded as president by Prince Albert, the husband of Queen Victoria. He, in turn, was succeeded by his eldest son Edward (the future Edward VII), followed by the future George V, the Duke of Connaught (one of Albert and Victoria's younger sons, and George V's uncle), the future Elizabeth II, her husband Prince Philip, and most recently their daughter Princess Anne.

In every case, the Society tried to maintain the royal connection. Many of them had had no other association with the Society before becoming president—Elizabeth had to be simultaneously appointed an honorary member to qualify. In a similar manner, the Society's Council arranged for the chairman in 1954, the year of its bicentenary, to be the direct descendant of its first president, Viscount Folkestone. Members of the Society even made an official visit to his seat at Longford Castle.[25] (The chairman for the centenary in 1854, by contrast, had been plain old Harry Chester.)

The Society's pursuit of associations with royalty also went international. Its Council in the late nineteenth century started appointing monarchs from around the world as members, often without even the formality of proposing and balloting. The Council exploited a bye-law in the Society's constitution, which allowed them to appoint persons 'distinguished in art, science, or manufactures'. They apparently stretched the definition to include anyone who ruled a country, and given the association of the Society with British royalty, most of the foreign monarchs accepted. They eventually even had their own membership category, of 'honorary royal members', which by 1914 had included the rulers of Belgium, Denmark, Germany, Greece, Norway, Persia, Portugal, Russia, Spain, and Sweden. Upon the outbreak of the First World War, the Society's secretary, Henry Trueman Wood, had to expunge the German Kaiser's name from the membership lists (along with anyone else of German or Austro-Hungarian nationality).[26] The Society even extended its pursuit of prestige to foreign republics, using the same procedure to appoint elected heads of state: US president Theodore Roosevelt, for example, and France's president during the First World War, Raymond Poincaré.[27] As with the Albert Medal and the Society's other commemorative medals, heads of state were not really honoured by their appointment as members—it was a way for the Society of Arts to gather prestige by association.

The Society of Arts itself even became 'Royal'. When the Society had acquired its royal charter in 1847, it had been an expression of permanence after its near-demise and rescue by Thomas Webster's reforms. It had, for a few years, occasionally been referred to in the press as the

'Royal Society of Arts'. But the privilege of putting 'Royal' in the name only became official in the early twentieth century. With its growing sense of self-importance, and with its growing similarity to learned societies, members of the Society must have looked with envy at the royally chartered learned societies, many of which were called 'Royal': the Royal Society, the Royal Institution, the Royal Academy, and even specialist groups like the Royal Photographic Society. The Society of Arts was even mother to many of these societies. Its seniority, members reasoned, deserved to be reflected in the name. In 1908 it became the Royal Society for the Encouragement of Arts, Manufactures, and Commerce—usually referred to as just the Royal Society of Arts, or simply the RSA. Its pursuit of greater distinction ironically made it less distinctive. Its use of 'Royal' and the acronym RSA became a source of confusion for the general public. The Society's staff have a list of the phone numbers of the Royal Society, the Royal Academy, and even Royal Sun Alliance, an insurance company, so that they can redirect callers to the intended recipients. Members of the public regularly turn up to the Society of Arts, looking for events that are at one of the other institutions. (I will continue to refer to the organisation as the Society of Arts, or the Society.)

More than any of its other actions to acquire greater prestige, however, it was the Society's next move that created the most confusion. A vocal minority of its members noted that learned societies, especially the older ones like the Royal Society, called their members 'fellows'. Fellows of the Royal Society could even signify their status as eminent scientists by placing the letters FRS after their names. Many of the other exclusive learned societies did the same. Crucially for the vocal minority, 'the term Fellow implied a higher standing than that of Member'. So in 1914 the Council of the Society of Arts decided to allow its members to call themselves fellows too. It was, after all, an ancient mother of societies: 'there seems no reason why members of so old a body as the Royal Society of Arts should not, if they wish, use the same title as that adopted by the majority of the younger and similar institutions'.[28] It also suggested the use of the letters FRSA after members' names. Members of the Society have referred to themselves as fellows ever since.

At the time, the Council of the Society felt that 'the two terms are obviously identical in meaning'. But in practice, they were a source of confusion. The term 'fellow' created a false aura of exclusivity. People began to append FRSA to their names, as though it was a kind of achievement, like receiving a doctorate or an order of merit. Some people seem to have attempted to use fellowship as a qualification, either accidentally or purposefully eliding it with the Society's examination certificates. The Society issued frequent notices to fellows on the appropriate use of the letters FRSA.[29] The term created the impression that people became fellows based on achievement rather than on intentions, while in practice nothing about the Society's membership had changed. Some of the Society's leaders expressed a wish to control the 'quality' of new fellows, to have entrants of higher status or influence.

In the late 1960s the Society's Council issued guidance to fellows wishing to nominate new people, stating that nominees ought to have at least a university degree or equivalent professional qualification. Yet the Council very soon backed down from this, instead recommending at least some 'evidence of comparable artistic, industrial, commercial or cultural achievement'—a definition so broad as to include just about anyone. Yet it was only ever guidance. The Council admitted that the only real check on applications was that the fellows decided whom to nominate, and some fellows readily nominated people they barely knew.[30] A membership committee still tried to exclude people it considered insufficiently worthy, with varying degrees of success. The Society did introduce some restrictions, for example in 1943 creating a lower age limit of 21 for fellowship, allowing people aged 18 to 21 become 'associates'—a sort of second tier of fellowship, much like that used by many learned societies.[31] Before this, there had never been any age limits. In 1965, it raised the minimum age for fellowship even higher, to 25.[32] These moves all tried to make the Society's membership more closely resemble that of an exclusive learned society.

Yet, overall, the Society continued to strive for more members rather than members who were more distinguished. One of the reasons it introduced its associateship for young people was that it introduced a special cheaper rate. It had also always relied on existing members nominating new people, or on the secretary simply writing to people who might be interested. In the late twentieth century, people sometimes received a letter or email that emphasised the Society's connection to its president, Prince Philip, informing them that their achievements had been recognised and that this was why they were being invited to join. Many recipients were flattered—it seemed as though they had been personally selected to something exclusive. Many joined as a result. Even today, even though the Society has long ceased this practice, some people have their organisations issue press releases about accepting an invitation to become a fellow.[33]

At first glance, fellowship increasingly resembled a sort of club—a membership that conferred benefits on the fellows, rather than fellows supporting the organisation. Those benefits were, however, very few. Fellows could vote for members of Council, received the *Journal*, received invitations to events and lectures, and had the use of the Society's library. Beyond this, however, the vision of the Society's fellowship as a club was increasingly just a perception rather than reality. To conform to changes in the law in 1963, the Society registered as a charity. This expressly limited the benefits that could be offered exclusively to fellows. Since then, the law has come to forbid essentially all discrimination by charities between fellows and the public. The Society does not, and indeed cannot, exclude the general public from the use of its library or coffee shop, though fellows of course retained some special rights, such as the ability to elect people to the Society's Council, or to vote on changes to its constitution at annual general meetings. Despite the image of exclusivity, members of the Society continued in reality to be subscribers, just as they always had been.

The image in fact diverged even further from reality. In one important respect, the Society had become markedly more inclusive. Since 1754, anyone could join the Society so long as they paid the subscription fee (and went through the formality of finding someone to nominate them). Only a handful of troublemakers were excluded in the late eighteenth century, and exclusions were almost unheard of from the 1840s onwards. The only real barrier to entry was thus the subscription fee—a barrier that was lowered significantly, through sheer inaction. The Society's original two-guinea annual subscription fee, set in 1754, remained unchanged until 1920. In today's money, when compared to the average wage, the Society thus allowed the price of membership to fall from about 3,800 pounds a year to only 230 pounds. The Society's only real barrier to entry dropped by about 94 per cent. Over the following years, the subscription fee barely kept up with inflation (at the time of writing, it is 178 pounds a year).[34]

The aura of exclusivity which had been created by the 'Royal' designation of the Society and its use of the term 'fellow' was at odds with reality. To some fellows, especially those who had been led to believe that had been invited to join the organisation based on their achievements, the true nature of the Society's fellowship sometimes seemed like a scam.[35] Whenever the Society's leaders exacerbated the contradiction by calling the Society's fellowship a mark of prestige, the organisation's reputation was put at risk.

Yet the aura of exclusivity had another major effect. Before it was called 'Royal' and used the term 'fellow', the popularity of the Society of Arts had been determined by its activity and perceived usefulness. Its membership had decreased in the late 1760s when it was associated with corruption over the fish land-carriage scheme and the actions of a few artists. It had increased in the mid-1780s when it began to publish its *Transactions* and advertised its usefulness as a means of diffusing knowledge. Likewise, its membership had declined in the 1830s when it could not compete with specialist learned societies for people's attention, and had risen again in the 1840s when it reformed itself. The Great Exhibition, the creation of the Union of Mechanics' Institutions, and its actions to promote the International Exhibition of 1862 had all attracted members. They joined mostly because they supported the Society's mission. As William Shipley had envisioned, people subscribed their time and money to the Society because it was seen to be benefitting the public. They wished to support its existing activities, or to direct it to their own projects for the public good. Of course, some people joined for other reasons too: because it gave them access to potential customers, or to a network of like-minded friends, or because simply allowed them to show off their public-spiritedness. Yet the underlying relationship had held true: the more the Society of Arts did, and the more useful it seemed, the more people joined. When it acquired its aura of exclusivity, that relationship was broken.

After the Society of Arts began to call its members 'fellows', its membership was able to rise regardless of the organisation's perceived usefulness. This was masked for a while by the two world wars—both seem to have killed off many members, or else made the subscription fees unaffordable. It was also masked for a while by the Society's popular campaigns to preserve ancient cottages and encourage industrial designers. At the point of its deepest crisis in the 1840s, the Society's membership had stood at just under 700, but by 1870 it had swelled to over 3,000. It hovered between about 3,000 and 3,500 right up until the mid-1930s. Since then, however, the overall trend has been for the Society's membership to rapidly increase. It stands today at almost 30,000. The Society achieved a tenfold increase in members over a century, with dramatic increases even in the 1950s to the 1970s—a period when it embarked on the fewest new initiatives, and was at its least visible.[36]

That is not to say that the Society's staff were not active. They continued to administer the prizes or bursaries for young industrial designers, each year having to find new sponsors and judging panels. They also continued to run the faculty of Royal Designers for Industry. Their biggest responsibility was the examination board. Before 1882, the number of examination candidates had never reached much more than two thousand in a given year; they had also sat the examinations for free. The Society agreed to continue to offer examinations in 1882 on the condition that it charge fees to cover the costs, and in the years that followed, the government passed measure after measure increasing the amount of money available for education. The system laid down by utilitarian reformers like James Booth in the mid-nineteenth century expanded. More teachers were paid to teach more pupils. The Society experienced a dramatic increase in examination candidates, along with higher revenues. By the early 1900s the number of candidates had increased over tenfold, to well over twenty thousand a year. The Society continued to mostly offer qualifications in commercial subjects: for skills like bookkeeping, shorthand, typewriting, and eventually the use of computers.

Many of the examinations were more specific subjects: for foreign languages for secretaries, for example, or for teaching English as a foreign language to immigrants.

The Society increasingly also examined people abroad. During both the world wars, the Society sent examination papers for free to soldiers held in German prisoner-of-war camps. In 1917, at Ruhleben, some papers were seized by the German censors because the test asked candidates to write a precis of the US ambassador's reports on the camps, some of which described poor treatment. The Society admitted that that examination paper 'ought not to have been sent to a prisoners' camp in Germany, and that the German censor was quite justified in suppressing it', but complained that the censors might have allowed the rest of the papers, which were otherwise harmless.[37] For some years after both wars, the Society's staff had to deal with enquiries from returned prisoners-of-war still waiting to hear whether they had passed. More and more of the Society's examinations were sat abroad, often in British colonies or former colonies in Africa and the West Indies.

By the 1930s, the Society was handling over one hundred thousand papers around the world each year; in the 1980s the figure increased to well over seven hundred thousand. The Society was forced to take on more and more staff. After the evacuations of the Second World War, many of the examinations staff even moved permanently out of the Adelphi, to their own offices. The examinations often generated a healthy surplus, much of it reinvested in keeping up with the increase in candidates, but some of it also used to subsidise the Society's other activities. In terms of its finances and staff, by the 1950s it had effectively become a large examination board with an entertaining discussion club attached.

One of the chairmen of Council, the former prime minister of Canada, R. B. Bennett, summarised the Society's appeal for much of the mid-twentieth century: it was a place for people like him to be active in retirement. 'I have commended it to many people who desire some little mental stimulation, a good magazine with up-to-date information and friendships that are not to be despised'. He became chairman, he explained, because of his seniority.[38] Indeed, the Society increasingly focused on finding ways to entertain its fellows. Its lectures and discussions continued to resemble those of a learned society, but were soon supplemented by film screenings and talks to entertain 'the children and grandchildren of fellows', some of which were delivered by popular children's radio presenters.[39] It also began to sell an annual Christmas card. The number of receptions proliferated. Before major meetings, fellows were often served sherry in the old library. After the meetings, they might adjourn there for tea. The Society soon began holding regular soirées with live music, 'to bring together men and women of achievement', which often featured live performances by the celebrated violinist Yehudi Menuhin.[40]

Even the Society's new initiatives seemed to be geared towards entertainment. In 1949 a famous cartoonist, H. M. Bateman, gave a lecture at the Society in which he suggested the creation of a permanent national collection of humorous art. The chairman of the Council immediately suggested that they hold an exhibition, the only reason being that it 'would be of great interest to Fellows of the Society and to their friends'.[41] The exhibition of humorous art took place later that year. Fourteen thousand people visited in the space of a few months, and it soon went on tour.[42] It was well liked by the newspaper critics, though one reported that the artists themselves were never seen to smile at each other's work.[43] Bateman's permanent collection, however, never materialised.[44] As far as the Society of Arts was concerned, the principal purpose was the entertainment of fellows.

Despite the occasional injection of some levity, the Society continued to take itself seriously. In the 1950s, the chairman of the Council acquired a badge of office, and for much of the mid-twentieth century the Society employed uniformed porters. Tail-coated and stately, they insisted on being the only ones allowed to stoke the building's fires.[45] Letters to the non-nobility were always addressed to so-and-so 'Esquire', instead of the ordinary 'Mr', and the letters after people's names were all listed in every publication. In the *Journal* from that period, it is common to find surnames followed by an acronym to denote an undergraduate degree (this had not been common practice from the late eighteenth through to the early twentieth centuries). Of the people who still remember the Society at that time, one of their most common comments is that it was an organisation from another age. Indeed, much of the Society's time was spent fulfilling the wishes of the dead.

The Society had long accepted donations and bequests. Many of them were related to the Society's activities, and were given to ensure continuation. In 1838, for example, a Mrs Hannah Acton had given five hundred pounds to fund two annual premiums for the best architectural drawings and models.[46] Its conditions were not unusual in the context of the kinds of premiums being awarded at the time. We have also seen how John Scott Russell gave the Society money so that it would award special premiums for art-manufactures. Yet in many cases the Society found itself carrying out the wishes of people who had been dead for over a century. Some of those people had not even been members. In 1831 a mysterious man deposited a parcel with the Society's secretary, and told him not to open it until he received further instructions. Those instructions finally arrived in 1844, when it turned out to be the will of a wealthy eccentric named George Swiney, who had bequeathed the huge sum of five thousand pounds (in today's money almost four million pounds).[47] The bequest came at a welcome time when the Society's financial situation was precarious. Yet Swiney had never been a member. He was a well-known recluse. The condition for his bequest was that every five years the Society award a silver goblet containing one hundred pounds for the best essay on jurisprudence, the theory or philosophy of law. Unusually, however, the prize was to be judged by members of the Society and fellows of the Royal College of Physicians, along 'with the wives of such of them as happen to be married'.[48] The Society carried out his request for the next 160 years (though it ignored the bit about the wives).

Administering the Swiney Cup every five years was not an onerous administrative burden, especially as it came with such a large amount of money. It even gave Henry Cole a chance to add his own interpretation. He had one of his artist friends, the Irish history painter Daniel Maclise, design the cup. But over the decades the Society accrued similar bequests. The administrative burden grew, taking up more and more of the staff's time. In 1924, the Society received a large bequest from the son of a civil servant, Thomas Gray, who had been the head of the Marine Department of the Board of Trade. The son wished to memorialise his father, who had died in 1890. Under the terms of the Thomas Gray Memorial Trust, the Society awarded prizes related to marine navigation, held lectures on the subject, and provided scholarships for deck boys and ordinary seamen wishing to qualify as ship's officers.

During the Second World War, the Society also began to use the trust to award prizes for deeds of professional merit in the merchant marine. The first went to James Wyld, the chief engineer of the oil tanker SS *Ohio*, which in 1942 was convoyed from Britain to Malta under heavy attack. The tanker's journey was part of Operation Pedestal, a mission to resupply Malta with aviation fuel so that it could be used to control the Mediterranean. Wyld managed to keep the tanker's engine going even after it was hit by a torpedo and a fire broke out in the pump room; he had to work in complete darkness. Yet the trust's prizes do not seem to have incentivised anyone to such acts of heroism. The awards were often given after the recipient had already received an official honour.[49] The main achievement of the awards was to continue to draw attention to the name of Thomas Gray. The Society continued to administer the prize until 1993, when it was handed over to a more appropriate organisation, the Marine Society. Similar trusts had the Society of Arts award prizes for work on industrial hygiene, improvements to motive power, to promising young cellists, and even for gardening—the philanthropist Violet Markham gave one thousand pounds for such a prize in memory of the architect of the Crystal Palace, her grandfather Joseph Paxton.[50]

Among the more unusual bequests was one from an artist, Katharine Maltwood. She bequeathed forty-two thousand pounds upon the death of her husband, who died in 1967 aged 101 (today, the bequest would be worth at least seven hundred thousand pounds).[51] Maltwood was obsessed with the mythical and occult, especially the folklore and Arthurian legends of the west of England. In the 1930s, aided by the advent of aerial photography, she had published a theory that the landscape around Glastonbury, in Somerset, formed a gigantic zodiac map that had been created by the Sumerians in 2700 BC. Maltwood claimed that the discovery of this 'Temple of the Stars' had come to her in a vision.

She became a fellow of the Society of Arts a few years later, and wanted her bequest to be used to pursue further research into her theory. The Society created a Katharine Maltwood Fund for Archaeological Research in Somerset. Thanks to the wishes of the eccentric deceased, for over twenty years the Society found itself bestowing research grants to archaeologists, most of whom would have pooh-poohed Maltwood's ideas. (The fund did, however, aid the Somerset Levels Project, which did much to initiate the sub-discipline of wetland archaeology.)[52]

By the late twentieth century, the long dead were even determining the Society's programme of lectures. The Society gave Atkinson memorial lectures on electrical engineering, Birdwood lectures on India, Bossom lectures on architecture, Cadman lectures on coal, Cook lectures on old master painters, Holland lectures on the Commonwealth, Matheson McWharrie lectures on Canada, Osborn lectures on town planning, Sharman lectures on overseas development, and Trueman Wood lectures on the application of science to industry. Many of these endowed lectures continued for decades. The full list goes on and on.[53]

Even the Society's members of Council found themselves busy administering the pet projects of their long-dead predecessors. Edwin Chadwick, for example, set up a trust to continue his interest in sanitary reform, with the Society's Council entitled to appoint one of the trustees.[54] By the mid-twentieth century, the Society was nominating representatives to the boards of museums, a hospital, various educational institutions, architectural groups, design advisory organisations, the British Film Institute, the Council for the Preservation of Rural England, and many more.[55] In a way, this gave the Society of Arts influence, but it had no clear sense of what to do with it.

The Society of Arts was in thrall to the past. In 1943, with the approach of the centenary of the Great Exhibition, the Society began to lobby the government to put on an exhibition in 1951 that would outdo the original. In the context of post-war reconstruction, however, such a project was out of the question. The government was not about to spend public funds on a massive exhibition when a third of all houses—four million homes—had been destroyed or damaged by wartime bombing.[56] The Society persisted in its lobbying, however, and the government's opinion seems to have been swayed in 1946 by the editor of the *News Chronicle*, Gerald Barry. Some kind of event in 1951, even if it was not a traditional large-scale exhibition, would be a way to show off the UK's recovery from the war.

But that was the extent of the Society's vision. Unlike the Great Exhibition of 1851, there was no equivalent figure to Henry Cole, and certainly no hidden agenda like that of spreading beauty to the masses. In 1946, as part of the Society's lobbying efforts, it even announced a five-hundred-guinea prize for the best essay on the purposes of a centenary event. Instead of having an agenda that would be served by an exhibition, the Society started with the idea of celebrating the centenary and would then work out why. Gerald Barry's initial ideas were similarly vague. When 1951 came around, the event would in many respects be the Great Exhibition's inverse.

Whereas the Great Exhibition had relied on private subscriptions, which had even been part of its appeal, the 1951 event was almost entirely funded by the government. The government also imposed its own agenda. Instead of being international, which was what had made the Great Exhibition so original, the 1951 event focused only on Britain. It was a chance for the government—an increasingly unpopular Labour government led by Clement Attlee—to lift spirits in the face of post-war austerity. 1951 was chosen to be a celebration of Britain's achievements, and a hopeful look to its future—a Festival of Britain.

The deputy prime minister, Herbert Morrison, took charge of the project. He was careful to avoid any overt celebrations of Labour's recent reforms, and all mention of the recently nationalised health service was avoided. Yet the Festival of Britain was a key piece in the government's construction of a new British identity. In the decades before the Second World War, the state had purposefully cultivated a sense of British identity that was closely intertwined with the empire overseas. The last great 'festival' had been the Festival of Empire, not of Britain, in 1911. Wembley Stadium, which was replaced in 2007, had originally been constructed for the British Empire Exhibition of 1924–25. The next empire exhibition had been held in Glasgow in 1938, just before the war. These exhibitions had all been nationalistic, but with the nation conceived of as encompassing entire British Empire, with Britain itself as the hub. We have also seen how the Society of Arts was one of many voluntary organisations that tried to educate the British about the empire overseas, so as to engender a sense of fellow feeling. As the historian David Edgerton has pointed out, however, the nationalism that became dominant after the Second World War was one focused on Britain alone. As the British Empire disintegrated, British identity needed to be redefined.[57]

This was easier said than done. Like the Society of Arts, the government began with the idea of holding the Festival of Britain, and then tried to clarify its vision. Herbert Morrison appointed Gerald Barry to be the Festival's director-general, responsible for its organisation—he had, after all, lobbied for it to happen. Defining Britain for the British was a task that was immense, not to mention vague. On 1 April 1948, the Society of Arts hosted the first meeting of the festival's executive committee, but Barry and his team had no idea where to start: 'that afternoon we sat before our blotting pads industriously doodling, in the hope perhaps that a coherent pattern might eventually emerge, on the same principle that if you set down twelve apes before twelve typewriters they will (or so it is said) in the course of infinity type out the complete works of Shakespeare.'[58]

In the end, the twelve apes succeeded. Instead of holding a single exhibition, Barry's team coordinated cultural activities throughout the country: locally run exhibitions of British art, music performances, sports events, village pageants, pleasure gardens, amusement parks, and film screenings. An escort aircraft carrier, the HMS *Campania*, was even repurposed and redecorated as a floating exhibition hall. The festival's activities centred on the South Bank of the Thames, in central London, where a large new concert hall was unveiled, the Royal Festival Hall. Visitors to the South Bank could also view a slender, rocket-like sculpture, the Skylon, suspended 15 metres from the ground, as well as an aluminium Dome of Discovery that showcased British designs, inventions, and scientific discoveries. The exhibits promoted a futuristic vision of continuing British genius, which the Labour government hoped would come to be associated with socialist planning. Yet despite the festival's futuristic overall agenda, the main individual contribution of the Society of Arts was rooted firmly in the past: they arranged for flagpoles to mark the site of the Great Exhibition in Hyde Park, and they hosted an exhibition in the Great Room that was about the practice of holding exhibitions.

The Festival of Britain could have been a platform for the Society to pursue further initiatives. It could have been an opportunity to demonstrate new usefulness to the public, as had happened in 1851. Instead, the Society's limited involvement meant it received very little credit. Its leaders did not have their own vision for the festival, so they allowed the centenary to be repurposed by others. But the Society's leaders did not have to provide any vision of their own. There was simply no cost to inaction.

Having developed the image of being a learned society with a prestigious fellowship, the number of members rose regardless. The Society's income from subscription fees rose, supplemented by donations, bequests, and surpluses from the examination board. The Society in the mid-twentieth century was more financially secure than ever. It had even, in 1922, been able to finally purchase its building in the Adelphi, which it had been leasing since 1774 (mostly thanks to a single anonymous donation of thirty thousand pounds—in today's money, depending on how you account for inflation, a figure somewhere between 1.5 and 5.5 million pounds).[59] Over the following years, the Society was able to purchase more and more of the block, easily paying for it from its reserves.[60] With more money and more members, the Society had little incentive to change. Its prestige and financial security had come at a cost.

Nonetheless, some people still saw the potential of the Society to do something more than just entertain its fellows or commemorate the dead. Its heightened prestige, even if it was based on confusion, might be put to greater use. It still had the potential to pursue new initiatives for the good of the public. Making the Society more useful again would, however, take decades of reform.

11

Rise of the Managers

UNLIKE THE LEARNED SOCIETIES with which it competed, the Society of Arts never had a permanent function—it was instead meant to find new things to improve. Yet in the mid-twentieth century the world around it was rapidly changing, often without its help. The utilitarian-supported reforms of the late nineteenth century had laid the foundations for state systems of education, health, and welfare, which grew in size and complexity. Reformers like Henry Cole had constructed finely tuned bureaucratic machines, constituted on a rational basis, that once set up could then be left to others to expand. By the mid-twentieth century, many of those systems were well-established and state-run. Overall, the utilitarians and their allies had succeeded in remaking the state. Yet if the Society was to find room for improvement, it would mostly have to involve making tweaks to existing systems rather than creating entirely new ones.

The membership of the Society had also changed. Whereas the 1840s had seen an influx to the Society of new professionals—civil engineers, patent agents, and professional inventors—in the early twentieth century it had seen an influx of the employees of large bureaucracies, especially large firms. Before the mid-nineteenth century, large firms had been rare. Before 1844 there had been severe restrictions on the number of partners that a company could have without requiring a special act of Parliament, and before 1855 partners in most companies had been personally liable for all of its debts. With the general introduction of limited liability, however, partners were liable only to the extent of the capital they had invested. Limited liability made it much easier for anyone to become a shareholder, to hold shares that were only a tiny fraction of the total value of the firm.

With firms able to attract much more investment from a mass of shareholders, the size of firms was able to increase dramatically. They were able to take advantage of efficiencies that only came from size, and the large firms often merged to become even larger still. Economies of scale were increasingly important, especially as the new manufacturing technologies of the 1940s to 70s required larger machinery and larger factory sizes in order to be efficient enough to remain competitive. In services, too, the 1960s saw the rise of the supermarket and dramatic changes to the retail industry. The bureaucracies needed to run these firms increased, such that in the mid-twentieth century many more people were the employees of large firms. Even the people who directed the bureaucracies were more often professional managers, rather than themselves being owners. Whereas the nineteenth century had seen the rise of owner–industrialists and a new class of self-employed professionals, the twentieth century saw the rise of manager employees.

The membership of the Society of Arts came to reflect the growth of both government and corporate bureaucracies. The Society's members were increasingly drawn from the civil service, middle management, and from the chairmen or directors of companies. These were the people often most keen to improve their status, whose fellowship of what appeared to be a learned society helped them stand out from their co-workers within an otherwise faceless bureaucracy, especially as they approached retirement. A typical week's influx of members might include the director of a hovercraft engineering company, a deputy secretary at the Ministry of Transport, the managing director of the Civil Aviation Authority, the vice-chancellor of a university, and the deputy chairman of a nationalised industry.[1] They were all members of a new managerial class.

The Society reacted to the trend by increasingly appealing to large firms for the sponsorship of its industrial design bursaries. It supplemented the bursaries with pre-agreed work experience, called attachment awards, using its connections to kick-start the winners' careers.[2]

In 1964 the Society also began to offer an award every few years for design management—recognition for bureaucracies that could maintain a high aesthetic standard throughout all of their operations, year after year.[3] Improving the country's design in the mid-twentieth century had to recognise managers and administrators, the people who made the decisions about when to hire designers. The winners of these awards included supermarkets like J. Sainsbury and Waitrose,[4] public bodies like London Transport, and the household furnishings manufacturer and retailer Conran & Co., later renamed Habitat, which won the award twice. The judges, mostly members of the Council of Industrial Design and Royal Designers for Industry, were impressed the first time by the items Conran manufactured, and the second time by the aesthetics of its shop-floor, merchandise, catalogues, leaflets, transport, and even advertisements.[5]

With the rise of the managerial class, it was not enough to just improve the supply of trained designers; the demand from firms and state-owned services had to be encouraged too. The Society of Arts even tried to resurrect the idea of the Union of Mechanics' Institutions, but for firms. It began to admit companies into a formal association, allowing them to nominate a few employees to have full membership rights. Very few firms joined, and the initiative did not last long—unlike with the union, there was no obvious benefit to the firms from joining the association.

Yet the new managerial class did not join the Society of Arts to represent the interests of their employers. The Society became an outlet for their wider, often cultural interests—their concerns for the public at large. Take the example of John Stratton, the chairman of the Fatstock Marketing Corporation Ltd., a meat retail company that owned butchers' shops throughout the country, its shares mostly owned by farmers. He had once been the managing director of a shoe manufacturer, Dolcis Ltd., and before that a civil servant. He used the Society of Arts to support both aesthetic beauty and music, to draw attention to the design of ever larger industrial farm buildings, to chair the judging panel on jewellery for the Industrial Design Bursaries Competition, and in 1974 to endow scholarships for string players to go abroad to study. Stratton was himself a keen amateur pianist, had been told that Britain was especially lacking in the quality of postgraduate study for musicians, and was worried that the worldwide inflation of the 1970s was making the career of a musician unaffordable.[6] (The music bursaries also included awards for singers, which came from corporate sponsorship, and briefly for choreographers and cellists. The awards were discontinued in 1991.)

The new managerial class also had a different way of pursuing reform. They had all learned to navigate complex bureaucracies, and many of them had been administrators in either industry or the military during the Second World War. They were planners, either in business or in government, and appreciated the difficulties of making changes. They feared, or had found from experience, that affecting one part of a system might inadvertently damage another. The certainties of the nineteenth century, of people like Henry Cole, bolstered by a utilitarian faith in reason, were gone. Tweaking a complex system might work in theory, but what if a crucial part had not been considered, or had been misunderstood? With the growth of bureaucracies, the number of records and statistics had also proliferated. Would-be reformers might drown in an ocean of data before they even decided what to change. Reforms required research, and lots of it.

Reforms also required discussion, perhaps more so than ever before. In the late nineteenth century, there had only been a few organisations in any given field of enquiry—the Society of Arts was often among the first, and groups had then splintered from it. By the mid-twentieth century, however, there was already a mass of specialist groups, which only seemed to keep growing: ever more learned societies, charities, pressure groups, lobbyists, trade unions, and professional organisations, not to mention government departments and regulatory bodies. In 1854 there had been about sixteen thousand civil servants; in the 1950s through to the 1980s there were usually between six and eight hundred thousand.[7] Any particular reform might attract the opposition of hundreds of small groups, let alone the large ones. Often, the smaller and more specialised the groups were, the better organised they could be.[8] A hasty reform, without consultation, might founder on the intransigence of coordinated opposition.

Many of the Society's members were themselves the members of such groups. John Stratton, for example, was chairman of the British Bacon Curers' Federation, and had also led the National Farmers' Union. Others had become used to constant negotiation with trade unions—following the Second World War, the unions were more powerful than ever, making industrial relations an essential part of management and politics. Unions frequently brought entire industries, sometimes the entire country, to a halt. For would-be reformers, successful changes would have to involve reconciling the competing interest groups, or at the very least negotiating coalitions to push them through.

A handful of members saw a new role for the Society of Arts. One of the most active was Arthur Reginald Newsom Roberts, who always went by A.R.N. Roberts, the public relations director of a chemical pesticide company, Plant Protection Ltd., which was a subsidiary of Imperial Chemical Industries, one of the largest manufacturing companies in the country. Roberts, like Stratton, was a member of the new managerial class. He likewise had interests beyond his industry. He was apparently a devotee of the late Arts and Crafts movement,[9] with a concern that the beauty of England's 'green and pleasant land' was under threat from ugly development.[10] For decades he would be the Society's representative on the Council for the Preservation of Rural England.[11]

Roberts joined the Society in 1943, and immediately had ideas about how the organisation might be more active. It looked as though the Second World War might soon be coming to an end, so Roberts approached the Society with a new initiative: to continue its campaign against ugliness in the countryside by advising on the erection of war memorials.[12] Roberts and others felt that the war memorials that followed the First World War had often been ill-considered and badly designed. They wished to prevent 'a widespread building of unsightly stone memorials similar to those which followed the last war'.[13] Yet the Society could not act in this alone, and nor could it make any decrees. With the proliferation of groups involved in the commissioning and design of war memorials, it instead brought the interested parties together for a conference.[14] Change was to be had through discussion, compromise, and coordination.

The result of the conference on war memorials was that the Society of Arts set up a War Memorials Advisory Council. Roberts acted as its secretary, assisted by one of the Society's members of staff. The Advisory Council's role—and thus the role of the Society of Arts—was to act as a clearing house for requests for information or advice on new memorials. Villages, regiments, and other groups wishing to commemorate their fallen were invited to write to the Advisory Council, who would put them in touch with one of almost fifty different specialist organisations. If a local authority needed advice on the best person to chisel the names on a plinth, Roberts would put them in touch with the Art Workers' Guild. If another group wanted to plant a memorial garden, Roberts might put them in touch with the Royal Horticultural Society.

The Advisory Council presented itself as having no specific agenda, but it in fact tried to ensure new war memorials conformed to their ideas of good taste. It was careful to exclude groups that it felt had poor aesthetic standards, for example by repeatedly refusing requests to join by the Guild of Memorial Craftsmen. The Advisory Council also issued a publication listing the desirable qualities in a war memorial, calling attention to the fact that they might benefit the living as well as commemorating the dead. Memorials might take the form of suitably labelled playing fields, swimming pools, village halls, homes for veterans, or newly planted forests (though they were careful not to suggest things that would be too utilitarian). They also recommended vellum books of remembrance, to be displayed in special rooms in village halls or churches. Roberts might put someone wanting one of these in touch with the Society of Scribes and Illuminators.[15]

The War Memorials Advisory Council called attention to these less obtrusive alternatives because they might reduce the demand for stone crosses. The fewer stone crosses in general, the fewer of them might be ugly: 'we are against any further crosses being put up on town and country greens' was a common opinion among its members.[16] Yet if local authorities insisted on erecting more stone crosses, and many of them did, Roberts and the Advisory Council did their best to prevent designs they considered ugly. When the town clerk of Dunstable wrote to them in 1948 to get their advice on some plans, Roberts sent the letter to the architect Edward Maufe (who designed Guildford Cathedral and the Air Forces Memorial). Maufe was appalled: 'I don't think I have ever seen a design more vulgar or ignorant.' He and Roberts agreed that 'it must be stopped'. The design was, as Roberts put it, 'the sort of thing for which we were formed to suppress'. Roberts tactfully suggested to Dunstable's town clerk that the design should be done by someone more experienced, and put him in touch with the Royal Institute of British Architects. Dunstable followed their advice.[17]

The War Memorials Advisory Council also pushed for a national or imperial war memorial, to be erected in central London. Roberts and Lord Chatfield, the former head of the British Navy, who was the Advisory Council's chairman, even visited the prime minister, Clement Attlee.[18] Their lobbying efforts, however, were rebuffed. Public opinion polls suggested that most people did not want any new stone monuments, which in the countryside was just as Roberts and the Advisory Council had hoped. Unfortunately for them, public opposition to monuments also extended to their proposed national memorial. The government would not act without evidence of public demand, and instead simply had the dates of the second war added to the Cenotaph on Whitehall. Defeated, the War Memorials Advisory Council ceased operations in 1948.

Yet the involvement of Roberts in the Society of Arts was just beginning. The success of the War Memorials Advisory Council in suppressing designs they did not like suggested a model by which the Society might be useful in the twentieth century. Its advantage was in being able to act as a convenor of diverse interests, as a neutral organisation that could call competing groups together to find common ground. Unlike the Royal Academy, which claimed to represent the interest of artists, or the Royal Institute of British Architects, which claimed to represent the interests of architects, the mission of the Society of Arts was so broad and vague that it could claim to represent the public as a whole. Although would-be reformers in control of the Society of Arts might have their own agendas, as Roberts had with war memorials, the Society's members were from such a diverse range of backgrounds that it seemed relatively neutral.

In 1945, A.R.N. Roberts was appointed to the Society's Council. In 1950, he seems to have persuaded his firm, Plant Protection Ltd., to endow a series of lectures on agricultural science.[19] Predictably, they mostly discussed the effects of pesticides. Roberts, however, was not interested in the Society of Arts as a learned society. Indeed, he saw himself as something of an outsider: 'although I am a member of the Council . . . it is very rarely that I am allowed to speak at it, because everybody knows that I have no real qualification to be on the committee of a learned society'.[20] Roberts instead wished the Society to be more proactive, to fulfil its potential role as a convenor and to otherwise push for change—to do in the twentieth century what it had done in the mid-nineteenth.

Roberts began to drag the Society towards action. He first tried to exploit the celebrations of its bicentenary, in which he found an ally in the highest of places: Queen Elizabeth II's husband, Prince Philip, the Duke of Edinburgh. When Elizabeth took the throne in 1952, Philip had been invited to succeed her as the Society's president. His first year was uneventful, but as a man in his early thirties he was much younger than the rest of the Society. He wished to do something useful, and cared little for the Society's aura of exclusivity. After all, in terms of aristocratic rank, he could not rise any higher. At the opening of its two-hundredth session in November 1953, Philip subtly reminded the Society to be active. 'There is no obsession with the past', he said, just after having welcomed the direct descendant of Viscount Folkestone as the new chairman. 'The Society remains essentially forward-looking and practical', he continued.[21] By paying these exaggerated compliments, Philip laid down a challenge to the Society's Council to live up to them. This was the chance Roberts needed.

Philip's words coincided with his announcement of a cash prize for the best essay on life in the year 2000—a first step in reminding the mostly elderly Council to think ahead.[22] The results were disappointing, and the first and second places were never awarded. Roberts took more practical steps. 'In keeping with the demand for a progressive future which was made by the President', the Society announced the formation of a Special Activities Committee, chaired by Roberts, which would collect and discuss proposals from fellows and the public about 'useful new action by the Society in matters of public interest'.[23]

This was what the Council itself was supposed to do, but it was increasingly bogged down in the day-to-day running of the Society's affairs. Roberts would also have had to wait his turn to ascend to the chairmanship, which was increasingly awarded based on seniority, and was in any case only for a maximum of two consecutive year-long terms (there were only a handful of exceptions to this rule).[24] Although having a Council had suited the likes of Henry Cole, who was able to dominate it for decades even when not the chairman, most people who joined it were happy to sit back and await their turn until the position of chairman opened up.

After all, with the Society's revenues and membership both rising, there was no pressure on the Council to do anything else. Satisfied by the increasing numbers and the Society's accumulating prestige, its members rarely, if ever, tried to vote anyone on the Council out of office. The norm was for members of Council to be inactive, with only a few exceptions. Already, by 1900, less than two decades after Cole's death, a new chairman at his inauguration explained that he accepted the position only because he had been told that there would not be much for him to do, and that in any case he would be absent for a quarter of his term because he was about to embark on a three-month trip to Egypt.[25] Faced with this kind of complacency on the Council, it made sense for Roberts to obtain a Special Activities Committee under his own control. He would be able to act without having to answer to people who were older or of higher status. Its members were to 'be drawn from the younger members of the Council', and not include any office-holders. In some cases, he would be able to circumvent the old men on the Council entirely.[26]

Over the next few years the Special Activities Committee explored new avenues for action. Its method was simply to consider 'spontaneous suggestions' made by the Society's fellows or by the members of the committee.[27] It considered whether the Society should try to raise the standard of television programmes, or whether it should do something about the lettering on road signs. In 1954, the Society was approached by the chair of the British Export Trade Research Organisation Ltd. (BETRO), Roger Falk. BETRO was an organisation set up by about sixty large firms in 1945, to provide information on the commercial possibilities in foreign markets. It was to be their in-common research arm, and even received a large one-off cash injection from the government. Yet it was often distrusted by many firms, particularly because of its state connections. Directors often preferred to rely on their gut feelings about the commercial possibilities of foreign markets, rather than relying on research. By 1952 it had failed due to lack of interest, but its promoters believed it had simply been ahead of its time.[28] Here seemed a promising opportunity for the Society of Arts, to demonstrate to firms that systematic market research would make it easier to find markets for exports.

From BETRO's remaining funds, Falk gave the Society money for an essay competition on the value of market research—the winner was supposed to go abroad to learn foreign marketing strategies. The would-be reformers in the Society hoped it would be a new version of its eighteenth-century premiums, but updated for the twentieth century. The Society assembled a few interested parties at a conference in 1955 to try to push the agenda (naturally, Roberts was one of the organisers). Yet it was a dead end. BETRO had already died, and there was no enthusiasm for its message. The Society could not act as a relatively impartial convenor, like it had with war memorials, because there were too few organisations to convene—market research was just not as interesting. In 1964, when BETRO's assets were finally disposed of, the fund was given to the Society in trust.[29] Rather than commemorating a dead person like the rest of its growing list of trusts to administer, the BETRO Trust commemorated a failed firm. (The trust appears to have lasted until 1986—over three times longer than the original company, which had failed after just seven years. The trust was used by the Society to fund lectures on export marketing, a few more travelling bursaries for marketers to learn from foreign companies, and even some research of its own.[30])

With the BETRO project, however, Roberts and the Special Activities Committee were just getting started. They seem to have discussed anything and everything that came their way. In 1955 the Society held an exhibition of European medals made in the previous twenty-five years, instigated by the president of the Royal Academy, the architect Albert Richardson, who was also on the Society's Council. Richardson used the chance to draw attention to how a wartime tax had affected medal artists. He complained that artists were already poorly paid, and that the purchase tax, introduced on luxury items in 1940 to prevent unnecessary waste, further deprived them of income by forcing them to raise prices. 'It is ridiculous, this socialistic tyranny of the purchase tax', he railed, 'abandon it at once!'[31] Here was a chance for the Special Activities Committee to take action—it successfully lobbied the chancellor to make gold and silver medals exempt.[32] It was a minor change, but at least the Society was taking action again.

The Special Activities Committee took on a series of other, seemingly random initiatives. Some of these were simply personal to the Society's members, or just to Roberts. By the late 1950s, he had been promoted to education officer for Imperial Chemical Industries. He was concerned with the quality of manuals and design specifications, so used the committee, and thus the Society, to do something about it. He got himself nominated as the Society's representative on committees of the City and Guilds of London Institute, which it had had a hand in founding. At his suggestion, the institute introduced examinations in technical authorship.[33]

Yet the Special Activities Committee's main achievement was in the same vein as the Society's action on war memorials: to convene disparate or conflicting interests, reach a consensus, and the form a coalition that could push agreed-upon reforms. Roberts, as someone concerned with preserving the beauty of the English countryside, was particularly taken with a couple of lectures at the Society, entitled 'Beauty in Danger'. One of the lectures was given by the architect Hugh Casson, who had been director of architecture for the Festival of Britain. Casson railed against ugliness—'a power so evil, so active in this country, that it really does almost threaten to become a danger to our society'. He shocked his audience with example after example of ugliness: 'ghastly' street lamps, mutilated trees, suburban sprawl, advertisements, car parks, 'a paralysing slime of bollards, signs and street furniture', and electrical pylons and cables running through the centre of old market towns, 'the whole place scribbled over as if by a great black pencil'. Worst of all, he said, this ugliness had been allowed to happen despite ubiquitous state planning. The government was more powerful than ever, since the Second World War touching every aspect of people's lives. Yet it had failed.[34]

The government had passed a law in 1947, the Town and Country Planning Act, which greatly strengthened its control over almost all new construction and renovation. The law required all construction to first obtain permission from local authorities, who employed town planners to decide each case—yet another group among the new class of bureaucrats and managers that had emerged in the twentieth century. Ten years on from the passage of the planning law, Casson's verdict was damning. Yet the answer was not to undo the system; the problem, he claimed, was that the planners were too few, too ill-equipped, and too reactive. Something had to be done. He called on his audience to 'recreate an environment of which we can all be proud'.[35]

The challenge, however, was in balancing concerns about ugliness—aesthetics—with the benefits of modern technology. Casson readily admitted that roads, electricity, street lamps, and industry all had their advantages. He also thought it would be unhelpful to find scapegoats. The spread of ugliness was nobody's particular fault; it was the fault of everybody. The issue was in negotiating the right balance, of reconciling the different interests. Here was a chance for the Society of Arts to play a role as convenor, to find out what the points of agreement and disagreement even were, before the negotiations could begin. Roberts immediately invited Casson to put some proposals before the Special Activities Committee.[36]

Casson's concerns, shared by Roberts, were similar to those the Society of Arts had had in the 1920s and 30s when it tried to save ancient cottages. But the problems of development and ugliness had seemingly only worsened, despite the fact that the government now actively sought to prevent them. Even the relevant government ministers were already on board. Duncan Sandys, the Minister for Housing and Local Government, in effect the person in charge of planning, opened a conference that Roberts organised for the Society in 1956 on the 'Perils and Prospects in Town and Country', despite the fact that on the same day Britain and France went to war with Egypt to try and force open the Suez Canal. Sandys was too distracted by the Suez Crisis to prepare his speech properly, but he still turned up and supported the conference's aim to 'wipe away squalor and ugliness'.[37] The problem was that having support from the top politicians like Sandys, a son-in-law of Winston Churchill, was no longer enough. Although the planners had the levers of power, they did not always work as intended. Preventing ugliness instead required the cooperation of everybody involved. As Casson put it, 'there must be constant and unceasing vigilance and preparedness on every citizen's part to speak up for beauty'.[38]

In the early 1960s, the movement took on more than just aesthetics. The Society's concerns for the environment had focused mostly on built surroundings—either preventing them from covering 'England's green and pleasant land', or ensuring that the things that were built were of a certain standard. Increasingly, however, they focused on the natural environment. The word 'environment' in the late 1950s had mostly been used to denote surroundings: landscape, the scenery. The Society played a role in adding further meaning to the term.

Increasingly, the Special Activities Committee spent its time 'considering the much wider problems created by modern development as a whole'.[39] The turning point, however, came from the intervention of the Society's president, Prince Philip. He had long been keen on the country sports of shooting, stalking, and wildfowling, but a passion for wildlife was awakened in 1956 while travelling on the Royal Yacht *Britannia* on a tour of Commonwealth countries for the Melbourne Olympic Games. On a particularly boring stretch of ocean between New Zealand and the Antarctic he began taking photographs of the birds. Philip soon became a devoted bird-watcher, and became friends with the conservationist Peter Scott.

In 1946, Scott had founded the Severn Wildfowl Trust, now the Wildfowl & Wetlands Trust, which held many of its early annual general meetings at the Society of Arts. By the late 1950s, he was famous as a BBC broadcaster on natural history (he was a major inspiration to a more recent famous natural history broadcaster, David Attenborough).[40] Scott also won a bronze medal for single-handed yachting, was an accomplished artist, and was the only son of the famous Antarctic explorer, Captain Robert Falcon Scott. It was in 1961, when Scott helped to found the World Wildlife Fund (now the World Wide Fund for Nature), that he got Prince Philip involved in the broader movement for conservation. Scott designed the fund's panda logo, and invited Philip to become the president of its appeal for donations in Britain. The purpose of the fund was to conserve wildlife across the world: to buy land where it was threatened, to pay people to guard it, and to educate people to take better care. Through the influence of Scott and his fellow nature enthusiasts, Philip's passion for birds became a passion for the conservation of all nature.[41] By 1963, Prince Philip was presiding over the Wildfowl Trust's meetings hosted at the Society of Arts, and was attending other groups of conservationists. (Incidentally, Scott also became Britain's gliding champion that year—yet another passion he imparted to the prince.)[42]

Britain's wildlife conservation trusts in 1960 were small. Collectively, they only had about three thousand members, with an additional ten thousand members of the Royal Society for the Protection of Birds.[43] Yet with the help of evangelists like Scott, using radio and television to spread concern, the number of trusts was growing. The government had intervened in 1949, with the creation of a system of national parks, run by the Nature Conservancy—changes instigated by Max Nicholson, yet another bird enthusiast and co-founder of the World Wildlife Fund, who also served as secretary to the executive committee for the Festival of Britain. Nicholson, in charge of the Nature Conservancy, persuaded the various conservation trusts to organise a 'National Nature Week' on

18–25 May 1963.[44] With funding from the World Wildlife Fund, they persuaded the Post Office to issue wildlife postage stamps, organised nature trails for schoolchildren, and held an exhibition at Alexandra Palace to highlight endangered species.[45]

The exhibition attracted forty-six thousand visitors, including Prince Philip. He was impressed at the range of organisations represented and asked the people manning the different stands whether they all knew one another. It turned out they did not. Here was an opportunity for convening the different groups. Philip asked Nicholson to put a conference together—a forum in which to thrash out any differences within the growing movement for conservation and agree on where they should concentrate their efforts. He wanted it to take place as soon as possible, to take advantage of the publicity and excitement generated by Nature Week. Without much time, Nicholson put together a conference in late 1963, entitled 'The Countryside in 1970'—a name chosen because it was forward-looking, but close enough to create a sense of urgency. The conference coincided almost perfectly with the Society's own efforts—the Special Activities Committee had commissioned a report on the impact of industrialisation on the countryside, which was also published in 1963. Instead of organising their own conference to discuss the report, they joined forced with Max Nicholson.[46]

The first conference in 1963 was rushed as Nicholson had not had much time to assemble everyone. At the very least, however, many of the participants forged connections for the very first time. It was a first step in building a coalition in favour of conservation. Philip suggested that the Society of Arts take on the organisation of future conferences, to keep alive the spirit of coordination. Unlike the Nature Conservancy, the Society could draw upon a much broader network—its growing membership in industry, the civil service, and further afield.[47] Two more conferences took place, in 1965 and in 1970, with the administrative burden shouldered by the Society.[48] They were large affairs, over multiple days, split into working groups to investigate a topic in detail and then report back to the whole. The last conference had 900 people representing 330 different organisations.[49] The topics included everything from pollution of the air and soil, to rubbish disposal, toxic waste in rivers, agriculture, and the pressures of a growing population. The task of the conferences was to bring these issues together into a coherent whole, to form a full picture of the danger to nature and to people too. The concern for beauty was combined with concerns for wildlife, health, and litter.

Before the mid-1960s, the term environmentalism had mostly referred to the belief that it was a person's education and upbringing, rather than their genes, that determined their behaviour. It was a term mostly used in debates about education. Over the course of the mid-1960s, however, the term took on a new meaning, more familiar today, of concern about protecting the natural world. Many years later, one of the main people involved said that Prince Philip's intervention had 'more or less invented the environment'.[50] That claim may be overstated, but the conferences played a role. At the very least, they spurred the kinds of conversations that led to new ideas.

The environmental movement had its roots in the instincts of thousands of people to preserve what they saw as important, for the benefit of wildlife they adored, or for their own enjoyment. It was over the course of the conferences, in Britain and in many other industrialised countries, that a new argument began to gain currency: that the conservation of nature was about benefitting humans, not just the wild species faced with extinction. The attitude of those who sought to conserve the beauty of the built environment, so focused on the aesthetic enjoyment of current and future generations of people, came to be applied to nature too. More seriously, 'The Countryside in 1970' conferences revealed the full extent of the danger to the natural world. In 1962, just before the first conference, the American biologist Rachel Carson published a book, *Silent Spring*, which documented the harmful effects of pesticides in US agriculture. The book caused widespread shock, especially the revelation that some chemicals were accumulating to dangerous levels in human breast milk. Prince Philip recommended the book publicly, and privately sent advance copies to government ministers.[51] The conferences reinforced the impact of the revelations still further.

By having the separate campaigners and experts present to one another, they found out about problems they had never heard of, or never even imagined—the full effects of the smogs, chemicals, oil spills, and pollution. As the shocking revelations accumulated, the arguments about human benefit from conserving nature went further still: to many, the problems seemed so massive and widespread, that failing to conserve nature might even threaten humans with extinction. It was with the emergence of this argument, surmised Philip, that the environmentalist movement truly began.[52] The term 'environment' came to mean a concern for the wellbeing of the entire planet, humans included.

Whether or not the conferences were directly responsible for the emergence of this new argument, they showed the Society of Arts how it could be useful. As Nicholson put it, 'out of a rabble of unrelated organizations unaware of one another's aims', the conferences created 'a brotherhood of constructively aware and active groups'. The Society, 'as an autonomous, independent body with no sectional interest to guard', seemed the ideal convenor.[53] As one chairman of the Society's Council put it, convening different and sometimes conflicting interest groups with a view to finding solutions was 'probably the most valuable service we can perform'.[54] Between conferences, the Society issued newsletters to the delegates describing the latest environmental disasters, the activities of voluntary groups, and new legislation. Study groups were appointed months before the conference to research the topics that would be discussed, to ensure that they would be able to argue from the best information. Prince Philip continued to play his part, hosting receptions or dinners, sometimes at the royal palaces.[55]

The Society also hosted smaller conferences on some of the more specific issues, offered more lectures on environmental topics, and sent delegations to the United States and Europe. Some members of the study groups attended a conference on natural beauty held by the US president in 1965 at the White House,[56] and it was on the suggestion of one of 'The Countryside in 1970' organisers that the Council of Europe designated 1970 European Conservation Year—a bid to raise public awareness internationally.[57] What had started as a small group of British bird-watchers was rapidly becoming a coordinated global movement.

Public awareness also rose in Britain. The combined membership of Britain's wildlife trusts, which in 1960 had stood at only three thousand, had by the mid-1970s risen to a hundred thousand. It doubled again in the following decade, and at the beginning of the twenty-first century stood at four hundred thousand. Other conservationist organisations saw similarly dramatic increases, and the 1970s saw the creation of new groups, like Friends of the Earth and Greenpeace, which sought to prevent damage to the environment as a whole.[58] At the 1970 general election, for the first time ever, polled voters cited the environment as an issue.[59] The incoming prime minister, Edward Heath, created a new Department for the Environment and spoke at that year's 'The Countryside in 1970' conference. Within a couple of years, some concerned members of the public had formed the forerunners to Britain's current Green Party.

'The Countryside in 1970' conferences also had a more concrete impact on government policy. At the second conference, in 1965, the delegates signed up to a broad set of proposals, and many of them found their way into law. One of the major concerns that year was that there was an impending new wave of environmental destruction. The first wave had been caused by the growth of industrial cities, the second by the expansion of railways, and the third by the sprawl of suburbs with the arrival of the car. The impending 'fourth wave' was an expected increase in leisure. The technological revolutions of the 1950s and 60s had caused rapid economic growth, coupled with policies that stressed full employment, leading to higher incomes and more time for holidays. With a larger population able to afford their own cars, and with the further expansion of the road network to accommodate them, the environmentalists feared a plague of tourists, 'weekend multitudes', who would issue from Britain's crowded cities to congest roads, drop litter, and disturb the quiet with the drone of car engines.[60]

To stem the impending tide, the environmentalists proposed the creation of country parks closer to the cities. If the tourists were 'like ants ... swarming out of cities', it made sense to have more convenient sites to act as honeypots—distractions for the leisure-seekers to prevent the ruination of places that were more beautiful and remote.[61] The proposals found their way into law with the Countryside Act of 1968.[62] Local authorities and Max Nicholson's Nature Conservancy were empowered to create more country parks as quickly as possible, 'before the scenery becomes a victim of its own beauty'.[63] More broadly, too, the comprehensive approach of 'The Countryside in 1970' conferences was reflected in the law's stipulation that the impact of government policies on the natural beauty of the countryside would have to be considered by every government department. Albeit vague, and without the teeth for enforcement, it was a clear signal of the state's intentions.[64] The stipulation meant that the government's concern for the environment no longer depended on the personal beliefs of the ministers or officials who happened to be in charge. Consideration of the environment was now explicitly mandated by law.

Prince Philip did not stop in 1970. He now saw a role for the Society of Arts as a permanent convenor for the environmental movement—a means of rationalising the mess of thousands of small groups, getting them to work together for the common cause. In 1971, he had the Society of Arts set up a committee for the environment, over which he presided personally. This step was unusually active compared to his predecessors as the Society's royal president, who were generally content to only show their faces at prize-givings and assorted ceremonies. Even Prince Albert, who had also been unusually active, did not chair committee meetings himself—he had usually just had a deputation sent to him instead. For Philip, the Society of Arts became the main tool for pursuing what he felt were the most useful reforms. Many years later he would refer to it privately as 'my RSA'.[65]

Philip's committee on the environment continued for decades, essentially acting as his personal environmental think-tank: of the nine other people who sat on it, he personally chose a third, another third were chosen by the Society's Council, and the final third were chosen by the committee itself.[66] Over the decades its members included Max Nicholson, a few other founders of major environmental organisations, some academics, planners, and even the natural history broadcaster David Attenborough.[67] It also had a dedicated member of the Society's staff—an assistant secretary for the environment. Philip still had an interest in design and some of the other activities of the Society, but the environment was his focus. After all, in his view the survival of the entire planet was at stake.

The purpose of the environment committee was to sustain the movement that had so successfully reached the public consciousness in 1970. They brought in more lecturers to the Society on environmental issues, including those with information on potential problems, such as the impact of industrial chemicals on cancer, or those claiming to have new solutions. They 'aimed at the enlightenment of the ignorant', as Philip put it.[68] They also convened more conferences, many of them on topics suggested by Prince Philip himself. His aim was to try and discuss issues that might arise in the future, before they became too urgent. The Society's conferences covered the fertility of the soil, world population, fish-farming, forestry, water conservation, renewable energy, and acid rain. They even held conferences on planned developments to Covent Garden, and in 1973 on the proposed Channel Tunnel, to connect Britain with France. Unlike the usual lectures of the Society, the conferences tended to end with resolutions that would be sent to the relevant officials, though they met with varying success.

The environment committee was not, however, a campaigning organisation. Nor did it try to demonise the people who caused damage to the environment. Prince Philip's approach was to try to involve them in finding solutions. He did not attack the firms who polluted, but rather sought to educate the people who ran them, to persuade them to take the concerns of others seriously, and to find technological solutions.

A feature of many of the conferences and lectures held by the Society was that they frequently involved state officials and the directors of large firms. They were given the chance to explain their decisions, to point out the trade-offs involved so that a solution or compromise might be reached. Electrical pylons and overhead wires, for example, might be ugly, but in 1960 the chairman of the state-owned Central Electricity Generating Board explained that it would be sixteen times as expensive to lay the cables underground, not to mention unreliable. There was also no cheaper insulator than the air, which was free. Either people had to be willing to pay more, or they would have to develop the technology to remove the problem.[69] By giving the vested interests a platform, and discussing the trade-offs seriously, Philip hoped to make environmental concerns respectable.

In 1983 the Society took a further step, hoping to encourage firms and state-owned businesses to find technological solutions to the problems they caused. The Society was approached by the Department of the Environment and a lobby group for firms, the Confederation of British Industry, about organising an award for new technologies that reduced pollution. The catchily titled 'Pollution Abatement Technology Awards' were used to draw attention to innovations and promote their widespread adoption. Their backing by government and business ensured they were taken seriously, with the Society taking on the administrative burden and providing an air of impartiality. The awards were environmental versions of the eighteenth-century premiums. They could reward individuals, but mostly recognised the achievements of corporate entities.

An oil company won an award for developing new ways to clean up oil spills, and chemical manufacturing giants won awards for reducing the use of solvents in painting cars and neutralising poisons like cyanide in toxic waste. State-run water providers won awards for finding ways to recycle sewage for agriculture, and an engineering company won an award for developing a quieter and more efficient aeroplane engine.[70] The awards were soon extended to cover more than just reducing pollution, to include the design of recyclable products, and even the export of environmental technologies to other countries.[71] By involving the polluting industries in the search for solutions, the Society's various awards were used by Philip as a 'tactical weapon' in his fight to preserve the environment.[72]

Yet some began to question whether there might be a deeper problem with the industries that damaged the environment, perhaps even with the kinds of people who ran them. In 1966, Prince Philip suggested that one of the buildings within Windsor Castle, a house attached to St George's Chapel, be used as a sort of staff college for Anglican clergymen. Very quickly, it began to do more than this, becoming a venue in which to host informal discussions between the leaders of government, firms, and religious organisations. St George's House, hidden away within the castle's walls, was a place where the managers of some of the largest and most powerful bureaucracies could discuss the country's problems in private. The organisers hoped that through free discussion at these 'consultations', the invited leaders might reach some solutions.

The person who ran the consultations in the early 1970s was Kenneth Adams, a former army major, who had also been the director of one of London's wharfs. It was as a dedicated member of the Church of England, however, that Adams became concerned about the relationship between industry and morality. He worried that the people who ran Britain's businesses, especially its manufactures, rarely considered the moral implications of their decisions. Just as in the eighteenth century members of the Society of Arts had worried about the morals of the aristocrats who governed them, and had used history painting to try to instil them with virtue, Adams sought a way to improve the morals of the people who ran Britain's twentieth-century economy.

Adams noticed that the managers and directors of firms often treated their jobs as distinct from the other facets of their lives. When it came to business they mostly acted as mere functionaries, enacting the interests of the firm's owners, often a disparate and anonymous mass of shareholders, rather than considering the wider public good. At a church gathering in the 1960s, Adams had been asked to speak about how to find time for good deeds—'the work of God'—in the forty hours a week that were supposedly left for that kind of activity after someone had finished working, eating, sleeping, and spending some time with the family. Adams was horrified. He spent the talk railing against the whole premise. Work itself, he argued, was a chance to do good.[73]

The problem, he found, was that people did not believe him. While he argued that all industry served a social purpose—it provided everything that people relied on to survive and to thrive—most people saw it as only a means of earning a living. 'Don't tell me that I do work of any social value like people who work in the Health Service—I only make underwear!' was a typical response.[74] For Adams, this was deeply troubling. If people could not see any social value to their work—after all, manufacturing underwear substantially benefits everyone who wears it—then they would be blind to the other opportunities their work provided to do good. They would also be blind to the harm they might do from doing work badly. At its root, the problem was that people in Britain were apathetic about industry, often even opposed to it. Britain's 'anti-industrial culture', Adams argued, was a source, if not *the* source, of all of industry's other malaises—its disregard for the environment, for a start, as well as the decline of British manufacturing, and even worsening relations between workers and their managers.

Britain's share of the world's manufactured exports halved between the late 1950s and late 1970s, from almost a fifth to under a tenth.[75] Meanwhile, its industries were frequently affected by strikes. At a time when almost all of Britain's electricity was derived from the burning of coal, and when all of Britain's coal-mining industry was controlled by a single state-owned corporation, a strike by its employees could bring the entire country to a standstill. In 1974, when the coal miners went on strike, the government tried to conserve the country's electricity by enforcing a three-day working week. Only a few essential services were exempt. To try to bring the strike to an end, the prime minister Edward Heath called a general election, hoping that it would demonstrate public opposition to the strike. His party ran under the slogan 'Who governs Britain?' but it turned out that the miners did: his party lost power. During the winter of 1978–79, nicknamed the 'Winter of Discontent', strikes by state employees meant that rubbish piled up in the streets, corpses were left unburied, and hospitals were reduced to only treating emergency cases.

For Kenneth Adams, these problems were not just to do with public policies—finding ways to restrain inflation, for example, or to reduce the power of trade unions. For Adams, the problems were all symptoms of Britain's anti-industrial culture. People would not do their jobs well if they thought their jobs were worthless, he argued. People would act unethically in their jobs if everyone else thought their jobs were evil anyway. To solve these problems, Adams formulated a plan to change the way that people in Britain thought about industry. If people valued industry, he believed, then the people who worked in industry would do their jobs better. If industry were to be held in high esteem, then they would raise their ethical standards to deserve that esteem too. He formulated a plan to change Britain's culture.

For the British public to value industry, they first needed to appreciate what it did. They needed to be educated about the fact that they all depended on one another's industry—underwear had to be manufactured by someone, after all, as did bread, steel, coal, or any of the other things people used. It was not just about the individual things people produced for one another, but the fact that the combination of their industry also benefitted them all collectively. People who worked in industry, Adams argued, were all contributing to a greater whole. Yet the public were not only ignorant of this, they were generally educated to believe the opposite. Schools and universities often insinuated that careers in industry or commerce were inferior to careers in government, academia, and professions like law, medicine, and science. People in industry 'genuinely believe that their work is not as good, not as worthy, not as virtuous', Adams argued. It meant that the people who went into industry were not expected to do good, and so they met those low expectations. The people who wished to do good also went into the other professions, leaving a dearth of people in industry who prioritised moral concerns.

Overall, Adams wished to bring an end to the public's 'disenchantment' with industry. This was partly about getting people in industry to behave better, to set a better example on the environment, on pay, working conditions, working relations, and corruption. The better industry behaved, and was seen to behave, the more it would deserve and thus be able to demand the public's esteem. Industry would have to play its part too, if it was to bring about a change in Britain's culture.[76]

Adams, by running the consultations at St George's House, persuaded a few industry lobby groups and business associations to draw up ethical codes of conduct for directors—moral guidelines by which to manage.[77] He was not alone, however, in wishing to improve the country's attitude towards industry. The government began annual competitions to recognise talented young engineers, and introduced more technical subjects to its school qualifications. The chief executives of a few large companies also set up an organisation, the Industry and Parliament Trust, to educate politicians. When it was set up in 1977, fewer than 15 per cent of MPs had any direct experience of industry. The trust arranged for a few politicians each year to spend a few weeks at firms, to gain an appreciation of the kinds of decisions managers faced.[78] Similar initiatives to educate schoolchildren about industry were set up by companies, trade unions, and individuals. Among the earliest was 'Young Enterprise', set up in 1962 by Walter Salomon, a German-born Jewish banker who had fled to London from the Nazis. Salomon's scheme had teenagers set up and run companies, under the guidance of professionals.[79]

Adams was therefore not alone in trying to solve the problem. Just like the conservationist movement of the 1950s and 60s, the attempt to raise the country's esteem for industry was a 'movement of a thousand blossoms'.[80] He believed, however, that the leaders of all those initiatives needed convening, to be brought together to share tactics and develop a strategy. Following the apparent success of the conservationist movement, the ideal organisation to convene the disparate groups seemed to be the Society of Arts. It was, Adams said, an 'independent body of repute'.[81] The Society's full title, alluding to the encouragement of manufactures and commerce, covered what Adams had in mind.

In 1979, Adams moved from St George's House to the Society of Arts, his salary paid for by an Australian-born Greek engineer and inventor, Demetri Comino. Adams thus became the Society's 'Comino Fellow', tasked with finding a way to convene the movement for improving British attitudes to industry. He was first inspired by the Society's past use of exhibitions. The Great Exhibition, he noted, had been a popular celebration of the products of industry—it must, he surmised, have encouraged the British public to hold industry in high esteem. Yet an exhibition in the 1980s would be too expensive, and extremely risky. There had been no major exhibitions of industry for decades. Even the world's fairs, the successors to the Great Exhibition of 1851, from the mid-twentieth century most commonly resembled the Festival of Britain—they were branding exercises for countries, emphasising culture rather than industry. They were increasingly used by governments to try to define their nations' special characteristics, to their own populations and to the rest of the world.

When Henry Cole had pushed for the Great Exhibition, however, he had not had twentieth-century technology at his disposal. Adams, unlike Henry Cole, could use television. In 1969, an art historian, Kenneth Clark, had written and presented a television series for the British Broadcasting Corporation called *Civilisation*. It aired on BBC2, run by David Attenborough, which at the time was the only channel broadcast in colour.[82] *Civilisation* was a huge success, attracting 2.5 million viewers in Britain, and double that figure when it was aired in the United States—unprecedentedly high numbers for a series about art. For the first time, in full colour, and right in their living rooms, the British public received an international guided tour of the history of western art from a leading expert on the subject. In terms of spreading beauty to the masses, Henry Cole could eat his heart out. In the years that followed, similarly sweeping television series, on science and the history of Britain, had also met with success.[83]

What was still missing, however, was a similar series about industry, about the role and development in world history of manufactures and commerce. Adams used the Society of Arts to try to produce such a programme. When it was aired, he would also use the Society to convene the various leaders of the pro-industry movement, so that it would be promoted by trade unions, firms, and schools. It would be, as he called it, a national 'teach-in'. Whereas Henry Cole had had the Crystal Palace, Kenneth Adams hoped that the television set in every British home would be his 'crystal box'.[84]

But the television series was never broadcast. A script was prepared, provisionally entitled *Homo Faber* or *The Art of the Impossible*,[85] and a company agreed to produce it.[86] The Society even announced that Channel 4, the newest of the television channels, had commissioned it.[87] But in 1983 Channel 4 ran out of funds and the project was shelved.[88] Foiled, Kenneth Adams instead sought to emulate a more recent endeavour of the Society of Arts: the apparent success of 'The Countryside in 1970' conferences, and especially its focus on the year 1970, which had seemed a watershed year for the environmental movement. Adams would still try to have his teach-in, even if he was denied his crystal box.[89] At his urging, the Society of Arts decided to designate the year 1986 as 'Industry Year', much as 1970 had been the European year of conservation. After that, he hoped, the pro-industry movement would be able to maintain momentum.

The Society did not have to get permission from anybody to name a year. Indeed, named days, months, and years, have all proliferated in general. But they did have widespread support for it. The Society was prestigious, and had a wide network of fellows, not to mention the connections it had made with lecturers, supporters of the industrial design bursaries, and through its conferences on the environment. The Royal Designers for Industry happened to celebrate their fiftieth anniversary during 1986—an 'Eye for Industry' exhibition of their work was, fittingly, held at the Victoria and Albert Museum, which used to be Henry Cole's South Kensington Museum and was funded by the Royal Commission for the Great Exhibition of 1851. The campaign had the backing of Prince Philip too—his environment committee held a conference on the role of industry in caring for the environment, which in 1987 was accompanied by a book and an exhibition, as well as talks with trade unionists about how they might contribute to environmental policy.[90]

To run the campaign, the Society hired a former businessman, Geoffrey Chandler. He was, by many accounts, a 'dynamo'.[91] Although Adams had initiated the campaign, he was most comfortable thinking or discussing things. Chandler was an organiser. In the late 1970s he had been a senior executive at a major oil company, Shell. Influenced by the discussions at St George's House, he had persuaded the company to publicly set out ethical guidelines on how to deal with social and environmental issues. (It was a step in the right direction, even if the company later often broke them.) After this, he ran the government's attempt to reconcile managers, trade unions, and civil servants, and form a national economic plan: the National Economic Development Office, often nicknamed 'Neddy'. As a respected businessman with contacts in government, he brought his own wide network to the Industry Year campaign.[92]

Chandler travelled the country, meeting with the local representatives of business groups, churches, and women's organisations, as well as visiting schools, firms, and local councils. As a representative of the Society of Arts, which did not formally represent any particular interest, he was an uncontroversial figure, able to persuade the disparate groups to form local committees. As Chandler pointed out, he would not have been able to do the same as a representative of a trade union, or of the Confederation of British Industry, the major business lobby group. Leadership from those groups in the campaign would have been too divisive.[93]

To the various local committees, Chandler distributed promotional pamphlets and other materials, including video cassettes with a film by a popular radio presenter, Brian Redhead. By January 1986, some 4,400 schools, 1,400 companies, and thousands of other organisations had promised their involvement in the campaign. Church leaders produced sermons to be given on the benefits of industry, for example, and teachers prepared advice for schools. All 26,000 schools in the country received the campaign's materials, distributed via the local education authorities. Overall, the campaign sent out some three million documents.[94]

Chandler persuaded other kinds of organisations to contribute too. The Archbishop of Canterbury conducted a service at St Paul's Cathedral on the theme of Industry Year, attended by Prince Philip and the queen.[95] The nationalised railway monopoly, British Rail, named one of its diesel-electric locomotives *Industry Year 1986* (despite the campaign's spirit of industrial cooperation, the naming was delayed by a few months due to strikes).[96] The Garden Gnomes Association even offered an industry-themed gnome display. The Post Office issued industry-themed stamps, though Chandler thought them 'aesthetically disappointing'.[97]

Yet for all that promotion, there was not much response from the public. By mid-1986, polls revealed that about 9 per cent of the population recognised the name 'Industry Year 1986' without any prompting. Journalists occasionally referenced the campaign, but usually just to make a point about its obscurity. 'Next week sees the start of Industry

11.1. Some of the stamps issued by the Royal Mail as part of the Industry Year 1986 campaign. RSA/PR/MC/100/15/3. Stamp designs © Royal Mail Group Limited.

Year, 1986', started one editorial. 'Not a lot of people know that. Not a lot of people care.'[98]

The campaign did, however, have some impact on culture. It was the basis of the plot for an award-winning novel, *Nice Work*, by David Lodge. Set in the fictional town of Rummidge, it began with a university English lecturer's secondment to a factory in 1986 as part of Industry Year, to shadow one of the factory's managers. Lodge used the book to examine the ideological divide between intellectuals and those who worked in industry, satirising academia's myopia. Lodge himself researched the book in 1986 by shadowing the manager of an engineering company.[99] It was the kind of reconciliation of intellectuals with industry that Adams had hoped for.

The Industry Year campaign also helped the pro-industry movement. Industries opened their doors to school visits, which often resulted in lasting connections between managers and teachers and allowed the visits to be repeated. Surveys suggested that the number of secondary schools with regular links to industry increased from around only a quarter to well over half.[100] Some of the hundreds of local pro-industry committees that Chandler helped to form in the years leading up to 1986 were also creative in how they forged new links. 'We're a bit daft up here in Rossendale', said one company director, who, as well as arranging for schoolchildren to visit factory floors, arranged with a few colleagues to attend the local school, sitting in on classes and playing football during the lunch break.[101] The companies that reached out to schools often 'shamed other companies into doing something' as well.[102]

The formation of hundreds of local committees was, in Chandler's view, the most important outcome of the Industry Year 1986 campaign. Although the Society of Arts would not be able to afford to continue sustaining them for long—the project was already one of the Society's most expensive ever—he hoped that another organisation might eventually take up the task. The Society continued to host Chandler until 1989, but the local committees were soon threatened. Although the campaign had been funded by the Society of Arts, Comino, and the Confederation for British Industry, most of the money came from the government.

In late 1987, the government unilaterally decided to take matters into its own hands. It offered state funds to support local partnerships between industry and schools, but insisted that the organisations to sustain them would have to tender for the privilege of receiving those funds. Rather than simply funding the hundreds of local committees that Chandler had helped to set up, the government replaced them. Although its scheme lasted only until 1990, by then the damage had been done. The personal connections that had formed between teachers and some company directors persisted, but many of the local committees to support and encourage more of them had in the meantime disbanded.[103] Industry Year's most promising outcome had, Chandler complained, been ruined by the meddling of government's 'third-rate dittos'.[104]

The Industry Year campaign ended in frustration for Adams and Chandler. They both moved on to other things.[105] Yet it demonstrated a new willingness in the Society of Arts to take on ambitious new projects, to try to make itself useful. The Special Activities Committee had disbanded in 1963, the same year as the first 'Countryside in 1970' conference. It is not entirely clear why, although Roberts perhaps simply felt that the Society's work on the environment was sufficiently important and time-consuming for him to give up trying to find new ideas. Apart from Prince Philip's work on the environment, throughout much of the 1960s and 70s the Society had otherwise just continued giving its lectures, running its annual industrial design competitions, and managing its trusts. The appointment of Kenneth Adams as Comino Fellow demonstrated a much greater openness to ambitious new ideas. But before the Society could do more, it would have to survive a self-imposed crisis.

12

Furious Brainstorming

THE SOCIETY'S RENEWED OPENNESS to ideas in the mid-1970s was led by its secretary, Christopher Lucas. For much of the Society's history, the post of secretary had usually been that of chief functionary—the head clerk to carry out the democratic will of its subscribers. Although the subscribers had elected the Society's founder, William Shipley, to be their first secretary, his job had almost entirely involved taking minutes at both the weekly general meetings and the various sub-committees. He had drawn up the lists of the subscribers and drafts for the advertisements of the premiums, and otherwise managed the Society's correspondence. There had been little time to do much else, even when assistant secretaries were appointed to share some of the burden. It was when Shipley was simply a subscriber, and no longer the secretary, that he seems to have developed most of his new suggestions for what the Society should encourage next. In any case, new initiatives tended to emerge from the debates among subscribers at their weekly meetings every Wednesday evening.

The secretaries did, however, have the opportunity to become more active in deciding the Society's direction. As the one person who had to be present at almost every single meeting, they knew most about the organisation's workings and could manipulate that knowledge to pursue their own initiatives. The extent to which they did this or were content to get on with administration very much depended upon the person in question. It was Arthur Aikin, for example, who in the early nineteenth century pioneered the practice of giving lectures that were for instruction and entertainment, in addition to the usual discussions of whether a particular improvement was worthy of a prize. We have also seen the way in which Francis Whishaw personally piloted the Society's exhibitions, and how John Scott Russell prompted its focus in the late 1840s on applying art to manufactures. It was also the Society's secretary towards the end of the nineteenth century, Henry Trueman Wood, who persuaded it to be involved in further international exhibitions.

Many of the others were content, as far as can be ascertained from the records, to simply carry out the suggestions thrown out by the deliberations of the Society's subscriber democracy, and then from 1846 its governing Council. Even the more passive among the secretaries did, however, have an influence on the Society's membership. As the functionaries in charge of the Society's correspondence, and especially for writing invitations to potential new members, they often exerted an influence on the kinds of people who became members. Samuel More used his connections among the late eighteenth century's inventors—people like John 'Iron Mad' Wilkinson or the pioneering Staffordshire potter Josiah Wedgwood—to recruit them as members. Francis Whishaw, himself an engineer, likewise used his connections among patent agents and engineers to help rescue the Society's decline in the 1840s.

In some cases, the secretary might combine their influence over recruitment with their ability to manipulate their unparalleled knowledge of the Society's administrative and electoral processes. This was difficult when the Society was a direct democracy, as there was no easy way for the secretary to consistently sway the voters at the meetings, week after week. They did not often have the opportunity to argue the merits of a particular course of action to the subscribers, instead being limited to reading out minutes, letters, and reports, or clarifying points of order. From 1846, however, with the establishment of the Council, the power of the secretary to sway the Society increased. When Henry Trueman Wood was promoted to secretary in 1879, he reminisced that 'the first thing I did was to try to get some thoroughly good men on the Council'.[1] Elections to Council were rarely competitive, so even just persuading people to stand for election and then undertaking some of the administrative hassle could immediately influence the Society's leadership.

When the Society had been a direct democracy, people had turned up in large numbers to vote at the annual general meetings. The election tallies, especially for well-paid positions like that for the secretary, often reached into the hundreds. Members had, after all, been in the habit of turning up and voting at ordinary meetings every week. Yet when nearly all decision-making was taken on by the Council, the Society's members gradually lost the habit of exercising their votes. Very few elections to the Society's Council seem to have ever been competitive, a notable exception being the 1850 election in which Henry Cole and his allies pushed out Thomas Webster so that the Society would continue to hold exhibitions of art-manufactures. Even this, however, had been when the Council was relatively new, when many members still retained their democratic habit. The elections became ever less contentious from then on, with very few people turning up to vote; even fewer when compared to the Society's growing membership.

As the influence of the Society's members over the Council declined, the influence of the secretary only grew. Indeed, very soon after it was formed, the Council took on the responsibility of hiring the secretary and other staff, rather than leaving it to the members to elect them. Having once been almost powerless elected officials, the Society's staff instead became influential hired appointees. The secretaries who were hired often reflected the interests of the chairman of the Council at the time. John Stratton, for example, who in the 1970s established the Society's scholarships for musicians, ensured that when a secretary retired during his tenure as chairman, the replacement they hired was the former manager of the Royal Opera Company, Keith Grant.

Yet more often, the influence ran the other way. The secretary could be in post for decades, whereas the chairmen of the Council were limited to only two year-long terms (with a few exceptions who had an additional year or two). The secretary generally long outlasted the chairman who appointed them, and if they did not get on well with a future chairman, as sometimes happened, they could usually afford to just wait them out and ensure the election of a chairman they liked more.[2] The make-up of the Council and its chairmen increasingly reflected the interests of the Society's secretary.[3]

Henry Trueman Wood, for example, remained in post for thirty-eight years. He had been a clerk at the Patent Office and was interested in new scientific inventions. So when he decided to get 'some thoroughly good men' on to the Council, this meant recruiting some of the country's most prominent men of science and invention. The Council's chairmen during his tenure included engineers like Frederick Bramwell and Douglas Galton, and the pioneer of underwater electric telegraph cables, Carl Wilhelm Siemens. It was during Wood's tenure that the Society's lectures included demonstrations of brand new technologies like the telephone and wireless teleprinting. The Albert Medal, too, was in those years mostly given to some of the world's most prominent scientists and inventors, from Thomas Edison to Marie Curie.

Over the course of the late nineteenth and early twentieth centuries, the Society's secretary thus became increasingly influential. This meant that when it hired an outsider, as it did in 1977 with Christopher Lucas, he was in a unique position to change things. Lucas had trained as an accountant, but had run the finances for an educational film-making company and then a radio station. He had never heard of the Society of Arts when in 1977 his wife spotted an advertisement in *The Times* for the job of secretary (Keith Grant had resigned after only a few years to direct the Design Council). Lucas applied, visiting the library to find out something about the organisation from its *Journal*. It is not entirely clear why the Society decided to hire Lucas—someone with little experience, who knew next to nothing about the organisation. Perhaps, he speculated, it was because he had worked in the arts and had a background in accounting—an apparent combination of culture and prudence. Little did they know, however, that Lucas was far from being a cautious accountant. He had only gone into accounting because at one point in his youth his father had taken ill, and Lucas had promised he would study something serious. His father recovered, and lived to a ripe old age, but Lucas stuck to his promise. He was, in fact, by inclination a risk-taker.[4]

Lucas was 39 when he took the job—relatively young compared to both the Society's Council and its membership. The organisation he

found seemed as though it was from another age. The working conditions of the staff when he arrived were 'almost Dickensian', many of
them working in tiny cubicles with cardboard partitions.[5] The people
who ran the industrial design competitions worked in especially 'abject
conditions', tucked away in a cramped basement. At the same time, the
Society had antiquated luxuries, such as a tea trolley with chocolate
biscuits for the staff, which did the rounds daily. It was tradition for the
secretary, assistant secretaries, and the editor of the *Journal* to sit around
at the appointed time and take tea. Lucas even discovered that there was
a special Society of Arts ticket to the London Zoo, for some reason kept
in the secretary's safe. Attitudes towards staff were, Lucas discovered,
'shocking, patriarchal'.[6] Almost all of the staff with managerial positions
were male, though most of the staff were women. They used only surnames. As one member of staff put it, 'underlings were underlings in
those days'.[7]

Lucas banished the tea trolley,[8] freed the ticket to London Zoo from
the safe and posted it on the noticeboard for anyone to use, and soon
had the cardboard partitions torn down. He introduced an air of infor-
mality: staff, for example, began to use their first names.[9] Some practices
were governed by committees of the Society's fellows or by the Council,
and so the pace of change was slow. Certainly, even in the late 1980s, the
Society could feel to newcomers as though they were stepping back into
the 1950s.[10] But when he could, Lucas acted by edict. He immediately
abolished, for example, the practice of addressing letters with the courtesy title 'Esq.'.[11] Some traditions did, however, stay intact. Since the
1950s it had become a custom for the first year of a chairman's two years
to go on a trip with the secretary abroad, their partners included. The
trips were ostensibly about fundraising and meeting the growing number of fellows abroad, but the trips were also just fun. (The tradition
seems only to have ended at some point in the 1990s.)

Lucas's reforms to the Society's day-to-day management were only
the beginning. The influence that had accumulated to the position of
secretary allowed him to make even more sweeping changes. Indeed,
his title was in 1992 changed to director.[12] By that time it was 'only a
cosmetic change', but it reflected the culmination of over a century of

the role's evolution. (The title was in 2006 changed again, to chief executive.) A director was no mere functionary, but responsible for formulating a vision of the Society's future. With the accumulated influence of his position, Lucas felt secure—so much so that he was willing even to stand up to the Society's president, Prince Philip.

On one occasion, a large oil company, Shell, offered to sponsor the Society's environmental awards. Philip was against. At a meeting of the environmental committee hosted at Buckingham Palace, Lucas contradicted him. The company's intentions, he argued, had integrity and their money should be used to support the environment. Philip eventually came round, but joked that he would know whom to blame if it all went wrong. As they were leaving, David Attenborough remarked to Lucas that few people would have to stood up to Philip. (Philip, who could be intimidating, reportedly invited industrialists to discussions at Buckingham Palace to berate them about their impact on the environment—he apparently often succeeded in using his royal position to awe them into acquiescence.)[13]

Having arrived into the security of the secretary's position, and unafraid to use it, Lucas began to focus the Society on attaining a new usefulness. He was, first of all, open to exploring new ideas. Under his direction, the Society explored a number of new initiatives. Many of them came to nothing—for example a proposal for a new museum in London devoted to building—but some of them were significant new projects.[14] Lucas was rarely the initiator, but he was open to exploring suggestions. The appointment of Kenneth Adams as Comino Fellow, along with the massive effort to promote Industry Year 1986, went ahead with Lucas's blessing and support. Adams, however, was not the only person involved with St George's House to approach Lucas with new ideas. Indeed, he was not even the first.

Lucas was also approached in the late 1970s by Peter Gorb, who had become involved with the Society through its promotion of design management. Gorb was academically educated—he attended Cambridge University and Harvard Business School—but he was also a trained craftsman and an experienced manager. He had helped run Burton Retail Group, after which he did an apprenticeship as a tailor and joined his family's textile manufacturing business in Wales. Having undergone both an academic and a hands-on technical education, and with his experience of industry, he became concerned that Britain's education system was deeply flawed, and worsening.

Schools seemed to be directing children towards academia and universities, teaching them knowledge, but not giving them the skills they needed for a fulfilling life, both in work and in leisure. Like Kenneth Adams, Gorb feared that Britain's education system was biased against industry. He also feared it was biased against otherwise fulfilling aspects of people's lives—anything to do with making and doing, rather than just thinking. As one supporter put it, applying the concept to theatre and music, 'the value of performing, doing, making something ourselves, however "badly" we do it, is often an infinitely more satisfying experience than listening to the most brilliant professional performer'.[15]

Gorb's own eclectic educational background convinced him that there should not be a rigid distinction between subjects that were intellectual and ones that were technical—there were advantages to be had from both. The stigma against vocational or hands-on technical education particularly needed to be removed. As with Adams's campaign to promote industry, Gorb wanted to change Britain's culture. He honed his ideas with a few friends at St George's House, particularly its warden, Charles Handy.

Handy took an academic interest in how managers could make the complex bureaucracies they ran more innovative, more rewarding for the people who worked for them, and more ethical in the decisions they took. Handy had been a marketing executive at Shell and then an economist, but by the late 1960s was teaching management at the London Business School. He and Gorb founded a department there, to research and teach 'design management'—the kinds of management practices that would ensure designers worked effectively alongside engineers, marketers, and others within an organisation (the field has evolved significantly since then, to encompass the design of services and systems as well as physical products).

By stressing design management as a new field, Gorb and Handy encouraged existing managers to hire more professional designers, and more broadly to take seriously the skills that they possessed. They hoped to change managers' attitudes, removing any stigma they had towards vocational training. They were not the first to develop the concept of design management, but were influential and early proponents. The Society of Arts was of interest to them both, given its long-standing competitions for industrial designers and its awards since the mid-1960s for design management.

Over a dinner with friends, Gorb, Handy, and a few others decided to take further action. They drew up a short manifesto, decrying Britain's over-intellectual culture: 'the idea of the "educated person" is that of a scholarly individual who has been neither educated nor trained to exercise useful skills; who is able to understand but not to act'. Young people were being encouraged to specialise, and were being taught only the skills associated with academia and science. What they lacked, Gorb and his friends thought, were the skills to apply their knowledge when they left education. They were leaving schools and universities unprepared for life, lacking capabilities like problem-solving, organising, cooperating, and exercising their creativity. More broadly, they lacked the capabilities associated with *doing,* rendering them unprepared to design, make things, cooperate in a team, or market goods and services—the skills essential to economic success. Gorb and his friends called for an education system that would stress those capabilities. They called their campaign Education for Capability.[16]

They wrote up their manifesto over dinner and drinks. The next morning, still a little hungover, Gorb visited Christopher Lucas at the Society of Arts to convince him to take up the idea. The Society, thought Gorb and his friends, would be the ideal organisation to take up their campaign: it was involved in design and its members included managers, educators, and civil servants. It might bridge the gap between the people who already made and designed things, and those who could do something to change the educational system. It also had the prestige to give the campaign a platform. Lucas agreed to help.

Education for Capability began as a series of lectures in late 1978, in which Handy and others set out their ideas. Gorb and his friends did not think that the practical education they favoured was entirely lacking; they did not want to invent an entirely new method of teaching. Instead, they wanted the Society to act as a repository of information about all the existing schemes throughout the country—a single organisation, or 'clearing house' that people could turn to for information. They began a recognition scheme 'to identify, publicize and encourage courses or programmes' that they felt were worthy: they awarded certificates to programmes like Young Enterprise, which had students managing their own businesses, or simply to courses that were introduced into schools' regular timetables. A few of the programmes were even given funding.[17]

Projects like these, alongside that for the Industry Year 1986 campaign, attracted new kinds of members to the Society. In the mid-twentieth century the Society had attracted managers and officials, many of whom had interests outside of their jobs—music, conservation, or the arts, for example. In the 1980s it attracted radicals—people who often had the same kinds of high-ranking roles, as managers, officials, or academics, but who wished to transform the systems within which they operated. Gorb and Handy fitted that role, and the reputation they created for the Society of Arts attracted more of their kind. Whereas a chairman of Council like John Stratton in the early 1970s would create a music scholarship as an addition to the existing curriculum—a chance for people who had graduated to then train abroad—in the 1980s the approach of people like Gorb and Handy would be to change the curriculum. Instead of wanting to supplement something, they wanted to change it. The Education for Capability movement attracted the kinds of people interested in alternative forms of education, such as home-schooling, or who worried that education was lacking when it came to certain hands-on skills, such as cooking, art, and theatre. It also attracted politicians—the Labour leader, Neil Kinnock, for example, spoke at the Society's 'recognition day' for educational schemes, held in 1986 to coincide with Industry Year. He used the chance to criticise the educational polices of the then Conservative government.[18]

Lucas's openness to ideas like Education for Capability and Industry Year 1986 began to change the Society's direction and membership. Yet such changes had almost happened before. In the late 1960s, for example, one chairman of Council, Walter Worboys, a former chair of the Council of Industrial Design, had attempted to do something very similar—his worries had been almost identical to those later pursued by Adams and Gorb, that Britain's culture was too anti-industrial and that vocational training and careers in industry needed to be made more attractive. His successor as chairman in the early 1970s also called for the Society to investigate reforms to education, expressing a critique almost identical to that of the Education for Capability manifesto. Unlike the projects that emanated from St George's House, however, these earlier campaigns went nowhere.[19] They did not result in the Society taking any concrete action.

What was different in the 1980s was not only that Lucas opened the Society to new ideas; he also created the conditions for those ideas to be pursued for longer. The key change occurred in 1987, when the Society of Arts finally ended its involvement with the examination board. As we have seen, by the mid-twentieth century the Society was essentially an examination board with a discussion club attached. The examination board, by charging fees, brought in most of the Society's revenue and the entirety of its surplus each year. It also employed most of its staff. It was in the decision to separate the examination board from the Society that Lucas's risk-taking nature became evident.

Separation from the examination board was financial suicide—a major self-imposed crisis, albeit one that was planned. The case for separation was not practical. It was moral. When the Society had begun its examinations, it had not charged fees, and when the Society was persuaded by the mechanics' institutions to continue the examinations in the 1880s, they did so on the condition of charging fees that would cover the costs and would allow anyone to sit them. At the time, the people who paid the fees had been the candidates themselves, or else the private institutions to which they subscribed. Over the course of the twentieth century, however, with the gradual growth of the state education system, an increasing proportion of the candidates who sat the Society's examinations had their fees paid for by the state. With the candidates being educated at state-funded institutions, and with their examination fees paid for by their institutions, by the 1980s the Society was in essence receiving an indirect state subsidy.

The process had been gradual, and few had noticed the change. But when the person who ran the examination board, Martin Cross, brought it to Lucas's attention, it was obvious that something had to be done. Indeed, people had begun to comment on the fact that the Society's other activities were benefitting from this subsidy—the social occasions and the traditional trips abroad, for example, were not obviously benefitting the public. This is not to say that the surplus generated by the examination board had always gone to the Society's other activities—in most years, it had in fact been reinvested. As the number of candidates increased in the post-war years to over half a million a year, the examinations had required new facilities, including computers. In some years, the subsidy had even been reversed, with the members' subscription funds subsidising the examination board. Yet this was less and less common, and once the indirect state subsidy had been pointed out, it simply seemed wrong.[20]

Thus, in 1987, the examination board was separated. The Society at a stroke lost three quarters of its staff, 150 people, as well as roughly 85 per cent of its revenue, including its entire operating surplus. It was suddenly in financial trouble. The separation was not total—the Society became sole shareholder, just over half of the board were appointed by the Society's Council, and the chairman of Council became the examination board's chairman too. In practice, however, this was only nominal control—the running of the examination board was in effect entirely handed over to the professionals, and the Society was deprived of the previously huge annual surplus. The loss of the surplus was only partly made up for by the examination board's payment to the Society of a royalty, for the use of the 'Royal Society of Arts' or 'RSA' brand. The royalty was a temporary measure, to aid the Society while it scrambled to adjust.[21]

The Society suddenly found itself in dire financial straits. It would eventually cash in on the examination board by selling its stake, but this would not happen for over a decade. The board was eventually sold in 1998 to a syndicate of the Oxford and Cambridge examination boards.

They merged to form OCR, standing for Oxford, Cambridge, and the RSA (at the time of writing OCR is one of England's principal five school examination boards). In the meantime, however, the Society needed to find alternative sources of income. Instead of cutting back, Lucas's approach was to take a risk and spend the Society's way out of the crisis. The organisation's principal, untapped asset was its building, to which it owned the freehold. He had, since his very first weeks as secretary, seen potential for the building to be put to better use.

When Lucas had arrived in 1977, the Society had just bought the freeholds to some of the adjoining buildings—it had done so easily, having accumulated surplus after surplus over the preceding decades. Lucas had allowed the leases of their tenants to lapse, extending the proportion of the buildings available for the Society's own use, and removing the staff from their previously Dickensian conditions. He had added extra floors to some of the buildings, and transformed one of the basements into a gallery in which to display the prize-winning entries of the industrial design competitions. Of all the Society's activities, Lucas most enjoyed collaborating with the Royal Designers for Industry. Although he had had no formal design training, redesigning the Society's house became one of his major passions. He had also seen potential uses for the Society's vaults, hidden deep under the block, which up until then had been used by a wine merchants' to store some million bottles of wine.

Lucas's solution to the sudden loss of income in 1987 was to convert the vaults into a conference centre and restaurant. Since becoming secretary, he had encouraged anyone who wished to hire out the Society's rooms, usually for functions or seminars. Indeed, he was at one point overhasty. A few months into his post, a publisher had hired out one of the rooms for a book launch—Lucas had happily agreed. On the day of the launch, however, a reporter from a tabloid newspaper, *The Sun*, turned up requesting an interview and revealed that the book being launched was pornographic. The Society's mishap was mentioned on the newspaper's infamous page 3, which from the 1970s for decades featured a topless woman.[22] The mishap was, however, a one-off. Lucas believed, though he did not have the evidence to support it, that the

Society might generate a surplus from hiring out more of its building. And the more space it had, the better.

The Society went on a donations drive to pay for the building work, but it was not enough. So Lucas took the bold step of mortgaging the Society's building. Having arrived at an organisation that had been financially secure, piling up surplus after surplus, and with cash to burn, Lucas put it into debt. Nonetheless, spending the Society's way out of the crisis worked. The vaults reopened as a restaurant and conference centre in 1990, and after a few years the gamble began to pay off. Indeed, at least a quarter to a third of the Society's income each year still comes from the hire of its house—the vaults and the Great Room are often even used for weddings. More significantly, they seem to have changed the way the Society was perceived—the building's atmosphere became more relaxed, while remaining business-like.[23] It was an attractive place for the managers or directors of firms. Indeed, the Society began to use the acronym 'RSA', reflecting a new trend among businesses for short logos.[24]

The separation of the examination board also gave Lucas the opportunity to focus the Society's activities. He began to abolish many of the endowed lecture series and bequests for premiums that had accumulated over the course of the late nineteenth and early twentieth centuries. He ended the postgraduate music scholarships as well as the lectures and prizes related to the Commonwealth, or otherwise handed trusts over to more appropriate, specialist organisations. This was the fate of the Thomas Gray fund for services to the merchant marine, and for the Katharine Maltwood fund for archaeological research in Somerset. Unless there was good reason to keep something, the Society would no longer administrate the wishes of the dead. As Charles Handy put it, by this point the chairman of Council, 'there is nothing like the prospect of financial adversity for focusing the mind'.[25]

The Society's activities after 1987 focused on where it felt it would be most useful. It was 'a year of furious brainstorming'.[26] Prince Philip's environment committee continued its work, and the Education for Capability movement's scope was widened further. From 1987, the Society would focus overwhelmingly on pursuing reforms to both of these areas. The industrial design competitions, in 1989 renamed the Student Design Awards, were also retained, as were the Royal Designers for Industry. The Society now attempted to find ways to combine the three areas. So long as a project could more or less fund itself, the Society would consider pursuing it. In this respect, the Student Design Awards were fortunate in that they were already by this stage mostly funded by corporate sponsors—the design team's long-serving director, Helen Auty, recalled at one point chasing a potential sponsor around a car park.[27]

Some of the campaigns of the mid-1980s also had unfinished business. Foremost of these was Kenneth Adams's ambitious attempt to reverse Britain's anti-industrial culture. Industry Year 1986 successfully forged connections between industries and schools, presumably also raising awareness among schoolchildren and teachers of the value of industry to their everyday lives. What the campaign had failed to do, however, was to reform industry. Adams and Chandler had wanted firms to demonstrate that they were actually worthy of esteem, by adopting the kinds of codes of conduct that Chandler had issued at Shell, as well as then actually sticking to them.

Companies, complained Chandler, failed to take the opportunity to 'articulate their purposes or principles'.[28] The only exception was the chairman of United Biscuits, who in 1987 issued operating principles for the company and stated that they would rather go out of business than break them (the company produced popular brands like McVitie's Penguin, Jaffa Cakes, and Jacob's Cream Crackers). It is unclear whether it continued to stick to those principles. The Society decided to take on the reform of business practices. Indeed, this had become a more urgent issue, as over the course of the late 1980s and early 1990s, many state-owned businesses were privatised. With more and more of the economy responsible to shareholders, it made sense to clarify what managers' responsibilities were.

Charles Handy suggested someone to take on the project of reforming firms, or rather of clarifying the responsibilities of managers. The person he suggested was Mark Goyder, yet another manager at a firm, but with an interest in social concerns. He had been active in local politics. Goyder was tasked with putting together an inquiry into the subject, to ask how the companies of the future should operate. The project was called 'Tomorrow's Company'.

If Goyder was to reform business practices, he would need to involve firms' managers, directors, and chairmen. He assembled a group of twenty-five of the most senior and influential, so that they might work out, through discussion, what kinds of ethical guidelines businesses should adopt. As directors and chairmen themselves, they were aware of the kinds of ethical dilemmas that others would face. If this high-powered group could agree on clear guidelines, then Goyder reasoned that other firms might simply adopt them. After all, it was easier to simply follow moral rules than have to come up with them from scratch. Perhaps, if ethical guidelines were clearly set out, then the managers and directors of firms would take responsibility for the impact their actions had on society, rather than focusing only on the immediate demands of their shareholders.

The dominant attitude at the time was that managers were responsible only to their shareholders. As long as they otherwise followed the law, then it made sense that they would be responsible to the people who actually owned the companies they managed. The mass of shareholders, however, usually expressed their will through prices. If they sold their shares, then that seemed to indicate worry about the company's direction, or at the very least disapproval of the actions of its managers. When shareholders sold, the price fell. Likewise, if people bought the company's shares, it seemed to indicate approval. This did, however, leave room for shareholders' wishes to be interpreted by managers. If they so chose, then they might still act in the interests of shareholders while also considering the impact of their decisions on the environment or society more broadly. The law was one thing, but managers might choose to be forces for good as well—on the environment, on relations between employees and employers, and in terms of adding other kinds of value to their communities.

The Tomorrow's Company inquiry reported in 1995. The twenty-five people assembled by Goyder had met and discussed things among themselves, as well as keeping diaries of the ethical dilemmas they faced.

They also engaged with the leaders of other firms and the public. Their conclusion was that firms should focus on their relationships with four other groups, in addition to shareholders. These 'stakeholders' were the firm's suppliers and customers, as well as its employees and the wider community. They also made an argument very similar to the one that 'The Countryside in 1970' conferences had helped to develop for the environment. Their experiences, they believed, suggested that the companies that valued all of their stakeholders actually performed better economically too. Just as the environmentalists argued that conservation was in everyone's long-term best interests, the Tomorrow's Company inquiry argued that it was in the best interests of shareholders for the companies they owned to act in the best interests of all stakeholders. It would be, they called it, 'enlightened capitalism'. Indeed, they argued, though they could not prove it, that if all firms acted in this way then it would be to the overall benefit of Britain's productivity and thus its overall economy too.

The problem with the Tomorrow's Company inquiry was that, although many directors agreed with it, they still felt constrained. They pointed out that, by law, the responsibilities of a company's directors were to its shareholders. This objection was, however, soon removed. One of the people who had sat on the inquiry was Stuart Hampson, the chairman of the John Lewis Partnership, a major retail company but also a worker-owned cooperative. The company was automatically responsible to some of its stakeholders, as the shareholders were themselves the employees. The kinds of questions that the inquiry asked were the ones that Hampson took for granted.

Nonetheless, Hampson said, serving on the inquiry was 'one of the most influential periods of my life'.[29] It drove home to him that the kind of approach dominant at the John Lewis Partnership could actually be applied to all firms. Worker-owned cooperatives, in other words, were not just oddities, exceptions to the general rule of what would count as the best practices for all companies. Some years later, when Hampson was asked to form part of the government's investigation into reforming company law, he took his chance. Alongside a group of mostly lawyers, he argued the Tomorrow's Company inquiry's case. The eventual result, the 2006 Companies Act, removed all objections to the inquiry's recommendations. The primary responsibility of a company directors was still to shareholders, the company's owners, but other stakeholders had to be taken into account too.[30] There was now no excuse for directors to not adopt the inquiry's recommendations. The problem now was encouraging them to do so, a task that Goyder took upon himself.

Having run the initial inquiry at the Society of Arts, in 1995 Goyder founded Tomorrow's Company as a separate organisation. Eventually, it would try to change attitudes among investors as well as managers. After all, the investors held the purse-strings, and many companies were owned in large part by pension funds. As with the Industry Year campaign, however, changing attitudes was difficult. One major obstacle was that few people disagreed with the inquiry's report. Everyone wanted to say that they would behave well, or that they already did. What mattered was whether they lived up to their rhetoric, though at least getting them to sign up the rhetoric seemed, to Goyder and Hampson, to be a start.

Other than trying to reform companies, the Society of Arts under Lucas focused overwhelmingly on three areas: education, the environment, and design. It also, increasingly, tried to combine them. Just as Tomorrow's Company tried to persuade firms to consider their impact on society in general, the Society did the same with designers. The Student Design Awards, for example, were increasingly focused on persuading designers to think about social and environmental issues. Contestants were asked to design products that would be easier to recycle, for example, or easier for disabled people to use. In 1999 a competition for a medical device was won by a design student, Matt McGrath, who had no experience of medicine. His submission was a reinvention of the laryngoscope, a device for seeing down the throat—within a few years it had become the basis for a company worth tens of millions of pounds.[31]

In some years, competitors were asked to design products that would make life easier for the elderly. The influence here, as with the Society's focus on the environment, seems to have partly come from Prince Philip. He complained to the Society's staff that he and the queen had to crawl on their bellies to put a tape into a video player, or that he found it difficult to turn a shower on at the right temperature. As Philip himself aged, he directed the Society's attention to the wider problem of Britain's ageing society.

For the Royal Designers for Industry, too, the terms were later changed to stress the need for societal impact. Having originally been focused on just beauty, the distinction also included other forms of design, such as effective engineering, as well as things like designing acoustics, or processes in service industries. With its changed terms of reference, some of those who were appointed felt that it was a role as well as an honour, that having made money or made things that worked well, they would now consider the wider implications of what they did. The Society's design staff also played their part, taking the RDIs on tours where they would pick up litter, for example, to remind the designers of the need to consider how the products they made would end up being discarded.

The Society in the 1990s seems to have explored initiative after initiative, many of them emerging from its members or the Council. The radicals and would-be educational reformers who had been introduced to the Society by the Education for Capability campaign often proposed new ideas or initiatives to the director, whereas the funding for them often came from the managers of firms who had become involved either through the Industry Year or the ensuing Tomorrow's Company campaign. Others still were brought into the Society because the director was keen to broaden its base of support.

For example, a catering entrepreneur and restaurateur, Prue Leith, was first brought into the Society when she received a letter nominating her for fellowship. As someone who had never completed a university degree, she felt flattered to have been invited to what she assumed was a learned society. She had never heard of the organisation before. Yet Christopher Lucas was, in the late 1980s, seeking to expand the Society's membership. This was partly about the financial imperative of needing to plug the shortfall of cash from separating from the examination board. It was also, however, about infusing the Society's membership with the kinds of people who had new and fresh ideas. Leith at the time was in her late forties, relatively young, at least compared with the rest of the members and especially the Council. She was also a woman, of whom there were very few among the fellowship at the time.

Although women had been allowed to be members of the Society since the very beginning, they had always been a tiny proportion of the total. They were also rarely in positions of influence. In the late nineteenth century, when the Society increasingly resembled an exclusive learned society, they had become especially few. It did not have any women on the Council until 1942, when it elected the electrical engineer Caroline Haslett, almost a hundred years after the Council had been created. As one of her contemporaries put it, 'it was with some apprehension' that they originally put her name forward for election.[32] It did not have a female chairman of Council until 1981, when it elected an influential headmistress, Diana Reader Harris. As for its first female secretary, it depends what counts. When the secretary during the Second World War was called up to serve in the military, one of his replacements as acting secretary was Jean Scott Rogers, who served in the post for three years. In terms of permanent posts, however, the Society's first female director was Penny Egan, who started the role in 1998.

It was largely thanks to Lucas's encouragement that many more women joined the Society's fellowship, and, more than that, became actively involved. With greater diversity, he hoped, would also come greater diversity of ideas. In the cases of both Prue Leith and Penny Egan, his encouragement would heavily influence the Society's activities in the 1990s.

Leith became more than just a passive member of the Society of Arts. Indeed, it was Egan, in charge of the Society's lecture programme in the late 1980s, who was responsible for getting her more closely involved. One of the many lectures funded by bequests was supposed to be about food, and Leith had become quite well known to the public because of a campaign she had waged to improve the quality of the meals served by British Railways. Egan invited her to speak. Leith, born in South Africa, had studied for a while in Paris and fallen in love with its food. In 1960, when she moved to Britain, she had found British restaurants to be shockingly poor. Food was, she said, something that people in

Britain did not talk about, like religion or sex. She was one of a small group of ambitious chefs and caterers who set out to change that, bringing high-quality food to Britain's services and high streets (and becoming rich in the process).

As well as providing Britain with better food herself, however, she was interested in encouraging others to do so as well. She set up a school of food and wine in the 1970s. Yet she was also appalled at the general state of cooking education. She had visited schools for talks and seen the state of packed lunches and school meals. The prevailing attitude in the 1960s and 70s, she feared, was that people were looking forward to a time when technology would supersede the need for food. One day, said some, the housewives of Britain would be freed from the drudgery of cooking, which was often seen as merely a chore. People would instead consume mass-produced pills with all the required nutrients—something akin to the food provided for astronauts. Leith was appalled.

Leith's concern was very akin to that of Gorb, Handy, and their friends. The core tenet of Education for Capability was that young people needed to be taught to do things, not just to study them. Although Gorb had focused primarily on design, Leith thought the same about food. Children, she thought, needed to learn to cook, to experience food's tastes, smells, touch, and sounds. Cooking was a skill necessary to stay alive, but it was also a skill that could make life more enjoyable. In common with the Education for Capability people, Leith thought that Britain's schools were too biased against hands-on skills, and in particular cooking. Indeed, she discovered that most 12-year-olds had never even learned to boil an egg.[33] She saw in the Society of Arts a potential platform she might use to change that.

Yet if she was to campaign to change Britain's education system, she would first need to gain some expertise of education. She had dropped out of university, and later joked that 'nobody would listen to someone whose qualifications were a 25-yard swimming certificate, a pony club badge and a cookery diploma.'[34] She therefore joined the Society's education committee. Although she had discovered that the Society was not in fact a learned society, it certainly appeared to many to be one. She would use the confusion to her advantage, while also learning everything she could about education from the lectures.

Christopher Lucas encouraged her to take things further. He was aware of her critique of education—as director, he attended almost every one of the Society's lectures and seminars—and encouraged her to use the Society to her advantage. Leith was elected to the Council, and Lucas later also urged her to become its chairman. When she expressed some misgivings, Lucas persuaded her that cooking involved all aspects of the Society's mission: it was an art, it was manufacture, and it involved commerce, not to mention science too. As ever, the breadth and vagueness of the Society's mission was exploited to suit an agenda.

Leith began in a way that was becoming routine for the Society in the late twentieth century, with a conference. She convened chefs, caterers, politicians, and teachers, to explore what might be done to encourage more cookery teaching in schools. Leith suspected that teaching primary school children might lead them to have better eating habits, to demand better food from their parents and schools, or else to make better food themselves. She also suspected that improving nutrition might also improve children's academic performance. Proving either of these hypotheses might help convince school authorities of the need to teach cooking. Yet conducting a proper study involved tracking children for years and then finding other ways to ensure that the experiment was valid. The campaign commissioned a study, but it was only limited in its scope. Even if it had confirmed Leith's hypotheses, the research might also have just been ignored.

To supplement the research, Leith decided to take more practical action. Her campaign became known as 'Focus on Food'.[35] The Society of Arts had many teachers among its members, so she convened some of them for another conference, to work out what kinds of materials they would need if they were to teach cooking. The suggestions included printed materials as well as a phone line that teachers might use to ask for support. The Society organised annual 'food weeks' for a few years, in which participating schools across the country would try to provide cooking lessons for their pupils. By 2001, when the food weeks were in their fourth year, they involved thirty thousand schools and some three

hundred thousand students and teachers. This approach, however, relied on teachers, many of whom were inexperienced at cooking.

Leith therefore also provided an ideal model of what teaching cookery in schools should look like. She took the approach that had informed
Henry Cole in his use of exhibitions, that people did not know what
they wanted until they had seen it. She would bring her ideal version of
food teaching directly to the schools, hopefully impressing the politicians responsible for funding them, as well as the children, parents, and
teachers. The idea was to prepare a bus, which would be able to open up
into a cookery teaching classroom with all the necessary facilities—after
all, as very few schools taught any cooking, they would not have what
was required.

The only problem was finding the money. It would cost about two
hundred thousand pounds to fit out a bus, not to mention the costs of
running it, including paying for petrol, the driver, two cookery teachers,
and the food. The research and food weeks needed funding too. The
money came from a business leader who had become involved with the
Society through Tomorrow's Company: Stuart Hampson. At the time,
Hampson was chairman of Waitrose, the supermarket (one branch of
the John Lewis Partnership, which he would also later head). Mark Goyder had got Hampson initially involved in the Society via Tomorrow's
Company, but it was Leith who persuaded him to join the Council.
Indeed, he would be among her successors as chairman. A couple of
days after the conference she held with the teachers, he had phoned to
say that Waitrose would be interested in funding the entire campaign.
Leith accepted.

Waitrose were to back the Focus on Food campaign for nine years,
though it never once requested any special branding or insisted on the
use of their ingredients. At one point, when Leith produced a promotional film, she ensured that the camera occasionally zoomed in on the
Waitrose logo. When she sent it to Hampson, however, he rang to tell
her there was a problem: he instructed her to take out all the zoom-ins.
For Hampson, the Focus on Food campaign was an opportunity for
Waitrose to act in the kind of way that he had called for as part of the
Tomorrow's Company inquiry. Waitrose, he argued, did not support the

campaign for the direct commercial benefit, but because a love of food among the nation's young was something that the company simply *should* use its resources to promote.

The Focus on Food buses were 'like a Tardis'.[36] They seemed to have more inside them than would seem possible, opening up when they arrived at a school to reveal sinks, tables, and chairs, along with the oven and hobs. They toured the country, mostly used to instruct and inspire teachers. They eventually expanded in number too, to serve other regions of the UK. The original started its campaign in London but was based in Halifax. Occasionally, the campaign featured celebrity chefs—after all, Leith had the contacts. At the launch in 1997, Anton Edelmann, the head chef of the Savoy, showed around thirty schoolchildren between the ages of 9 and 10 how to prepare meatballs, while Albert Roux, the first restaurateur in the UK to gain three Michelin stars, showed them how to make bread.[37] The kids were, Leith said, 'mesmerised'.[38] On another occasion, the campaign arranged for a group of children to cook a meal at No. 10 Downing Street, the home of the prime minister. It seems to have had the desired effect: in 2001, the government created a fund to train teachers to teach cookery.[39]

After nine years Waitrose ended its funding of the campaign. By this stage, Hampson was chair of the overall John Lewis Partnership rather than just Waitrose, so it was no longer up to him. Funding for the buses had also been moved to Waitrose's marketing department, who decided the expense was too much to bear. As Leith later complained, such a partnership might not have occurred in 2019, as many companies have their marketers in charge of their funds for social outreach. The food buses do, however, at the time of writing still travel the country. The Society ended its involvement after five years, in 2002, but the member of staff who ran the campaign, a design and cookery teacher named Anita Cormac, continued under a separate charity, also called Focus on Food. Some of the buses were also eventually acquired by the Soil Association, a group that campaigns in favour of growing food organically, under the project heading Food for Life. They send the buses to schools to educate children about both cooking and the choice of healthy ingredients too.

Cooking, however, was not the only kind of vocational training that the Society stressed. Penny Egan, before coming to work for the Society in 1986 to run its lecture series, was interested in the visual arts. She had worked for the Victoria and Albert Museum and some other arts-related organisations. Lucas encouraged her to pursue her interest in the arts through the Society, to restore it to the list of things that the Society encouraged, especially if it could be combined with its other activities.

As with cooking, one of the Society's principal agendas in the 1990s was to encourage schools to teach the arts, particularly when it involved some kind of physical activity—art, music, dance, drama. For example, it encouraged the teaching of Shakespeare in primary schools. The Society found ways to make Shakespeare's work seem less daunting, both to primary school teachers, who might lack the confidence to teach it, as well as to students under the age of 11. The Society worked with the Royal Shakespeare Company to make Shakespeare more fun. They hoped that if schoolchildren had more familiarity with Shakespeare's work when they were younger, they would find the arts more enjoyable when they reached secondary school.[40]

In a similar vein, in 1994 the Society of Arts held a competition with a radio station, Classic FM, for the best new compositions for young people. Egan and her colleagues noted that school orchestras often lacked certain instruments, so they wanted music that would be more flexible in terms of the kinds of instruments used, as well as the technical proficiency required to play the instruments well. If they could make playing good music less demanding, they hoped that young people would be more likely to play it, though in the end the submissions were 'generally disappointing'.[41]

The Society's new focus on the arts was also combined with its interest in the environment, both natural and built. One of the Society's projects in 1990 was to encourage architects, landscape designers, and engineers to collaborate with artists. It was called Art for Architecture. Although many buildings hung paintings on the walls or might even have sculptures, artists were rarely involved in the actual design of the buildings themselves. The Society thus attempted to bridge the divide between the specialisms, to see if it would improve the built environment. Ideally, they hoped, the contributions of an artist and an architect in a building would be indistinguishable. By the time the project ended in 2004, it had funded over 135 collaborations, including the interior refurbishment of the Royal Court Theatre in London, which was well received by critics, though some of the collaborations were more difficult. One artist was asked to help design a waste disposal unit, which he called 'applying lipstick to a gorilla', though he later changed his mind.[42]

In terms of the natural environment, some members in the early 2000s suggested that the Society draw attention to the waste of electronic and electrical equipment (WEEE), to coincide with the European Union's implemention of targets to reduce it. The Society commissioned a 23-foot-tall sculpture, the 'WEEE Man',[43] made entirely from such waste—'a towering figure made of washing machines, mobile phones and other electronic gadgetry'.[44] It weighed over 3 tonnes—the average amount of electrical waste that a person in the UK was expected to produce over the course of their lifetime, most of which went to landfill. The WEEE Man was intended to look like he was dragging himself back out of landfill, a monster of each person's own creation.[45] It was on display in front of London's City Hall for a month, before being toured around the country. It ended up at the Eden Project, in Cornwall.

In terms of public art, however, it was in the combination of Penny Egan's and Prue Leith's interests that the Society had a more prominent impact. While taking taxis on her way to the Society, Leith had in the 1990s noticed that one of the four plinths on Trafalgar Square stood empty. The others had sculptures of generals and a king. It bothered her—'why on earth don't they put back whatever it is that they took down?', she asked in a letter to a newspaper. She discovered it had never had anything on it. The fourth plinth had been intended for William IV, but the project had run out of funds. Since 1841 it had simply stood empty.

Leith called for something to be put on it, which sparked a public debate. Suggestions in the newspapers included famous footballers, Winnie-the-Pooh, Margaret Thatcher on a tank, and even a gigantic pigeon—Trafalgar Square's most multitudinous resident. Many suggested

Queen Elizabeth II, but it was a convention to never erect statues of the monarch while he or she was still alive: this would have to wait until she died. Leith felt out of her depth, so approached the Society of Arts. Perhaps they would be able to resolve the disagreements.

It became Leith's pet project, albeit with the support of Egan and the Society's member of staff responsible for the arts, Michaela Crimmin.[46] They assembled a panel of art experts to consider the public's suggestions. Their decision was not to decide on any one sculpture—it was simply too contentious an issue—but instead to have temporary sculptures. If people did not like the one that was on display at any one time, they would be able vote or lobby for a different one the next time. Such a scheme would also, they hoped, be a chance to encourage contemporary sculptors, whose works were rarely so public. Whatever was on the fourth plinth would be in one of the most visited spots in London. Just as the Society had been used to promote contemporary artists in the 1760s with exhibitions, in the 1990s it did the same for sculptors with the plinth. Just as it had once promoted history painting, a form of art addressed to the public, it would now give sculptors their own opportunity to do the same.

The Society's project soon received promises of funding. Artists' agents offered to pay for the sculptures that would go on display, expecting to then sell smaller maquettes—getting a sculpture on the fourth plinth would be effective advertising. The process of approval, however, was more onerous. They consulted all and any organisation that might declare an interest. Then, once Leith and her panel had commissioned three sculptures, to be displayed one after another, each one of them requiring their own separate planning permissions. Leith had to seek approval from some thirteen separate organisations, from the government department that controlled the site, to the Mayor of London, the borough council, and various national arts organisations.

Most obstructive, however, was the Fine Art Commission, chaired by Norman St John-Stevas, a former Conservative politician. He seems to have wished the plinth to be reserved for the Queen Mother, who was still alive so could not yet have a statue. He repeatedly refused to meet with Leith, or to allow her to present the proposal to the commission. Leith eventually manoeuvred him into accepting a presentation, pointing out to his colleagues that it said in their brochure they were open to all ideas. Foiled, St John-Stevas tried instead to have a private lunch with Leith, but she insisted on a formal presentation to the commission. When they were finally asked to present, however, Leith and Egan were left waiting for almost three quarters of their allotted hour, which was just before lunch. Given only ten minutes, St John-Stevas did not allow them to present and gave most of the time to one of the proposal's opponents. He ignored Egan entirely and introduced Leith as a 'famous cook who has somehow got herself into the art business'.

Leith and Egan openly protested at their treatment and insisted that the Fine Art Commission still vote on whether to approve their plans at its next meeting. In the meantime, they lobbied them individually. It paid off. Leith received a call from one of the commissioners saying that they had been overwhelmingly in favour of the proposals but out of deference for their chairman had decided not to take a stance. It was enough to go ahead. Foiled again, however, St John-Stevas wrote to Leith informing her that the commission had voted against. Knowing the truth, she responded by requesting the minutes. He did not reply.

After five years of consultations and committees, Leith finally got her wish: in 1999 the first sculpture was placed on the plinth, sparking both admiration and uproar. The artist, Mark Wallinger, had produced a life-size cast of a man, entirely in white—Jesus Christ flayed, bound, and crowned with thorns. It was entitled *Ecce Homo*, 'behold the man', after the words Pontius Pilate reportedly used when Jesus was prepared for crucifixion. As the cast was life-size, it seemed tiny, especially when compared to the larger-than-life statues on the other plinths. The plinth dwarfed him. Some thought it blasphemous for depicting Jesus as so frail, others endearing.[47]

Some art critics saw the fourth plinth sculptures as positive, giving a chance for public sculpture to be improved. They noted how older statues 'plunge their subjects into oblivion': the king and generals on the other three plinths were almost entirely unheard of, and frequently ignored. (One of the generals' claims to fame today is a pun he did not make: upon conquering Sind, in present-day Pakistan, newspapers reported that he had announced it with the Latin message *peccavi*, meaning 'I have sinned'.)[48] Other critics saw the fourth plinth as a reversal of the progress modern art had made, forcing contemporary sculpture, which had once 'gleefully subverted' all convention, back into the confines of an ancient medium.[49] Regardless, the fourth plinth provoked debate, and still does. Twenty years on, the contemporary sculptures continue (though from 2004 they were organised by the office of the Mayor of London and publicly funded, rather than self-supporting as Leith had intended).

The Society also promoted education more broadly, in addition to focusing on the arts or on practical skills like cooking. The Society led projects calling for more teaching of pre-schoolers, and at the other end of the scale for more teaching of adults. They wished adults to be able to receive training in short courses, which they envisaged being sold using vouchers by major retailers, in much the same way as airlines issued air miles. Many major companies signed up. The project, called the 'Campaign for Learning', aimed to provide for adults who may have received a poor or patchy education during their childhoods (indeed, much like it had in the 1850s under Harry Chester). The major problem it sought to solve, however, was that many people did not want to go to school. 'I was made to feel a fool at school: I won't go to college to be made a fool of again' were the words, from a boy in Bristol, that had inspired the campaign.[50] The supply of learning opportunities was better than it ever had been; the problem in the 1990s was one of demand. Once again, the Society attempted to bring about a change in widespread and deeply rooted attitudes—indeed, just as it had designated 1986 the Year of Industry, it briefly considered organising a 'Year of Learning'. It wished to make Britain a 'learning society'. In 1997 the Campaign for Learning became an independent charity, which at the time of writing still exists.

In addition to encouraging adults and pre-schoolers, the Society also sought to address the problem at another of its roots, by attempting to prevent children in schools from becoming disaffected in the first place.[51] The Society's campaigners believed that the answer lay in the tenets of the Education for Capability manifesto. They argued that an education focused on doing was not just better than one focused on the acquisition of knowledge—it was also more enjoyable. Whereas in the 1990s the Society's projects to pursue this had mostly focused on hands-on skills, by the early 2000s it also emphasised skills like ethical decision-making, self-reliance, teamwork, and managing time or stress. These all coalesced into a curriculum, called 'Opening Minds'.[52] The problem was persuading the government to adopt it.

Although the British state had been involved in education since the nineteenth century, its role had mostly been that of funder—first of school buildings, later of teachers, and soon everything else. Since 1988, however, the state also determined what was taught: it established a national curriculum. If schools were to adopt the Society's alternative curriculum, they would need convincing. The Society consulted teachers, convening them for discussions about how best to implement the Opening Minds curriculum and persuading them to pilot it. The difficulty, however, was in ensuring that the curriculum was interpreted in the same way across different schools and by different teachers. A subject-specific curriculum was easy to define—for much of it, one can simply list the facts that a student demonstrates they know. On the other hand, the Opening Minds curriculum was difficult to communicate, especially to the people expected to teach it. Teachers were purposefully encouraged to blur the lines between different subjects when teaching skills like research or teamwork—easier said than done.

The Society's chance to resolve this came, however, in 2002, when the government created a new kind of school: academies. These were state schools that were exempted from the national curriculum, which could also be sponsored by private organisations. They remained mostly state-funded, but the sponsors could exert an influence over the academy's curriculum. In 2006, the Society decided to sponsor its own academy—a school in which to hone its Opening Minds curriculum. The 'RSA Academy' opened in 2008 in Tipton, in the West Midlands, and in the following years the Society decided to sponsor more—at the time of writing, there are seven.

The Society's academies did not, however, fulfil all the dreams of the campaign for Opening Minds. They soon discovered limits to how far one can experiment with children's education without worrying their parents and state regulators—academies were still, after all, state schools. Most significantly, there was the challenge of assessment. In a world in which qualifications matter, the pupils at the academies still needed to pass their examinations, which were still largely determined by the government. It was too great a challenge for the schools to reinvent the curriculum entirely and operate outside of the system. Instead, only aspects of the Opening Minds agenda have remained. The academies are no longer sponsored directly by the Society—a separate charitable company called RSA Academies was created in 2011—but they retain their connection. The RSA Academies ensure that their pupils receive education in the arts, which the Society helps them to provide, for example by drawing upon its connections with designers.

The 'furious brainstorming' of 1987 seemed, by the early 2000s, to have borne fruit. The Society pursued project after project, some of them ineffectual, but many of them spinning off as separate organisations to continue their work. It was a period of rapid experimentation, spurred on by the fact that the projects had drawn in such a diverse array of people, from environmentalists and designers, to educational radicals and company directors. As Penny Egan put it, 'where else could you find Greenpeace sitting down at the same dinner table as Shell?'[53] On the whole, the Society was open to ideas. Some of its leaders felt, however, that it could do more. By the year 2000, the number of members stood at well over twenty thousand, yet they were largely passive.

Most of its projects came from members of the Council, like Prue Leith, or from the interests of the Society's staff. A few initiatives, like the WEEE man, simply came from its members, but these were the exception rather than the rule. Indeed, the members seemed, to many of the Society's leaders, like an untapped resource. Over twenty thousand people who were passionate about improving the world around them would have a lot of ideas. If they were encouraged to collaborate with one another, too, the possibilities for benefitting the public were endless. The Society frequently convened different interest groups, but it had the potential to create mass movements.

13

Building a Social Movement?

THE SEPARATION of the examination board did more than change the Society's activities. The strain on its finances forced it to consider the nature of its membership. Just as it had been before 1882, when the examination board began charging fees, the Society once again became reliant on the subscriptions of its members. The Society needed to expand its membership—it was a financial necessity. To do so, it had to become more inclusive. The perception of the organisation as an exclusive learned society was to be put to the test.

Although the membership had expanded dramatically over the course of the twentieth century, it had largely been a by-product of the Society's prestige. Bolstered by the surpluses from the examination board, the Society often appeared to be successful even when it did little to make itself useful to the public. This is not to say, however, that some of its leaders had not tried to make it more active. As we have seen, A.R.N. Roberts tried to do so in the 1950s with his Special Activities Committee. Prince Philip, too, in 1958 urged the Council 'most strongly to take a searching look at what it is doing in this country to see if the Society's aims and objects are in fact being pursued in the most suitable and rewarding manner'.[1] His meaning could not have been plainer—he was frustrated at its complacency, and instructed it to do something about it.

One of the responses was to search for new initiatives, often adopting suggestions that came the way of their leaders, as happened in the case of the Special Activities Committee. The Society also responded by trying to reform its membership, to make it a source of new ideas. The Special Activities Committee in 1955 adopted the suggestion of one member to hold evening discussion meetings. The idea was that the usual late-afternoon meetings of the Society were inconvenient for anyone other than retirees. They were also often formal—the Society's aura of exclusivity could be off-putting to a younger crowd.

Roberts and his committee decided to organise later evening discussions, to be both informal and attractive to younger members. With more young members, they hoped, the Society would have a source of fresh ideas about how the organisation might benefit the public.[2] The evening discussions were popular, but only with the usual older members. This may have been due to the nature of the topics they chose to discuss—the third session was on 'The Future of Shop Design and Window Display'. With this 'disappointing' response, the discussions were discontinued in only their second year.[3]

Yet the Special Activities Committee persisted. Another similar suggestion was for the institution of the Benjamin Franklin Medal—it was originally intended to be specifically for younger people, who might have made a name for themselves in a limited circle, and who might be encouraged further by the honour.[4] The medal was intended to be useful, a means of drawing in the young. But this lasted only a few years. The first recipient, in 1957, was a 46-year-old scientist, Freddie Williams, who had already been elected to a fellowship of the Royal Society. The second recipient, the actor Peter Ustinov, was younger at 37, but he had already won a Golden Globe, an Emmy, and a Tony. Williams and Ustinov must have seemed young to the Council of the Society of Arts, but the medal's third recipient was 72, had already been knighted, and was soon to be made a baronet (a hereditary knight).[5] The Benjamin Franklin Medal very rapidly, if not immediately, became another version of the Albert Medal, used by the Society to accrue honour to itself by associating itself with the great and the good. This proposal by the Special Activities Committee did not survive contact with the Society's 1950s tuft-hunters.

Meanwhile, in response to Prince Philip's call for the Society to 'take a searching look at what it is doing', the Council formed a Future Policy of the Society Committee. Predictably, one of its members was A.R.N. Roberts. It was this committee that recommended the Society bring companies into association, to try to emulate the 1850s Union of Mechanics' Institutions. The committee also suggested other ways to introduce more young people to its membership. One of these was to award an associateship—a junior form of the Society's membership—to young people who performed especially well in certain examinations.[6]

Another, more significant, recommendation was that the Society should have more of a presence outside London. The Society began to form regional committees, starting with Birmingham in 1960, which eventually became a West Midlands committee. The idea was that by having members meet with one another throughout the rest of the country, their discussions would lead to new ideas and initiatives for the Society to adopt. The members meeting outside London might even collaborate on initiatives of their own, to be useful to the public more locally. Successful local initiatives might then be adopted on a national basis by the Society as a whole.[7]

But in practice, the creation of the regional committees mostly resulted in smaller, local versions of what the Society was already perceived to be: an exclusive learned society or discussion club, largely for the benefit of its own members. There were some exceptions to this rule—a few of the regional committees occasionally pursued campaigns in their localities—but on the whole, within a few years most of their meetings involved group visits to exhibitions, tours of factories, the occasional speech from a grandee, and dinner receptions with sherry, evening dress required. The regions became bastions of the Society's aura of exclusivity.[8]

One proposed solution, to redirect the attentions of the regional committees towards more useful ends, was to involve them more closely in the operations of the Society. In 1980, the Society's constitution was amended so that chairs of some of the regional committees would be entitled to sit on the Council.[9] In 1999 the link was strengthened further, with all eleven regional chairs entitled to a seat.[10] The Society's leaders hoped that this move 'towards greater democracy' would result in a 'stronger two-way flow of ideas', though at the same time they made the

Council less powerful. To reflect changes to charity law, they created a Board of Trustees. The Council still had a role in appointing the trustees, but it became more advisory, focused on developing programmes and initiatives.[11]

Rather than changing the make-up of membership in the regions, however, greater representation on the Council only entrenched a perceived hierarchy, with an often tiny group of members in each region getting themselves and their friends elected to positions of apparent honour. By the early 2000s, the regional chairs—usually male retirees—presided over their meetings wearing ornate badges of office. Although the regions had been established to draw in the young, their formality instead often drove them away.[12]

Meanwhile, in the late 1990s Penny Egan tried to bring the Society to the regions, hoping that this would encourage the members there to become more involved. She based some of the staff for its projects in cities outside London. The Focus on Food campaign, for example, was largely based in Halifax at a former carpet factory complex, the Dean Clough Mills, which had been converted into a centre for the arts by an industrialist-turned-pianist and composer named Ernest Hall. It was from Dean Clough that the cooking buses ranged.[13] Other staffed offices were set up by the Society in Birmingham and Bristol, but they did not last long. They were financially unsustainable.

Nonetheless, the separation of the examination board created the conditions for reform. Although Roberts and others had tried to inject some energy into the Society's membership, it had never been a necessity. In 1987, the Society at a stroke became dependent on having a large number of subscribers, just as it had in the period 1754–1882. The conversion of the Society's vaults into a conference centre offset some of the lost revenue, but the main source would be from the members. And the more useful the Society seemed, the more members it would attract—the original relationship between usefulness and membership was at least somewhat restored. As Charles Handy put it, in the immediate aftermath of the separation 'the need to ask for financial support in turn required us to explain more precisely and more publicly why the Society existed'.[14]

From 1987 the Society began to send mission statements and manifestos to its members, calling for greater engagement. Its leaders no longer wanted members to simply receive the *Journal* passively, but rather to send in ideas and projects, to involve themselves in the Society's various campaigns. The Society's exclusivity began to weaken—it had to, if the organisation wished to survive. There was no room for the complacency of the 1950s. Christopher Lucas pushed for the selection criteria for new members to be loosened, so that more people could be nominated and allowed in (though this went back and forth in an ongoing battle with the membership committee).[15] The chairman wrote to every fellow, asking them each to nominate one or two new people.[16] In 1986 the fellowship records were computerised, and from 1990 there was even a fellowship director—a member of staff dedicated to communicating with members.[17] The technology to more easily reach the Society's tens of thousands of members had coincided with the structural change that made that communication necessary.

Slowest to change, however, was the Society's perception of itself. Its leaders still continued to refer to the organisation as 'a learned society'—the term persisted right up until the twenty-first century.[18] Indeed, although Lucas had lowered the barriers to becoming a fellow, he still, at least publicly, stressed that the 'quality' of fellows would be maintained.[19] The chairman in 1987 said that the Society's drive to increase membership would take place 'without impairing the standards of accomplishment' it had hitherto used.[20]

It was in the late 2000s that this began to change. Much as it had in 1977 with Lucas, the Society once again decided to bring in an outsider. In 2006 it hired Matthew Taylor to be its chief executive (the title replaced that of director). Taylor was head-hunted for the job, but he knew very little about the Society. He had been a local politician, run think-tanks, and briefly been the chief policy adviser to the prime minister, Tony Blair. What he noticed about the Society, however, was that it had a huge number of members who did not seem to be particularly involved. Here, he felt, was the potential to combine the Society's think-tank elements—its staff produced report after report—with a membership in the tens of thousands.

Instead of convening differing interests and persuading people to act, much of the Society's activity had become focused on simply 'calling' for things to happen. It pursued initiatives, but often failed to use its members to support them. The Society might publish a report, send out a press release, perhaps even mark the occasion by posting a blog. Then nothing else happened and the Society moved on. It seemed to Taylor that if the membership could be properly harnessed, it might be used as a ready-made social movement, to take initiatives further and actually change things.

Taylor was not the first to see the fellowship in this way. Although the Society had often drawn upon some of its high-status members when convening people for commissions, panels and conferences, it had also tried to engage with the members in greater numbers. To coincide with the 150th anniversary of the Great Exhibition, in the years up to 2001 Christopher Lucas had tried to create network of volunteer groups across the country. He noted that a million young people between the ages of 16 and 24 were not in school, training or work, and that meanwhile the retired and semi-retired might benefit from more opportunities for volunteering. He hoped that, instead of holding a physical exhibition—an investment in a building—people would instead use 2001 to invest in their social connections. The idea was that they would introduce vocational qualifications for the young people out of work, to recognise the skills they might gain through volunteering. It would give young people something to show to potential employers, while also involving them in the life of their communities. It would, Lucas hoped, prevent them from becoming disconnected from the rest of society.[21] 'Project 2001' was the sort of thing that might have been easy to pull off, had the Society been fully engaged with its members, instantly able to assemble those who were interested in a common goal. The campaign had little trouble getting funding from businesses, but Lucas had hoped the campaign would involve 2,000 volunteering projects across the country. Instead, they gathered just over 220.[22]

Similarly, to coincide with the Society's 250th anniversary in 2004, Egan acquired sponsorship from a major coffee chain, Starbucks, for a

'Coffee House Challenge'. Just as the Society had had its first meeting in a coffee house, she hoped that fellows would meet in coffee shops across the country to debate how they might solve the most pressing issues the public faced. But the event ignored the Society's existing local networks, wishing to avoid the formality of many of the regional committees. The Coffee House Challenge did involve existing members, but it was also about acquiring new ones—the sort of people who might join to benefit the public instead of pursuing status. (This was still, however, a point of contention among the Society's leaders. The chairman at the time, Paul Judge, insisted that the Challenge culminate in a large and expensive gala at the Royal Albert Hall, to which they tried to invite Bill Clinton and Nelson Mandela.)

The Coffee House Challenge meetings generated plenty of debate and ideas, though unlike in 1754, those who took part did not have much say in what the Society did. The meetings may have taken place in coffee shops, but that was where the resemblance ended—the Society did not suddenly revert back to being a direct democracy. Nonetheless, it did mark a reversion in the Society's approach to its membership. Its leaders began to stress how fellows of the Society were not members of a club or learned society, but rather people 'who subscribe to its mission and . . . help to forward it'.[23] They once again began to stress that being a fellow was about intentions, not achievements.

This change accelerated when Taylor became chief executive. He dispensed with as many formalities as he could find. The offices at the Adelphi became open-plan, with staff attending weekly meetings. The chains of office worn by the chairman and president were soon banished to the archives, as were those used by the chairs of the regional committees. Taylor even joked about abolishing the title 'fellow', though he worried that a reversion to the use of 'member' would leave the letters after the members' names as MRSA (a type of lethal bacteria often found in hospitals).

By 2018 there was no mention of the letters 'FRSA' as an inducement to join the Society. The letters were nowhere to be seen on its 'Join the Fellowship' web page. Taylor wanted different people to join—those who wished to serve the public rather than obsess over status. Indeed, membership of the Society again became explicitly about intentions rather than achievements. 'While many fellows have achieved recognition for their contribution in a particular field', wrote Taylor, 'this is not the defining criterion for becoming a fellow. Our ethos is inclusive; we value all who positively impact society'.[24]

Taylor's changes to the Society affected its other activities too. The Student Design Awards became focused on benefitting society more widely, accelerating the trend that had begun in the 1990s. By the late 2010s, the competition might typically call for the design of a service to encourage parents to embrace shared parental leave, or for the design of a product that reduces the impact of loneliness on mental health.[25] The Society's focus on design was less about aesthetics, more about encouraging designers to apply their skills to solving social issues.

Taylor made similar changes to the Albert Medal. From 2008 the Society awarded it to people who set up charities or volunteer groups, or who enabled those kinds of organisations to thrive. Instead of pursuing status, the Albert Medal became about giving its recipients encouragement—it was offered to people who had not already received many, if any, accolades (much like the original intentions behind the Benjamin Franklin Medal, though this time the change stuck, for at least a decade).[26] In 2009, for example, the Albert Medal was awarded to Zarine Kharas, the co-founder and chief executive of an online platform for donating to charity, JustGiving. She received the medal well before she was made a dame.

The Society also changed in appearance. The entrance hall was opened out to become lighter and more spacious. The Great Room, which for years had had fixed rows of seating for the lectures, became an open space. Chairs could be brought in, but the default was for people to move around and talk to one another. In 2018, some of the house's lower floors were also opened out to become a coffee house (named Rawthmells in honour of the venue of the Society's first meeting in 1754). It was designed to promote discussion and collaboration between the Society's members and interested members of the public (as a charity, the Society was not allowed to exclude the public from the coffee house even if it had wanted to). The house at the Adelphi was redesigned to reflect Taylor's vision of it as a place where social movements could be born.

The Society also became more visible online. In 2009, a member of staff noticed an artist, Andrew Park, who drew on a whiteboard to illustrate people's lectures as complex cartoons. Taylor was intrigued, and at the time a fan of short, popular videos of lectures that were receiving millions of views online, called TED Talks. The Society commissioned Park to combine them: a few of the Society's lectures were illustrated with Park's cartoon-like animations. This new artistic medium, called whiteboard animation, gave those lectures extraordinary popularity—the first few were watched 9 million times in a matter of months.

The content of the lectures also changed, as did articles in the *Journal*, to reflect Taylor's interest in using the members as a social movement. They were increasingly devoted to discussing new theories about organisation, the nature of society, and the way people's minds work—things that needed to be understood in order to better harness the Society's members as activists. Rather than creating change, however, Taylor became increasingly frustrated that the Society seemed only to be discussing it. Its research staff continued to produce reports, on drugs, crime, immigration, and even taxi drivers, all of which continued to be ignored. The staff debated with one another on the Society's blog, about the purpose of the organisation. Indeed, the Society came no closer to using its members as a social movement, with researchers sometimes actively avoiding them—when there were well over twenty thousand members, there were inevitably a few with strong opinions.

There was also resistance to Taylor's changes. When he visited one regional event, he noticed the chairman was still wearing a chain of office. Taylor made him hand it over at the end. On another occasion, Taylor attended the annual general meeting of a region, only to find that it was a 1950s-style dinner dance, complete with fob watches, waistcoats and pearls. When he left early, he received a letter from the chair of the committee demanding an apology for leaving before the loyal toast.

Taylor tried to do too much, too quickly. He was, he admitted, perhaps too irreverent, with unrealistic expectations. Whereas Lucas and

Egan had patiently compromised and negotiated to eventually get their way, Taylor was frustrated at the slow pace of change—he was used to the rapidity of the Downing Street team. In the late 2000s many members resigned, feeling ignored.

In 2010 he also almost lost control. Taylor had found that opposition to his reforms most often came from the chairs of the regional committees. The Council by this stage was mostly advisory, but the Society's administration and finances were controlled by the Board of Trustees. Many of the trustees were elected by members, some were appointed. The elections for the trustees had extremely low turnout—never above 2 per cent of members—and were dominated by the regional chairs. The elected trustees were generally opposed to Taylor's reforms.

That year, Taylor attempted to make the Board of Trustees entirely appointed.[27] It only made matters worse. At the annual general meeting, some of the regional chairs accused Taylor of attempting to shut down democracy, using the chance to criticise his management in general.[28] They filed a protest motion, proposing that the entire board be elected. Had that happened, Taylor would have come under pressure to resign. The protest motion only narrowly failed.

Taylor compromised, but once the issue of the constitution had been raised, it took years to fully resolve. Nonetheless, he eventually managed to get the regional committees abolished. The Council, in 2009 relabelled the Fellowship Council, became directly elected, with a few of its number appointed (to ensure that it was diverse in terms of gender, ethnicity, age, area, and even the kinds of projects its members were interested in). Taylor's vision was that the Fellowship Council would lead the way in convening the Society's members, though it took time. For many years, the Fellowship Council continued to be a place where his opponents voiced their concerns.

Yet Taylor hired many more staff to talk to the members, to encourage them to become involved with the Society, as well as to collaborate with one another on projects for the public good. If the Society was to use its members to build momentum for campaigns, it had to take the time and effort to build working relationships with them. Although the regional committees were abolished, members still met throughout the country, with the support of the Society's staff. With that support, the regions no longer needed to create their own hierarchies.

By 2018, Taylor felt that his reforms were finally working. The membership, having fallen for a few years, eventually recovered and then expanded to just under thirty thousand. The people who joined were increasingly activists. Having removed so many of the Society's associations with status, it attracted people with different priorities. And it became more diverse. It was still mostly middle-aged and male, but since at least the 1970s, under Christopher Lucas, the Society's leaders had made a public and concerted effort to make the membership more representative of the population as a whole. By the time Egan took over in 1998, the proportion of female members was around a fifth.[29] By 2018, it had risen to a third.

To incentivise members to become more active, the Society soon also offered small grants for new charitable projects, or for endeavours that needed some extra money to be increased in scale. The Fellowship Council were given the final say on which of the projects received funding. These 'Catalyst' grants gradually grew in size as the quality of the submissions also seemed to increase. By 2018, the Society was confident in offering grants as high as ten thousand pounds, not just in Britain, but around the world. The fellowship became increasingly global too. In 2018, for example, the largest grant was awarded to Soumya Dabriwal, in India, for a campaign to make menstruation less taboo. It was the eighteenth-century premium system, reinvented. Indeed, one project that received a two-thousand-pound grant, the Chatty Café Scheme, had further echoes of the Society's origins. To combat loneliness, one of the Society's members from Manchester, Alexandra Hoskyn, persuaded a major coffee-shop chain, Costa, to begin designating tables in its shops as places to talk—on those tables, someone could put up a discrete sign letting others know that they would be happy to have some company.[30]

Overall, Taylor's vision was that the Society, itself an organisation for the public good, would become a generator of similar, more specialised organisations. Whereas in the late nineteenth century the Society had been considered a mother of learned and professional societies, Taylor hoped that in the twenty-first century it might become a mother of charities and social movements. The Society's research increasingly reflected that agenda too, investigating how to get individuals to collaborate with one another for the common good, to act to improve the world around them rather than accept their lot.

The Society's focus was increasingly on how to 'empower' the population, in education, in work, and in leisure, as well as how to remove barriers to individuals taking action. Its researchers campaigned for the state to provide a universal basic income, so that nobody would be too poor to take the initiative to better the world around them. All social reformers, after all, require time and money to support themselves. Likewise, the Society's research focused on ensuring that individual citizens had routes through which to make their voices heard. Taylor and his staff at the Society argued that the managers of powerful bureaucracies should at least consult panels of citizens, to ensure they were not blind to the concerns of different stakeholders when making decisions that affected the country. The Society, having run some trials, in 2018 persuaded the Bank of England to create such a panel.[31] The Society's campaigns thus focused on improving the agency of individuals—allowing more people to be the authors of their own lives.

Likewise, in the late 2010s, the Society campaigned for the creation of consumer-owned local banks—ones that would invest locally and be more responsive to customers than a large, impersonal bureaucracy. Rather than lobbying existing firms to change their structure, or for the government to enforce their ideas, the Society instead drew upon its network of members to help create entirely new banks. It convened local members to introduce the banks to potential customers and investors, as well as connecting the banks to members who were experienced managers who might sit on the boards of directors. Indeed, the staff member who directed the project, Tony Greenham, in 2018 left the Society to be the executive director of one of the new community banks, South West Mutual (at the time of writing, the bank is seeking regulatory approval).[32]

For Taylor, these were examples of the Society using its members appropriately—convening, communicating, and acting in partnership—rather than just relying on them to pay their subscription fees. It remains to be seen whether this latest incarnation of the Society will last. But, ultimately, the success and influence of the organisation depends on it. Many of the Society's activities have involved seeking to change hearts and minds, to bring about changes in the way people think, the things that they value, and thus the ways that they act. This was as true of the efforts in the eighteenth century to persuade people to buy contemporary art or to plant more trees or to invent devices that saved the lives of workers, as it was of the campaigns in the mid-nineteenth century to persuade people to seek beauty in their every-day household objects or to value education. It was just as true for the twentieth-century campaigns to change people's attitudes to their built and natural environments, as well as towards industry. And it was when those campaigns succeeded that the Society was at its most influential. The success of the 1840s exhibitions led to the Great Exhibition, and the success of the Great Exhibition inspired others to use the Society to form the Union of Institutions and create public examinations.

Those efforts to change hearts and minds succeeded when the priorities and efforts of the Society's leaders most aligned with those its members. In the Society's first hundred years, achieving this was straightforward. After all, every member had an equal vote in what the Society did. It had no shortage of ideas for things to change, and the majority ruled. The leaders were simply those members who spoke out for their ideas and took the initiative. Otherwise, they had no special access or power. Even the Society's presidents merely cast tie-breaking votes, their sole privilege in meetings being that they could wear a hat. There was little to distinguish the leaders from other members, other than that they most often turned up to the general meetings and sat upon committees. For would-be reformers who sought to direct the Society towards their own agendas, what mattered most was their ability to argue their case before the assembled subscribers. They had to be orators, or at least have friends who could make their case for them. They also needed persistence. William Shipley kept on attending early meetings even when nobody else turned up, and his persistence ultimately paid off. The artists in the 1760s who tried to use the Society to hold exhibitions or to create a Royal Academy were not persistent enough.

With the reforms of the 1840s, the skills needed to sway the Society changed. The frequent votes before subscribers were replaced by the work of a restricted Council and various small sub-committees. Whereas the massed subscribers had had a multitude of opinions and ideas for change, the default for the closed-off committees was inertia. Those who most successfully managed to direct the Society to their own agendas were thus those who could both gain access to the group and then take the initiative. Utilitarians like Cole and Booth had an influence on the Society that was far larger than their numbers merited, largely because of their willingness to shoulder additional responsibilities. Those who sat on the Council and various sub-committees were of course generous with their time. They did plenty of work. But the utilitarians were among the few who proposed new committees, committed additional time and energy, and ensured that they were the people who turned up most often. They were the few who took on the burdens of drafting commit- tee reports, ensuring that they had the final say over everything the So- ciety produced. Once access had been gained to the Council, influence went to those who showed up. For Prue Leith, for example, it did not take much to sway the Society to her agenda.

What also mattered was support from members, especially when it came to disputes over the future direction of the Society. This was obvi- ously the case when the Society was a direct democracy, when the rela- tive strength and persistence of factions could make the difference week after week, vote after vote. Later, too, Cole was successful in his contest with Thomas Webster over the future of the Society's exhibitions be- cause he brought in so many of his friends as members—artists, manu- facturers, and other would-be reformers. Webster was ultimately out- voted. James Booth discovered the value of allies when the rest of the Council forced him to resign as chairman, and Matthew Taylor's re- forms in the 2010s were threatened because he failed to first unite mem- bers around his vision.

But although the Society's leaders might persuade the organisation to do something, it was only when they pursued wider alliances that the

Society's campaigns had the greatest chance of success. The Great Exhibition drew upon pre-existing mass movements rather than trying to create one from scratch. It appealed to free traders, radicals, and pacifists, not just the much smaller group who shared Henry Cole's particular enthusiasm for art-manufactures. The same applied to later initiatives, like the campaign to preserve ancient cottages and the series of conferences on 'The Countryside in 1970'. A wide coalition may not have guaranteed success—the Industry Year campaign had plenty of good will and still disappointed its founders—but it was nonetheless necessary. In general, the Society experienced the most influence when it tapped into much larger underlying movements, engaging existing members and inspiring new people to join.

The Society's recent moves towards re-engaging the membership are thus crucial to its continued relevance. On a basic level, it needs the members to survive financially. It was when it found alternative major sources of income, especially from the examination board and bequests, that it allowed itself to fall into a period of relative inactivity. Although some of its leaders continued to take the initiative, as with the formation of Roberts's Special Activities Committee, these initiatives were short-lived. There was insufficient pressure for the Society to reinvent itself to stay relevant. It was only with the removal of those alternatives, when it separated from the examination board, that it was forced to reconsider its priorities.

Yet financial dependence on the members is not enough to keep the Society relevant. It only matters if members mostly join because the Society seems an effective tool with which to serve the public good, rather than because they get the personal prestige associated with the letters FRSA. It is only with the removal of the Society's aura of exclusivity that the size of its membership may again become a direct indicator of the organisation's influence.

Just as importantly, the Society needs its members as a source of ideas. The constant struggle for the Society has been to find the next thing to improve, to find yet another trail to blaze. In this sense, the more voices heard, the better. In the eighteenth century every member had an equal say. Even with the more restricted structures of the

Council and Board of Trustees, the Society remained open to new ideas. The latest incarnation of the Society will require something more, as it seeks to work with members to actively pursue initiatives and transform ideas into change. If those efforts succeed, the Society's influence will likely again increase. There are some initial signs that they are working. The government, for example, in 2016 appointed Taylor to lead an independent review into modern work practices. But it remains to be seen whether this is the start of a new trend.

It will be a matter for a future historian to explore whether the latest incarnation of the Society will last, and what it will seek to improve next. Ultimately, that will all depend on the individuals who will try to use it to serve the public good. They will have their own concerns and priorities, each filtered through the ideologies they will happen to hold. The Society has never been party-political, though its members have from time to time used the organisation to advance ideological agendas, from mercantilism to free trade, from utilitarianism to environmentalism. As in the past, they will sometimes be misguided, and at other times right. And their scope may well change too. The Society's history mostly involved seeking to change a nation, Britain. As it gains members abroad, they may try to use it to change the rest of the world too. Regardless, the Society is likely here to stay. It may lapse back into being an organisation that seeks to entertain its members and bolster their social status. Its leaders may fail to continue adapting it, internally, to be a tool that serves the public good. Just as in 1754, and ever since, its usefulness to the public will depend upon the public-spiritedness and initiative of those who choose to be involved.

ACKNOWLEDGEMENTS

THIS PROJECT BEGAN because the Society of Arts was in search of a history. Fortuitously, I had just written a little about it in my PhD thesis, and through sheer chance it came to the Society's attention: Indy Johar deserves credit for making the introduction after we met over coffee. Thus, like the Society itself, my writing this book began in a coffee house. Thanks to Indy's introduction, I turned up to a meeting with Matthew Taylor, the Society's chief executive, thinking I was just going to have a brief chat. I showed up in shorts, t-shirt, and sandals, as casual as one can be. And to my surprise, at the end of our conversation, Matthew and the Society's archivist, Eve Watson, asked me to write the book. Thank you to Matthew for bravely asking me to portray the Society 'warts and all', for holding true to that request even after reading the manuscript, and to the Society's trustees for backing the project too.

Thank you also to Eve for her unremitting support and advice, and her staunch championing of the Society's archive, which is still very fortunately in-house. It would not have been possible to write the book without the easy and unrestricted access that she allowed me. I have been like a kid in a candy store. I have been so spoiled, that I cannot help but feel restricted when I visit another archive and have to follow all the usual rules for new visitors. Thank you also to the volunteers—Lyn Dunn, Pat Hammett, Jill Penegar—who help keep the archive going and continue to make it ever better. Some people think that an archive is just a room full of boxes and old papers, but it requires immense work to maintain and there is always something new to be done.

Through my connection with the archive, I had the opportunity to meet many researchers who came to use it, or had used it before. My conversations with them have been invaluable, though they are too numerous to mention. Anthony Howe perhaps deserves special mention, for having looked over some of my manuscript (and caught some very embarrassing errors), and because fate seems to have had something in store for us: we were both commissioned to write entries for the *Oxford Dictionary of National Biography*, him on the founders of the Great Exhibition, and I on one of them, Francis Whishaw, at the very same time. Thus we both happened to use the RSA archive on the very same day for the very same purpose. Perhaps fate couldn't decide which of us, given our near-identical names, was supposed to do this.

I am also grateful to many of the Society's staff. They have made me feel extremely welcome as historian-in-residence, and through thousands of conversations I hope I have gained some insight into its modern workings. I would especially like to thank Nicholas Bull, the in-house lawyer, for our many kitchen conversations. Nina Bolognesi also ensured that I faced only open doors when it came to contacting people. My especial thanks also go to a number of people who were very generous with their time so that I could quiz them about the Society, including Melanie Andrews, Helen Auty, Penny Egan, Stuart Hampson, Charles and Liz Handy, Prue Leith, Christopher Lucas, and His Royal Highness the Duke of Edinburgh. And thank you to Daniel de Búrca for coming up with the title.

The Society's fellows, too, have been exceptionally supportive. My thanks go to Susan Bennett, Nicholas Cambridge, and others at the William Shipley Group for the Society's History, who very kindly furnished me with their publications. I relied heavily on the work they promote. A cursory look at the book's bibliography will also reveal the reoccurring name of the group's founder, and my predecessor as the Society's historian, David G. C. Allan. I was very unfortunate to have never met him, starting my work less than a year after he died. He was one of the tallest giants upon whose shoulders I stood in order to see a little further.

I also had the privilege of collaborating with the artist Andrew Park on a mural of the Society's history, which can now be found on the bottom floor of Rawthmells, the new coffee house in the Society's basement. His requests for information and copy, as well as the evolution of the image he created, often aided immensely in the structuring of the book and in finding some very special details. I would never have discovered that the prison reformer John Howard had promoted a premium for ventilators, had it not been for one of Andrew's queries.

Thank you also to Sarah Caro, Charlie Allen, and Hannah Paul at Princeton University Press, who ably shepherded the proposal and manuscript through the review process, as well as to all those who gave advice and support throughout that process—Joanne Paul, Julian Mueller, Dan D'Amico, Gianna Englert, and Joel Mokyr. I am also grateful to the anonymous peer-reviewers of the proposal and manuscript. Reviewer 1, who later revealed himself to be Martin Daunton, remained with the project all the way from initial proposal to corrected manuscript, all the time providing invaluable comments. My thanks also go to Tash Siddiqui, for some extraordinarily patient and diligent copy-editing.

A friend once told me that there are two stages to writing a book: one is research, the other is 'oh ****! I have no time left!' This turned out to be very true, and I only got through those last few months thanks to a few individuals. One was my research assistant Diego Rodriguez Mejias, supported by an excellent scheme—a summer research fellowship for undergraduates run by my then employer King's College London—who learned far more than is healthy about the London fish market of the 1760s and the life and times of Henry Cole. Jodie Altham also contributed magnificent research assistance in covering the Society's connection to the Arts and Crafts movement and the evolution of the Student Design Awards, as well as providing feedback on some chapters. Laurence Scales, who often shares my passion for the history of technology over a pint or two, read every chapter and provided extremely thorough comments, sometimes at short notice. I think I got only a handful of split infinitives past him. A large part of getting me through the final weeks was the occasional 20-minute break to watch *Brooklyn Nine-Nine*. Thank you to the cast and creators for such an uplifting comedic masterpiece. Last, but by no means least, thank you to Claire Matheson. In the final months she read every word, and quite literally kept me alive.

Despite all this help, I probably made mistakes. They are frustratingly easy to make—a typo in my notes here, a misremembered or misread source there. They are all my own, and hopefully not too embarrassing.

ABBREVIATIONS

Committee Minutes

Minutes of sub-committees of the Society of Arts: RSA/AD/MA/104/12

Council Minutes

Minutes of the Council of the Society of Arts: RSA/AD/MA/100/12/02

Jnl

Journal of the Society of Arts / Journal of the Royal Society of Arts
/ RSA Journal. They are a continuous series (1852–2018)

Minutes

Minutes of the general meetings of the Society
of Arts: RSA/AD/MA/100/12/01

ODNB

Online Oxford Dictionary of National Biography, http://www.oxforddnb.com

Trans

Transactions of the Society of Arts, Volumes 1–57
(1783–1851): RSA/PR/GE/112/13/11–67

NOTES

Introduction

1. Jnl, Vol. 98, No. 4808 (18 November 1949), 3–20.

Chapter One. Patrons of the Nation

1. Porter, *Enlightenment* frames an English enlightenment in these terms; see also Slack, *The Invention of Improvement* for a discussion of the invention and evolution of the term 'improvement'.

2. Sprat, *History of the Royal Society*, 6.

3. Ibid., 35.

4. Mokyr, 'The Intellectual Origins of Modern Economic Growth', 289.

5. Sprat, *History of the Royal Society*, 5.

6. Wootton, *The Invention of Science*; Sprat, *History of the Royal Society*, 73, 99; for a slightly dissenting view, see Shapin, *The Scientific Revolution* and Shapin, *A Social History of Truth*, which stress the diversity of practices used to gain acceptance for knowledge. Shapin points out that facts were often 'made' as much as they were discovered.

7. Sprat, *History of the Royal Society*, 23–24. Please note that throughout the text I have occasionally 'corrected' the spellings and grammar in seventeenth- and eighteenth-century quotations. This is to make their words more comprehensible to modern eyes, and wishing to prevent them from appearing in any way quaint. I have, of course, not changed the meanings of the quotations in any way.

8. For detail about the overlap in membership with the Society of Arts, see: Allan, *The Society of Antiquaries and the Society for the Encouragement of Arts, Manufactures and Commerce: An Account of Shared Memberships and Interests from the Mid-18th to the Early 21st Centuries*; for a general overview of antiquarianism in eighteenth-century Britain, see: Sweet, *Antiquaries*.

9. Allan, *William Shipley*, 169.

10. Thoresby, *The Diary of Ralph Thoresby*, 2:117.

11. Clark, *British Clubs and Societies 1580–1800*.

12. Sprat, *History of the Royal Society*, 61; Lyons, *The Royal Society, 1660–1940*, 41. A 'Georgical Committee' to deal with agriculture was set up by the Royal Society in 1664.

13. See: Ochs, 'The Royal Society of London's History of Trades Programme' for a fuller discussion.

14. Sprat, *History of the Royal Society*, 75.

15. Patent No. 143, 3 March 1664, under the name of its treasurer, Abraham Hill; see also: Hunter, *Establishing the New Science*, 89.

16. For examples, see: Ochs, 'The Royal Society of London's History of Trades Programme'.

17. Hunter, *Science and the Shape of Orthodoxy*, 178; Hunter, *Establishing the New Science*, 311–12.

18. Allan, *William Shipley*, 14–15.

19. Jacob and Stewart, *Practical Matter*, 28–29.

20. On the British (Newton-influenced) natural philosophy as different from Descartes's approach, see: Mokyr, *A Culture of Growth*, 103–5.

21. RSA/PR/GE/118/134, 'Three Letters', Letter 1.

22. Hilaire-Pérez, 'Transferts Technologiques, Droit et Territoire', 554, n.36; Bertucci, *Artisanal Enlightenment*, 84.

23. RSA/PR/GE/118/134, 'Three Letters', Letter 1, p. 4.

24. This is often referred to in the secondary literature as a 'chamber of arts', but this was in fact the term to be used for the physical meeting place of what was otherwise to be called the 'society'.

25. Harris, 'French Industrial Policy under the Ancien Regime and the Pursuit of the British Example', 95.

26. For a comprehensive treatment of both schemes, see: Paul, *The South Sea Bubble*.

27. Bertucci, *Artisanal Enlightenment*, 77–92.

28. Bertucci and Courcelle, 'Artisanal Knowledge, Expertise, and Patronage in Early Eighteenth-Century Paris'; Bertucci, *Artisanal Enlightenment*, 136–38.

29. Maxwell, *Select Transactions of the Honourable the Society of Improvers in the Knowledge of Agriculture in Scotland*, x; Smout, 'A New Look at the Scottish Improvers'.

30. Prior, *A List of the Absentees of Ireland, and the Yearly Value of Their Estates and Incomes Spent Abroad. With Observations on the Present State and Condition of That Kingdom*, 15–16, 21.

31. Clarke, 'Thomas Prior, 1681–1751', 339.

32. Allan and Schofield, *Stephen Hales*, 119.

33. Swift, *The Works of Jonathan Swift*, 12:204.

34. Shadwell, *The Virtuoso*, 47.

35. See for example: Sprat, *History of the Royal Society*, 26–27: natural philosophers were scornfully derided as 'men of another world, only fit companions for the shadow, and their own melancholy whimsies'.

36. Ibid., 119.

37. Allan and Schofield, *Stephen Hales*, 83–85.

38. Hales, *A Description of Ventilators*, vii.

39. Samuel Johnson reportedly tried this unsuccessfully. Hawkins, *The Life of Samuel Johnson, LL.D.*, 516. The *Gray's Inn Journal*, 77 describes Slaughter's as 'this little asylum of the [French] refugees'.

40. Allan, *William Shipley*, 26–30.

41. Ibid., 169.

42. Ibid., 185: this is from a crossed-out passage in the manuscript letter Baker sent to Shipley.

43. Theobald, 'Account of the Society of Arts', 1.

44. Allan, *William Shipley*, 24–25.

45. For an overview of the concept, see: Miller, *Defining the Common Good*.

46. RSA/PR/GE/110/1/42.

47. Allan, *William Shipley*, 46.

48. Smith, *Wealth of Nations*, book I, chapter 10, part II, 130: 'people of the same trade seldom meet . . . but the conversation ends in a conspiracy against the public, or in some contrivance to raise prices'.

49. There are echoes here of the work of Bernard Mandeville, though Shipley's approach was very different. Mandeville in the opening decades of the eighteenth century controversially challenged the distinction between virtue and vice, arguing that material wealth and progress depended upon 'vices' like self-interest. Although Shipley and the Society of Arts sought to harness self-interest for the public good, however, they also sought to make the population more virtuous.

50. RSA/PR/GE/110/1/42.

51. *London Advertiser and Literary Gazette*, 21 March 1751, Issue 16.

52. RSA/PR/GE/110/2/103.

53. *The Gray's Inn Journal*, 75.

54. Anderson, *Imagined Communities*.

55. Sprat, *History of the Royal Society*, 63: 'they openly profess, not to lay the foundation of an English, Scotch, Irish, Popish, or Protestant Philosophy; but a Philosophy of Mankind'.

56. RSA/PR/GE/110/1/42: 'will not only unite in one common band all real patriots, or as I should then call them the Patrons of the Nation, but will in time I hope utterly extirpate all party distinctions, the bane of society and civil government'.

57. RSA/AD/MA/100/10/109.

58. *The Gray's Inn Journal*, 128.

59. RSA/PR/GE/110/1/42.

60. *The Gray's Inn Journal*, 130.

61. Allan and Schofield, *Stephen Hales*, 100.

62. Musson and Robinson, *Science and Technology in the Industrial Revolution*, 378–81. Shipley seems to have already known some of Hales's opinions of his scheme even before Baker put them in touch, suggesting that someone had already made the introduction—Yeoman is the most plausible candidate.

63. Loft, 'Peers, Parliament and Power under the Revolution Constitution, 1685–1720', 117, 303; Theobald, 'Account of the Society of Arts', 2.

64. There is evidence that Shipley managed to also get the support of the Earl of Halifax, who was president of the Board of Trade. A newspaper report in early March, for example, names Halifax and the Bishop of Worcester as supporters. Yet Halifax would not actually become a member of the Society until 1760, six years later. See: *Derby Mercury*, Friday 8 March 1754.

65. £3,782 on measuringworth.com, using labour value. Labour value essentially denotes the price in terms of what the average worker at the time could buy.

66. Allan, *William Shipley*, 56. See also: Minutes, July–September 1754.

67. Allan, 'The Society of Arts and Government, 1754–1800'.

68. Cross, 'Early Contacts of the Society of Arts with Russia (i): Corresponding Members in Russia'; Braun, 'Some Notes on the Germanic Association of the Society of Arts in the Eighteenth Century'; Braun, 'Some Notes on the Germanic Associations of the Society of Arts in the Eighteenth Century: (ii) Relations with German Societies; Leipzig (1764), Celle (1764), Karlsruhe (1765), Hamburg (1765)'.

69. Hudson and Luckhurst, *The Royal Society of Arts, 1754–1954*, 12; Allan, 'Artists and the Society in the 18th Century (ii): Members and Premiums in the First Decade, 1755–64', 271 gives a figure of 2,136 members in 1764. Allan was responsible for card-cataloguing the membership records up to 1800, so his estimate is likely to be the most accurate.

70. Mallet, 'Nicholas Crisp, Founding Member of the Society of Arts, Part II: Crisp and the Society', 92.

71. Allan, 'Robert Marsham, 2nd Baron Romney (d. 1793) and the Society'.

72. There was originally a 'treasurer', though in 1759 this post was abolished and the responsibility was merged with that of the 'collector' of subscriptions and handed over to Shipley. Shipley held the responsibilities of secretary, collector and register all at once between November 1755 and March 1757, with George Box as assistant secretary in 1755 too. In March 1757 Shipley was replaced as secretary by George Box, but continued as collector until March 1760 (when Box also took this over), and as register until he resigned from all posts in October 1760. Thereafter, all the responsibilities were elected separately. See: Allan, *William Shipley*, 68–70.

73. Minutes, 1760–61, 37, 81.

74. An example of someone who was excluded was John Hill, who had libelled many of the fellows of the Royal Society, including Henry Baker, one of the Society of Arts founders. Shipley was scandalised by John Hill even before the Society of Arts began.

75. Humphry Davy to [John Hodgson], 12 July 1816, MS: Northumberland Archives (Woodhorn), SANT/BEQ/18/11/13/391–8. Unpublished—my thanks to Frank A.J.L. James for providing me with this reference.

76. *The Gray's Inn Journal*, 87.

77. Cross, 'Early Contacts of the Society of Arts with Russia (iii): The Visit of a Russian Serf', 336; Minutes 1763–64, 88.

78. Eger and Peltz, *Brilliant Women*, 104, 127–28; Davies, *Catharine Macaulay and Mercy Otis Warren*, 174–75; O'Brien, *Women and Enlightenment in Eighteenth-Century Britain*, 153; Montagu, *The Letters of Mrs. Elizabeth Montagu*, 37: 'the men are all become military, and the ladies politicians. I do not like such times.'

79. There is no evidence that they ever voted in person. See Minutes 1760, 16, in which it is stated that female members of the Society were allowed to vote by proxy so long as the proxy was a member. See RSA/AD/MA/100/10/387 and 398 for letters from female members appointing someone to vote on their behalves by proxy in 1770.

80. Kippis, *Biographia Britannica*, IV:2266.

81. Abbott, 'Dr. Johnson and the Society (i)'; Kippis, *Biographia Britannica*, IV:2266.

82. Grosley, *A Tour to London, or, New Observations on England and Its Inhabitants*, 2:14–15. Judging by the other details given by Grosley in terms of the timing and committee chair, the 'lusty hatter' responsible for the speeches was likely a certain hosier of Friday Street, London, named Edward Stanley.

83. Allan, *The Houses of the Royal Society of Arts: A History and a Guide*, 3–5.

84. Ibid., 5.

85. Minutes, 1760–61, 8.

86. Minutes, 1760–61, 33.

87. Smollett, *The Expedition of Humphry Clinker*, 127.

88. Allan, *William Shipley*, 43.

89. Ibid., 46, 180.

90. Minutes, 1759–60, 17.

91. Tierney, 'Robert Dodsley: The First Printer and Stationer to the Society', 285–87.

Chapter Two. Exciting an Emulation

1. Findlay and O'Rourke, *Power and Plenty*, 366–67.

2. Dossie, *Memoirs of Agriculture, and Other Oeconomical Arts*, I:33.

3. Dickinson, *A Companion to Eighteenth-Century Britain*, 314.

4. Hogarth, *Marriage A-La Mode: 1. The Marriage Settlement*, 1745, oil on canvas, in the National Gallery, London.

5. Allan, 'The Laudable Association of Antigallicans'.

6. Louis Philippe Boitard, *The Imports of Great Britain from France*, 1757, etching and engraving on paper, British Galleries, Room 53a, Case 5, Victoria and Albert Museum. https://collections.vam.ac.uk/item/O1240590/the-imports-of-great-britain-engraving-boitard-louis-philippe/.

7. Brewer, *The Pleasures of the Imagination*; Berg, *Luxury and Pleasure in Eighteenth-Century Britain*.

8. Kitson, 'Hogarth's "Apology for Painters"', 98.

9. Hudson and Luckhurst, *The Royal Society of Arts, 1754–1954*, 90.

10. Trans, Vol. 22, 154.

11. Trans, Vol. 1, 10–11.

12. Dossie, *Memoirs of Agriculture, and Other Oeconomical Arts*, I:192–94.

13. RSA/PR/GE/110/1/45.

14. Dossie, *Memoirs of Agriculture, and Other Oeconomical Arts*, I:149.

15. RSA/AD/MA/100/12/01/01, 3.

16. Dossie, *Memoirs of Agriculture, and Other Oeconomical Arts*, I:33.

17. Bennett, *Cultivating the Human Faculties*, 26–49.

18. De Freitas, 'The Society and Wood Engraving in the Eighteenth Century'; De Freitas, 'The Society and Illustration during Two Centuries'.

19. Berg, *Luxury and Pleasure in Eighteenth-Century Britain*, 93.

20. Hargraves, *Candidates for Fame*, 83.

21. Gwynn, *An Essay on Design*, 24.

22. Reynolds, *The Discourses of Sir Joshua Reynolds*, 4.

23. Ibid., 37–38.

24. Ibid., 48–50.

25. Samuel Johnson, *Idler*, No. 45, Saturday 24 February, 1759.

26. Cheere, *The Plan of an Academy for the Better Cultivation, Improvement and Encouragement of Painting, Sculpture, Architecture, and the Arts of Design in General*, iv.

27. Barrell, *The Political Theory of Painting from Reynolds to Hazlitt*, 11; Pressly, *The Artist as Original Genius*, 1; for an overview of many of the debates among artists in the period, see also Solkin, *Painting for Money*.

28. Sunderland, 'Samuel Johnson and History Painting'.

29. In 1761 this was changed to British, with Irish history added a few years after that. The artists originally proposed specific subjects from both British and classical history, as well as an allegorical work on commerce, but the Society resolved it should be limited to English history only. Minutes 1758–59, 154–55.

30. Taylor, *Art for the Nation*, 8.

31. Dossie, *Memoirs of Agriculture, and Other Oeconomical Arts*, I:vi; Berg, *Luxury and Pleasure in Eighteenth-Century Britain*, 94.

32. Fordham, *British Art and the Seven Years' War*, 6.

33. Hoock, *The King's Artists*, 98.

34. Hargraves, *Candidates for Fame*, 12–13.

35. Coutu, *Then and Now*, 113.

36. Smith, *The Company of Artists*, 24.

37. Coutu, *Then and Now*, 95, 113.

38. Allan, 'Artists and the Society in the 18th Century (i) The Foundation and Henry Cheere's Plan for an Academy'.

39. Pressly, *The Artist as Original Genius*, 15.

40. Kitson, 'Hogarth's "Apology for Painters" ', 76, 96, 99.

41. Allan, 'Artists and the Society in the 18th Century (i) The Foundation and Henry Cheere's Plan for an Academy', 205.

42. Scott, *Leviathan*, 312–14.

43. Hargraves, *Candidates for Fame*, 7.

44. Taylor, *Art for the Nation*, 1.

45. Trans, Vol. 1, 48.

46. Ackermann, *Microcosm of London*, 3:49.

47. Minutes, 1756, 84.

48. Lady Louisa Augusta Greville, who in 1758 at the time of her first win was the daughter of the earl of Brooke, who was then made earl of Warwick the following year.

49. Ackermann, *Microcosm of London*, 3:49.

50. *The Times*, 11 June 1853.

51. RSA/AD/MA/305/10/37, Letter from 'Modestus', 3 February 1796.

52. 1847–48 Premium List.

53. Crow, *Painters and Public Life in Eighteenth-Century Paris*, 1.

54. Bayer and Page, *The Development of the Art Market in England*, 56–57.

55. Hargraves, *Candidates for Fame*, 22.

56. Minutes, 1759–60, 4, 9.

57. Bayer and Page, *The Development of the Art Market in England*, 57.

58. Committee Minutes, Polite Arts, 3 March 1760, 63.

59. Hargraves, *Candidates for Fame*, 24–25.

60. 'Papers of SAGB', 122.

61. Bayer and Page, *The Development of the Art Market in England*, 58.

62. Committee Minutes, Exhibition, 19 April 1760, 107.

63. 'Papers of SAGB', 119, shows a bill to Mr Woodin, the Society's landlord, for 13s for broken windows; Committee Minutes, Affair of the Porter, 10 May 1760, 127. Morgan was apparently a very large man, so perhaps his assailant came off the worse for the encounter. See description of him as a 'great officer', an allusion to his size: *St. James's Chronicle*, 31 January–2 February 1764.

64. 'Papers of SAGB', 122.

65. Gwynn, *London and Westminster Improved, Illustrated by Plans*, 25.

66. Ibid., 22; Hargraves, *Candidates for Fame*, 16.

67. 'Papers of SAGB', 123.

68. Hargraves, *Candidates for Fame*, 26; a subsequent general meeting overturned this, but also tried to redirect it to other uses.

69. Minutes, 1760–61, 127, 142.

70. Minutes, 1760–61, 142.

71. Hoock, *The King's Artists*, 19.

72. Minutes, 1761–62, 119.

73. Minutes, 1763–64, 104–5. This is the most likely explanation of the debates based on the minutes, contra Hargraves.

74. Hargraves, *Candidates for Fame*, 52; *Public Advertiser*, 17 March 1764.

75. Minutes, 1763–64, 107, 151.

76. Taylor, 'Sea Pieces and Scandal'.

77. Hargraves, *Candidates for Fame*, 65–69, 85.

78. Taylor, *Art for the Nation*, 15–19; Conlin, ' "At the Expense of the Public": The Sign Painters' Exhibition of 1762 and the Public Sphere'.

79. *St. James's Chronicle*, 27–29 April 1762: 'the door-keepers refreshed themselves at Mother's Red-Cap's; as also did the Society, at the Old Hat at Ealing—at the expence of the public'.

80. Hargraves, *Candidates for Fame*, 167–69.

81. Ibid., 29.

82. Ibid., 64.

83. Coutu, *Then and Now*, 123; Hargraves, *Candidates for Fame*, 90–91.

84. Trans, Vol. 1, 47–48.

85. Hargraves, *Candidates for Fame*, 101 refers to this as 'blatant theft'.

86. Warner, 'John Everett Millais and the Society of Arts': it was not a drawing of the Battle of Bannockburn as is often claimed.

87. Millais, *The Life and Letters of Sir John Everett Millais*, 14.

88. Minutes, 1758–59, 49.

89. Minutes, 1759–60, 24–25, 27.

90. Smith, *Nollekens and His Times*, 32–33.

91. Cox-Johnson, 'Patrons to a Sculptor: The Society and John Bacon, R.A.'.

92. Minutes, 1758–59, 146.

93. Committee Minutes, Fine Arts, 21 April 1845.

94. Allan, *The Houses of the Royal Society of Arts: A History and a Guide*.

95. Pressly, *James Barry's Murals at the Royal Society of Arts*, 11.

96. Ibid., 12.

97. Ibid., 4.

98. Barry, *An Account of a Series of Pictures, in the Great Room of the Society of Arts, Manufactures, and Commerce, at the Adelphi*, 181.

99. Pressly, *James Barry's Murals at the Royal Society of Arts*, 72.

100. Personal interview with David Luckhurst.

Chapter Three. Peculiar Genius

1. Smith, *A Selection of the Correspondence of Linnaeus, and Other Naturalists*, 459.

2. Anonymous, *The Antigallican Privateer*.

3. See, for example, the works of Brewer, *The Sinews of Power*; Ashworth, *Customs and Excise: Trade, Production and Consumption in England, 1640–1845*; Hoppit, *Britain's Political Economies*.

4. Allan, 'The Society of Arts and Government, 1754–1800'.

5. Wade, *A Proposal for Improving and Adorning the Island of Great Britain*, 31.

6. Findlay and O'Rourke, *Power and Plenty*, 256.

7. Albion, *Forests And Sea Power*, 9; *Penny Magazine*, Vol. 12, 275.

8. Albion, *Forests And Sea Power*, 7–9, 10.

9. Evelyn, *Silva*.

10. Wade, *A Proposal for Improving and Adorning the Island of Great Britain*, 22.

11. Albion, *Forests and Sea Power*, viii.

12. Dossie, *Memoirs of Agriculture, and Other Oeconomical Arts*, I:38.

13. Albion, *Forests and Sea Power*, 7; *Shipbuilder's Assistant*, 1769, 57.

14. Wade, *A Proposal for Improving and Adorning the Island of Great Britain*, 8.

15. Ibid., 46.

16. Britain et al., *A Collection of Statutes Connected with the General Administration of the Law*, 280–84.

17. Minutes, 1757, 216.

18. Minutes, 1757, 13–14.

19. Wade, *A Proposal for Improving and Adorning the Island of Great Britain*, 53.

20. Ibid., 6–9.

21. Dossie, *Memoirs of Agriculture, and Other Oeconomical Arts*, I:39.

22. Trans, Vol. 30, 97.

23. Trans, Vol. 21, 107–8, 111.

24. Trans, Vol. 27, 23.

25. Trans, Vol. 32, v.

26. Dossie, *Memoirs of Agriculture, and Other Oeconomical Arts*, I:40.

27. Wood, *A History of the Royal Society of Arts*, 150, estimated fifty million, but I have re-counted the figure, often looking beyond the headline figures in the transactions for more detail.

28. Tucker, *A Brief Essay on Trade*, 92–95; Beer, *British Colonial Policy, 1754–1765*.

29. Allan, ' "Dear and Serviceable to Each Other" '.

30. Franklin and Sparks, *The Works of Benjamin Franklin*, 4:225.

31. Green, 'Translating Hemp into a Transatlantic "Band of Reciprocal Interest" '.

32. Dossie, *Memoirs of Agriculture, and Other Oeconomical Arts*, I:264; Smith, *A Selection of the Correspondence of Linnaeus, and Other Naturalists*, 438.

33. There was considerable debate at the time over whether or not the necessaries of life should be taxed as much as luxuries. On the one hand, it was believed that wages should be as low as possible to encourage people to industry—otherwise, some economic theorists believed, the poor would simply spend their surplus on luxuries and alcohol. On the other hand, some believed that wages should be high relative to the cost of necessaries so that greater consumption would stimulate Britain's industries. They still wished wages to be low, but with cheaper necessaries of life so that the living standards of workers rose. The Society's members seem to have sided with this latter position, made, for example, by people like Malachy Postlethwayt. An overview of some of the debate, at least as so far as it applied to tax, is provided in Ashworth, *Customs and Excise*, 60–62.

34. Dossie, *Memoirs of Agriculture, and Other Oeconomical Arts*, I:76.

35. Ibid., I:46.

36. Ibid., I:187.

37. Minutes, 1760–61, 235–37, 280, 284; Minutes, 1761–62, 10 for the motion to stop it happening again. See also Stern, 'The Society of Arts and the Improvement of Whaling, Part 2: The Edulcoration of Train Oil' for a full account of the tests on edulcoration.

38. Dossie, *Memoirs of Agriculture, and Other Oeconomical Arts*, I:82.

39. See, for example, Hogarth's *O the Roast Beef of Old England ('The Gate of Calais')*, 1748.

40. Dossie, *Memoirs of Agriculture, and Other Oeconomical Arts*, I:59–60.

41. Ibid., I:82–85.

42. Committee Minutes, Mechanics, 1 March 1764.

43. Dossie, *Memoirs of Agriculture, and Other Oeconomical Arts*, I:89, 93–94.

44. Allan and Abbott, ' "Compassion and Horror in Every Humane Mind": Samuel Johnson, the Society of Arts, and Eighteenth-Century Prostitution'.

45. Henderson and Ferguson, *Life of James Ferguson, F.R.S., in a Brief Autobiographical Account, and Further Extended Memoir*, 227.

46. For a recent overview, see: Paskins, 'Sentimental Industry: The Society of Arts and the Encouragement of Public Useful Knowledge, 1754–1848', 46–72.

47. Minutes, 1763–64, 79; Minutes, 1764–65, 2; see also: *St. James's Chronicle*, 31 January–2 February 1764.

48. *Gazetteer and New Daily Advertiser*, 24 January 1767.

49. See, for example: Khan, 'Prestige and Profit'.

50. Minutes, 1762, 138.

51. E.g. see Humphrey Jackson's patent for isinglass—Minutes, 1761, 268, 275, 288; Minutes, 1761–62, 1, 61.

52. For further and detailed discussion of the Society's relationship with patents, see also: Harrison, *Encouraging Innovation in the Eighteenth and Nineteenth Centuries*.

53. Trans, Vol. 40, 135–50.

54. Minutes, 1767–68, 106.

55. RSA/SC/EL/1/154.

56. RSA/SC/EL/5/254.

57. Committee Minutes, Mechanics, 16 February 1775, 30–31.

58. Trans, Vol. 47, xxvii.

59. Trans, Vol. 47, 185.

60. Howes, 'Why Innovation Accelerated in Britain 1651–1851', 89–96.

61. Minutes, 1758–59, 10.

62. RSA/PR/GE/118/201/693–5.

63. Minutes, 1830–31, 75; Minutes, 1832–33, 105; RSA/SC/EL/3/36.

64. Minutes, 1762–63, 141.

65. Schofield, 'The Society of Arts and the Lunar Society of Birmingham (i)'; Schofield, 'The Society of Arts and the Lunar Society of Birmingham (ii)'.

66. Trans, Vol. 38, 24.

67. Allan, 'The Society of Arts and the Committee of the Privy Council for Trade, 1786–1815', parts i–iv.

68. Even £10 and £15 notes had only been introduced by the Bank of England in 1759 to compensate for the shortages of gold and silver brought on by the Seven Years' War. £5 notes were only issued from 1793

69. McGowen, 'Managing the Gallows'.

70. McGowen, 'The Bank of England and the Policing of Forgery 1797–1821', 255–56; Mockford, '"They Are Exactly as Bank Notes Are"', 130.

71. *Report on Preventing Forgery*, 5.

72. RSA/PR/AR/103/10/452.

73. Hewitt, 'Beware of Imitations'.

Chapter Four. Jack of All Trades

1. Dutton, *The Patent System and Inventive Activity During the Industrial Revolution, 1750–1852*; MacLeod, *Inventing the Industrial Revolution*.

2. See, for example, 4 December 1839, 5 February 1840 (initially too few, but eventually enough turned up), 1 April 1840, 3 June 1840 in Minutes.

3. Committee Minutes, Miscellaneous, 1841, 33–34.

4. E.g. Trans, Vol. 53, Part I, 3–9. At the time it was referred to as voltatyping.

5. E.g. Trans, Vol. 53, Part II, 10–18.

6. Moe, *Governance, Growth and Global Leadership*, 79.

7. Wyatt, *A Report on the Eleventh French Exposition of the Products of Industry*, 9.

8. *The Times*, 7 June 1849.

9. *The Times*, 15 November 1849.

10. The conversazioni seem to have been started in the late 1830s—they first appear in Trans, Vol. 52, for the years 1837–38.

11. Harrison, *Encouraging Innovation in the Eighteenth and Nineteenth Centuries*, 177–79.

12. Bottomley, *The British Patent System during the Industrial Revolution 1700–1852*, 87–88.

13. Webster and his allies also believed that the law of patents had changed since the 1760s. Webster, for example, in 1844 compiled influential case reports on patents and made much of a particular court case, Liardet v. Johnson (1778), which was said to have set the precedent for patent specifications to be sufficiently detailed. But this was incorrect, and has created a persistent myth. Webster actually accidentally got the outcome of that case wrong—it had gone the other way. More recent research reveals that the case law for detailed specifications was already developing before the Society of Arts was even founded. See: Bottomley, *The British Patent System during the Industrial Revolution 1700–1852*, 90–91.

14. *The Repertory of Arts and Manufactures* (1794–1819) was perhaps the first, and certainly the best known. It soon had lots of competition.

15. Data derived from Woodcroft, *Titles of Patents of Invention, Chronologically Arranged*. In 1760–69 there were 204 patents, compared to 2,451 in 1830–39.

16. Wood, *A History of the Royal Society of Arts*, 347–48. The secretary in question was W. A. Graham.

17. Since the heyday of membership in the 1760s, when it reached a peak of over 2,000 members in 1764, the Society's membership had rapidly declined. This may have been related to the splits from the artists in the 1760s, as well as the scandal over the fish land-carriage scheme. It had fallen to under 1,500 by 1766, to under 500 by 1776 (though with over 1,000 members in arrears). For much of the early 1780s there just over 300 members, but following the publication of the *Transactions* from 1783 it slowly recovered. By 1800 there were 625. Allan and Abbott, *The Virtuoso Tribe of Arts and Sciences*, 365–66. It recovered to over 1,000 members in the early nineteenth century. Allan, 'RSA: A Chronological History', 69 shows there was then a steady decline again in the 1820s. From 1,701 subscribers in 1820, it declined to 1,236 by 1831, to 802 by 1840, and to 685 by 1843, at which point the Society experienced its major crisis.

18. Harrison, *Encouraging Innovation in the Eighteenth and Nineteenth Centuries*, 143, n.6. There were 260 recruits in the four years 1842–45, an increase of at least a third; the membership doubled in the years 1842–52.

19. Ibid., 143–44, n.6. Among the more prominent names added to the Society's membership lists in this period were engineers and inventors like Henry Bessemer, William Capmael, Joseph Whitworth, Bennet Woodcroft, John Scott Russell, Benjamin Fothergill, William Cubitt, William Newton and William Newton Jnr, Richard Prosser, William Fairbairn, and George Bodmer.

20. Pressly, *James Barry's Murals at the Royal Society of Arts*, 22; see *The Times*, 18 January 1830, for her 'perfectly' recollecting the prize-giving of Sir Thomas Lawrence, who became president of the Royal Academy.

21. Wood, *A History of the Royal Society of Arts*, 343.

22. E.g. in *The Times*, 20 March 1850 and 1 January 1851.

23. *The Times*, 8 March 1849.

24. Whishaw, *The Railways of Great Britain and Ireland Practically Described and Illustrated*, v.

25. Jnl, Vol. 46, No. 2353 (24 December 1897), 97–116.

26. Bouin and Chanut, *Histoire Française Des Foires et Des Expositions Universelles*, 39.

27. Kusamitsu, 'Great Exhibitions before 1851'.

28. For example, the National Repository of 1828, and its successor the Museum of National Manufactures of 1834.

29. The oft-cited notion that Whishaw intended to pay for this entirely from his own money is absurd—the sum of £300 was twice his annual salary. It seems to arise from a slight misreading of Wood, *A History of the Royal Society of Arts*, 403, and of Whishaw's own account—Whishaw instead bore the expense of the 6 December conversazione (see below), with which this is often confused. Little is known about Joseph Woods (d.1849), not to be confused with the architect and botanist of the same name. Woods is almost certainly the anonymous 'gentleman, being desirous of promoting the arts' described in the competition's newspaper advertisements (e.g. *The Times*, 27 November 1844). It is of course possible that Whishaw was to provide some of the money.

30. *The Art-Union, Monthly Journal of the Fine Arts, the Arts Decorative and Ornamental*, 1 January 1845, 20.

31. *The Athenaeum*, 4 January 1845, 16.

32. The misunderstanding seems to stem from a misreading of Whishaw's own account. See: RSA/PR/MC/107/10/11, Vol. II, 664. It is worth noting that Whishaw did refer to this event as an 'exposition'—the French word—before the fact: see Committee Minutes, Miscellaneous, 4 December 1844.

33. *The Art-Union, Monthly Journal of the Fine Arts, the Arts Decorative and Ornamental*, 1 January 1845, 20.

34. Whishaw only asked permission to use the rooms two days before: see Committee Minutes, Miscellaneous, 4 December 1844.

35. The 'aeolian attachment' invented by American mechanic Obed Mitchell Coleman. See *The Standard*, 29 January 1845. The person who played the piano seems to have been the composer and conductor Julius Benedict.

36. *The Standard*, 29 January 1845.

37. *Morning Post*, 19 April 1844.

38. Whishaw himself later stated that 'about 800' people attended (see RSA/PR/MC/107/10/11, Vol. II); but the estimate of at least 1,000 people is from *The Civil Engineer and Architect's Journal*, February 1845, 63.

39. Committee Minutes, Miscellaneous, 21 May 1845.

40. Hobhouse, *Prince Albert, His Life and Work*, iv.

41. Committee Minutes, Miscellaneous, 4 June 1845.

42. Committee Minutes, Miscellaneous, 14 July 1845.

43. In this instance the plan was to use much cheaper chemically treated wooden rails instead of iron—it eventually turned out that they could not withstand the wear and tear of the heavy engines.

44. Council Minutes, 9 June 1846.

45. Council Minutes, 6 May 1846.

46. RSA/PR/MC/107/10/11, Earliest Proceedings, Vol. II, Whishaw's memorandum, 671–72.

47. Auerbach, *The Great Exhibition of 1851*, 11–12.

Chapter Five. The Greatest Beauty for the Greatest Number

1. Bonython and Burton, *The Great Exhibitor*, 1.

2. Ibid., 29–32.

3. The politician in question was Charles Buller MP, an overt Benthamite.

4. Thomas, *Postal Pleasures*, 10–14; Bonython and Burton, *The Great Exhibitor*, 54–55.

5. Bonython and Burton, *The Great Exhibitor*, 57.

6. Ibid., 59 reports that he collected 262,809 signatures on 2,007 petitions. The total votes cast at the general election of 1837 numbered 798,025.

7. Summerfield, 'The Making of The Home Treasury'.

8. Bonython and Burton, *The Great Exhibitor*, 64–65. The quotation is from Rowland Hill's diary, but they were of the same opinion, Cole having commissioned the design.

9. Summerfield, 'The Making of The Home Treasury'; Summerly, *Traditional Nursery Songs of England With Pictures by Eminent Modern Artists*, Preface: ' the legend more as a fairy tale than a lecture'.

10. Shales, 'Toying with Design Reform'; Bonython and Burton, *The Great Exhibitor*, 89.

11. Bonython and Burton, *The Great Exhibitor*, 84.

12. Committee Minutes, Fine Arts, 22 May 1846.

13. Cooper, 'For the Public Good: Henry Cole, His Circle and the Development of the South Kensington Estate', 36.

14. Cole, *Fifty Years*, 1:24: the comment applied to the arrangement of physical space, but it might just as well have applied to Cole's meetings with Albert.

15. Bonython and Burton, *The Great Exhibitor*, 94.

16. Trans, Vol. 56, 1–4.

17. Allan, *The Houses of the Royal Society of Arts: A History and a Guide*, 19–20.

18. Heleniak, 'William Mulready, RA (1786–1863) and the Society of Arts (i)', 468.

19. Trans, Vol. 56, 73–77.

20. Mulready won a silver palette in 1801 for a drawing; J. C. Horsley won the silver medal in 1830 for a chalk drawing from a bust, when he was about 13; Charles Eastlake won a silver medal in 1810 for a drawing of Cupid and Psyche and thus came to the attention of a perpetual member of the Society, Jeremiah Harman, who gave him his first commission.

21. RSA/SC/EX/1/77, A Catalogue of the Select Specimens of British Manufactures and Decorative Art, Exhibited at the house of the Society of Arts, London in the Month of March, 1847, 3.

22. Cooper, 'For the Public Good: Henry Cole, His Circle and the Development of the South Kensington Estate', 40.

23. *The Times*, 27 March 1848.

24. Heleniak, 'William Mulready, RA (1786–1863) and the Society of Arts (ii)'.

25. Auerbach, *The Great Exhibition of 1851*, 20.

26. *The Times*, 14 June 1847.

27. Cole, *Fifty Years*, 1:121–22.

28. Technically, the 1848 exhibition had also charged entry of a shilling on Saturdays. But the 1849 exhibition was the first to entirely dispense with free entry.

29. *The Times*, 8 March 1849.

30. The MP in question was Thomas Milner Gibson, a passionate free trader who in later years would collaborate often with Cole on his utilitarian campaigns. It is not clear whether Gibson was himself influenced by utilitarianism, but as was so often the case Cole found common ground with free traders and radicals to push through his desired reforms.

31. Auerbach, *The Great Exhibition of 1851*, 21.

32. Bonython and Burton, *The Great Exhibitor*, 111–14.

33. Cole, *Fifty Years*, 1:120.

Chapter Six. For the Masses, by the Masses

1. For a recent overview of mercantilism, see Magnusson, *The Political Economy of Mercantilism*. It is worth noting that mercantilism itself was never a coherent 'school' of thought, but rather a series of attitudes and beliefs regarding economic policy. See Magnusson, *Mercantilist Economics*, 10 for the difference between mercantilism as a trend in economic thought as opposed to the narrower definition used here, to describe a set of policies involving protectionism and import-substitution.

2. Bullionism was still widespread, especially among the Society's members, but writers such as Josiah Child, Charles Davenant, and Nicholas Barbon had stressed employment. They argued that the country should produce and export especially valuable goods, and import as little of them as they could, so that such jobs would go to domestic workers rather than foreign ones. Thus, alongside many who believed in the importance of a balance of trade, were those who believed in the importance of a 'balance of labour'. These 'reformed mercantilists', however, still thought that the best means to achieve a better balance of labour was through achieving a favourable balance of trade.

3. For an overview, see: Irwin, *Against the Tide*.

4. Adam Smith joined the Society of Arts on 1 November 1775 and left in February 1777. He was proposed by the deist Henry Dodwell.

5. Howe, *Free Trade and Liberal England, 1846–1946*, 29–30.

6. https://www.historyofparliamentonline.org/volume/1820–1832/constituencies/dunwich (accessed 26 October 2018).

7. James, 'Michael Faraday, The City Philosophical Society and The Society of Arts'.

8. Minutes, 7 May 1817, 243–45.

9. Bonython and Burton, *The Great Exhibitor*, 60.

10. Restrictions at the universities of Oxford and Cambridge were not fully abolished until the Universities Tests Act in 1871.

11. For a discussion of 'manliness' in the free trade movement, see: Kuchta, *The Three-Piece Suit and Modern Masculinity*, 158.

12. *The Economist*, Vol. 2, Issue 35, 20 April 1844, 704.

13. *The Standard*, Friday 9 May 1845.

14. *Morning Post*, Friday 9 May 1845.

15. Wood, *A History of the Royal Society of Arts*, gives the date as 1848, but the first advertisement in the Society's *Transactions* is in 1835.

16. Trans, Vol. 35, 210.

17. Wyatt, *A Report on the Eleventh French Exposition of the Products of Industry*.

18. *The Times*, 18 October 1849.

19. Ibid.

20. Ibid. (see Cole's speech in particular).

21. Bonython and Burton, *The Great Exhibitor*, 116.

22. *The Times*, 21 December 1849.

23. *The Times*, 18 October 1849.

24. *The Times*, 22 March 1850, comment by Earl of Carlisle (formerly Lord Morpeth).

25. *The Times*, 18 October 1849 (Cole's speech, quoting the opinion of James Black & Co).

26. *The Times*, 15 November 1849.

27. *The Times*, 26 January 1850.

28. Mabon, 'John Scott Russell and Henry Cole: Aspects of a Personal Rivalry at the Society of Arts, (i) 1844–49'; Mabon, 'John Scott Russell and Henry Cole: Aspects of a Personal Rivalry at the Society of Arts, (ii) 1849–50'.

29. Bonython and Burton, *The Great Exhibitor*, 124–25.

30. Committee Minutes, Joint Agriculture and Chemistry, 14 April 1845, 8 June 1846.

31. Bonython and Burton, *The Great Exhibitor*, 101.

32. Gage, 'Turner and the Society of Arts'. Turner won a greater silver palette in 1793 for a landscape drawing of Lodge Farm, near Hambleton, Surrey. It does not seem to have survived.

33. Bell, 'The Society's William Etty Exhibition of 1849'.

34. ODNB.

35. The Society did hold other exhibitions to individual artists—in 1855 for John James Chalon, and in 1860 for William Ross—but these were both posthumous (Chalon's still-living brother Alfred was only somewhat featured alongside him).

36. *The Times*, 20 March 1850.

37. Bonython and Burton, *The Great Exhibitor*, 101–102.

38. Cole, *Fifty Years*, 1:189–92.

39. Bonython and Burton, *The Great Exhibitor*, 133.

40. Ibid., 128–29.

41. Trans, Vol. 53, 97–101.

42. Bonython and Burton, *The Great Exhibitor*, 134–35.

43. *The Times*, 25 October 1850; however, that construction was a lot noisier once the glass started to be put in place.

44. *The Times*, 1 January 1851, 'The Crystal Palace'.

45. Cole, *Fifty Years*, 1:173; Cowper speech to Society of Arts, as described in: *The Times*, 1 January 1851, 'The Crystal Palace'.

46. The window tax, begun in 1696, was repealed in the summer of 1851.

47. *The Times*, 1 January 1851, 'The Crystal Palace'.

Chapter Seven. A System to Force down the General Throat

1. According to the census of 1851, the combined population of England, Scotland, Wales, the surrounding islands, and those in the armed forces, was 21,121,967. The total number of visitors to the Great Exhibition was 6,039,195. See: Cheshire, 'The Results of the Census of Great Britain in 1851, with a Description of the Machinery and Processes Employed to Obtain the Returns; Also an Appendix of Tables of Reference'.

2. *The Times*, 9 July 1851.

3. The population of Newcastle-upon-Tyne in 1851 was 87,784. Cheshire, 'The Results of the Census of Great Britain in 1851, with a Description of the Machinery and Processes Employed to Obtain the Returns; Also an Appendix of Tables of Reference'.

4. Cole, *Fifty Years*, 1:199.

5. Martin, *The Life of His Royal Highness the Prince Consort*, II:361–62.

6. The two corps were amalgamated in 1855.

7. *First Report of the Commissioners for the Exhibition of 1851*, 47–49.

8. Bonython and Burton, *The Great Exhibitor*, 137.

9. As well as Cole, the especially influential utilitarians in the Society included Edwin Chadwick and James Booth, who were directly influenced by Bentham. We shall meet them properly in the following pages. A few other utilitarians, like Joseph Hume and Henry Brougham, had also long been influential members of the Society and lent their support to its later reforms. Their close friends were also important, often finding their way onto committees. Henry Cole, for example, was rarely listed on any committee without Charles Wentworth Dilke (1810–69, confusingly the second of three generations of that name, whose father also happened to be a Benthamite). From the 1860s, one often finds Cole's son-in-law George C. T. Bartley. Frequent collaborators with the small group of utilitarian reformers included radicals like William Tooke, free traders like Richard Cobden and Thomas Milner Gibson, and other liberal politicians like Samuel Morton Peto and Earl Granville. On issues like patent reform, the utilitarians also worked with inventors like Bennet Woodcroft and patent agents like Thomas Webster; in the case of copyright reform, they worked with influential artists like Charles Eastlake.

10. RSA/PR/GE/121/10/40, 2 December 1850, First Report on the Principles of Jurisprudence which should regulate the Recognition of the Rights of Inventors.

11. Cole, *Fifty Years*, 1:275.

12. The radicals on the committee included the 2nd Marquess of Northampton, as well as the 3rd Earl of Radnor. Both were supporters of parliamentary reform and the abolition of slavery. Radnor also opposed the Corn Laws, favoured the disestablishment of the Church of England, and advocated universal male suffrage with annual parliaments. The committee also featured frequent supporters of the Society such as the radical MPs Thomas Milner Gibson and Samuel Morton Peto. Even a Conservative MP on the committee, Henry Thomas Hope, was a free trader. Cole also involved friends from the world of art and manufactures, such as Owen Jones and Herbert Minton. Although he was not involved via the Society of Arts committee,

the utilitarian Lord Brougham played an influential role in getting the proposed patent law passed.

13. Harrison, 'Bennet Woodcroft at the Society of Arts, 1845–57 Part I: Reform of the Society and of the Patent System'.

14. Bottomley, *The British Patent System during the Industrial Revolution 1700–1852*, 62 gives the estimate of £380 for a patent covering the UK in 1846. I have used www.measuringworth .com/ppoweruk/ (accessed 25 October 2018) for the price conversion, which is the same site used by Bottomley. The exact quantity given in the conversion from pounds in 1851 to pounds in 2017, in terms of labour value, is £297,200. Labour value essentially denotes the price in terms of what the average worker at the time could buy. An alternative measure, real price, gives a value of £39,550. Both measures have their problems, as changes to technology have radically changed what money can buy. All such conversions should be taken with a rock of salt. I have used labour value because it is used by Bottomley and best illustrates the point that patents were beyond the means of the average labourer.

15. Ibid., 64; conversion from www.measuringworth.com/ppoweruk/ (accessed 25 October 2018) from pounds in 1852 to pounds in 2017, giving a labour value of £19,380.

16. Ibid., 64 records 455 patents in 1851, which increased to 2,187 patents in 1853—a figure 4.8 times higher.

17. Jnl, Vol. 9, No. 418 (23 November 1860), 9, the chairman's address, apparently quoting Lord Palmerston.

18. Jnl, Vol. 9, No. 449 (28 June 1861), 576.

19. Cooper, *Art and Modern Copyright*, 23–35.

20. Bale, 'Artistic Copyright', 301 contains a detailed account of the passage of the law by Basil Field, who was involved with the reform.

21. Allan, ' "Barkiss [sic] Is Willin" '.

22. *The Times*, 26 May 1851; also *The Times*, 7 February 1851, 'Public Waterclosets and Urinals'.

23. Jackson, *Dirty Old London*, 155–81 gives an account of Londoners' toilet-related habits in the nineteenth century, also describing the Society's campaign for public conveniences.

24. *The Times*, 7 February 1851: 'Public Waterclosets and Urinals'.

25. *The Times*, 24 February 1851.

26. To be precise, the ladies' waiting rooms had 704,528 visits; the men's 827,820.

27. *The Times*, 26 May 1851.

28. *The Times*, 1 May 1851.

29. *The Times*, 13 June 1851.

30. Cole, *Fifty Years*, 1:197.

31. *The Times*, 6 April 1853, quoting a translation of *Le Constitutionnel*.

32. *The Times*, 13 May 1853; for further discussion of the initial Anglo-French rivalry, see Wildman, 'Great, Greater? Greatest??'

33. For the Chicago exhibition—the 'World's Columbian Exposition'—which celebrated, a year late, the four-hundredth anniversary of the discovery of America by Columbus, the members of the Council of the Society of Arts were appointed the Royal Commissioners to manage the British section. Hudson and Luckhurst, *The Royal Society of Arts, 1754–1954*, 213–15.

34. Fisher, 'Sir Henry Trueman Wood, Written by His Daughter, Freda Fisher', chapter III, 23.

35. For context on the International Exhibition of 1862, see: Agnew, 'The 1862 London International Exhibition'; Davis et al., *Almost Forgotten*; Bonython and Burton, *The Great Exhibitor*, 185.

36. Crouzet, *The Victorian Economy*, 206. The US North's blockade of the Confederacy's ports began the cotton famine, but it was soon exacerbated by the Confederacy's embargo.

37. *The Times*, 6 December 1849, 'The Great Exhibition of 1851'.

38. They were at first made honorary corresponding members, and Cole in 1852 changed their status to ordinary corresponding members.

39. The association was chaired by the 2nd Earl Granville, a staunch free trader and supporter of the Great Exhibition as vice-president of the Board of Trade. Among Cole's utilitarian-influenced allies in the association were Charles Wentworth Dilke, Dilke's father, the Anglican archbishop of Dublin Richard Whately, and the politician Charles Pelham Villiers, who was also a prominent free trader and radical. The association also included Sir Stafford Northcote, later famous with Charles Trevelyan for their reforms to the civil service on broadly Benthamite lines. Among the radicals and free traders were the MPs George Moffatt, who had been a supporter of Rowland Hill's postal reforms, and Thomas Milner Gibson.

40. Haltern, 'The Society of Arts and Some International Aspects of the Great Exhibition of 1851 (i)'. The Universal Postal Union was originally known as the General Postal Union, but has since expanded. Almost every country in the world is now a member.

41. Hudson and Luckhurst, *The Royal Society of Arts, 1754–1954*, 324.

42. Jnl, Vol. 15, No. 742 (8 February 1867), 175; Cole's first mention of this to the Society appears to have been in 1863, signed F. S. (presumably Felix Summerly): Jnl, Vol. 12, No. 576 (4 December 1863), 52.

43. Letter by Cole, as Felix Summerly, Jnl, Vol. 13, No. 676 (3 November 1865), 761–62.

44. Bessemer, *Sir Henry Bessemer, F.R.S.*, 318–22.

45. See Cole's letter as Felix Summerly: Jnl, Vol. 21, No. 1047 (13 December 1872), 71.

46. Jnl, Vol. 1, No. 18 (25 March 1853), 205: 'Memorial of the Council . . . to the Lords Commissioners of Her Majesty's Treasury'.

47. One of these plans came from Cole's ally Charles Wentworth Dilke.

48. *The Times*, 3 December 1852, 3.

49. Quinn, *Utilitarianism and the Art School in Nineteenth-Century Britain*, 27–32. Alongside Ewart, the Bentham-influenced 'Philosophical Radicals' in Parliament in the 1820s and 30s included Joseph Hume, John Bowring, Charles Buller, Lord Henry Brougham, and Charles Villiers. Ewart led the committee that in 1836 recommended the creation of the schools of design.

50. *The Times*, 20 October 1851.

51. Ibid.

52. *The Times*, 19 May 1852.

53. *The Times*, 20 October 1851.

54. Weintraub, *Uncrowned King*, 322.

55. *Second Report of the Commissioners for the Exhibition of 1851*, 10. Conversion using

Measuringworth.com—the figure is for 2017, the last year available. I have used the labour cost measure, as it gives an idea of how many people might be employed by such a sum. The 'real cost', which attempts to take into account changes to the prices of particular goods that could be bought with it, would be £25 million. The 'economic cost'—which compares the sum to the size of the economy as a whole—would today be worth £769 million. This may actually be the best measure, but all of them have their flaws. In any case, the surplus was huge.

56. *The Times*, 15 September 1851.

57. *Second Report of the Commissioners for the Exhibition of 1851*, 13–15.

58. *The Times*, 30 July 1851.

59. Hobhouse, *Prince Albert, His Life and Work*, 91.

60. Bonython and Burton, *The Great Exhibitor*, 146.

61. Ibid., 148.

62. Ibid., 167.

63. Ibid., 150.

64. 'Upwards of seven million boxes' sold by 1869, 17 years after the prizes were awarded in 1852, according to a letter from Rogers's son. See: Jnl, Vol. 18, No. 892 (24 December 1869), 101.

65. Jeremiah, 'The Society of Arts and the National Drawing Education Campaign: (iii) The Provision of Drawing Aids'.

66. Bonython and Burton, *The Great Exhibitor*, 154–55.

67. Cole, *Fifty Years*, 1:285–86. The article was not by Dickens himself, but by Henry Morley.

68. Cooper, 'For the Public Good: Henry Cole, His Circle and the Development of the South Kensington Estate', 111.

69. Ibid., 130. The evolution of the South Kensington Museum into the Victoria and Albert Museum is more complex than that. They are widely considered the same institution, though, arguably, only the art and design collections of the South Kensington Museum evolved into the V&A.

70. Harrison, 'Bennet Woodcroft at the Society of Arts, 1845–57 Part 3: Models, Exhibitions and Museums'. Again, the evolution of the Museum of Patents, and later Patent Office Museum, is rather complicated. At one point it was part of the South Kensington Museum, before the art and design collections were split into the Art Museum (soon the Victoria and Albert Museum) and the scientific collections became the Science Museum. Nonetheless, the collection of inventions that opened in 1857 is widely considered the origin of the Science Museum.

71. Bonython and Burton, *The Great Exhibitor*, 250.

72. Jnl, Vol. 3, No. 131 (25 May 1855), 487–502. The collection was assembled by Edward Solly, a chemist who was very briefly the Society's secretary. See 494–95 for a brief catalogue of what was on show in the Society's repository before the collection was sent to South Kensington.

73. For example, in 1855 it lobbied unsuccessfully for the government to purchase the collection of Ralph Bernal. See: Bonython and Burton, *The Great Exhibitor*, 161–62.

74. Bonython and Burton, 179; Cole, *Fifty Years*, 2:292–93.

75. Bonython and Burton, *The Great Exhibitor*, 260–61; Jnl, Vol. 87, No. 4534 (13 October 1939), 1167–68.

76. Bonython and Burton, *The Great Exhibitor*, 247.

77. Cole, *Fifty Years*, 2:290.

78. Trevelyan, *The British Army in 1868*, 8.

79. Jnl, Vol. 17, No. 872 (6 August 1869), 730.

80. Jnl, Vol. 19, No. 957 (24 March 1871), 357–74 gives a summary of arguments in favour of military drill in schools. The quotation in the original is in Latin: 'mens sana corpore in sano', 362.

81. Jnl, Vol. 19, No. 949 (27 January 1871), 187.

82. Jnl, Vol. 24, No. 1200 (19 November 1875), 16, letter from Edwin Chadwick.

83. Jnl, Vol. 19, No. 957 (24 March 1871), 360.

84. Jnl, Vol. 17, No. 848 (19 February 1869), 205–22, here 207.

85. Jnl, Vol. 17, No. 872 (6 August 1869), 727.

86. Jnl, Vol. 18, No. 918 (24 June 1870), 693–96.

87. See rejections from various officials and politicians: Council Minutes, Vol. 19, 6 and 59, and RSA/PR/GE/119/22 Bundle 5/7—War Office 14 7 7. The drill reviews were continued by the London School Board, but only briefly.

88. Butterworth, 'The Society and the Department of Science and Art: (iii) Other Relationships'.

89. Cole, *Fifty Years*, 1:386.

Chapter Eight. An Education for the Whole People

1. Kelly, 'The Origin of Mechanics' Institutes', notes that the movement was not the offspring of a single mind. See also the ODNB entry for George Birkbeck: the working-class radicals who criticised Birkbeck were J. C. Robertson and Thomas Hodgskin, who had first conceived of the London Mechanics' Institution.

2. Godard, *George Birkbeck, the Pioneer of Popular Education*, 90–92; Birkbeck, *Mathematics Practically Applied*, i–vi.

3. Jeremiah, 'The Society of Arts and the National Drawing Education Campaign: (ii) The Working of the Drawing Committee'.

4. Stephens, 'The Society of Arts and The Warrington Mechanics' Institution: (i) An Institute in Union', 240.

5. Miller, 'The Society of Arts and Wigan Mechanics' Institute in the Nineteenth Century', 116.

6. The first appears to have been the West Riding of Yorkshire Union of Mechanics' Institutes, founded in 1837 by Edward Baines. Another early one was the Union of Lancashire and Cheshire Institutes, founded in 1839, which is sometimes erroneously referred to as the first.

7. Paz, 'The Composition of the Education Committee of the Privy Council, 1839–1856'; Newbould, 'The Whigs, the Church, and Education, 1839'. The government had its own reasons for the reform, but as an idea it appears to have been introduced by Henry Brougham. Brougham was part of Jeremy Bentham's inner circle as a youth and was later responsible for utilitarian reforms to the law. He was a popular champion of mechanics' institutions, though he was a vocal critic of the Great Exhibition. Brougham was supported in 1839 by other Benthamite 'Philosophical Radicals', namely John Arthur Roebuck and Thomas Wyse.

8. Hurt, 'Harry Chester (1806–68) (i): The Early Years'.

9. Hurt, 'Harry Chester (1806–68) (ii): The Middle Years'.

10. *The Times*, 19 May 1852.

11. *The Times*, 27 February 1852, 'The Society of Arts'.

12. Jnl, Vol. 3, No. 137 (6 July 1855), 567–90.

13. *The Times*, 19 June 1854.

14. Layton, 'The Educational Exhibition of 1854: (i) The Origins'; Layton, "The Educational Exhibition of 1854: (ii) The Opening'; *The Times*, 12 August 1854.

15. ODNB entry for James Hole.

16. For a summary see: Jnl, Vol. 1, No. 34 (15 July 1853), 413–24.

17. Hurt, 'The Society of Arts and the Elementary Education Act of 1870'.

18. Hurt, 'Harry Chester (1806–68) (i): The Early Years'.

19. Hudson and Luckhurst, *The Royal Society of Arts, 1754–1954*, 237.

20. *The Times*, 19 May 1852, 'The Society of Arts': see comments by the Marquis of Lansdowne that there were 70,000 members of 446 mechanics' institutions in the country, of which the Society had taken in some 350. Proportionately, that would have given the Union of Institutions a combined membership of 54,600. I have given 50,000 as a reasonable underestimate—similar figures were given throughout the period but membership was never stable.

21. Dutton and King, 'The Society of Arts and the Preston Strike, 1853–54 Part I'.

22. Jnl, Vol. 2, No. 63, Supplement (3 February 1854).

23. Dutton and King, 'The Society of Arts and the Preston Strike, 1853–54 Part II'; Dutton and King, 'The Society of Arts and the Preston Strike, 1853–54 Part III'.

24. See: Loftus, 'Limited Liability, Market Democracy, and the Social Organization of Production in Mid-Nineteenth-Century Britain'.

25. For an outline of the law, see: Chaplin, 'The Origins of the 1855/6 Introduction of General Limited Liability in England', 4–8.

26. Jnl, Vol. 2, No. 80 (2 June 1854), 483.

27. Walker, *The Development of the Mechanics' Institute Movement in Britain and Beyond*, 117–18.

28. Loftus, 'Limited Liability, Market Democracy, and the Social Organization of Production in Mid-Nineteenth-Century Britain', 87.

29. Jnl, Vol. 2, No. 56 (16 December 1853), 65–80.

30. Jnl, Vol. 2, No. 52 (18 November 1853), 1–16.

31. Ibid., 6.

32. Foden, 'The Revered James Booth and the Genesis of the Examinations of the Royal Society of Arts, Part I'.

33. Foden, *The Examiner: James Booth and the Origins of Common Examinations*, 90–91.

34. Jeremiah, 'The Society of Arts and the National Drawing Education Campaign: (iv) Drawing Conceived as Part of General Education'.

35. Watts, 'Cambridge Local Examinations 1858–1945', 41.

36. Foden, 'The Revered James Booth and the Genesis of the Examinations of the Royal Society of Arts, Part II'.

37. Foden, *The Examiner: James Booth and the Origins of Common Examinations*, 77.

38. Foden, 'The Founding of a Tradition: James Booth and the Society's Examinations (i)'.

39. Foden, *The Examiner: James Booth and the Origins of Common Examinations*, 63.

40. Foden, 'The Founding of a Tradition: James Booth and the Society's Examinations (ii)'.

41. Hudson and Luckhurst, *The Royal Society of Arts, 1754–1954*, 246 seems to be the first to claim Medcraft was a chimney sweep. Foden, *The Examiner: James Booth and the Origins of Common Examinations*, 123 repeats the claim, also adding that he came back the next year. I have been unable to trace any evidence of this. If he was the William Miles Medhurst who took the Society's later examinations in Geography in 1859, he is described as an assistant foreman, not a chimney sweep: Jnl, Vol. 7, No. 342 (10 June 1859), 515.

42. See: Foden, *The Examiner: James Booth and the Origins of Common Examinations* for a full account of Booth and his reforms. Chapter 8, 124–39 gives a comprehensive account of the 1856 examination.

43. Watts, 'Cambridge Local Examinations 1858–1945', 42; Foden, *The Examiner: James Booth and the Origins of Common Examinations*, 150–52.

44. Watts, 'Cambridge Local Examinations 1858–1945', 42.

45. Foden, 'The Founding of a Tradition: James Booth and the Society's Examinations (ii)'.

46. Ibid.

47. Foden, *The Examiner: James Booth and the Origins of Common Examinations*, 171–72.

48. Foden, 'The Founding of a Tradition: James Booth and the Society's Examinations (i)'.

49. According to Butterworth, 'The Society and the Department of Science and Art: (i) Beginnings', it was Playfair's idea, though many other accounts stress the roles of the people who remained to implement the system: John Donnelly and Henry Cole.

50. Ibid.

51. Bonython and Burton, *The Great Exhibitor*, 199–200.

52. Jnl, Vol. 3, No. 113 (19 January 1854), 133.

53. Jnl, Vol. 3, No. 134 (15 June 1855), 538.

54. Jnl, Vol. 20, No. 1027 (26 July 1872), 725–52.

55. Jnl, Vol. 24, No. 1200 (19 November 1875), 16.

56. *The Times*, 9 June 1853.

57. Foden, 'Colleges, Schools and the Society's Examinations', 209.

58. Fisher, 'Sir Henry Trueman Wood, Written by His Daughter, Freda Fisher', part I, 10.

59. Jnl, Vol. 34, No. 1754 (2 July 1886), 859.

60. Jnl, Vol. 62, No. 3214 (26 June 1914), 692.

61. *The Times*, 26 September 1855.

62. The original reason the Society began its investigations into the water supply in 1873 was that they were worried about the recent Chicago fire and whether such a catastrophe might also occur in London. They wanted to ensure there was adequate water for fire-fighting. Chadwick soon directed this line of inquiry into one about public health and sewage. Hudson and Luckhurst, *The Royal Society of Arts, 1754–1954*, 306–9 provides an overview. For Chadwick's influence see: Jnl, Vol. 26, No. 1305 (23 November 1877), 6.

63. Jnl, Vol. 25, No. 1272 (6 April 1877), 461.

64. Jnl, Vol. 26, No. 1333 (7 June 1878), 664.

65. Pearce, 'Thomas Twining (1806–1895): The Determined Improver (iii) Economic Museums'.

66. Jnl, Vol. 24, No. 1200 (19 November 1875), 14.

67. Committee Minutes, 1866–69, 201–9.

68. Jnl, Vol. 21, No. 1069 (16 May 1873), 502–3.

69. Jnl, Vol. 23, No. 1183 (23 July 1875), 773.

70. For an overview of the act and the Society's role in the lead-up to it, see: Hurt, 'The Society of Arts and the Elementary Education Act of 1870'.

71. Kamm, *Indicative Past*, chapter 3.

72. Council Minutes, Vol. 17, 102.

73. Jnl, Vol. 19, No. 979 (25 August 1871), 719.

74. Ibid.

75. Council Minutes, Vol. 17, 163–64.

76. *The Graphic*, 11 May 1872, Issue 128.

77. ODNB entry on The Girls' Public Day School Company.

78. Jnl, Vol. 19, No. 939 (18 November 1870), 14.

79. Jnl, Vol. 7, No. 338 (13 May 1859), 443–58.

80. Rainbow, 'The Rise of Popular Music Education in Nineteenth-Century England', 25.

81. He also gave a lecture there on 24 July 1854, entitled 'On Music as an Element of Education'.

82. Elected 29 November 1854. He seems to have been elected again on 29 June 1859.

83. Jnl, Vol. 14, No. 704 (18 May 1866), 453–68.

84. Jnl, Vol. 2, No. 88 (18 July 1854), 628–9; see also Jnl, Vol. 15, No. 778 (18 October 1867), 717–28, in which Hullah was credited at a conference on church music for having been responsible for the musical revival.

85. Jnl, Vol. 14, No. 704 (18 May 1866), 453–68; evidence by Harry Chester on Hullah's system, 455.

86. See Haynes, *A History of Performing Pitch* for an exhaustive history of efforts to standardise musical pitch.

87. Charles Wentworth Dilke introduced the idea to the Council, but Harry Chester drew his attention to the change. See Chester's letter in Jnl, Vol. 7, No. 338 (13 May 1859), 453.

88. Or, at least, that was their intention. In fact, they measured it from C (=528) from which the measurement of A differed. Although this corresponded to A=440 for pianos, for orchestras it corresponded to 444. See: Jnl, Vol. 88, No. 4570 (20 September 1940), 851–52.

89. Bonython and Burton, *The Great Exhibitor*, 272.

90. Skidmore, 'The Society and the National Training School for Music'; see also Hobhouse, *The Crystal Palace and the Great Exhibition*, 187–90.

Chapter Nine. A Society against Ugliness

1. *The Times*, 18 October 1849, 'Exhibition of the Industry of All Nations', Cole's comments.

2. Ibid.

3. *The Times*, 20 October 1851.

4. Chatterjee became a life member of the Society of Arts in 1917, a member of the Council in 1928, and was chairman of Council 1939–41.

5. The first Indian member appears to have been the civil engineer Ardaseer Cursetjee, who became a life member in 1840. He was elected an associate of the Institution of Civil Engineers the same year, and the following year he became the first Indian to be elected a fellow of the Royal Society. The first Indian member of a royally chartered society in London, however, appears to be Manockjee Cursetjee, who became a member of the Royal Asiatic Society in 1835. For Naoroji, see: Jnl, Vol. 10, No. 472 (6 December 1861), 40—his name is written in the announcement as Dadabhai Navroji.

6. See, for example, Jnl, Vol. 19, No. 952 (17 February 1871), 239–58; Jnl, Vol. 16, No. 794 (7 February 1868), 232. David Ochterlony Dyce Sombre, an Anglo-Indian, was technically the first person of Indian descent elected to the British Parliament, but he was soon removed from office due to election bribery.

7. It is almost impossible to say for sure who the first black member of the Society was, without a painstaking and systematic investigation of thousands of membership records. One early black African member, however, was William Thomas George Lawson, of Sierra Leone, who became a member in 1866: Jnl, Vol. 16, No. 835 (20 November 1868), 20. He trained as a civil engineer in Britain, and in 1883 was briefly Prince Regent of Little Popo. He is the earliest I have been able to identify, but this does not mean he was the first. Later early black African members include the mining entrepreneur Thomas Birch Freeman Sam (not to be confused with the more famous Thomas Birch Freeman, presumably a namesake), who became a member in 1898, followed by Adegboyega Edun (1903), Rev. Jacob Anaman (1903), John Augustus Abayomi-Cole (1904), and Adebiyi Tepowa (1905). It is also worth noting that one of the intellectual founders of African nationalism, Africanus Horton, participated in the discussion after a talk at the Society in 1882, on the subject of the gold fields of West Africa—see Jnl, Vol. 30, No. 1541 (2 June 1882), 777–96.

8. The Times, 18 June 1852.

9. Jnl, Vol. 69, No. 3560 (11 February 1921), 177–88; Jnl, Vol. 56, No. 2896 (22 May 1908), 696–97; Jnl, Vol. 61, No. 3136 (27 December 1912), 150–51.

10. Jnl, Vol. 96, No. 4756 (21 November 1947), 6–18.

11. The Times, 19 May 1852.

12. The Times, 18 May 1853.

13. Bonython and Burton, The Great Exhibitor, 144; Haltern, 'The Society of Arts and Some International Aspects of the Great Exhibition of 1851 (ii)'; Davies, 'The Society of Arts and the Dublin Exhibition of 1853'.

14. Head, 'Indian Crafts and Western Design from the Seventeenth Century to the Present'.

15. Jnl, Vol. 82, No. 4270 (21 September 1934), 1106.

16. Jnl, Vol. 58, No. 3023 (28 October 1910), 1048–49.

17. This was in 1881. The Society held an exhibition at the Royal Albert Hall of art-furniture. The hall was by this stage managed by Cole's son, Wentworth Cole. Henry Cole, however, died the following year. A committee was then re-established in 1886.

18. For the manifesto of the Society for the Protection of Ancient Buildings, see: https://www.spab.org.uk/about-us/spab-manifesto (accessed 20 November 2018).

19. Hansard, 17 July 1863, https://api.parliament.uk/historic-hansard/commons/1863/jul/17/residences-of-deceased-celebrities (accessed 29 November 2018).

20. Jnl, Vol. 14, No. 703 (11 May 1866), 437–52.

21. List begins: Jnl Vol. 15, No. 774 (20 September 1867), 669–80.

22. Jnl, Vol. 14, No. 713 (20 July 1866), 577–88.

23. For an overview of the history of blue plaques, see: Cole, *Lived in London*.

24. Jnl, Vol. 68, No. 3506 (30 January 1920), 165–75.

25. Jnl, Vol. 68, No. 3528 (2 July 1920), 529.

26. Jnl, Vol. 75, No. 3887 (20 May 1927), 630–35.

27. Baines's draft for Baldwin, along with associated correspondence, are at the time of writing in the possession of Richard Ford, a dealer in manuscripts and letters. See item description: https://www.richardfordmanuscripts.co.uk/catalogue/6277 (accessed 1 December 2018).

28. Jnl, Vol. 75, No. 3873 (11 February 1927), 305.

29. Jnl, Vol. 78, No. 4024 (3 January 1930), 202.

30. Jnl, Vol. 78, No. 4027 (24 January 1930), 277.

31. Jnl, Vol. 78, No. 4024 (3 January 1930), 202.

32. Jnl, Vol. 78, No. 4027 (24 January 1930), 277.

33. Rycroft, 'Lewis Foreman Day (1845–1910) and the Society of Arts'.

34. Jackson, *Twentieth-Century Pattern Design*, 22; Jnl, Vol. 60, No. 3092 (23 February 1912), 406.

35. Jnl, Vol. 60, No. 3092 (23 February 1912), 409.

36. Jnl, Vol. 69, No. 3565 (18 March 1921), 277.

37. Jnl, Vol. 147, No. 5489 (1999), 8–12.

38. Summerfield, 'Cadbury's Chocolate Boxes and the Royal Society of Arts' Annual Competitions of Industrial Designs, 1924–1933'.

39. Jnl, Vol. 103, No. 4947 (18 March 1955), 260.

40. Jnl, Vol. 81, No. 4190 (10 March 1933), 388–92.

41. Jnl, Vol. 83, No. 4288 (25 January 1935), 245–53.

42. RSA/PR/DE/101/10/1, correspondence between Milne and Henry Japp.

43. For an outline of events, see: Jnl, Vol. 85, No. 4382 (13 November 1936), 10–24.

Chapter Ten. 'A Society of Snobs'

1. At a meeting on 21 March 1862, a general meeting of members requested that the Council find a way to commemorate Albert in a way that would not detract from the subscriptions towards the Albert Memorial. Their report was presented and discussed the following year: Jnl, Vol. 11, No. 534 (13 February 1863), 215–17.

2. Skidmore, 'The Award of The Society's Albert Medal to Napoleon III'.

3. Since 1961, the Benjamin Franklin Medal has been awarded in alternate years to someone from the UK and someone from the US.

4. These associations with Benjamin Franklin, as well as many other aspects of the Society's re-engagement with the United States, were due to Simon Lissim, a Ukrainian-born designer and art professor who lived in New York.

5. The comparison was explicit: see Jnl, Vol. 11, No. 534 (13 February 1863), 215.

6. The Hartnett Medal was endowed in 1985, by Laurence Hartnett, an English engineer who

had moved to Australia to develop its aircraft, munitions, and automotive industries. The last award appears to have been in 2004.

7. *Punch*, Vol. 69, 25 December 1875, 265.

8. These were just a handful of the lectures given to the Society in the first few months of the 1907–8 session—a year I chose entirely at random. Jnl, Vol. 56, No. 2870 (22 November 1907), 1–2.

9. Jnl, Vol. 2, No. 66 (24 February 1854), 245.

10. Marconi was not the only inventor of the radio—or rather, wireless telegraphy by electric waves. His main contribution, however, was to hugely extend its range and thus make it practical. Marconi was the Society's chairman of Council in 1924.

11. Jnl, Vol. 26, No. 1306 (30 November 1877), 17–26. Bell gave three lectures to the Society: his first two in 1877 on the telephone, and a third in 1880 on the photophone.

12. Jnl, Vol. 26, No. 1336 (28 June 1878), 749.

13. Jnl, Vol. 69, No. 3550 (3 December 1920), 24–36 and Jnl, Vol. 69, No. 3581 (8 July 1921), 542.

14. See, for example, the inaugural addresses of its chairmen: in 1963 (Sir Hilary Blood, with the title 'The Encouragement of Arts, Manufactures and Commerce: A Learned Society Looks at its Role'); in 1972 (John Stratton, 'this learned Society'); in 1975 (Lord Roger Nathan, 'ancient learned society'). It was only in 1985, with the inaugural address of Sir Peter Baldwin, that the error was explicitly recognised: 'it is not a learned society, or not a very learned one'. Yet reference to the Society by its leaders or staff as a 'learned society' persisted well into the 1990s.

15. They left the petition letter out in the Great Room for members to sign, and advertised it in the Society's weekly proceedings.

16. *The Times*, 31 December 1852.

17. The proposal was made by Peter Le Neve Foster, who within a few months would become secretary of the Society of Arts (1853 to 1879). He was apparently accompanied by a deputation from the Society's Council to make the offer, consisting of Lyon Playfair, the scientist involved in the Department of Science and Art, and James Booth, the driving force behind the Society's early examinations. For more on Le Neve Foster, see Stirling, 'Peter Le Neve Foster and Photography'.

18. Stirling, 'The Society of Arts' Photographic Exhibition of 1852'; Roberts, '"The Exertions of Mr. Fenton": Roger Fenton and the Founding of the Photographic Society'; Johnston, 'The Origins of the Photographic Society'.

19. For example, when Britain joined the Crimean War in 1854, Prince Albert suggested to the commander of the British troops that he take a photographer with him; through Albert and the Society of Arts, the general was introduced to the Photographic Society's secretary, Roger Fenton. See: *The Times*, 23 March 1854. It was Fenton who undertook the trip to Crimea, which made him world-famous. It was the first war to be captured by photography (though he presented it as a series of heroic portraits, instead of the gruesome reality).

20. From 1866 to 1938. When the Wright brothers visited London in 1909 to receive the Aeronautical Society's gold medal, the Society of Arts first hosted a lecture by F. W. Lanchester on 'Aerial Flight', after which they had the award ceremony and a banquet of the members of both societies and the Aero Club at the Ritz Hotel.

21. Jnl, Vol. 29, No. 1461 (19 November 1880), 6.

22. Wood was secretary 1879–1917. Before this, he had been a member of staff since 1872, including the editor of the *Journal*.

23. Allan, 'The "Red Doctor" amongst the Virtuosi: Karl Marx and the Society Part (ii)', 310.

24. Greenwood, 'Notes from Over the Sea'.

25. Jnl, Vol. 102, No. 4930 (23 July 1954), 695–96.

26. J.S.S., 'Some Royal Members of the Society, 1770–1915 (ii)'.

27. Roosevelt was an ex-president when he was appointed a life member on 9 May 1910—he had left office the previous year. Poincaré, however, had just been elected, in 1913, and became an honorary member.

28. Jnl, Vol. 62, No. 3214 (26 June 1914), 693.

29. See, for example: Jnl, Vol. 109, No. 5054 (January 1961), 74; Jnl, Vol. 110, No. 5073 (August 1962), 615; Jnl, Vol. 120, No. 5188 (March 1972), 201; Jnl, Vol. 136, No. 5384 (July 1988), 528. There is even an entire box in the archive devoted to the misuse of the letters FRSA: RSA/AD/ MA/900/10/2.

30. See, for example: Jnl, Vol. 120, No. 5189 (April 1972), 269–70.

31. Jnl, Vol. 91, No. 4643 (9 July 1943), 414–30.

32. Jnl, Vol. 113, No. 5107 (June 1965), 460–61.

33. Just a quick search on Google reveals hundreds of such announcements on company and university websites. I will not embarrass any fellows by citing specific examples.

34. Measuringworth.com—£2 2s in 1920, converted to 2017 figures, using labour earnings measure comes to £232.60. The same calculation for 1754 yields a figure of £3,782. The precise percentage drop was 93.8%, but such figures are imprecise at the best of times. They do, however, give an overall impression of the scale of the change. In 1920 the fee was increased to 3 guineas (£349 in modern labour earnings), and in 1952 to 4 guineas (a drop in real terms, to £294.10). In 1969 the Council obtained an amendment to the bye-laws so that it would be able to unilaterally determine the subscription fee.

35. Personal interview with Matthew Taylor (18 October 2018).

36. In 1950, the number of fellows stood at just over 5,000. It passed 6,000 in 1957, 7,000 in 1963, and 10,000 in 1973, despite the fact that around 400 fellows either resigned or died each year.

37. Jnl, Vol. 65, No. 3388 (26 October 1917), 808; see *Further Correspondence with the United States Ambassador Respecting the Treatment of British Prisoners of War and Interned Civilians in Germany*, 42 for an example of bad treatment being described.

38. Jnl, Vol. 94, No. 4721 (5 July 1946), 502.

39. Personal interview with David Luckhurst (25 July 2018), who mentioned David McCulloch aka 'Uncle Mac'. For McCulloch's lecture, see: Jnl, Vol. 95, No. 4745 (20 June 1947), 501–3.

40. Jnl, Vol. 118, No. 5163 (February 1970), 120.

41. Jnl, Vol. 97, No. 4799 (15 July 1949), 640.

42. Jnl, Vol. 97, No. 4804 (23 September 1949), 833.

43. See press clippings, and some cartoons about the exhibition: Jnl, Vol. 97, No. 4800 (29 July 1949), 672–77.

44. There is now a Cartoon Museum in London, but it opened only in 2006.

45. Personal interview with David Luckhurst (25 July 2018); personal interview with Helen Auty (17 July 2018).

46. *Morning Chronicle*, Issue 21260 (3 January 1838).

47. Measuringworth.com: £3,954,000 in labour earnings.

48. *Gentleman's Magazine*, Vol. 23 (1845), 133–35. Swiney's original stipulation in 1831 was that the Society give an award for the greatest amount of waste land brought into arable cultivation. This would have been in keeping with many of the Society's premiums. But it was discovered that he had made an amendment to his will in 1835 to stipulate the prize for jurisprudence. The Society's secretary had actually opened the package before 1844, but at the time had been unable to find Swiney's address.

49. For example, Wyld had already been awarded the Distinguised Service Order for his services. The second year's recipient was the engineer Gerard Gordon Allan, who risked his life to prevent an oil tanker from exploding when it was torpedoed. He had already been awarded an MBE (Membership of the Order of the British Empire) when he received the Society's award. Jnl, Vol. 92, No. 4664 (28 April 1944), 253–54.

50. Jnl, Vol. 100, No. 4861 (30 November 1951), 27; the prize was later offered as a bursary for young gardeners, and appears to have been last awarded in 1988. Markham endowed the prize on the centenary of the Great Exhibition.

51. Measuringworth.com. The real wealth figure is £724,600. In terms of labour earnings, it would be worth £1.3m. As ever, all such conversions are indicative and should not be treated with precision.

52. In 1989 the remainder of the fund was handed over to the Somerset Archaeological and Natural History Society, which continues to run it. The Somerset Levels Project was run by John and Brony Coles—their projects received numerous awards for their work inspiring the sub-discipline.

53. Among the best-known were the Cantor lectures, after Dr Edward Theodore Cantor. He had been the superintendent of lunatic asylums in Calcutta (present-day Kolkata) in India. Yet he had not devoted his bequest of £4500 to any particular purpose—the Society itself decided to use it to endow a lecture series. Jnl, Vol. 9, No. 418 (23 November 1860), 4–5. The first Cantor lecture was in 1862; the last seems to have been in 2000.

54. The Edwin Chadwick Trust still exists today. It now mostly awards prizes to students at University College London and the London School of Hygiene and Tropical Medicine for conducting research into public health.

55. E.g. Charing Cross Hospital, the Chadwick Trust, the Sir John Soane Museum, the British Film Institute, the National Film Library, the National Register of Industrial Art Designers, the London Society, the Institute of Physics, the Standards Committee of the Directorate of Post-War Building, the Council of the City and Guilds of London Institute.

56. Conekin, *The Autobiography of a Nation*, 28.

57. Edgerton, *Rise and Fall of the British Nation*, Introduction.

58. Jnl, Vol. 100, No. 4880 (22 August 1952), 667–704 for Barry's description of events leading up to the Festival of Britain, here 674.

59. Measuringworth.com: the labour cost was £5,647,000, the real cost was £1,557,000.

60. It took a 99-year lease of the rest of the three houses adjacent to it on John Adam Street and Adam Street in 1957, with a deal to buy out the freehold in 1977 if they so wished, which they did.

Chapter Eleven. Rise of the Managers

1. *The Times*, 16 February 1961.

2. These were introduced in 1977. See report: Jnl, Vol. 127, No. 5278 (September 1979), 607–9.

3. The idea appears to have originated with the Council of Industrial Design, but it was Prince Philip's suggestion that it be organised by the Society of Arts. They were accordingly known as the Presidential Awards for Design Management. They ended in 1986, when the scheme was taken over by *The Financial Times* and The London Business School. The last reference I was able to find to it online was in 2001. It is unclear whether it was handed on or simply discontinued. See Philip on the award's beginnings and aims: Jnl, Vol. 113, No. 5109 (August 1965), 657–74.

4. At the time of writing, these supermarkets are called Sainsbury's and Waitrose and Partners. I have given the names they had at the time they won the award, in 1967 and 1972, respectively.

5. Jnl, Vol. 124, No. 5234 (January 1976), 75.

6. Jnl Vol. 124, No. 5244 (November 1976), 695–702; Jnl, Vol. 123, No. 5222 (January 1975), 48.

7. https://www.civilservant.org.uk/library/2012_Civil-Service-Reform-Context.pdf (accessed 24 November 2018).

8. This is a basic tenet of public choice theory: Olson, *The Logic of Collective Action.*

9. He was later commissioned by the London County Council to write a history of the Arts and Crafts architect W. R. Lethaby. *The Times*, 4 May 1962.

10. Jnl, Vol. 92, No. 4667 (9 June 1944), 322–40, see especially 338 where the chairman of the Conference on War Memorials says: 'It is very largely due to him [Roberts] that we are holding this Conference, because he . . . brought the whole idea to our notice, and Mr Roberts has helped a great deal in the organisation of it.' Roberts explicitly then states: 'Let us not be shamed to keep ever before us Blake's vision of a holy city in England's green and pleasant land.'

11. The first reference to this is in 1949 when he and John Alexander Milne were the representatives. He was still listed as one of the representatives on the CPRE as late as 1973.

12. Council Minutes, 13 December 1943.

13. RSA/PR/GE/117/12, 22 May 1945.

14. Council Minutes, 14 February 1944. The suggestion to achieve this with a conference seems to have come from Sir Frank Brown (13 March 1944). The conference was agreed after discussion with Brown and Roberts to take place on 27 April.

15. For a brief overview, see Creaton, *'A Guide and Light to Future Generations': The RSA and the Design of Memorials.*

16. E.g. W. H. Roberts of the Oswald Stoll Foundation in Jnl, Vol. 92, No. 4667 (9 June 1944), 322–40, here 337; Dudley Daymond of the Ecclesiological Society, 330.

17. Creaton, 'A Guide and Light to Future Generations': The RSA and the Design of Memorials, 20–21.

18. Chatfield was originally the president of the War Memorial Advisory Council and the chemist E. F. Armstrong (also the Society of Arts' president and chairman) was chairman. Armstrong died in 1945, however, and Chatfield replaced him as chairman.

19. Fernhurst lectures, named after Plant Protection Ltd.'s agricultural research station. Council Minutes, 25 November 1948, record a letter from the secretary of the company to establish the lecture series. It is not clear whether Roberts himself suggested this to his company, but he seems to have been at almost every lecture, was its director of public relations, and almost always had the last word in the discussions to thank the chair.

20. Jnl, Vol. 102, No. 4927 (11 June 1954), 571.

21. Jnl, Vol. 102, No. 4913 (27 November 1953), 6.

22. This was decided at an extraordinary meeting of the Council that Prince Philip hosted at Buckingham Palace. Staff, 'Looking Ahead to A.D. 2000'.

23. Jnl, Vol. 103, No. 4956 (22 July 1955), 614. See also: Council Minutes 10 May 1954. Roberts originally proposed the Special Affairs Committee as the Public Affairs Committee, 'in response to the articles in the press analysing the difficulties the RSA faces on its bicentenary'. I was unable to track down the articles in question, but it seems Prince Philip's words may have seemed ironic to the press. The decision was taken 14 June 1954.

24. Thomas Phillips (four terms, 1859–63), Lord Henry Lennox (four terms, 1868–72), Richard Webster (four terms, 1890–94), John Alexander Milne (three terms, 1932–35), E. F. Armstrong (three terms 1943–45, though he died in his third term), Ernest Goodale (three terms, 1949–52). NB: the list of chairmen in Hudson and Luckhurst, The Royal Society of Arts, 1754–1954, Appendix A, 372–74, rather confusingly only give the years in which their terms started, e.g. the Earl of Radnor is listed for just 1953, when in fact he served 1953–54, having started his year-long term in the middle of the year. The dates for the chairmen's terms on the RSA's staircase at the time of writing are a complete mess, half of them taken from Hudson and Luckhurst, but since the 1970s unable to decide which system to adopt.

25. Jnl, Vol. 49, No. 2505 (23 November 1900), 16.

26. Council Minutes, 14 June 1954: the Special Activities Committee met at the discretion of its chairman, Roberts. It could consider when to communicate with the press on behalf of the Society, and in urgent cases needed only the approval of the chairman of Council.

27. Committee Minutes, Special Activities, 28 July 1954, 282.

28. Tiratsoo, 'The Government, Full Employment and the Politics of Industrial Efficiency in Britain, 1945–1951', 66–67.

29. Jnl, Vol. 112, No. 5097 (August 1964), 645.

30. The funds were handed over to the examination board to fund an annual prize for the best UK student undertaking the study of languages for commercial use.

31. Jnl, Vol. 103, No. 4954 (24 June 1955), 552.

32. Jnl, Vol. 104, No. 4982 (20 July 1956), 653–70.

33. Jnl, Vol. 105, No. 5008 (19 July 1957), 679–702.

34. Jnl, Vol. 104, No. 4981 (6 July 1956), 627–45.

35. Ibid.

36. Ibid., 645.

37. Jnl, Vol. 105, No. 4993 (21 December 1956), 73–120. The conference took place on 31 October 1956. Britain and France had issued their ultimatum to Egypt on the night of 30 October, and began their bombing on the evening of the 31st.

38. Ibid.

39. Jnl, Vol. 108, No. 5049 (August 1960), 658.

40. Jnl, Vol. 142, No. 5448 (April 1994), 78.

41. For Prince Philip's own account of events, see: Cantell, *The RSA and the Environment: 30 Years of Identifying the Dilemmas, Led by HRH The Duke of Edinburgh*, 7–8.

42. Parker, *Prince Philip*, 340; Seward, *My Husband and I*, 236.

43. Adams, *Against Extinction*, 61.

44. Sheail, *An Environmental History of Twentieth-Century Britain*, 138; the organising body of the different groups was the Council for Nature, but Sheail relates that it was mostly at Max Nicholson's urging that they held Nature Week.

45. Wilson, 'The British Environmental Movement: The Development of an Environmental Consciousness and Environmental Activism, 1945–1975', 120; the exhibition was The Observer Wildlife Exhibition.

46. Jnl, Vol. 112, No. 5089 (December 1963), 18–19.

47. The Society was not as involved in the first conference of 1963. It hosted a drinks reception for the attendees on the evening of 4 November, and otherwise had a delegation present. Ibid., 7–8.

48. Jnl, Vol. 113, No. 5101 (December 1964), 9.

49. Sheail, *Nature Conservation in Britain*, 147–53.

50. Jnl, Vol. 141, No. 5439 (May 1993), 342: comment by Lord Hayter.

51. Sheail, *An Environmental History of Twentieth-Century Britain*, 235; Classified Ad, *The Observer*, 3 March 1963, with Prince Philip's quotation: 'I strongly recommend Silent Spring if you want to see what is going on.'

52. Cantell, *The RSA and the Environment: 30 Years of Identifying the Dilemmas, Led by HRH The Duke of Edinburgh*, 8.

53. Ibid., 15.

54. Jnl, Vol. 122, No. 5209 (December 1973), 12.

55. Jnl, Vol. 116, No. 5145 (August 1968), 725–26.

56. RSA/PR/EN/104/13/2: a review of preparatory studies for the second conference on 'The Countryside in 1970' 10–12/11/1965, 7.

57. Cantell, *The RSA and the Environment: 30 Years of Identifying the Dilemmas, Led by HRH The Duke of Edinburgh*, 13; Wilson, 'The British Environmental Movement: The Development of an Environmental Consciousness and Environmental Activism, 1945–1975', 313. European Conservation year 1970 was the suggestion of Robert Boote, the secretary to the Countryside in 1970 movement from 1966–71, who also became director-general of the Nature Conservancy Council, which replaced Nicholson's Nature Conservancy in 1973.

58. Adams, *Against Extinction*, 61.

59. Wilson, 'The British Environmental Movement: The Development of an Environmental Consciousness and Environmental Activism, 1945–1975', 124.

60. Sheail, *An Environmental History of Twentieth-Century Britain*, 139–45; the term 'fourth wave' was coined by Michael Dower in 1965.

61. Lambert, 'The History of the Country Park, 1966–2005', 44–45.

62. Wilson, 'The British Environmental Movement: The Development of an Environmental Consciousness and Environmental Activism, 1945–1975', 124.

63. Lambert, 'The History of the Country Park, 1966–2005', 45.

64. Adams, *Future Nature*, 18.

65. Personal interview with Prue Leith (20 November 2018).

66. Cantell, *The RSA and the Environment: 30 Years of Identifying the Dilemmas, Led by HRH The Duke of Edinburgh*, 16. When the committee first met in 1972, it consisted of Philip, Lord Hayter (its chairman), and Lord Brabourne, a television and film producer, whose wife was Philip's cousin (Philip was the godfather to their son, the next Lord Brabourne).

67. For a complete list 1971–93, see ibid., 47.

68. RSA/PR/EN/107/10/1, letter from Prince Philip dated 20 October 1976, 2.

69. Jnl, Vol. 108, No. 5043 (February 1960), 180–210.

70. For a comprehensive list of winners, see: Cantell, *The RSA and the Environment: 30 Years of Identifying the Dilemmas, Led by HRH The Duke of Edinburgh*, 50–54.

71. In 1987, due to funding from the European Commisson, they became the Better Environment Awards for Industry. From 1993 they were no longer run by the Society, instead forming an environmental category in the Queen's Awards for Enterprise, the highest official awards for British businesses. The Society from 1993 ran a new award, the Environmental Management Awards, but these were only continued until 1995. The application records for the awards between 1983 and 1990 were handed over to the London Science Museum in 1995.

72. Jnl, Vol. 132, No. 5333 (April 1984), 284.

73. Jnl, Vol. 138, No. 5412 (November 1990), 826.

74. Ibid.

75. Jnl, Vol. 128, No. 5289 (August 1980), 590.

76. For Adams's full initial statement of aims to the RSA see: Jnl, Vol. 128, No. 5289 (August 1980), 589–602. For added detail in later talks, see: Jnl, Vol. 134, No. 5355 (February 1986), 164–81; Jnl, Vol. 138, No. 5412 (November 1990), 826–34.

77. Jnl, Vol. 134, No. 5355 (February 1986), 165: Adams lists the Watkinson Committee of the Confederation of British Industry, the Professional Standards Committee of the British Institute of Management, and guidelines by the Institute of Directors. The Vice-President of the British Institute of Management was explicit about the role of Adams in their 1970s code of best practice (175).

78. Brook, 'The Industry and Parliament Trust'.

79. ODNB entry for Walter Salomon.

80. Jnl, Vol. 134, No. 5355 (February 1986), 171.

81. Jnl, Vol. 128, No. 5289 (August 1980), 597.

82. BBC2 became the first colour channel on 1 July 1967. *Civilisation* was aired on BBC2 23 February–18 May 1969. BBC1 and ITV, the other two channels, broadcast in colour for the first time in late 1969.

83. Adams singled out *The Ascent of Man* (1973), which was about science, and *Royal Heritage* (1977), about the history of Britain. He might also have singled out David Attenborough's *Life on Earth* (1979), on natural history, which would have a global audience of 500m.

84. Jnl, Vol. 128, No. 5289 (August 1980), 598.

85. This is the title on the script in Christopher Lucas's possession.

86. Jnl, Vol. 129, No. 5301 (August 1981), 547.

87. Jnl, Vol. 129, No. 5304 (November 1981), 759.

88. Jnl, Vol. 132, No. 5329 (December 1983), 40.

89. Adams developed a number of other proposals as Comino Fellow, too. One was to establish a National Industrial Broadcasting Trust, to ensure that the press and media presented about industry more, as well as more favourably.

90. The campaign was called, appropriately, 'Industry: Caring for the Environment'.

91. Personal interview with Christopher Lucas (9 August 2018).

92. Mason, 'Sir Geoffrey Chandler Obituary'.

93. Chandler, *Industry Year 1986: An Attempt to Change a Culture—Its Allies and Obstacles*, 18.

94. Ibid., 21.

95. Jnl, Vol.134, No. 5389, (1 June 1986), 423.

96. For detailed commentary by a railway enthusiast, see: https://www.flickr.com/photos/ingythewingy/34027795280/ (accessed 23 November 2018).

97. Chandler, *Industry Year 1986: An Attempt to Change a Culture—Its Allies and Obstacles*, 24.

98. Keegan, 'How Having Lost the Art of Manufacturing We Could Regain It (from next Week)'.

99. Nightingale, 'The Tools a Writer Used for Building An Industrial Novel'.

100. The estimates differed. The Department of Education and Science suggested 90% of secondary schools had some kind of link in 1987, though the CBI put the figure for regular links at 63%. Chandler, *Industry Year 1986: An Attempt to Change a Culture—Its Allies and Obstacles*, 42.

101. Correspondent, 'Where Bosses Are Going Back to School'.

102. Meade-King, 'This Year, next Year'.

103. The initial scheme, launched in 1988, was the Enterprise and Education Initiative. It was replaced in 1990 by the Education Business Partnership Initiative. See: Connell et al., *The Vocational Quest*, 219–21. Chandler, *Industry Year 1986: An Attempt to Change a Culture—Its Allies and Obstacles*, 43–46 points out that a Foundation for Education Business Partnerships was also founded to continue the campaign's work in 1990, but died after only a few months. Rather than attempting to simply support local collaborations, it had tried to rationalise and coordinate them. The local committees had no enthusiasm for this kind of management from the centre, so they did not respond.

104. Retirement tribute book for Christopher Lucas, in his possession, 11.

105. Adams concentrated his efforts on changing the clergy's attitudes to industry, while Chandler founded a business-related branch of Amnesty International, trying to get firms to make more ethical decisions when it came to supply chains and human rights.

Chapter Twelve. Furious Brainstorming

1. *The Observer*, 7 October 1917, 'Royal Society of Arts: Reminiscences of Forty Years the Retirement of Sir H. Trueman Wood'.

2. Personal interviews with Christopher Lucas (9 August 2018), Penny Egan (30 July 2018), Matthew Taylor (18 October 2018). Nearly all the post-1846 secretaries seem to have had at least one chairman they did not get on with, starting right from the beginning. Henry Cole had a major row with John Scott Russell. David Luckhurst (personal interview 25 July 2018) related that his father Kenneth Luckhurst always frowned whenever he heard the name of the one-time chairman, the chemist E. F. Armstrong.

3. There was no clear point at which the position of secretary became especially powerful. It was an incremental change, and thus provoked no direct opposition. Internal divisions between secretaries and chairmen instead usually revolved around specific actions or just conflicting personalities. By the time a chairman might try to challenge the secretary's accumulation of influence, it was usually already too late.

4. Personal interview with Christopher Lucas (9 August 2018). His father, Philip Gadesden Lucas (1902–81), was an English aviator and test pilot, who won the George Medal for keeping his cool when a Hawker Typohoon prototype he was testing in 1941 suffered a structural failure mid-flight. Perhaps the risk-taking ran in the family.

5. Jnl, Vol. 150, No. 5506 (April 2003), 61. This is the judgement of the librarian, who joined two years after Lucas. In a personal interview with Lucas, he used exactly the same term.

6. Personal interview with Christopher Lucas (9 August 2018).

7. Personal interview with Helen Auty (17 July 2018).

8. Penny Egan, who joined the Society's staff in 1986, recalls the tea trolley. So it must have been abolished at some point after that. Lucas's changes were, therefore, not immediate.

9. Personal interview with Helen Auty (17 July 2018).

10. Personal interview with Penny Egan (30 July 2018).

11. Personal interview with Christopher Lucas (9 August 2018).

12. Technically, one of Lucas's predecessors, Kenneth Luckhurst, had in 1961 been appointed director. This was, however, due to the fact that he was in poor health and unable to continue as secretary. He had suffered a stroke in the late 1950s. The position of director was thus a mark of esteem—in practice he acted as a sort of adviser, but died in 1962. Personal interview with David Luckhurst (25 July 2018).

13. Personal interview with Christopher Lucas (9 August 2018).

14. Jnl, Vol. 129, No. 5298 (May 1981), 380.

15. Jnl, Vol. 131, No. 5317 (December 1982), 29.

16. Thompson, ' "Education for Capability" '.

17. For the three lectures and discussion see: Jnl, Vol. 127, No. 5271 (February 1979), 117–57.

18. Jnl, Vol. 135, No. 5367 (February 1987), 238–45.

19. In the case of Worboys, whose project was called Project Manager-Technologists, it may have foundered because he died in office as chairman, in 1969. Nonetheless, his successor James Taylor did express support for it in his 1969 and 1970 inaugural addresses, along with his own calls for a campaign to do with education.

20. There were also some practical considerations, but they were minor in comparison to the financial damage that the decision inflicted. They were, in effect, practical consolations for a moral decision: firstly, some recent judicial rulings had suggested that the examination fees might be liable for Value Added Tax if the surpluses were used for anything other than the examination board's own purposes. Secondly, it was felt that the decision might sooner or later be forced upon them by the government. With the creation in 1986 of the National Council of Vocational Qualifications, a regulatory body to accredit vocational qualifications like those offered by the Society, it was expected that they might soon insist on the Society's examinations being separated in order to remain accredited.

21. Jnl, Vol. 137, No. 5399 (October 1989), 686.

22. Jnl, Vol. 142, No. 5454 (November 1994), 11.

23. Jnl, Vol. 150, No. 5506 (April 2003), 61.

24. This was adopted in 1987, the year of the separation from the examination board.

25. Jnl, Vol. 136, No. 5385 (August 1988), 629–44.

26. Jnl, Vol. 137, No. 5389 (December 1988), 2.

27. Personal interview with Helen Auty (17 July 2018). Auty joined the Society's staff in 1960. Except for a brief gap 1964–66, she remained on the staff until 1999, retaining a link with the RDI faculty for a further year. I have relied heavily on my interview with her for impressions of how the Society changed during the period.

28. Chandler, *Industry Year 1986: An Attempt to Change a Culture—Its Allies and Obstacles*, 33, 48.

29. Personal interview with Stuart Hampson (12 September 2018).

30. Sheikh, *A Guide to The Companies Act 2006*, 34, 164–65.

31. 'Monday Interview'.

32. Jnl, Vol. 105, No. 4995 (18 January 1957), 148.

33. Jnl, RSA Annual Report 1998/99 (1998/99), 17.

34. Leith, *Relish*, 379.

35. Jnl, Vol. 146, No. 5485 (1998), 37; most details in the following section are taken from a personal interview with Prue Leith (20 November 2018), corroborated by checking the *Journal* and Leith's autobiography, *Relish*.

36. Personal interview with Stuart Hampson (12 September 2018).

37. Jnl, Vol. 145, No. 5483 (November–December 1997), 10–25.

38. Personal interview with Prue Leith (20 November 2018).

39. Jnl, Vol. 148, No. 5499 (2001), 38–39.

40. *The Times*, 21 April 1994, 'Teach the Bard to five-year-olds'.

41. Jnl, Vol. 142, No. 5455 (December 1994), 10.

42. Jnl, Vol. 146, No. 5487 (1998), 22–25.

43. The idea came from Hugh Knowles, who worked for a sustainable development charity, and the idea was proposed to the RSA by Mark Fremantle, who was then studying for an MBA. The project was directed by Robert Holdway and David Walker, of Giraffe Innovation, a consultancy. The designer was Paul Bonomini, and the funder was Canon Europe, a major producer of electronic equipment.

44. Jnl, Vol. 152, No. 5516 (April 2005), 22–27.

45. Comment from the designer, Paul Bonomini: 'I designed him to look like he's dragging himself out of landfill, coming back from the dead. He's there to reminds us of this monster that we're creating when we dump these goods rather than recycle them.' https://www.edenproject.com/visit/whats-here/giant-sculpture-made-of-waste (accessed 26 November 2018).

46. Again, much of this section is based on a personal interview with Prue Leith (20 November 2018), corroborated by her autobiography, *Relish*, and the *Journal*.

47. For a selection of opinions see: Jnl, Vol. 147, No. 5490 (1999), 10–13.

48. Jnl, Vol. 148, No. 5492 (2000), 24–31.

49. https://www.theguardian.com/artanddesign/jonathanjonesblog/2017/mar/21/fourth-plinth-trafalgar-square-heather-phillipson-michael-rakowitz (accessed 27/11/18)

50. Jnl, Vol. 143, No. 5457 (March 1995), 9–19 gives a useful summary of many of the education committee's efforts.

51. Jnl, Vol. 148, No. 5498 (2001), 47–49.

52. 'RSA Opening Minds Competence Framework'.

53. Jnl, RSA Annual Report 1998/99 (1998/99), 6.

Chapter Thirteen. Building a Social Movement

1. Copy of letter, 25 June 1958, from James Orr to Alfred Bossom, communicating Philip's wishes, inserted into Council Minutes, November 1958; see also: Jnl, Vol. 107, No. 5037 (August 1959), 602.

2. Jnl, Vol. 103, No. 4956 (22 July 1955), 614–15.

3. Jnl, Vol. 104, No. 4982 (20 July 1956), 653–70.

4. The suggestion was made by one of the early members of the Special Advisory Committee, Lord Halsbury.

5. This was Sir George Nelson. He was chairman of English Electric, and was raised to the peerage a year after he received the Benjamin Franklin Medal.

6. Initial discussion: Jnl, Vol. 107, No. 5037 (August 1959), 602–3; decision announced: Jnl, Vol. 110, No. 5066 (January 1962), pp. 72–74.

7. Jnl, Vol. 108, No. 5049 (August 1960), 657: the Birmingham meeting held in May 1960, the beginning of the West Midlands region.

8. For example, in 1964–65 the Midlands Centre's meetings involved a sherry party, a tour of the Shell-BP building in Birmingham, and dinner and a talk about motor-car design at a university: Jnl, Vol. 112, No. 5097 (August 1964), 630, 633–656; likewise, the North West Centre's meetings involved luncheon with a university vice-chancellor, a visit to a television studio, and a dinner with evening dress: Jnl, Vol. 112, No. 5091 (February 1964), 141. These kinds of events were entirely typical of the regional committees' activities right into the early twenty-first century.

9. Jnl, Vol. 128, No. 5292 (November 1980), 791–96.

10. Jnl, Vol. 147, No. 5489 (1999), 4–5.

11. Jnl, RSA Annual Report 1998/99 (1998/99), 5.

12. Personal interview with Matthew Taylor (18 October 2018).

13. Moggach, 'The Cooking Bus Goes Round and Round'.

14. Jnl, Vol. 136, No. 5385 (August 1988), 629.

15. E.g. Jnl, Vol. 136, No. 5385 (August 1988), 632: after there had been a temporary dispensation from the usual criteria in 1987, the membership committee responded in 1988 by then having the criteria stress 'accomplishment'.

16. Jnl, Vol. 135, No. 5373 (August 1987), 641.

17. Jnl, Vol. 143, No. 5456 (January–February 1995), 25.

18. Jnl, RSA Annual Report 1998/99 (1998/99), 5.

19. Jnl, Vol. 143, No. 5456 (January–February 1995), 25.

20. Jnl, Vol. 135, No. 5373 (August 1987), 642.

21. Summary: Jnl, Vol. 143, No. 5459 (May 1995), 56–59.

22. Jnl, RSA Annual Report 2000 (2000), 17.

23. Jnl, Vol. 151, No. 5510 (January 2004), 19.

24. https://www.thersa.org/fellowship/join-the-fellowship (accessed 27 November 2018).

25. https://www.thersa.org/action-and-research/rsa-projects/design/student-design-awards/design-briefs (accessed 27 November 2018).

26. https://www.thersa.org/discover/publications-and-articles/matthew-taylor-blog/2008/01/the-albert-medal (accessed 10 October 2018).

27. Personal interview with Matthew Taylor (18 October 2018).

28. 'City Spy'.

29. Jnl, RSA Annual Report 1996/97 (1996/97), 13.

30. https://www.huffingtonpost.co.uk/entry/chatty-cafe-costa-becomes-first-uk-chain-to-roll-out-scheme-tackling-loneliness_uk_5b684d2fe4b0fd5c73dbb25a?guccounter=1 (accessed 20 November 2018).

31. https://www.bankofengland.co.uk/-/media/boe/files/speech/2018/climbing-the-public-engagement-ladder.pdf (accessed 20 November 2018).

32. https://www.thersa.org/discover/publications-and-articles/rsa-blogs/2018/11/a-regional-banking-revolution-for-the-21st-century (accessed 20 November 2018).

BIBLIOGRAPHY

Abbott, John L. 'Dr. Johnson and the Society (i)'. *Journal of the Royal Society of Arts* 115, No. 5129 (1967): 392–400.

Ackermann, Rudolph. *The Microcosm of London: Or, London in Miniature*. Vol. 3. London: R. Ackermann, 1808.

Adams, W. M. *Against Extinction: The Story of Conservation*. London: Earthscan, 2013.

———. *Future Nature: A Vision for Conservation*. Abingdon: Routledge, 2004.

Agnew, John. 'The 1862 London International Exhibition: Machinery on Show and Its Message'. *The International Journal for the History of Engineering & Technology* 85, No. 1 (January 2015): 1–30. https://doi.org/10.1179/1758120614Z.00000000053.

Albion, Robert Greenhalgh. *Forests And Sea Power: The Timber Problem of the Royal Navy 1652–1862*. Cambridge, MA: Harvard University Press, 1926. http://archive.org/details /ForestsAndSeaPower.

Allan, D.G.C. 'Artists and the Society in the 18th Century (i) The Foundation and Henry Cheere's Plan for an Academy'. *Journal of the Royal Society of Arts* 132, No. 5331 (1984): 200–207.

———. 'Artists and the Society in the 18th Century (ii): Members and Premiums in the First Decade, 1755–64'. *Journal of the Royal Society of Arts* 132, no. 5332 (1984): 271–76.

———. ' "Barkiss [sic] Is Willin": Some Dickensian Associations of the Society of Arts'. *RSA Journal* 142, No. 5446 (1994): 45–49.

———. ' "Dear and Serviceable to Each Other": Benjamin Franklin and the Royal Society of Arts'. *Proceedings of the American Philosophical Society* 144, No. 3 (2000): 245–66.

———. 'Robert Marsham, 2nd Baron Romney (d. 1793) and the Society'. *RSA Journal* 143, No. 5456 (1995): 67–69.

———. *RSA: A Chronological History of the Royal Society for the Encouragement of Arts, Manufactures and Commerce*. London: Royal Society of Arts, 1998.

———. *The Houses of the Royal Society of Arts: A History and a Guide*. London: Royal Society of Arts, 1974.

———. 'The Laudable Association of Antigallicans'. *RSA Journal* 137, No. 5398 (1989): 623–28.

———. 'The "Red Doctor" amongst the Virtuosi: Karl Marx and the Society Part (ii)'. *Journal of the Royal Society of Arts* 129, No. 5297 (1981): 309–11.

———. *The Society of Antiquaries and the Society for the Encouragement of Arts, Manufactures and Commerce: An Account of Shared Memberships and Interests from the Mid-18th to the Early 21st Centuries.* The William Shipley Group for RSA History, Occasional paper 23, 2012.

Allan, D.G.C. 'The Society of Arts and Government, 1754–1800: Public Encouragement of Arts, Manufactures, and Commerce in Eighteenth-Century England'. *Eighteenth-Century Studies* 7, No. 4 (July 1974): 434–52. https://doi.org/10.2307/3031598.

———. 'The Society of Arts and the Committee of the Privy Council for Trade, 1786–1815 (i)'. *Journal of the Royal Society of Arts* 109, No. 5057 (1961): 386–94.

———. 'The Society of Arts and the Committee of the Privy Council for Trade, 1786–1815 (ii)'. *Journal of the Royal Society of Arts* 109, No. 5060 (1961): 628–32.

———. 'The Society of Arts and the Committee of the Privy Council for Trade, 1786–1815 (iii)'. *Journal of the Royal Society of Arts* 109, No. 5062 (1961): 806–10.

———. 'The Society of Arts and the Committee of the Privy Council for Trade, 1786–1815 (iv)'. *Journal of the Royal Society of Arts* 109, No. 5064 (1961): 979–80.

———. *William Shipley: Founder of the Royal Society of Arts; a Biography with Documents.* 1st edition. London: Hutchinson, 1968.

Allan, D.G.C., and John L. Abbott. ' "Compassion and Horror in Every Humane Mind": Samuel Johnson, the Society of Arts, and Eighteenth-Century Prostitution'. In *The Virtuoso Tribe of Arts and Sciences: Studies in the Eighteenth Century Work and Membership of the London Society of Arts,* edited by D.G.C. Allan and John L. Abbott, 1st edition, 18–37. Athens: University of Georgia Press, 1991.

Allan, D.G.C., and John L. Abbott, eds. *The Virtuoso Tribe of Arts and Sciences: Studies in the Eighteenth Century Work and Membership of the London Society of Arts.* 1st edition. Athens: University of Georgia Press, 1991.

Allan, D.G.C., and Robert E. Schofield. *Stephen Hales, Scientist and Philanthropist.* London: Scolar Press, 1980.

Anderson, Benedict. *Imagined Communities: Reflections on the Origin and Spread of Nationalism.* Revised edition. London and New York: Verso Books, 2006.

Anonymous. *The Antigallican Privateer: Being a Genuine Narrative from Her Leaving Deptford, September 17, 1756, to the Present Time. Containing, among Other Particulars, an Account of the Taking the Duke de Penthievre East-India-Man, Which Was Afterwards Detained at Cadiz; and the Proceedings Thereupon. To Which Is Added A Letter from the Escurial to Lord W—. Shewing the General Sentiments of the Spaniards, in Relation to the War between England and France.* London: J. Reason, 1757. http://archive.org/details/cihm_20244.

Ashworth, William J. *Customs and Excise: Trade, Production and Consumption in England, 1640–1845.* Oxford: Oxford University Press, 2003. http://www.oxfordscholarship.com/view/10.1093/acprof:oso/9780199259212.001.0001/acprof-9780199259212?rskey=yg7JxG&result=25&q=.

Auerbach, Jeffrey A. *The Great Exhibition of 1851: A Nation on Display.* New Haven: Yale University Press, 1999.

Bale, Edwin. 'Artistic Copyright'. *The Journal of the Society of Arts* 48, No. 2466 (1900): 293–308.

Barrell, John. *The Political Theory of Painting from Reynolds to Hazlitt: The Body of the Public.* New Haven: Yale University Press, 1995.

Barry, James. *An Account of a Series of Pictures, in the Great Room of the Society of Arts, Manufactures, and Commerce, at the Adelphi*. London: William Adlard, 1783.

Bayer, Thomas M., and John R. Page. *The Development of the Art Market in England: Money as Muse, 1730–1900*. Abingdon: Routledge, 2015.

Beer, George Louis. *British Colonial Policy, 1754–1765*. Cambridge: Cambridge University Press, 2010.

Bell, Roger. 'The Society's William Etty Exhibition of 1849'. *RSA Journal* 138, No. 5408 (1990): 557–61.

Bennett, Susan, ed. *Cultivating the Human Faculties: James Barry (1741–1806) and the Society of Arts*. Cranbury, NJ: Associated University Presses, 2008.

Berg, Maxine. *Luxury and Pleasure in Eighteenth-Century Britain*. Oxford: Oxford University Press, 2007. http://www.oxfordscholarship.com/view/10.1093/acprof:oso/9780199215287.001.0001/acprof-9780199215287.

Bertucci, Paola. *Artisanal Enlightenment: Science and the Mechanical Arts in Old Regime France*. New Haven and London: Yale University Press, 2017.

Bertucci, Paola, and Olivier Courcelle. 'Artisanal Knowledge, Expertise, and Patronage in Early Eighteenth-Century Paris: The Société Des Arts (1728–36)'. *Eighteenth-Century Studies* 48, No. 2 (2015): 159–79. https://doi.org/10.1353/ecs.2015.0006.

Bessemer, Henry. *Sir Henry Bessemer, F.R.S.: An Autobiography; with a Concluding Chapter*. London: Offices of 'Engineering', 1905. http://archive.org/details/sirhenrybessemer00bessuoft.

Birkbeck, George. *Mathematics Practically Applied to the Useful and Fine Arts, by Baron Charles Dupin, Adapted to the State of the Arts in England*. London and Edinburgh: Charles and William Tait, 1827.

Bonython, Elizabeth, and Anthony Burton. *The Great Exhibitor: The Life and Work of Henry Cole*. London: V&A Publication, 2003.

Bottomley, Sean. *The British Patent System during the Industrial Revolution 1700–1852: From Privilege to Property*. Cambridge: Cambridge University Press, 2014.

Bouin, Philippe, and Christian-Philippe Chanut. *Histoire Française Des Foires et Des Expositions Universelles*. Paris: Baudouin, 1980.

Braun, Hans Joachim. 'Some Notes on the Germanic Association of the Society of Arts in the Eighteenth Century'. *Journal of the Royal Society of Arts* 119, No. 5179 (1971): 476–80.

———. 'Some Notes on the Germanic Associations of the Society of Arts in the Eighteenth Century: (ii) Relations with German Societies; Leipzig (1764), Celle (1764), Karlsruhe (1765), Hamburg (1765)'. *Journal of the Royal Society of Arts* 119, No. 5180 (1971): 558–62.

Brewer, John. *The Pleasures of the Imagination: English Culture in the Eighteenth Century*. 1st edition. Abingdon: Routledge, 2013.

———. *The Sinews of Power: War, Money and the English State 1688–1783*. 1st edition. Abingdon: Routledge, 1989.

Britain, Great, William David Evans, Anthony Hammond, and Thomas Colpitts Granger. *A Collection of Statutes Connected with the General Administration of the Law: Arranged According to the Order of Subjects, with Notes*. London: W. H. Bond, 1836.

Brook, Rosemary. 'The Industry and Parliament Trust: Contributing to Better Government and

Greater Prosperity of UK Plc'. *Journal of Communication Management* 4, No. 1 (March 1999): 57–63. https://doi.org/10.1108/eb023507.

Butterworth, Harry. 'The Society and the Department of Science and Art: (i) Beginnings'. *Journal of the Royal Society of Arts* 133, No. 5344 (1985): 296–301.

———. 'The Society and the Department of Science and Art: (iii) Other Relationships'. *Journal of the Royal Society of Arts* 133, No. 5346 (1985): 422–26.

Cantell, Timothy, ed. *The RSA and the Environment: 30 Years of Identifying the Dilemmas, Led by HRH The Duke of Edinburgh*. London: RSA, 1993.

Chandler, Geoffrey. *Industry Year 1986: An Attempt to Change a Culture—Its Allies and Obstacles*. London: Royal Society of Arts, 2003.

Chaplin, Julia Elizabeth. 'The Origins of the 1855/6 Introduction of General Limited Liability in England'. PhD thesis, University of East Anglia, 2016.

Cheere, Henry. *The Plan of an Academy for the Better Cultivation, Improvement and Encouragement of Painting, Sculpture, Architecture, and the Arts of Design in General*, London: 1755.

Cheshire, Edward. 'The Results of the Census of Great Britain in 1851, with a Description of the Machinery and Processes Employed to Obtain the Returns; Also an Appendix of Tables of Reference'. *Journal of the Statistical Society of London* 17, No. 1 (1854): 45–72. https://doi.org/10.2307/2338356.

'City Spy: Ruffled Feathers at Luke Johnson's RSA'. *Evening Standard*, 10 December 2010. http://www.standard.co.uk/business/city-spy-ruffled-feathers-at-luke-johnson-s-rsa-6545759.html.

Clark, Peter. *British Clubs and Societies 1580–1800: The Origins of an Associational World*. Oxford: Oxford University Press, 2000.

Clarke, Desmond. 'Thomas Prior, 1681–1751: Founder of the Royal Dublin Society'. *Studies: An Irish Quarterly Review* 40, No. 159 (1951): 334–44.

Cole, Emily, ed. *Lived in London: Blue Plaques and the Stories Behind Them*. New Haven and London: Yale University Press, 2009.

Cole, Henry. *Fifty Years of Public Work of Sir Henry Cole, K.C.B., Accounted for in His Deeds, Speeches and Writings*. Edited by Henrietta Cole and Alan Summerly Cole. 2 vols. London: George Bell and Sons, 1884. http://archive.org/details/cu31924098820883.

Conekin, Becky. *The Autobiography of a Nation: The 1951 Exhibition of Britain, Representing Britain in the Post-War World*. Manchester: Manchester University Press, 2003.

Conlin, Jonathan. ' "At the Expense of the Public": The Sign Painters' Exhibition of 1762 and the Public Sphere'. *Eighteenth-Century Studies* 36, No. 1 (2002): 1–21.

Connell, Helen, Nicholas Lowe, Malcolm Skilbeck, and Kirsteen Tait. *The Vocational Quest: New Directions in Education and Training*. Abingdon: Routledge, 2002.

Cooper, Ann. 'For the Public Good: Henry Cole, His Circle and the Development of the South Kensington Estate'. PhD thesis, The Open University, 1992.

Cooper, Elena. *Art and Modern Copyright: The Contested Image*. Cambridge: Cambridge University Press, 2018.

Coutu, Joan. *Then and Now: Collecting and Classicism in Eighteenth-Century England*. Montreal: McGill-Queen's University Press, 2015.

Cox-Johnson, Ann. 'Patrons to a Sculptor: The Society and John Bacon, R.A'. *Journal of the Royal Society of Arts* 110, No. 5073 (1962): 705–10.

Creaton, Heather. *'A Guide and Light to Future Generations': The RSA and the Design of Memorials.* The William Shipley Group for RSA History, Occasional paper 19, 2011.

Cross, A. G. 'Early Contacts of the Society of Arts with Russia (i): Corresponding Members in Russia'. *Journal of the Royal Society of Arts* 124, No. 5236 (1976): 203–7.

———. 'Early Contacts of the Society of Arts with Russia (iii): The Visit of a Russian Serf'. *Journal of the Royal Society of Arts* 124, No. 5238 (1976): 334–36.

Crouzet, Francois. *The Victorian Economy.* Abingdon: Routledge, 2013.

Crow, Thomas E. *Painters and Public Life in Eighteenth-Century Paris.* New Haven: Yale University Press, 1985.

Davies, A. C. 'The Society of Arts and the Dublin Exhibition of 1853'. *Journal of the Royal Society of Arts* 123, No. 5227 (1975): 430–36.

Davies, Kate. *Catharine Macaulay and Mercy Otis Warren: The Revolutionary Atlantic and the Politics of Gender.* Oxford: Oxford University Press, 2005.

Davis, John R., Dale Dishon, Mark Jones, Julius Bryant, Charlotte Gere, Judy Rudoe, Max Donnelly, John Agnew, Anthony Burton, and David G. C. Allan. *Almost Forgotten: The International Exhibition of 1862.* Vol. 38. The Decorative Arts Society: 1850 to the Present, 2014.

De Freitas, Leo John. 'The Society and Illustration during Two Centuries'. *RSA Journal* 139, No. 5418 (1991): 405–11.

———. 'The Society and Wood Engraving in the Eighteenth Century'. In *The Virtuoso Tribe of Arts and Sciences: Studies in the Eighteenth Century Work and Membership of the London Society of Arts,* edited by D.G.C. Allan and John L. Abbott, 1st edition, 132–40. Athens: University of Georgia Press, 1991.

Dickinson, H. T., ed. *A Companion to Eighteenth-Century Britain.* Hoboken, NJ: Wiley-Blackwell, 2008.

Dossie, Robert. *Memoirs of Agriculture, and Other Oeconomical Arts.* Vol. 1. London: J. Nourse, 1768.

Dutton, H. I. *The Patent System and Inventive Activity During the Industrial Revolution, 1750–1852.* Manchester: Manchester University Press, 1984.

Dutton, H. I., and J. E. King. 'The Society of Arts and the Preston Strike, 1853–54 Part I'. *Journal of the Royal Society of Arts* 127, No. 5276 (1979): 506–8.

———. 'The Society of Arts and the Preston Strike, 1853–54 Part II'. *Journal of the Royal Society of Arts* 127, No. 5277 (1979): 593–99.

———. 'The Society of Arts and the Preston Strike, 1853–54 Part III'. *Journal of the Royal Society of Arts* 127, No. 5278 (1979): 654–58.

Edgerton, David. *The Rise and Fall of the British Nation: A Twentieth-Century History.* London: Allen Lane, 2018.

Eger, Elizabeth, and Lucy Peltz. *Brilliant Women: 18th-Century Bluestockings.* London: National Portrait Gallery, 2008.

Evelyn, John. *Silva: Or, a Discourse of Forest-Trees, and the Propagation of Timber in His Majesty's Dominions.* York: J. Walthoe, 1729.

Findlay, Ronald, and Kevin H. O'Rourke. *Power and Plenty: Trade, War, and the World Economy in the Second Millennium*. Princeton, NJ: Princeton University Press, 2009.

First Report of the Commissioners for the Exhibition of 1851. London: Spicer Brothers; W. Clowes & Sons, 1852.

Fisher, Freda. 'Sir Henry Trueman Wood, Written by His Daughter, Freda Fisher'. Typescript. Library of the Royal Society of Arts, c.1928–40.

Foden, F. E. 'The Revered James Booth and the Genesis of the Examinations of the Royal Society of Arts, Part I'. *Journal of the Royal Society of Arts* 118, No. 5169 (1970): 577–83.

———. 'The Revered James Booth and the Genesis of the Examinations of the Royal Society of Arts, Part II'. *Journal of the Royal Society of Arts* 118, No. 5170 (1970): 645–49.

Foden, Frank. 'Colleges, Schools and the Society's Examinations'. *RSA Journal* 140, No. 5426 (1992): 207–9.

———. *The Examiner: James Booth and the Origins of Common Examinations*. Leeds: Leeds Studies in Adult and Continuing Education, 1989.

———. 'The Founding of a Tradition: James Booth and the Society's Examinations (i)'. *Journal of the Royal Society of Arts* 135, No. 5370 (1987): 458–64.

———. 'The Founding of a Tradition: James Booth and the Society's Examinations (ii)'. *Journal of the Royal Society of Arts* 135, No. 5371 (1987): 526–31.

Fordham, Douglas. *British Art and the Seven Years' War: Allegiance and Autonomy*. Philadelphia: University of Pennsylvania Press, 2010.

Franklin, Benjamin, and Jared Sparks. *The Works of Benjamin Franklin: Containing Several Political and Historical Tracts Not Included in Any Former Edition, and Many Letters, Official and Private Not Hitherto Published*. Vol. 4. Boston: Tappan, Whittemore, and Mason, 1837.

Further Correspondence with the United States Ambassador Respecting the Treatment of British Prisoners of War and Interned Civilians in Germany. Miscellaneous, No. 26, 1916. London: H. M. Stationery Office, 1916. https://catalog.hathitrust.org/Record/000447271.

Gage, John. 'Turner and the Society of Arts'. *Journal of the Royal Society of Arts* 111, No. 5086 (1963): 842–46.

Godard, John George. *George Birkbeck, the Pioneer of Popular Education: A Memoir and a Review*. London: Bemrose & Sons, 1884. http://archive.org/details/georgebirkbeckpi00godauoft.

The Gray's Inn Journal. Edited by Charles Ranger. 1753.

Green, Georgina. 'Translating Hemp into a Transatlantic "Band of Reciprocal Interest": The Society for the Encouragement of Arts, Manufactures and Commerce as a 1760s' Actor Network'. *Journal for Eighteenth-Century Studies* 38, No. 4 (2015): 483–95. https://doi.org/10.1111/1754-0208.12351.

Greenwood, Grace. 'Notes from Over the Sea: Reception of the Royal Society of Art—Some of the Notable Private Receptions in London—the Oddest And most Incongruous of Them All—Its Variety and the Greatness of Its People'. *New York Times*, 3 September 1876.

Grosley, Pierre Jean. *A Tour to London, or, New Observations on England and Its Inhabitants*. Translated by Thomas Nugent. Vol. 2. London : Lockyer Davis, 1772. http://hdl.handle.net/2027/chi.16538079.

Gwynn, John. *An Essay on Design: Including Proposals for Erecting a Public Academy to Be Sup-*

ported by Voluntary Subscription (till a Royal Foundation Can Be Obtain'd) for Educating the British Youth in Drawing, and the Several Arts Depending Thereon. London, John Brindley, 1749. http://archive.org/details/gri_33125010931885.

———. *London and Westminster Improved, Illustrated by Plans : To Which Is Prefixed, a Discourse on Publick Magnificence, with Observations on the State of Arts and Artists in This Kingdom, Wherein the Study of the Polite Arts Is Recommended as Necessary to a Liberal Education: Concluded by Some Proposals Relative to Places Not Laid down in the Plans*. London: n.p., 1766. http://archive.org/details/gri_33125008677664.

Hales, Stephen. *A Description of Ventilators: Whereby Great Quantities of Fresh Air May with Ease Be Conveyed Into Mines, Goals, Hospitals, Work-Houses and Ships, in Exchange for Their Noxious Air*. London: W. Innys, R. Manby, and T. Woodward, 1743.

Halsall, Martyn. 'Where Bosses Are Going Back to School'. *The Guardian*, 12 October 1987.

Haltern, Utz. 'The Society of Arts and Some International Aspects of the Great Exhibition of 1851 (i)'. *Journal of the Royal Society of Arts* 116, No. 5142 (1968): 536–42.

———. 'The Society of Arts and Some International Aspects of the Great Exhibition of 1851 (ii)'. *Journal of the Royal Society of Arts* 116, No. 5143 (1968): 618–22.

Hargraves, Matthew. *Candidates for Fame: The Society of Artists for Great Britain, 1760–1791*. 1st edition. New Haven and London: Yale University Press, 2006.

Harris, J. R. 'French Industrial Policy under the Ancien Regime and the Pursuit of the British Example'. *Histoire, Économie et Société* 12, No. 1 (1993): 93–100.

Harrison, James. 'Bennet Woodcroft at the Society of Arts, 1845–57 Part 1: Reform of the Society and of the Patent System'. *Journal of the Royal Society of Arts* 128, No. 5284 (1980): 231–36.

———. 'Bennet Woodcroft at the Society of Arts, 1845–57 Part 3: Models, Exhibitions and Museums'. *Journal of the Royal Society of Arts* 128, No. 5286 (1980): 375–82.

———. *Encouraging Innovation in the Eighteenth and Nineteenth Centuries: The Society of Arts and Patents, 1754–1904*. Gunnislake: High View, 2006.

Hawkins, Sir John. *The Life of Samuel Johnson, LL.D.* London: J. Buckland, 1787.

Haynes, Bruce. *A History of Performing Pitch: The Story of "A."* Lanham, MD: Scarecrow Press, 2002.

Head, Raymond. 'Indian Crafts and Western Design from the Seventeenth Century to the Present'. *RSA Journal* 136, No. 5378 (1988): 116–31.

Heleniak, Kathryn M. 'William Mulready, RA (1786–1863) and the Society of Arts (i)'. *Journal of the Royal Society of Arts* 124, No. 5240 (1976): 464–69.

———. 'William Mulready, RA (1786–1863) and the Society of Arts (ii)'. *Journal of the Royal Society of Arts* 124, No. 5241 (1976): 558–62.

Henderson, Ebenezer, and James Ferguson. *Life of James Ferguson, F.R.S., in a Brief Autobiographical Account, and Further Extended Memoir: With Numerous Notes and Illustrative Engravings*. Edinburgh, London and Glasgow: Fullarton, 1870.

Hewitt, Virginia. 'Beware of Imitations: The Campaign for a New Bank of England Note, 1797–1821'. *The Numismatic Chronicle (1966-)* 158 (1998): 197–222.

Hilaire-Pérez, Liliane. 'Transferts Technologiques, Droit et Territoire: Le Cas Franco-Anglais Au XVIIIe Siècle'. *Revue d'histoire Moderne et Contemporaine* 44, No. 4 (1997): 547–79.

Hobhouse, Hermione. *Crystal Palace and the Great Exhibition: Art, Science, and Productive Industry—A History of the Royal Commission for the Exhibition of 1851*. 2nd edition. London and New York: Continuum International Publishing Group, 2002.

————. *Prince Albert, His Life and Work*. London: H. Hamilton, 1984.

Hoock, Holger. *The King's Artists: The Royal Academy of Arts and the Politics of British Culture 1760–1840*. Oxford: Clarendon Press, 2003.

Hoppit, Julian. *Britain's Political Economies: Parliament and Economic Life, 1660–1800*. Cambridge and New York: Cambridge University Press, 2017.

Howe, Anthony. *Free Trade and Liberal England, 1846–1946*. Oxford: Clarendon Press, 1997.

Howes, Anton. 'Why Innovation Accelerated in Britain 1651–1851'. PhD thesis, King's College London, 2016.

Hudson, Derek, and Kenneth W. Luckhurst. *The Royal Society of Arts, 1754–1954*. 1st edition. London: John Murray, 1954.

Hunter, Michael C. W. *Establishing the New Science: The Experience of the Early Royal Society*. Woodbridge: The Boydell Press, 1989.

————. *Science and the Shape of Orthodoxy: Intellectual Change in Late Seventeenth-Century Britain*. Woodbridge: The Boydell Press, 1995.

Hurt, J. S. 'Harry Chester (1806–68) (i): The Early Years'. *Journal of the Royal Society of Arts* 116, No. 5138 (1968): 155–60.

————. 'Harry Chester (1806–68) (ii): The Middle Years'. *Journal of the Royal Society of Arts* 116, No. 5139 (1968): 258–64.

————. 'The Society of Arts and the Elementary Education Act of 1870'. *Journal of the Royal Society of Arts* 129, No. 5298 (1981): 380–86.

Irwin, Douglas A. *Against the Tide: An Intellectual History of Free Trade*. Princeton, NJ: Princeton University Press, 1998.

Jackson, Lee. *Dirty Old London: The Victorian Fight Against Filth*. New Haven and London: Yale University Press, 2014.

Jackson, Lesley. *Twentieth-Century Pattern Design*. New York: Princeton Architectural Press, 2002.

Jacob, Margaret C., and Larry Stewart. *Practical Matter: Newton's Science in the Service of Industry and Empire 1687–1851*. Cambridge, MA: Harvard University Press, 2004.

James, Frank A.J.L. 'Michael Faraday, The City Philosophical Society and The Society of Arts'. *RSA Journal* 140, No. 5426 (1992): 192–99.

Jeremiah, David. 'The Society of Arts and the National Drawing Education Campaign: (ii) The Working of the Drawing Committee'. *Journal of the Royal Society of Arts* 117, No. 5153 (1969): 365–67.

————. 'The Society of Arts and the National Drawing Education Campaign: (iii) The Provision of Drawing Aids'. *Journal of the Royal Society of Arts* 117, No. 5154 (1969): 439–42.

————. 'The Society of Arts and the National Drawing Education Campaign: (iv) Drawing Conceived as Part of General Education'. *Journal of the Royal Society of Arts* 117, no. 5155 (1969): 506–10.

Johnston, Dudley J. 'The Origins of the Photographic Society'. *Journal of the Royal Society of Arts* 87, No. 4518 (1939): 831–37.

J.S.S. 'Some Royal Members of the Society, 1770–1915 (ii)'. *Journal of the Royal Society of Arts* 123, No. 5222 (1975): 93–99.

Kamm, Josephine. *Indicative Past: A Hundred Years of the Girls' Public Day School Trust*. Abingdon: Routledge, 2013.

Keegan, Victor. 'How Having Lost the Art of Manufacturing We Could Regain It (from next Week)'. *The Guardian*, 23 December 1985.

Kelly, Thomas. 'The Origin of Mechanics' Institutes'. *British Journal of Educational Studies* 1, No. 1 (November 1952): 17–27. https://doi.org/10.1080/00071005.1952.9972880.

Khan, B. Zorina. 'Prestige and Profit: The Royal Society of Arts and Incentives for Innovation, 1750–1850'. Working Paper. National Bureau of Economic Research, January 2017. https://doi.org/10.3386/w23042.

Kippis, Andrew. *Biographia Britannica: Or, the Lives of the Most Eminent Persons Who Have Flourished in Great Britain and Ireland, from the Earliest Age, to the Present Times*. 2nd edition. Vol. 4. London: Rivington and Marshall, 1789.

Kitson, Michael. 'Hogarth's "Apology for Painters" '. *The Volume of the Walpole Society* 41 (1966): 46–111.

Kuchta, David. *The Three-Piece Suit and Modern Masculinity: England, 1550–1850*. Berkeley and London: University of California Press, 2002.

Kusamitsu, Toshio. 'Great Exhibitions before 1851'. *History Workshop*, No. 9 (1980): 70–89.

Lambert, David. 'The History of the Country Park, 1966–2005: Towards a Renaissance?' *Landscape Research* 31, No. 1 (January 2006): 43–62.

Layton, David. 'The Educational Exhibition of 1854: (i) The Origins'. *Journal of the Royal Society of Arts* 120, No. 5187 (1972): 183–87.

———. 'The Educational Exhibition of 1854: (ii) The Opening'. *Journal of the Royal Society of Arts* 120, No. 5188 (1972): 250–56.

Leith, Prue. *Relish: My Life on a Plate*. London: Quercus, 2012.

Loft, Philip. 'Peers, Parliament and Power under the Revolution Constitution, 1685–1720'. PhD thesis, University College London, 2015.

Loftus, Donna. 'Limited Liability, Market Democracy, and the Social Organization of Production in Mid-Nineteenth-Century Britain'. In *Victorian Investments: New Perspectives on Finance and Culture*, edited by Nancy Henry and Cannon Schmitt, 79–97. Bloomington and Indianapolis: Indiana University Press, 2009.

Lyons, Henry. *The Royal Society, 1660–1940*. Cambridge: Cambridge University Press, 2015.

Mabon, G. P. 'John Scott Russell and Henry Cole: Aspects of a Personal Rivalry at the Society of Arts, (i) 1844–49'. *Journal of the Royal Society of Arts* 115, No. 5127 (1967): 203–11.

———. 'John Scott Russell and Henry Cole: Aspects of a Personal Rivalry at the Society of Arts, (ii) 1849–50." *Journal of the Royal Society of Arts* 115, No. 5128 (1967): 299–302.

MacLeod, Christine. *Inventing the Industrial Revolution: The English Patent System, 1660–1800*. Cambridge: Cambridge University Press, 2002.

Magnusson, Lars, ed. *Mercantilist Economics*. Berlin: Springer Science & Business Media, 2012.

———. *The Political Economy of Mercantilism*. Abingdon: Routledge, 2015.

Mallet, J.V.G. 'Nicholas Crisp, Founding Member of the Society of Arts, Part II: Crisp and the Society'. *Journal of the Royal Society of Arts* 121, No. 5198 (1973): 91–96.

Martin, Theodore. *The Life of His Royal Highness the Prince Consort*. Vol. II. London: D. Appleton & Co., 1876. http://archive.org/details/lifehisroyalhig05martgoog.

Mason, Peter. 'Sir Geoffrey Chandler Obituary'. *The Guardian*, Business Section, 10 April 2011. https://www.theguardian.com/business/2011/apr/10/sir-geoffrey-chandler-obituary.

Maxwell, Robert. *Select Transactions of the Honourable the Society of Improvers in the Knowledge of Agriculture in Scotland: Directing the Husbandry of the Different Soils for the Most Profitable Purposes, and Containing Other Directions, Receipts and Descriptions: Together with an Account of the Society's Endeavours to Promote Our Manufactures*. Edinburgh: Sands, Brymer, Murray and Cochran, 1743.

McGowen, Randall. 'Managing the Gallows: The Bank of England and the Death Penalty, 1797–1821'. *Law and History Review* 25, No. 2 (2007): 241–82.

———. 'The Bank of England and the Policing of Forgery 1797–1821'. *Past & Present*, No. 186 (2005): 81–116.

Meade-King, Maggy. 'This Year, next Year'. *The Guardian*, 31 December 1986.

Millais, John Guille. *The Life and Letters of Sir John Everett Millais*. London: Methuen, 1899. http://archive.org/details/lifelettersofsir01milliala.

Miller, Allan. 'The Society of Arts and Wigan Mechanics' Institute in the Nineteenth Century'. *Journal of the Royal Society of Arts* 128, No. 5282 (1980): 113–17.

Miller, Peter N. *Defining the Common Good: Empire, Religion and Philosophy in Eighteenth-Century Britain*. Cambridge: Cambridge University Press, 2004.

Mockford, Jack. ' "They Are Exactly as Bank Notes Are": Perceptions and Technologies of Bank Note Forgery During the Bank Restriction Period, 1797–1821', PhD thesis, University of Hertfordshire, 2014. http://uhra.herts.ac.uk/handle/2299/15308.

Moe, Espen. *Governance, Growth and Global Leadership: The Role of the State in Technological Progress, 1750–2000*. Farnham: Ashgate Publishing, 2013.

Moggach, Tom. 'The Cooking Bus Goes Round and Round'. *The Guardian*, Society Section, 7 February 2006. https://www.theguardian.com/society/2006/feb/07/health.schoolmeals.

Mokyr, Joel. *A Culture of Growth: The Origins of the Modern Economy*. Princeton, NJ: Princeton University Press, 2016.

———. 'The Intellectual Origins of Modern Economic Growth'. *The Journal of Economic History* 65, No. 2 (June 2005): 285–351. https://jstor.org/stable/3875064.

'Monday Interview: Matt McGrath, Aircraft Medical'. *The Scotsman*, 23 November 2015. https://www.scotsman.com/business/management/monday-interview-matt-mcgrath-aircraft-medical-1-3955572.

Montagu, Elizabeth Robinson. *The Letters of Mrs. Elizabeth Montagu: With Some of the Letters of Her Correspondents*. London: T. Cadell and W. Davies, 1813.

Musson, A. E., and Eric Robinson. *Science and Technology in the Industrial Revolution*. Manchester: Manchester University Press, 1969.

Newbould, Ian D. C. 'The Whigs, the Church, and Education, 1839'. *Journal of British Studies* 26, No. 3 (1987): 332–46.

Nightingale, Benedict. 'The Tools a Writer Used for Building An Industrial Novel'. *The New York Times*, Books Section, 16 October 1989. https://www.nytimes.com/1989/10/16/books/the-tools-a-writer-used-for-building-an-industrial-novel.html.

O'Brien, Karen Elisabeth. *Women and Enlightenment in Eighteenth-Century Britain*. Cambridge: Cambridge University Press, 2009.

Ochs, Kathleen H. 'The Royal Society of London's History of Trades Programme: An Early Episode in Applied Science'. *Notes and Records of the Royal Society of London* 39, No. 2 (1985): 129–58.

Olson, M. *The Logic of Collective Action: Public Goods and the Theory of Groups*. Revised edition. Cambridge, MA: Harvard University Press, 1974.

'The Papers of the Society of Artists of Great Britain'. *The Volume of the Walpole Society* 6 (1917): 113–30.

Parker, John. *Prince Philip: A Critical Biography*. Leicester: Ulverscroft Large Print Books, 1992.

Paskins, Matthew. 'Sentimental Industry: The Society of Arts and the Encouragement of Public Useful Knowledge, 1754–1848'. PhD thesis, University College London, 2014.

Paul, Helen. *The South Sea Bubble: An Economic History of Its Origins and Consequences*. 1st edition. Abingdon: Routledge, 2010.

Paz, D. G. 'The Composition of the Education Committee of the Privy Council, 1839–1856'. *Journal of Educational Administration and History* 8, No. 2 (July 1976): 1–8. https://doi.org /10.1080/0022062760080201.

Pearce, Brian Louis. 'Thomas Twining (1806–1895): The Determined Improver (iii) Economic Museums'. *RSA Journal* 136, No. 5377 (1987): 62–65.

Porter, Roy. *Enlightenment: Britain and the Creation of the Modern World*. New edition. London: Penguin, 2001.

Pressly, William L. *The Artist as Original Genius: Shakespeare's "Fine Frenzy" in Late Eighteenth-Century British Art*. Newark, DE: University of Delaware Press, 2008.

———. *James Barry's Murals at the Royal Society of Arts: Envisioning a New Public Art*. Cork, Ireland: Cork University Press, 2014.

Prior, Thomas. *A List of the Absentees of Ireland, and the Yearly Value of Their Estates and Incomes Spent Abroad. With Observations on the Present State and Condition of That Kingdom*, Dublin: R. Gunne, 1729.

Quinn, Malcolm. *Utilitarianism and the Art School in Nineteenth-Century Britain*. Abingdon: Routledge, 2015.

Rainbow, Bernarr. 'The Rise of Popular Music Education in Nineteenth-Century England'. *Victorian Studies* 30, No. 1 (1986): 25–49.

Report of the Committee of the Society of Arts, &c., Together with the Approved Communications and Evidence Upon the Same, Relative to the Mode of Preventing the Forgery of Bank Notes. London, n.p., 1819.

Reynolds, Sir Joshua. *The Discourses of Sir Joshua Reynolds*. London: James Carpenter, 1842.

Roberts, Pam. ' "The Exertions of Mr. Fenton": Roger Fenton and the Founding of the Photographic Society'. In *All the Mighty World: The Photographs of Roger Fenton, 1852–1860*, edited by Gordon Baldwin, Malcolm Daniel, and Sarah Greenough, 211–20. New Haven and London: Yale University Press, 2004.

'RSA Opening Minds Competence Framework'. http://www.rsaopeningminds.org.uk/about -rsa-openingminds/competences/. Accessed 27 November 2018.

Rycroft, Elizabeth. 'Lewis Foreman Day (1845–1910) and the Society of Arts'. *RSA Journal* 140, No. 5428 (1992): 333–36.

Schofield, Robert E. 'The Society of Arts and the Lunar Society of Birmingham (i)'. *Journal of the Royal Society of Arts* 107, No. 5035 (1959): 507–14.

———. 'The Society of Arts and the Lunar Society of Birmingham (ii)'. *Journal of the Royal Society of Arts* 107, No. 5037 (1959): 666–71.

Scott, David. *Leviathan: The Rise of Britain as a World Power*. Glasgow: William Collins, 2014.

Second Report of the Commissioners for the Exhibition of 1851. London: Her Majesty's Stationery Office, 1852.

Seward, Ingrid. *My Husband and I: The Inside Story of 70 Years of the Royal Marriage*. New York: Simon and Schuster, 2017.

Shadwell, Thomas. *The Virtuoso* (1676). Lincoln, NE: University of Nebraska Press, 1966.

Shales, Ezra. 'Toying with Design Reform: Henry Cole and Instructive Play for Children'. *Journal of Design History* 22, No. 1 (2009): 3–26.

Shapin, Steven. *A Social History of Truth: Civility and Science in Seventeenth-Century England*. 2nd edition. Chicago: University of Chicago Press, 1995.

———. *The Scientific Revolution*. New edition. Chicago: University of Chicago Press, 1998.

Sheail, John. *An Environmental History of Twentieth-Century Britain*. London: Macmillan International Higher Education, 2002.

———. *Nature Conservation in Britain: The Formative Years*. London: Stationery Office, 1998.

Sheikh, Saleem. *A Guide to The Companies Act 2006*. Abingdon: Routledge, 2013.

Skidmore, J. S. 'The Award of The Society's Albert Medal to Napoleon III'. *RSA Journal* 137, No. 5398 (1989): 652–57.

Skidmore, John. 'The Society and the National Training School for Music'. *RSA Journal* 140, No. 5426 (1992): 203–7.

Slack, Paul. *The Invention of Improvement: Information and Material Progress in Seventeenth-Century England*. Oxford: Oxford University Press, 2014.

Smith, Adam. *An Inquiry into the Nature and Causes of the Wealth of Nations*. Edited by Edwin Cannan. 5th edition. London: Methuen & Co. Ltd., 1904. https://www.econlib.org/library/Smith/smWN.html.

Smith, Charles Saumarez. *The Company of Artists: The Origins of the Royal Academy of Arts in London*. London: Bloomsbury/Modern Art Press, 2012.

Smith, James Edward. *A Selection of the Correspondence of Linnaeus, and Other Naturalists: From the Original Manuscripts*. London: Longman, Hurst, Rees, Orme, and Brown, 1821.

Smith, John Thomas. *Nollekens and His Times*. Edited by Edmund Gosse. London: Richard Bentley & Son, 1895. http://archive.org/details/nollekenshistime00smitrich.

Smollett, Tobias George. *The Expedition of Humphry Clinker*. London: J. F. Dove, 1825.

Smout, T. C. 'A New Look at the Scottish Improvers'. *Scottish Historical Review* 91, No. 1 (April 2012): 125–49. https://doi.org/10.3366/shr.2012.0074.

Solkin, David H. *Painting for Money: Visual Arts and the Public Sphere in Eighteenth-Century England*. 1st edition. New Haven: Yale University Press, 1993.

Sprat, Thomas. *The History of the Royal Society of London, for the Improving of Natural Knowledge*. London: T. R., 1667.

Staff, Our London. 'Looking Ahead to A.D. 2000: Duke Announces Bicentenary Competition of Royal Society of Arts'. *The Manchester Guardian*, 19 November 1953.

Stephens, W. B. 'The Society of Arts and The Warrington Mechanics' Institution: (i) An Institute in Union'. *Journal of the Royal Society of Arts* 111, No. 5079 (1963): 239–43.

Stern, Walter M. 'The Society of Arts and the Improvement of Whaling, Part 2: The Edulcoration of Train Oil'. *Journal of the Royal Society of Arts* 128, No. 5291 (1980): 770–76.

Stirling, A. J. 'The Society of Arts' Photographic Exhibition of 1852'. *Journal of the Royal Society of Arts* 131, No. 5317 (1982): 54–58.

Stirling, Alec. 'Peter Le Neve Foster and Photography'. *RSA Journal* 142, No. 5454 (1994): 67–70.

Summerfield, Angela. 'Cadbury's Chocolate Boxes and the Royal Society of Arts' Annual Competitions of Industrial Designs, 1924–1933'. *RSA Journal* 144, No. 5466 (1996): 57–59.

Summerfield, Geoffrey. 'The Making of The Home Treasury'. *Children's Literature* 8, No. 1 (1980): 35–52. https://doi.org/10.1353/chl.0.0466.

Summerly, Felix, ed. *Traditional Nursery Songs of England With Pictures by Eminent Modern Artists*. London: Joseph Cundall, 1843. http://archive.org/details/traditionalnurse30418gut.

Sunderland, John. 'Samuel Johnson and History Painting'. *Journal of the Royal Society of Arts* 134, No. 5364 (1986): 832–41.

Sweet, Rosemary. *Antiquaries: The Discovery of the Past in Eighteenth-Century Britain*. 1st edition. London and New York: Continuum, 2004.

Swift, Jonathan. *The Works of Jonathan Swift*. Vol. 12. Edinburgh: Archibald Constable & Co., 1814.

Taylor, Brandon. *Art for the Nation: Exhibitions and the London Public, 1747–2001*. Manchester: Manchester University Press, 1999.

Taylor, James. 'Sea Pieces and Scandal: The Society of Arts' Encouragement of Maritime Art, 1764–70'. *RSA Journal* 144, No. 5473 (1996): 32–34.

Theobald, James. 'An Account of the Rise and Progress of the Society of London for the Encouragement of Arts, Manufactures & Commerce'. In 'Chronological Register', Correspondence, 1758. MR 24 a. Society of Antiquaries of London.

Thomas, Kate. *Postal Pleasures: Sex, Scandal, and Victorian Letters*. New York: Oxford University Press, 2012.

Thompson, Keith. ' "Education for Capability": A Critique'. *British Journal of Educational Studies* 32, No. 3 (1984): 203–12. https://doi.org/10.2307/3121573.

Thoresby, Ralph. *The Diary of Ralph Thoresby*. Edited by Joseph Hunter. Vol. 2. London: H. Colburn and R. Bentley, 1830.

Tierney, James E. 'Robert Dodsley: The First Printer and Stationer to the Society'. In *The Virtuoso Tribe of Arts and Sciences: Studies in the Eighteenth Century Work and Membership of the London Society of Arts*, edited by D.G.C. Allan and John L. Abbott, 1st edition, 281–92. Athens: University of Georgia Press, 1991.

Tiratsoo, Nick. 'The Government, Full Employment and the Politics of Industrial Efficiency in Britain, 1945–1951'. In *Governance, Industry and Labour Markets in Britain and France: The Modernizing State*, edited by Robert Salais and Noel Whiteside, 52–71. Abingdon: Routledge, 2015.

Trevelyan, Charles E. *The British Army in 1868*. London: Longmans, Green, and Co., 1868. http://archive.org/details/britisharmyin18600trev.

Tucker, Josiah. *A Brief Essay on the Advantages and Disadvantages Which Respectively Attend France and Great Britain, with Regard to Trade*. London: T. Trye, 1753. http://archive.org/details/briefessayonadva00tuck.

Wade, Edward. *A Proposal for Improving and Adorning the Island of Great Britain: For the Maintenance of Our Navy and Shipping, Etc., by Parochial Plantations of Timber and Other Trees, Upon the Forests, Chaces, Commons, and Waste Grounds Throughout the Kingdom*. London: R. and J. Dodsley, 1755.

Walker, Martyn. *The Development of the Mechanics' Institute Movement in Britain and Beyond: Supporting Further Education for the Adult Working Classes*. 1st edition. Abingdon: Routledge, 2016.

Warner, Malcolm. 'John Everett Millais and the Society of Arts'. *Journal of the Royal Society of Arts* 124, No. 5244 (1976): 754–58.

Watts, Andrew. 'Cambridge Local Examinations 1858–1945'. In *Examining the World: A History of the University of Cambridge Local Examinations Syndicate*, edited by Sandra Raban, 36–70. Cambridge: Cambridge University Press, 2008.

Weintraub, Stanley. *Uncrowned King: The Life of Prince Albert*. New York: Simon and Schuster, 2000.

Whishaw, Francis. *The Railways of Great Britain and Ireland Practically Described and Illustrated*. London: John Weale, 1842.

Wildman, Stephen. 'Great, Greater? Greatest??: Anglo-French Rivalry at The Great Exhibitions of 1851, 1855 and 1862'. *RSA Journal* 137, No. 5398 (1989): 660–64.

Wilson, Mark. 'The British Environmental Movement: The Development of an Environmental Consciousness and Environmental Activism, 1945–1975'. PhD thesis, Northumbria University, 2014.

Wood, Henry Trueman. *A History of the Royal Society of Arts*. London: J. Murray, 1913.

Woodcroft, Bennet. *Titles of Patents of Invention, Chronologically Arranged: From March 2, 1617 (14 James I.) to October 1, 1852 (16 Victoriae)*. London: The Queen's Printing Office, 1854.

Wootton, David. *The Invention of Science: A New History of the Scientific Revolution*. 1st edition. London: Allen Lane, 2015.

Wyatt, Matthew Digby. *A Report on the Eleventh French Exposition of the Products of Industry*. London: Chapman and Hall, 1849. http://archive.org/details/reportoneleventh00wyat.

INDEX

A NOTE ON THE TYPE

This book has been composed in Arno, an Old-style serif typeface in the classic Venetian tradition, designed by Robert Slimbach at Adobe.